Knowledge In Minds:
Individual and Collective
Processes in Cognition

A. L. Wilkes
University of Dundee, UK

Psychology Press
An imprint of Erlbaum (UK) Taylor & Francis

Psychology Press, Publishers
27 Church Road
Hove
East Sussex, BN3 2FA
UK

British Library Cataloguing in Publication Data

A catalogue record for this book is available from the British Library

ISBN 0-86377-439-3

Printed and bound in the United Kingdom by TJ Press (Padstow) Ltd.

Contents

Preface

A tradition has arisen where the standard text in cognitive psychology spends a lot of time on the preliminaries of cognition (e.g. attention; perceptual segmentation; lexical access; syntactic parsing) and then, just as the central story seems to be about to start, it stops. Having toiled their way through the foothills, its readers are abruptly deserted just as the view opens out. Recent practice apart, there is no reason why cognitive texts should follow this pattern. Indeed, some 15 years ago, Norman (1980, p.4) wrote deploring the failure of cognitive scientists to respond to the rich dimensions of their chosen subject. He observed then how:

> The human is an animate organism with a biological basis and an evolutionary and cultural history. Moreover, the human is a social animal, interacting with others, with the environment and with itself. [Yet] The core disciplines of cognitive science have tended to ignore these aspects of behaviour.

Needless to say, these comments are still valid and the present book is one attempt at responding to this challenge. The base camps are taken for granted and the journey strikes out from there. What has resulted is a circuitous detour that starts off within cognitive science, diverts into developmental psychology and social psychology and ends up in territory that is normally occupied by historians and evolutionary biologists.

Although there is no particular virtue in breadth *per se* it does encourage making cross connections between topics that are not normally treated together. One of the central issues to come deals with the potential impact of newly acquired information on pre-existing knowledge and the surprising limitations that can attend this process. Cross connections within a complex knowledge base are not made automatically. If they are to be made at all, the new input needs to be repeatedly addressed in different contexts. Breadth cannot guarantee cross fertilisation of ideas but it does engender some of its prior conditions. One aim, therefore, has been to see how key issues in cognition transfer to new and sometimes unusual contexts of application. For example, the manner in which we cope with the accumulation of knowledge is first addressed at the level of the individual knower. It is then reconsidered both in the context of the transmission of information from the host culture to the individual learner and again in the transmission of knowledge from one generation to the next. Another, and related, aim has been to show how individually defined cognitive mechanisms need to be assessed with reference to the social and historical contexts in which they operate. The individual and collective perspectives serve to inform each other; neither is sufficient in itself. There are aspects of our thinking that fall within the purview of cognitive mechanisms derived from the study of individual minds. Equally, there are other aspects that derive from the distributed modes of cognition that arise from locating the individual within a host culture.

The question of exactly how such arguments should be pieced together to provide an account of "knowledge in mind(s)" has no single answer—what has emerged here is but one of the many possible versions that can be assembled from the available data. The book has been written for final year psychology students although it should also be of interest to students in other disciplines including cognitive science, education, and philosophy. For the last group of readers, one point needs to be made clear at the outset. What is dubbed as "knowledge" throughout this book does not refer exclusively to "true and justified beliefs"—as the sterner writings of the philosophers would have it—but to the multiple products of learning, thinking, and reflective processes which we accumulate over the years. These conceptual products may be internally consistent but most probably they are not. They may be justified but most probably they have been taken on faith. Some may even be true.

I am grateful to Gerry Mathews and Suzanne Zeedyk for reading and commenting on individual chapters and to Nick Wade and Alan Kennedy who read and commented on larger sections of the book. In particular, I am grateful to Phil Johnson-Laird, K. Manktelow, and D. Over for their detailed comments on the whole manuscript—which was way in excess of the agreed word limits. Paring it down has helped to clarify the central arguments but it has also meant that their insightful proposals for introducing new content has met with a more muted response than they deserved. For this, the responsibility is clearly my own. I am also indebted to Elizabeth Evans for expert help in constructing the tables and Gary Thompson who prepared most of the figures.

It has taken far longer than I expected to write this book. It grew in the telling. Meanwhile, political circumstances arose that called upon universities to justify their existence by producing a body of discrete publications within a specified period of time. On these terms, the present project could hardly have been more misconceived. There again, the book can also be read as an account of what is wrong with this collective approach to the accumulation of knowledge.

Figure and Table Acknowledgements

Figures

2.2	Allyn & Bacon
3.2	From *Memory and Cognition*, 1975, Vol.3 (5), pp.569–575, printed by permission of Psychonomic Society, Inc.
3.3	© 1985 American Psychological Association. Reprinted by permission of the publisher and the author.
3.4	© 1992 Academic Press, Inc. Reprinted by permission of the publisher and the author.
4.1	© 1992 Lawrence Erlbaum Associates, Inc. Reprinted by permission of the publisher and the author.
4.2	Reprinted by permission of Lawrence Erlbaum Associates, Inc. and the author.
4.4/4.5	Harvard University Press. © 1990 by the President and Fellows of Harvard College. Reprinted by permission.
5.2a/b	© 1988 HarperCollins. Reprinted by permission of the publisher and the author.
5.4	© 1986 MIT Press. Reprinted by permission.
5.5	© 1991 Lawrence Erlbaum Associates, Inc. Reprinted by permission of the publisher and the author.
6.1	© 1983 Lawrence Erlbaum Associates, Inc. Reprinted by permission.
10.1	© 1990 MIT Press. Reprinted by permission.
12.1	© 1981 Lawrence Erlbaum Associates, Inc. Reprinted by permission of the publisher and the author.
13.1	© 1992 by PUP. Reproduced by permission of Princeton University Press.
14.1	Reprinted from *Cognition, 51*, pp.131–176, 1994, with the kind permission of Elsevier Science – NL, Sara Burgerhartstraat 25, 1055 KV Amsterdam.

Tables

5.2a/b	© 1986 MIT Press. Reprinted by permission.
10.5	© 1989 American Psychological Association. Reprinted by permission of the publisher and the author.
11.1	© 1985 American Psychological Association. Reprinted by permission.
14.2	Harvard University Press. © 1991 by the President and Fellows of Harvard College. Reprinted by permission.

For my parents, Josiah Lawson and Doris Evelyn Wilkes, who believed in what was possible

SECTION ONE
Knowledge in mind

CHAPTER ONE

Mind acknowledged

In the course of a lifetime, each of us will acquire a large and diverse repertoire of knowledge about the properties of the world in which we live—the products of mental processes that commenced their work at birth (or before) and then just kept on going and expanding. During a typical day, we will have been called upon to recognise countless objects, people, and places; to participate in numerous conversations; to work any variety of tools and machines; to engage in subtly varied forms of social interaction; to take decisions; solve problems and, all the while, to learn something new from each transaction. It is the same the next day and the day after that.

Estimating the total amount of information that is likely to be laid down over this alloted span presents an intriguing exercise (e.g. Landauer, 1986) but global estimates of this total soon take on astronomical dimensions that convey little beyond the awesome scope of a lifetime's cognitive endeavour. By the same token, the same might be said for the potential dimensions of our current task of chronicling "knowledge in mind". However, we are not about to embark on an encyclopaedic survey of human knowledge in all its forms. Rather, the aim is to enquire into the variety of mechanisms and processes that service this remarkable achievement and sustain its cumulative growth. There will be quite enough here to keep us occupied.

The principal benefit arising from this unremitting cognitive activity lies, of course, in the fact that knowledge once acquired can be deployed to further our own ends. As Francis Bacon has famously observed, "knowledge is power". Famous, it may be, but the aphorism gets the equation only partly right. Knowledge can certainly confer power when it is used to select courses of action that will best further our current needs but our deliberations are not always quite so measured and dispassionate. There are many occasions when we act precipitately, without knowledge aforethought, or when we misinterpret what is going on. Possession of the relevant knowledge carries no guarantee that it will always be to hand when needed and, just as complete ignorance can render us ineffective, so too can the failure to deploy what we already know. If knowledge is to confer power it must be combined with effective procedures for putting it to work.

FUNCTIONS OF MIND

Whatever overall cognitive architecture is eventually judged as apposite for the human mind it must be one that is capable of implementing a rich variety of cognitive functions if we are to process the flow of external events in a manner that allows us to intervene as and when we judge necessary. There is no agreed and definitive account of what all this would entail but candidate inventories have been proposed, such as the listing in Table 1.1, which has been taken from Newell, Rosenbloom and Laird (1990).

TABLE 1.1
Requirements on the cognitive architecture

1. Behave flexibly as a function of the environment
2. Exhibit adaptive (rational, goal oriented) behaviour
3. Operate in real time
4. Operate in a rich, complex, detailed environment
   (a) perceive an immense amount of changing detail
   (b) use vast amounts of knowledge
   (c) control a motor system of many degrees of freedom
5. Use symbols and abstractions
6. Use language, both natural and artificial
7. Learn from the environment and from experience
8. Acquire capabilities through development
9. Live autonomously within a social community
10. Exhibit self-awareness and a sense of self

From Newell, Rosenbloom, and Laird, 1990.

The first four entries address the constraints on cognitive processes that arise from the press of events in the external world to which they must respond. The next four entries refer to the internal representations through which cognitive functions are realised and the role of experience in creating the skills for using these internal resources. The last two entries underscore the point that human cognition is situated in a social as well as a physical context. Much of our knowledge is acquired indirectly through our membership of social communities and, by benefiting vicariously from the experiences of others, we are not doomed to repeating past mistakes.

Obviously, a number of the requirements listed in Table 1.1 are likely to reveal considerable overlap once they have been unpacked but we will have plenty of opportunity later to explore beneath the surface of these issues. For the present, we can simply note that, taken together, these requirements identify a lower bound against which putative, psychological models of mind can be assessed. In principle, failure to address any one of these issues should be enough to rule a particular cognitive model out of court as a serious contender for modelling the human mind. In practice, we find there are no models on offer that are capable of accounting for all of these requirements equally well. Furthermore, none of the contenders seriously attempts to measure up to the neuroanatomical complexities of the brain through which they must work their effects. Partly, this is because too little of this anatomical detail is known but it also arises from an historical bias towards ideas drawn from the physical sciences rather than biological science. While recognising, therefore, that many of the fundamental questions relating to cognitive functioning still remain to be answered, there are enough answers already in place for an interesting story to be told.

In the course of the following chapters I intend to provide a general survey of what cognitive psychology has to say about these matters. In particular, it will mean addressing how we encode our knowledge of the world; how we put it to use in different circumstances; how we manage the organisational changes associated with cumulative learning and, ultimately, how this individual cognitive activity is influenced by our membership within a wider, social community that is collectively concerned with much the same problems.

SECTION ONE: Knowledge in mind

The first section (Chapters 1–5) sets out differing views on the basic properties of the human cognitive architecture and the representational codes used to store knowledge in memory. The classical treatment of mind interprets cognitive activity as a process of symbol manipulation and its already deep historical roots have been further reinforced by the analogies that can be drawn between mental processes and the operations of general-purpose digital computers. A major part of the present chapter, therefore, deals with the properties of symbol systems and their role in computational processes.

Chapter 2 provides a review of the role played by symbolic codes in representing our general knowledge of the world. Here propositions and schemas are instanced as higher-order encoding units adapted for handling complex bodies of knowledge. These codes are essentially "amodal" in that they are not tied to any specific sensory modality whereas our subjective experience of mental imagery seems to license the existence of additional, modality-specific codes. Consequently, Chapter 3 reviews some of the evidence in favour of dual coding in memory while referring to the running debates that have dogged this area of research. In Chapter 4, the assumptions behind "production system architectures" are described along with two example architectures (ACT* and SOAR) that have been designed to put stored knowledge to work in furtherance of the organism's goals. Chapter 5 concludes this section by setting out the assumptions behind connectionist architectures for cognition. Unlike production models, where cognitive operations are predicated upon the manipulation of internalised symbols, connectionist models make no such assumptions and they have constituted a powerful challenge to the ascendancy of classical symbol models for modelling cognition.

Both classical and connectionist models of cognition are open to the criticism that they are too narrow in scope—they focus exclusively on the individual case and, even then, their terms of reference are distinctly limited. The remaining sections provide an elaboration on this critical theme.

SECTION TWO: Memory dynamics and the accumulation of knowledge

The three chapters comprising this section are concerned with the problems posed by the cumulative nature of knowledge in mind. The acquisition of new knowledge can have significant implications for things that we already know and we are enjoined to find ways of updating this prior knowledge while at the same time avoiding the risk of either destroying the functional integrity of the memory records involved or being drawn into an endless quest for internal consistency.

Chapter 6 focuses on specific aspects of cumulative memory (e.g. interference, reality monitoring, and metacognitive processing) as these apply in the context of day-to-day functioning. It also addresses the issue of memory updating as when newly acquired information serves to question prior information that has previously been held in good faith.

Chapter 7 stays with the theme of cumulative memory, this time as it relates to the long-term processes of cognitive reorganisation and change. After reviewing the development of mnemonic functions in children, the discussion concentrates on the factors that initiate and constrain the direction of cognitive growth.

Chapter 8 concludes this section by discussing the role of affective processes in directing the course of cognitive activity. The affective valence assigned to particular bodies of knowledge can influence the ease and frequency with which they are brought to mind. In this respect, affect can play a significant role in determining the content of our current thoughts and hence in determining which components of our knowledge are likely to participate in the formation of new knowledge structures.

SECTION THREE: Acquiring and manipulating knowledge

A central property of the human mind is that it can selectively enrich itself by seeking out new information to supplement what it already knows and by engaging its contents in critical examination and re-evaluation. Both of these functions are addressed in this section. Chapter 9 deals with the ways in which individual knowledge may be augmented through the comprehension of written text and Chapter 10 looks at strategies for evaluating extant knowledge as evidenced in decision making, problem solving, and reasoning.

SECTION FOUR: Knowledge in minds

The final section aims to round out the preceding account by bringing the social and historical dimensions of knowledge formation into the picture. Chapter 11 starts the reassessment off by relocating the individual thinker within the wider social context and gives voice to criticisms of the "cognitivism" espoused by theories that insist on treating cognition as a purely private process encapsulated within the individual head. It is argued that there are collective aspects of social cognition that resist assimilation to explanatory principles based on the individual case.

Chapter 12 expands on this theme by discussing how individual and collective principles jointly participate in the educational procedures that are used to initiate new members into the culture of the host society. Chapter 13 then applies the same mode of analysis to the cumulative transmission of knowledge from one generation to the next. The historical record dealing with the manner in which ideas have changed across generations provides an important, additional data base wherein individual and collective patterns of growth can be compared. It also testifies to the intricate interplay that exists between individual and collective modes of cognitive activity.

Finally, in Chapter 14, a move is made towards redressing the non-biological slant that accompanies the majority of theorising about human cognition. In particular, this chapter introduces evolutionary arguments dealing with the manner in which individual cognitive processes and the host culture have interacted in shaping the structure of the modern mind.

Evidently, this means we are embarking on a broad and circuitous detour through the psychological literature. In compensation, it is hoped that the reader who stays the course will not only gain some impression of the psychological "forests" that can be formed from the individual trees, but also a sense of the wider landscape in which both are set. We will start by asking how folk psychological or common sense accounts of knowledge in mind have gradually come to be transformed into the "authorised" versions associated with classical symbol theory. Although this will take us rather briskly though a daunting array of technical arguments, there will be additional opportunities to look at these arguments again in what is to come.

FOLK PSYCHOLOGY

In our everyday life all of us (there may be a few exceptions) approach our transactions with the world armed with a naive or folk-psychological theory which holds that people's behaviour can be predicted from the contents of their mental states. We use this theory when we try to predict how people are likely to behave and we do so while being completely indifferent to the psychological mechanisms through which these states achieve their effects. The folk psychologist (if he or she were uncharacteristically pressed for justification) would argue something to the effect that people harbour beliefs about their world which they use to guide and direct their behaviour. Changes in these belief states will bring about changes in how they behave and, consequently, their current state of mind provides a good basis for guessing what they are likely to do next. This folk perspective is deeply rooted in our social traditions and it underpins our understanding of what it means to be a human agent acting in a physical and social world. If we believe that the train for Edinburgh is due to leave the station at 12.00 p.m. and we wish to go to that destination, we try to be there at the appropriate time.

As an "explanation" of human behaviour, folk psychology has the signal virtues of being both succinct and relatively comprehensible and it has been employed in making sense of human behaviour, with a few changes in content, for a very long time. Nonetheless, despite their longevity, explanations of behaviour that assign a causal role to the content of mental states are fraught with difficulties and ambiguities, especially if it is further assumed that there can be a direct mapping onto neurological states. Critics such as Churchland (1981) and Stich (1983) have expressed serious doubts as to whether a scientific account of mind can ever hope to use folk psychology as its touchstone. For Churchland, the very longevity of folk explanation is taken as evidence of its theoretically stagnant state and eloquent proof that it presents an obstacle to a more enlightened and scientific account of mind. For Stich, any science of mind that clung to folk-psychological principles would be as far from the mark as an astronomy that tried to preserve and refine ancient cosmological arguments employing concentric glass spheres.

Nonetheless, the case against folk-psychological explanations seems less persuasive once we question whether folk psychology and folk cosmology are really equivalent in the sense intended by this disparaging comparison. Clark (1987) has argued that they are not comparable; naive psychology is to be likened, not to theories of remote space, but to much more down to earth matters such as naive physics. Both naive psychology and naive physics employ primitive concepts to describe the world and they do so in a manner that partitions direct experience in a meaningful way. Naive physics was never intended to do the work of theoretical physics, rather it provides the mobile individual with functional insights into physical principles at a level that allows for adaptive movement. In the same way, naive psychology provides the user with a rough grasp of the basic psychological principles that are relevant for social interaction.

In which case, the parochial and unchanging nature of naive psychology, far from being evidence of its inadequacy, now turns out to be a potent argument in its defence as stated by Clark, (1987, p.147):

Any innate competence for psychological understanding which humans have developed will of course be geared to understanding the psychological regularities involved in the waking behaviour of normal human agents ... Parochiality then, is par for the course, and need not diminish our faith in naive psychology within its intended domain of application ... lack of change and development is precisely what we would expect of a theory which is formed on the basis of an innately specified competence which to some extent prestructures the space of our possible naive psychological understanding.

It may be that the concepts of folk psychology will not feature explicitly in scientific explanations of mind but it seems entirely reasonable that as new scientific accounts emerge, they should throw light on why the ascription of inner desires and beliefs should be so useful for our mundane understanding of the world in which we live.

REPRESENTATIONAL THEORY OF MIND

The "classical symbol model" of mind attempts to place the beliefs and desires of folk psychology onto a secure, scientific footing by interpreting human cognitive activity as operations over internalised representations—thought utilises internal symbols that map onto the salient features of the external world. Mental states such as belief and doubt (the basic currency of folk explanations) entail the tokening in the brain of internalised representations and the flow of cognitive activity arises as these representations interact to produce new versions that can be recombined in their turn. We solve problems by internally representing the initial state and goal state and by finding operators that will allow us to trace a path between them; we understand discourse by abstracting its ideational content and by using our background knowledge of the topic to create situation models of what it is about. In each case, we find internal representations and the rules for their manipulation being proposed as the hard currency of cognitive transactions. Rorty, 1980, (who is not a proponent of this view), describes it (p.3) as construing the mind:

> ... as a great mirror containing various representations ...
> To know is to represent accurately what is outside the mind;
> so to understand the possibility and nature of knowledge is
> to understand the way in which the mind is able to construct
> such representations.

Mental states such as "knowing that" or "believing that" are to be understood as "propositional attitudes" where a particular attitude (believe, know etc) is adopted to propositional contents that relate to external states in the world. Not all internal states take on this referential function—being hungry does not refer beyond itself—but a belief must incorporate some assertion about the world. When I assert, "I believe that the world is round", the accompanying mental state consists of tokening the propositional content ("that the world is round") and adopting an attitude of belief towards it. Although this may seem an overly pedantic exercise in philosophical analysis, later on we shall find that the distinction being made is extremely relevant to our ability to read other people's minds.

As all cognitive activity occurs within a physical device (the brain) its implementation must observe physical laws and this restriction immediately presents us with a major problem. If we wish to assign causal properties to the contents of beliefs the process must be one that is compatible with the physical workings of the brain. Yet the ethereal content of a belief seems to occupy a different world to the material substance of the brain and its operative laws. It is one of the major claims of classical symbol models that they can bridge this gap, although to understand how it is done we must first sketch in some of the historical background.

The fall and rise of mental representations

The origins of the representational account of mind can be traced back to Descartes who was also instrumental in identifying some of the difficulties it brings in its wake. Cartesian doubt recognised that if we can only know about the world and its properties indirectly via internal representations, then we cannot be sure that the representations are really what we think they are and not something else. We cannot stand to one side of the representational process and compare the "real" thing against the supposed copy. It also recognised that postulating mental copies of external states can introduce the paradox of an infinite regress, calling as it does for a mind's "eye" that "sees" our inner images only to pass on what it sees to yet another eye and so on. In the event, these problems persisted, unresolved, as matters of philosophical debate to be passed on, still unresolved, to theoretical psychology once it diverged from philosophy in the mid nineteenth century.

The fledgling psychological laboratories that were established towards the end of the nineteenth century pinned much of their faith on introspection as the tool of choice for unlocking the mysteries of mental life. It was assumed that subjects performing a set task, such as judging weights, could look inwards upon their mental processing at the time and then report whatever mental content was present, thus generating data that could be used to identify how the judgement was reached. If thought proceeded according to mental contents combining according to specific laws, introspection should yield a description of these same laws in operation. In practice, matters turned out to be not so simple. Far from unlocking the secrets of mental activity, introspection often came up with a null return on just those tasks, like thinking, where an explanatory foothold was most required. Kulpe and his colleagues at Wurzburg (see Humphrey, 1951) consistently found that their subjects reported that ideas simply came to them when required—there was no necessary accompanying mental content. At the critical moment when a response was being sought, instead of a rich body of conscious content for introspection to seize upon, the procedure seemed to run off silently and automatically.

Progress would be made when empirical enquiry could come to terms with the unconscious determining tendencies identified by Kulpe but, at the time, this outcome lay beyond the powers of the investigative tools available. In any case, radical behaviourism was soon to throw overboard both introspection and its concerns with mental activity, leaving the problems of mental representation to slumber on as challenges for the generation to come.

The audit has yet to be closed on the behaviourist legacy and by no means all of the entries are likely to stack up in the debit column. That said, however, the behaviourist movement did little towards creating a clearer and more coherent account of mind because its avowed purpose was to restrict psychological analysis to the correlation of stimulus inputs with behavioural outputs, dispensing with the need to account for mental processes altogether. In place of speculation about mental representations, the behaviourists offered instead a form of statistical modelling; how an organism behaved was determined by the frequency with which associative linkages had been formed between what it perceived and its repertoire of responses.

Despite the temptation to lump all behaviourist writers in one camp, it was never a monolithic movement. The explanatory systems put forward by Hull, Tolman, and Skinner differed in many important respects and it is a mistake to think that one voice, usually Skinner's, can speak for them all. Tolman, and eventually Hull, were both willing to speculate about internal events mediating between a stimulus and a response, but Skinner adamantly resisted such compromise to the end—as one of his last papers attacking contemporary cognitive psychology makes clear.

In this paper (Skinner, 1989), he turns to etymology (the history of word meaning) to cast light on the "true" significance carried by a word. Etymology is presented as "the archeology of thought" and, as we dig into this past, we find that words now taken as referring to inner mental states can be traced back to a time when they either referred to behaviour or to the eliciting situations. In their fall from grace, words that referred to observable situations or behaviour lost their original meaning and took on spurious overtones, including mental representation. Adopting these distorted concepts, in Skinner's eyes, inevitably resulted in explanations of mind that were fundamentally misconceived. As an example of this flawed reasoning, Skinner (1989, p.13) singles out the mental term "purpose" which, when subjected to etymological analysis, reveals a typical distortion:

> Originally a synonym of propose the word purpose has caused a great deal of trouble. Like other words suggesting probable action, it seems to point to the future. The future cannot be acting now, however, and elsewhere in science purpose has given way to words referring to past consequences.

For Skinner, little or no progress into these matters had been made since the time of Descartes and all attempts to found explanations of cognition on systems of mental representations would turn out now and in the future to be hopelessly misguided.

The counter-reaction to behaviourism occurred around the mid 1950s prompted (negatively) by the inadequacies of behavioural explanations of complex skills such as language and (positively) by the possibility of exploiting the new metaphors for mind being provided by an increasingly sophisticated technology. As Skinner's objections to mental states rest on the claim that they cannot be given a rigorously scientific treatment any evidence to the contrary strikes at the heart of the debate. In fact, George Miller (1983) specifically selected "purpose" as a telling illustration of how newly devised mechanical devices, such as servo-mechanisms, helped to bring mental representation back onto the psychological agenda. Servo-mechanisms, Miller claims (1983, p.24), can be seen as a purely mechanical instantiation of purposive behaviour because:

> With the servo principle it was possible to build machines that seemed to behave purposefully; the engineers talked about these machines as seeking goals ... It has a goal in the old teleological sense that scientists had ruled out on the grounds that the future cannot control the present. But in the servo systems (of big guns) the future position of that gun controls the present motion of the gun in a very real perfectly intelligible sense. So suddenly, a mentalistic notion like purpose was given a physicalistic instantiation.

It seems that Skinner was wrong. The key properties of certain mental terms could indeed be expressed in a perfectly coherent and scientifically respectable manner and this claim was to become a central tenet of the cognitive psychology that followed.

It is assumed that the mind operates by creating internal representations that have both semantic and syntactic properties. Representations can map onto reality in some meaningful way (they have a semantics) and they can combine together in lawful ways (they have a syntax) to produce new representations that also possess semantic and syntactic properties. Precisely how mental representations come to exhibit semantic and syntactic properties raises difficult and, as yet, unanswered questions (e.g. Stich, 1992). It is far from clear just what it is about mental representations that enables them to stand proxy for external things. Nor do we really understand how they can enter into sequences of transformations yet remain in step with states in the outer world. However, something approaching an intelligible picture is beginning to emerge.

The traditional view held that mental representations acquire their representational function by virtue of their similarity to the things they represent. We know what the image of a car stands for because we can "see" its meaning directly. This is clearly not very satisfactory. As well as the infinite regress implicit in this line of argument, any appeal to the specificity of visual images (they are images of something) seems to preclude the possibility of mental abstraction. How can an image of a car stand for all cars when it is bound to resemble some actual instance more closely than it resembles the general category? Worse yet, there is an awkward arbitrariness to the representational process which featural similarity arguments totally fail to address (Cummins, 1989). Evidently, something other than isomorphism is required which will allow representations to stand at some remove from their referents while still retaining their representational function. How this might be achieved is easier to appreciate if we look beyond the isolated symbol and ask instead how symbol systems can work collectively in the mapping of a referent domain.

In the *public* domain, numerals are used to represent numbers and historically we find that a variety of different numeral systems have been employed for this purpose. For example, Arabic and Roman numerals differ in the shape of the symbols they employ and in the rules governing the construction of complex numerals from simpler versions. They also differ in the transparency of their mapping function as compared, say, with a tally system where each tally mark stands for each item counted and the actual quantities and their representations increase in step together. Using the tally system it is relatively transparent that the operation of addition produces a sum that is the union of the component tokens and conversely for subtraction. But a price has to be paid for this notational explicitness. As the quantities increase in size, so the tally marks have to increase exactly in step—a state of affairs that is hardly conducive to error-free and efficient computation.

The Roman numeral system provides its users with more flexibility but now instead of the single tally mark we have a variety of coding forms that all need to be learned (e.g. I =1; V = 5; X = 10; L = 50; C = 100; D = 500; M = 1000) and we also need to learn more complex rules governing their combination. Within the Arabic system, however, just learning 10 symbols and the "many for one" and the "one for many" substitution rules allows us to read or write any number. It may take more time and effort to learn the system but, once learned, it can function as a powerful computational tool for those who have mastered its rules.

Such representational systems are likely to evolve new features as they respond to the pressures occasioned by their actual use; new-found applications prompt revisions in the notational system which then license another round of applications and revisions (Nickerson, 1988). The tally system may have a relatively transparent relationship to the incremental physical states it represents but this is not the reason why it works. Rather, it can function as a notational system because of the way in which transformations in the two domains remain in step with each other. Hence, in the Roman and Arabic notations, where transparency has been traded against a gain in computational efficiency, this loss in transparency does not impair their coding function. On the contrary, it actually boosts their representational utility. Representation, therefore, does not demand isomorphism and we can expect to find other representational systems that have developed along similar lines to numeral systems. The elements in these systems need resemble their referents in only the most abstract of ways yet they will perform their representational function perfectly well provided the combinatorial and mapping rules are faithfully observed. Further crucial insight into the formal properties of representational systems and, more especially, into the algorithms that can put them to work, has stemmed from developments within the history of computing.

COMPUTER METAPHORS OF MIND

After the Second World War, Alan Turing in Britain and John von Neumann in America were both working on proposals for building a machine that could be programmed to carry out different tasks—finally bringing to fruition a scientific project that had first been envisaged by Babbage in the previous century. Charles Babbage formulated his ambitious goals while engaged with a fellow scientist (Herschel) in the tedious chore of checking astronomical calculations. Detecting errors in mathematical and astronomical tables was not only tedious, it was also expensive. In a lecture to the Royal Institution in 1835, Dionysius Lardner (1835, p.80) lamented how:

... within 6 years it was necessary to compute the tables of the sun three times [while] the tables of the moon computed for the Board of Longitude in 1770 at an expense of nearly £4,000 were speedily rendered useless.

Responding to this necessary but uninspiring task prompted Babbage to speculate about a device that would substitute mechanical accuracy for human fallibility. Starting with the aim of constructing a "difference engine" which would calculate navigational and astronomical tables automatically, Babbage then progressed to the idea of an "analytical engine" which would calculate any arithmetical operation assigned to it by the operator. Babbage did not manage to complete his project and it was some hundred years later that Turing and von Neumann brought it to a conclusion in the form of the general-purpose digital computer. An important fall-out accompanying this technical development was the translation of the hitherto intuitive and ambiguous notion of cognitive activity as "operations on symbols" into the precise steps of an "algorithmic procedure".

Algorithms refer to "step by step procedures that mechanically produce a solution to any problem out of a certain class of problems" (Groner, Groner, & Bischoff, 1983, p.5) and we have already mentioned some of the algorithms of arithmetic when we referred to addition and subtraction. However, conceiving of computations as formalised step by step procedures has had significant implications that extend well beyond the confines of mathematics.

Exactly what is meant by "mechanical step by step procedures" or "computability" can be understood through the work conducted by Turing in the 1930s. Shortly before the Second World War, Turing (1936) published an account of a hypothetical device whose functioning could be completely determined by a finite list of internal rules. Turing's biographer, Hodges (1983, p.98), describes this hypothetical machine (now termed a Turing machine) as a device that:

> ... would work away by itself, reading and writing, moving to and fro, all in accordance with the way in which it was constructed. At every step, its behaviour would be completely determined by the configuration it was in and the symbol it had read.

The significance of such a machine is that it illustrates exactly what it means for a task to be carried out algorithmically (see Fig. 1.1).

The device consists of a tape of indefinite length divided into discrete cells in which a simple character may be written (say, 0 or 1). There is a read/write mechanism capable of reading a cell entry, writing a new

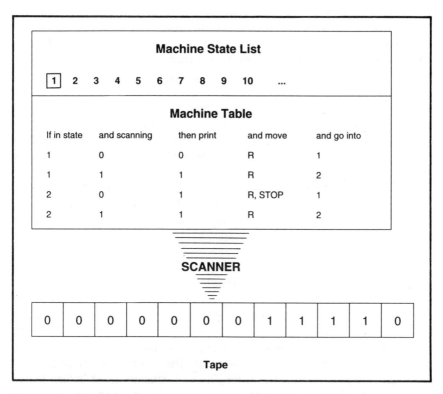

FIG. 1.1. Example Turing machine. (Adapted from Stillings et al., 1987.)

character and then moving one cell to the right or left after this has been done. The device also contains a machine table which includes a finite list of the internal states the machine can take up and, associated with each of these states, a set of rules which specify the action to be taken when the machine reads a particular character.

As an illustration, consider the task of incrementing a tally score by just one unit. The machine table for performing this task would take the form set out in Fig. 1.1 which depicts the initial tally score by a series of entries in the cells on the tape. The machine starts off in state 1 at the tape position indicated and, on reading a 0 on the tape, it leaves it unchanged and moves on to the next cell. It continues in this fashion until it reaches the first 1. Here (being in state 1 and reading 1) it leaves the cell entry unchanged, goes into state 2 and moves right. Remaining in state 2 it continues to work along the 1s until it encounters 0. At this point, being in state 2 and reading 0, it prints a 1, moves to the right and stops.

A device with this machine table will increment any tally score and Turing machines with different machine tables can be set up to handle different (and more complex) tasks. In fact, as the manner in which each different version operates can itself be expressed as a code on an input tape, it is possible to devise a version that will mimic any other version— giving rise to what is termed a Universal Turing machine (for a more detailed commentary, see Penrose, 1990). Computability can thus be defined through the operations of a Turing machine. And, so far as is known, in the prescription for a Universal Turing machine, any function that is computable lies within the power of this simple hypothetical device.

During the Second World War, Turing was assigned to the code-breaking unit at Bletchley. Eventually, these wartime experiences, coupled with his earlier work into mathematical logic, combined to form the blueprints for the digital computers that began to appear in the 1940s.

Von Neumann is credited with designing the basic architecture of the first generation of computers to actually be built. This design called for a memory and a central processing unit (CPU) that served to oversee the sequencing of the computing operations. The memory contained information stored in specific locations and the CPU could read what was held in a location once it was given the address. The device worked serially, moving from one address to another, and at each address it operated in some way on the information it encountered before being redirected to do further work at a new memory location. Memory addresses could contain instructions as well as data and by changing the instructions, different programs could be set up. Now, as Babbage had partially foreseen, we find that a single device can perform a variety of computable tasks.

This device has presented an irresistible attraction as a metaphor for the human mind, as minds and digital computers appeared to share a number of functional principles in common. The computer performs a set task by manipulating symbols to form new versions until the algorithm has run its course. Similarly, cognitive activity can also be interpreted as the manipulation of mental symbols under the control of the appropriate algorithms designed to meet the organism's needs. In fact, both Turing and von Neumann had appreciated the significance of computer architectures for explaining psychological phenomena and both men had foreseen the computer as reconstructing mind in its own image.

With the advent of the first generation of computer models for mind many of the traditional difficulties historically associated with mental representations appeared to recede. The infinite regress associated with a copy theory of perception could now be avoided by postulating that intelligent systems arise in aggregate from the workings of less intelligent subsystems. Working from the top down, at each change of level, the amount of intelligence required to carry out a task is diminished, until ultimately, a level is reached where processing can be carried out by simple physical elements (e.g. neurones) without reference to meaning at all. Whatever intelligence there is in the system resides in the aggregate, it does not have to be reduplicated at each operating level (Dennett, 1983).

If we accept that significant parallels can be drawn between the operations of minds and computers this is to propose that there is a level of description on which both serve the same functions, despite the glaring differences in their physical make-up. This "functionalist" view holds that computers and minds both exist in order to manipulate information and we can afford to ignore their vastly different evolutionary histories. For some observers, adopting this functionalist stance was a serious mistake—it only served to divorce cognitive theorising even further from its biological roots (e.g. Edelman, 1992). For other critics, functionalism made the mistake of ignoring the social context in which most of human cognition occurs (e.g. Bruner, 1990). And, functionalism has been criticised on both of these grounds (e.g. Lakoff, 1987). Nonetheless, for many observers, it was exactly this development that heralded *the* breakthrough that finally secured cognitive science a place within the wider scientific community.

PHYSICAL SYMBOL SYSTEMS

We embarked upon this historical detour as a consequence of asking how the propositional content of belief states could be made to play a causal role in cognition. We can now address the solution to this question which depends on exploiting the properties of what are termed "physical symbol systems". Stated baldly, it is claimed that the gap between the content of thought and the physics of the brain can be bridged by interpreting cognitive activity as operations over symbols that are *physically* tokened in the brain. Newell (1980, p.136) refers to this insight as being on a par with other great advances in the history of science:

> The physical symbol system is to our enterprise [cognitive science] what the theory of evolution is to all biology, the cell doctrine to cellular biology; the notion of germs to the scientific concept of disease, the notion of tectonic plates to structural geology.

The physical symbol system provides for a multilevel descriptive framework wherein the beliefs of folk psychology can eventually be grounded within the physical operations of the brain. Each descriptive level addresses a particular aspect of the system's behaviour and as top-level processes are translated into operations at lower levels so the account moves closer to the physical mechanisms that actually do the work. At the topmost level, we can describe the behaviour of the system in its environment as being guided by whatever knowledge concerning that world it deems relevant for achieving its goals. Below this level there are other levels which serve to clarify the procedures and mechanisms through which the enterprise works. Precisely how many levels of description are judged appropriate varies from theorist to theorist but, for the moment, we will follow Anderson (1990) in postulating four levels, where each descriptive level is appropriate for accounting for different psychological phenomena.

It is at the *rational* or knowledge level that questions concerning human rationality apply, as it is here that we can refer to an agent selecting actions in furtherance of its goals. Predictions at this level can be made without recourse to computational operations occurring at other levels. It provides a framework within which the products of these computations can be used for predictive purposes but it does so in ignorance of the details of the actual processing that needs to take place. Operating on this level we can comment on different cognitive functions in the light of the past history of the organism; refer to the knowledge the system has acquired from functioning in its environment and refer to the information that is needed to establish goals and select plans for their achievement. It is at this level that the beliefs and desires of folk psychology find their natural home.

At the next level down, the *algorithmic* level provides an abstract account of the computational steps through which plans are executed. At this level, the focus of concern shifts to questions dealing with the translation of knowledge representations into symbol systems and deciding which algorithms are being used to achieve particular outcomes. For example, we might derive the answer to "8 × 10" by adding 10 onto itself 8 times. Or again, we might arrive at the same answer by recalling the product directly. In fact, we could be told to use one method rather than the other, indicating that our goals and beliefs can continue to influence operations at this level. Below this descriptive level, however, such "cognitive penetrability" ceases to apply.

At the third, *implementational* level, concern focuses on the way in which the operations of the algorithmic level are to be implemented. Operations at this level are cognitively impenetrable because they are unaffected by what the organism knows. We may choose which objects we wish to count and which to ignore, but the time it takes to activate and compare the appropriate tokens in memory will not be affected by the organism's goals or beliefs. The actual process of scanning memory for the appropriate associate of "10 × 8" is affected neither by what we know nor want. We cannot reasonably be exhorted to speed the scanning process up or, for that matter, to slow it down. Operations at the implementational level are conducted over symbol tokens and the course of these operations is guided by their syntax not by their meanings. Thus, it is not necessary for a calculating device to "know" what it is doing when it performs arithmetical operations—in the sense of decoding what its symbols mean in the external world. Rather, in following the steps of the relevant algorithm, the device simply transforms its internal codes according to set rules which relate to their structural patterns not their mathematical meaning. However, it is in the nature of these rules that correspondences exist between the syntactic structure of the symbol strings and particular functions which can be defined at the mathematical level. Consequently, it is possible to invest the computed products with particular meanings even though these will have played no part in the computations themselves. It is at the implementational level that questions concerning the comparative durations of different cognitive tasks and their likely error rates can be formulated.

Finally, as the system has to be realised in some physical form, there is a further *biological* level of description dealing with the physical nature of the implementational device itself. For minds, this means referring to the neural circuits of the brain. At this level yet another set of psychological issues arise, this time relating to such questions as the effects of brain damage or different drug regimes on the outcomes of particular cognitive operations.

According to Anderson, only the algorithmic level and the biological level are to be credited as psychologically real. The latter because brains are needed to create minds, the former because the only way we can account for human intelligence is via a physical symbol system. Even so, the rational level is useful because it offers us another way of looking at cognition by suggesting possible constraints that have led to the emergence of particular cognitive architectures. Cognitive mechanisms have not just been thrown together but have evolved in response to environmental pressures and this evolutionary history can be important when it comes to deciding between different candidate mechanisms, any of which could compute the same function. In resolving this identifiability problem, reference to the constraints set by possible adaptive costs and benefits may be critical in allowing us to choose one mechanism over another. The implementational level, on the other hand, is only an approximate way of talking about activity occurring at the biological level.

Needless to say, every step in this argument has been and remains the subject of disagreement and debate. For connectionists such as McClelland and Rumelhart, Anderson's arguments are essentially the wrong way around; only the microcognitive level dealing with neural networks is psychologically real and the macrocognitive descriptions can offer no more than approximate accounts of what is going on at this level.

Which levels of description are emphasised, therefore, will carry significant implications for the properties ascribed to other levels. Furthermore, the division between classical and connectionist models is not the only source of dissent. A similar reassessment of the properties attributed to different descriptive levels arises if we go beyond the rational level by locating individual cognition within the wider, social context. Newell (1990) makes reference to a social level of cognition but fails to pursue its implications for redefining the properties ascribed to other levels. However, other commentators such as Hutchins (1995) and Salomon (1993) have been far less reticent in pursuing this argument. They note that by proposing a Collective or Socially Distributed level of description for cognition it is possible to observe how the cognitive load associated with specific tasks can be off-loaded from individuals onto the artefacts and practices of the social institutions of which they are members. These varying perspectives on cognitive activity have been reproduced in Table 1.2 which indicates where the descriptive levels and their varying labels coincide.

The tensions between classical, connectionist, and socially distributed models of cognition will resurface at a number of points in

TABLE 1.2
Levels of cognitive theory

Hutchins	Newell	Anderson	Rumelhart and McClelland
Socially distributed level	Social level		
	Knowledge level	Rational level	
	Program/Symbol level	Algorithm	Macrotheory/Rules
	Register transfer level	Implementation	Microtheory/PDP models
	Device	Biological level	

Adapted from Anderson, 1990.

the account that follows. However, at this stage it will be useful to take stock by setting out some of the strengths and weaknesses associated with the classical symbol account of mental functioning.

Design properties of classical symbol models of mind

If we raise our sights beyond the minutiae of rival theoretical models, it is evident that the historical record provides ample testimony to the productivity of the human mind. There appears to be no limit to the number of thoughts we can entertain and, by and large, our thoughts are internally coherent. We can make a good stab at understanding the (possibly) novel thought that "Green ideas and red emotions sleep furiously" and, if we can do this, we should have no trouble with "red ideas and green emotions" doing the same thing. At the very least, therefore, putative models of mind must be capable of accommodating these remarkable properties. They must explain how it is possible for our thinking to be open-ended or "productive" while remaining coherent or systematic. In fact, on both of these fronts, classical symbol models can supply what seems to be required. To see why and how this is the case, we will again have recourse to the design properties of numeral systems.

One of the principal features of the major numeral systems is that they are capable of generating an infinite output—there is no number that, in principle, falls outside the scope of their generative rules. Both the Roman and Arabic systems cope with the feature of productivity by allowing for complex (molecular) symbols to be created out of simpler (atomic) forms. Naturally, if this is to work, the combinations must not occur at random and there must be specific rules that enable us to determine which combinations are lawful and which are illegal. To take an example from Johnson-Laird (1988), we find that within the Roman numeral system the symbol (XIV) can be decomposed into the constituents, (X) and (IV). This hierarchical constituency is important and we would soon find that matters have gone badly wrong should these constituency relationships be violated. If we were to take (X) and (IV) as the constituents of (XIV) on one occasion and (XI) and (V) as its constituents on some other occasion, this would call the whole representational system into question. On the other hand, so long as the combinatorial rules are faithfully and consistently observed, the productivity of the system can be exploited to the full.

The presence of hierarchical constituency also contributes to the coherence or "systematicity" of a numeral system. It would be a strange representational system that could handle, say, "10 × 4" but not "10 × 2 × 2" or "10 × 8". In the first two cases the operations are equivalent and, in the second, they are very closely linked. These correspondences derive from the way in which the molecular symbols are formed from atomic symbols that retain their meaning as they enter into the different constituent combinations. Hence, both productivity and systematicity ultimately depend on the combinatorial properties of symbols.

The design features of productivity and systematicity are not unique to numeral systems; they also characterise spoken language and, by implication, the inner thoughts that are being expressed. There is a "language of thought" which also exploits the combinatorial properties of symbols and, because of this resource, human minds are capable of entertaining an infinite variety of thoughts—albeit many may be trivial and banal. Furthermore, not only can we generate an open-ended set of internal mental states, we are also capable of registering which constructions should be treated as equivalent and how they can enter into logical inferences. These fundamental properties of human thought have been forcefully expounded by Fodor and Pylyshyn (1988) and, as they are at pains to stress, any alternative (non-symbolic) contenders for modelling cognition need to be assessed on the extent to which they too can account for these same properties of mind.

Criticisms of classical models

Although the concept of a physical symbol system has dominated cognitive theorising to the extent of qualifying as the classical theory of mind, there still remain many commentators who are not happy to be drawn along in its wake. These critics have mounted their attack on the classical stance on a number of fronts but most especially with regard to:

1. Its exclusive emphasis on cognition as based on algorithmic procedures.
2. Its assumption that information is encoded and tokened in symbolic form in the mind/brain.
3. Its "brittleness" in application as evidenced by the susceptibility of its computational processes to breakdown in the presence of error or noise.
4. Its signal failure to take the neurological structure of the brain into account as a major constraint during theory construction.

We will look briefly at each of these objections and then, even more briefly, we will refer to the manner in which connectionist models provide an alternative perspective on the properties of cognition.

Dreyfus and Dreyfus (1988) have argued that when people perform many real-world tasks they tend to fall back on everyday "common sense" which is not easily modelled by formal rules. Common sense is less a matter of rule application and "more a matter of knowing what to do in a vast number of special cases"—cases where it is improbable that there is an appropriate algorithm to hand. Hofstadter (1988) makes the same point when he cites the case of inviting a friend to dinner who then fails to turn up. At first, we look for reasonable causes why the expected guest should be absent (e.g. the friend has had a memory lapse, so we try to phone up), but as the hour gets later, we start to entertain less obvious hypotheses (e.g. do we have the right date?) until, with the guest still missing and all our efforts unrewarded, we start to entertain less probable possibilities (e.g. questioning the validity of our recall that we passed on the invitation in the first place or, at limit, wondering if the friend could be a figment of our imagination). Hofstadter asks how it is that we exercise our common sense in such situations. How do we manage to sample the space of possibilities in a plausible order, starting with sensible ideas first and then moving to the wilder extremes? As such situations are likely to be unique but not necessarily infrequent, it is difficult to see how any algorithm could underlie these common-sense exertions. There is an inflexibility to classical explanations that sits awkwardly with the malleability of everyday thought and behaviour.

Other objections have hinged upon the inadequacy of "mere" symbol manipulation as providing a basis for explaining mental activity. Searle (e.g. 1980) has repeatedly expressed his doubts about the utility of treating mental states as "no more than" a system for implementing the right sort of program. His Chinese room example rests on the case where someone (who does not understand Chinese) responds to questions written in Chinese simply by consulting a list of rules to determine the correct answer. For Searle, such symbol manipulation could proceed perfectly well without *ever* engaging with meaning and, in consequence, we are being provided with no more than shallow caricature of what is really happening in the mind. Searle's Chinese room conundrum has provoked a number of rebuttals and defences of the functionalism he is attacking (e.g. Boden 1988) but it is difficult to dismiss his concern that something is missing entirely out of hand.

Yet other critics are also sceptical about treating thinking as algorithmic but choose to locate the faultlines somewhat differently. For example, Penrose (1989, 1990, 1994) has expressed severe doubts that thinking can be squared with the physics of the brain simply by calling upon algorithmic processes. He cites mathematical reasoning as a paradigm case where non-algorithmic processes are at work. In particular, Penrose refers to Gödel's incompleteness theorem which holds that for any collection of axioms for arithmetic there will always be certain conclusions that cannot be proved. For Penrose, this means that Gödel's thinking must have followed a course that could not be modelled using an algorithmic procedure, otherwise this would mean violating the theorem itself. And, if it is conceded that Gödel reached his conclusion by some non-algorithmic means, the creative insight involved can hardly be unique to the mathematical domain (Penrose, 1990, p.699):

> It must have been useful for such things as the conception of mammoth traps and the like—or for apes perceiving the value of tools. It is the elusive quality of understanding (and things related to it) that has this non-algorithmic character—and that is what Gödel's theorem demonstrates, albeit (of necessity) in a particularly sophisticated context.

Unfortunately, the introduction of such an ill-defined term as "insight" does little to advance the clarity of Penrose's argument and matters do not improve when he goes on to appeal to the special (but equally mysterious) properties attendant on human consciousness. Nonetheless, although these counter-arguments may have problems of their own, they are effective in exposing particular areas where symbol metaphors have to push and strain to keep up with the phenomenology of thought.

CONNECTIONIST MODELS OF COGNITION

Searle's argument that merely providing a physical instantiation of a computer program fails to capture the properties of the human mind has been criticised as a retreat into vitalism. On the other hand, it can also be interpreted as an appeal for greater attention to be paid to the biological context in which human cognition is set (Flanagan, 1991). A similar critique has been mounted by proponents of connectionist models of cognition who advocate using the neurological structure of the brain as the source of theoretical inspiration rather than the internal workings of the digital computer. We will refer to the properties of connectionist models in Chapter 5 but it will help to round off this preliminary account if we anticipate some of the arguments against classical models that have emanated from this source.

At the outset, it needs to be said that, like behaviourism, connectionism is a broad church; respect for the neurophysiological make-up of the brain may provide its central credo but its practioners have adopted this ideology with varying degrees of fervour. Consequently, the claim that connectionist modelling is "neurally inspired" needs to be treated with caution. In the absence of detailed understanding of neurological functioning, many connectionist theorists have been perfectly content to look for their inspiration from physics and engineering, *in lieu*.

The entry in Table 1.2 for Rumelhart and McClelland referred to just two levels of description applying to cognitive phenomena: a microcognitive level and a macrocognitive level. In fact, the balance within this dichotomy is distinctly unequal because the macrocognitive level is seen as no more than an approximate way of talking about cognitive operations that are best described on the microcognitive level. Although it may be possible to describe the operations of cognition in terms of rules for manipulating symbol structures, ultimately this offers us little more than a flag of convenience. Rather, the real work is being carried out at the level of neural nets—a microcognitive level that classical models have failed to exploit in any detail. Thus, connectionist models of human cognition present a radical break from the classical models discussed earlier and they have fostered in their wake a second generation of computer metaphors for mind.

Whereas classical models place great stress on rule-governed operations, connectionist models place their stress on the importance of recognition processes in cognitive processing. We know what to do in a given situation because we recognise it as similar to situations we have encountered before. Such recognition is possible because previous experiences have left their impression on the neural networks engaged in computing the response. Over time, units within the network will have come to excite or inhibit the neighbouring units to which they are connected and it is this pattern of interconnections that encodes the organism's knowledge of its environment. When the organism encounters a familiar input, units in an input layer in the network become active and this activation then spreads out around the network until eventually certain units in a response layer are turned on which happen to have been associated with the input on previous occasions. Whatever knowledge is being deployed to determine the appropriate response, it does not reside in the form of mental representations, but rather in the way in which the neural units in the network have become interconnected, one with another.

Associationist explanations of this kind have exercised a compelling attraction for many generations of psychologists. The demise of behaviourism involved one version of associationism being rejected; the advent of connectionism has now resurrected another version to take its place. For connectionists, the lessons of experience work their effects, not by establishing new internal representations or processing rules, but by establishing new weights on a network's connections. This supplies the knowledge that is required for performing different mental computations and it comes neither in symbolic form nor in the form of specialised rules. Classical models were wrong in making mental processes dependent on syntactically driven symbol manipulations, rather they involve dynamic state changes in neural networks which are best described in numerical or statistical terms.

Despite their relatively recent resurgence, connectionist accounts have already made impressive inroads into the modelling of various forms of cognitive activity. Connectionist models now exist for simulating speech perception (McClelland & Elman, 1986); concept formation (Gluck & Bower, 1988), and schema recognition in narrative text (Bookman & Alterman, 1991) as well as for many other cognitive activities that were hitherto the primary concern of classical symbol models. It would seem then that with the advent of connectionist models, we are faced with a radical alternative to the classical symbol model and a competitive struggle can be expected to ensue as the two camps strive for theoretical supremacy. A more considered reaction, however, would be to try to see where each has strengths that the other lacks. Classical symbol models are particularly suited to handling higher cognitive activities such as thinking, planning, and problem solving. Connectionist models are most obviously suited to modelling cognitive tasks where multiple constraints need to be simultaneously satisfied, as in the control of motor performance and many aspects of perception and recognition. There are certainly areas where genuinely different explanations for the same phenomena are being proposed but this state of affairs is only to be welcomed. As we will see, conceptual conflict can be an important prerequisite for theoretical change and growth.

To progress from here, we need to descend from this bird's eye view of cognition in order to try and get to grips with it on the ground. In the next few chapters, therefore, we will look more closely at how both the classical and connectionist frameworks have been used to specify cognitive architectures capable of sustaining, if not the full range of cognitive phenomena set out in Table 1.1, then at least a significant subset of these vital mental functions.

CHAPTER TWO

Encoding general knowledge

The typical adult can expect to call upon an extensive store of general knowledge relating to the scenes and events occurring in the surrounding world. The contents of this store will mainly have been acquired via direct perception of the environment but a significant proportion will also have been acquired, less directly, through communication with others or as a result of reflecting on past acquisitions. Whatever its source, knowledge of the manner in which the properties of external events cluster together enables us to set the daily round of activity against a background of contextual information that invests it with meaning. An encounter with a heavy woven fabric, if categorised as a "carpet", leads to the expectation that the item belongs on the floor and can be walked upon with impunity. Had the categorisation followed a different course, say, the item had been classed as a "tapestry", we would expect to find it hung on the wall and kept well out of harm's way. In each case, a perceptual parsing of the object in question generates a structural description which is then used to select whichever category provides the best fit. The net result is that the flow of experience becomes channelled into known and familiar territory.

Precisely how information is transferred between the perceptual and cognitive systems is, to say the least, a contentious issue. Accordingly, we will take up the account at a relatively late stage in the processing cycle where stimulus inputs have been converted into a structural description constructed around their component features. Our primary concern in this chapter is to understand how this welter of information comes to be encoded in long-term memory in a form that enables us to convert our specific experiences into generalised knowledge.

STRUCTURAL DESCRIPTIONS

A significant contribution to the understanding of stimulus configurations came from a group of psychologists (since termed the Gestalt psychologists) in the earlier part of this century. In a series of demonstrations they showed how elements in simple visual displays entered into different groupings according to general principles such as similarity and proximity. The displays in Fig. 2.1a reveal that while in principle there are various ways of segregating the rows in each array, one version tends to be favoured over the rest. In the top row, the dots are equally spaced and there is no obvious perceptual grouping to be discerned. In the second line, where the spacing is unequal, elements that are closer together combine to form distinct groups. In the third line, where proximity has been held constant but the size of the elements varies, it is similarity in size that determines how the elements will be grouped.

In Fig. 2.1b, it is evident that the principles of proximity and similarity are overridden when a connecting line is added to component elements in the display. In the top line of Fig. 2.1b, although the elements are equidistant, the elements connected by a horizontal line now group together to form a pair. In the second line, the same device overrides proximity effects, just as in the third line, it overrides similarity (see Palmer & Rock, 1994).

In other words, the structural descriptions assigned to a stimulus configuration encode information about the part–whole constituents that make up the display. Although there may be a number of ways of compiling this signature, it is likely to take the same form each time the

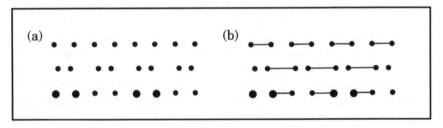

FIG. 2.1. (a) Grouping by proximity and similarity; (b) Grouping via connectedness. (Adapted from Palmer & Rock, 1994.)

stimulus occurs. This means that we are predisposed to recognise recurrent regularities in our environment and, as others are likely to have the same predispositions as ourselves, these regularities can be shared around. This is not just true for simple visual displays. Similar constraints apply to all types of stimulus configuration and the resulting structural descriptions come to play a crucial role in determining which events are recognised as having occurred before and, hence, how our general knowledge is likely to accumulate over time.

Consider the deceptively simple case of learning a serial string of 12 random letters by reading it aloud from a card and then recalling it from memory. Most subjects will require a number of read and recall attempts before they can reproduce the list without error and this gives us the opportunity to observe their spontaneous encoding strategies as they set about the task. If the subjects are tape-recorded while reading and recalling, we soon find that extended pauses start to appear at specific points in the list. The locations of these pauses tend to be consistent from one reading to the next and they mark the grouping boundaries that arise as the learner tries to impose a part–whole constituent structure on the input. At recall, the same grouping patterns reappear, implying that the extended pauses mark the boundaries of the subjective chunks the learner has selected for encoding the input. Typically, random lists tend to be partitioned into groups of three items; groups with two or four items are less common, while groups featuring more than four items tend to be avoided altogether (Wilkes, Lloyd, & Simpson, 1972). Thus, a typical reading of a 12-item list would consist of the subject running quickly through the first three items, pausing, and then repeating the same routine for the remainder of the items. There are occasional variations—for eight-item lists a grouping in fours tends to be preferred—but overall, the triplet pattern stands out as the majority choice (see also Ryan, 1969, and Broadbent, 1975). The upshot of this encoding activity is to convert a random list into a more manageable hierarchical format which can be stored in long-term memory ready to be unpacked whenever the original list content needs to be consulted.

The customary interpretation of such grouping behaviour has been that it enables the learner to overcome the bottleneck imposed by the limited capacity of working memory. Converting a list of 9 or 12 items into three or four chunks effectively reduces the immediate memory load by transforming each string into a condensed format. However, alleviating immediate memory load is not the whole story. The structural format assigned to a list also determines whether or not subsequent lists will be categorised as the same or different. That is, the hierarchical structure assigned to a list is on a par with the individual items and their serial order in determining whether two lists will be treated as identical. If we vary a list's constituent structure, while leaving its elements and their serial order unchanged, this has the effect of creating a new list for each of the variant groupings. As it is possible to impose a particular grouping pattern on a printed list by introducing double spacing between items at the intended group boundaries, we can steer subjects away from their preferred groupings towards other patterns chosen by the experimenter. When faced by spatially grouped lists, subjects normally adjust their reading to accommodate their extended pauses at the spatial break and their recall output is also adjusted to match this reading. Consequently, we can observe what happens when subjects attempt to memorise a serial list whose grouping structure alters from one trial to the next. Although, on the surface, this is an apparently minor change, the manipulation is quite sufficient to halt cumulative learning in its tracks.

Wilkes (1972) arranged for two groups of subjects to learn a list of 15 letters via the read and recall procedure. Subjects in the consistent group saw their list spatially grouped into threes on all trials. Subjects in the inconsistent group experienced a triplet spacing on trial 1 but, thereafter, the spatial grouping altered from trial to trial. Thus consistent subjects saw the sequence (LDT CKG BSY FQW ZHV) on each trial. Subjects in the inconsistent condition only saw this sequence on their first trial. Thereafter, the spatial grouping changed (e.g, LDTC KG BSY FQWZ HV) and it continued to change from one trial to the next.

Subjects in the consistent group took on average 8.4 "read and recall" attempts to learn their list whereas subjects in the inconsistent condition took on average 18.5 attempts to reach the same learning criterion. Although these group averages seem to imply that under the inconsistent condition the learning criterion was eventually met, closer inspection revealed that the group measure was highly misleading. In fact, the subjects who slavishly grouped their reading in accordance with the changing spatial pattern on each trial *never* actually learned their list at all. These subjects were stopped after 28 abortive attempts and it was this score that was entered for averaging. The only subjects from the inconsistent condition who did manage to learn the list were those who ignored the imposed spatial grouping and substituted a constant version of their own—in effect, they transferred themselves into the consistent, experimental condition. It seems that the subjects who faithfully shadowed the changing groupings had been enticed into categorising their list afresh on each trial and this was quite sufficient to prevent them from deriving any cumulative benefit from the repeated exposures (see also Bower & Winzenz, 1969).

The Gestalt groupings depicted in Fig. 2.1 are examples of perceptual categories—they constitute ways of literally seeing the world—whereas the groupings imposed on serial lists appear closer to the linguistic categories that are derived from socially sanctioned distinctions. To make the distinction clear, consider another example drawn from the field of colour vision. Different cultures may subdivide the colour spectrum in different ways, perhaps employing two, five, or more linguistic categories. Each arrangement has the effect of drawing the native speaker's attention to whichever distinctions the parent culture has deemed significant. Nonetheless, the information provided by the visual system ultimately constrains how these colour labels will be distributed. Visual perception defines the range of possibilities within which structural descriptions can be formulated but, within that range, we may be steered towards adopting certain choices over others (Mehler & Dupoux, 1994). We will have a little more to say about perceptual categories in the following chapter and at the end of the book but the bulk of the present discussion is concerned with the culturally driven categorisations that accompany language acquisition and vocabulary growth.

The gist of the argument, so far, has been that events are encoded in a form that allows us to recognise when the same input has been repeated. As a result, we can proceed to impose a degree of control on the flux of experience by categorising together discrete inputs that share a common structural description. This strategy leads to a major gain in cognitive economy, as each newly categorised input can then be treated as equivalent to the other instances stored under the same description and not as a unique event each time it is encountered. Over time, by reflecting on the properties that matched instances have in common, we can proceed to induce the generic versions that constitute our general knowledge of the world.

THE PROCESS OF CATEGORISATION

Barsalou (1992) divides the act of categorising an entity into five basic steps where the first step consists of forming a structural description as described in the previous section. Subsequent steps involve:

2. Searching long-term memory for categories with similar structural properties.
3. Choosing which category offers the best fit to the input.
4. Using the knowledge represented by this category to draw inferences about the new input.
5. Storing this input with the category for future use.

Exactly how steps 2–4 are conducted will depend on how our repertoire of categorial knowledge is represented in long-term memory and this is an issue that has provided considerable scope for disagreement. Originally, it had been assumed that categories are organised around strict definitions which serve to specify the necessary and sufficient features associated with class membership. Unfortunately, in this form, the traditional position does not stand up very well to critical scrutiny. It works in certain cases but not others. Defining "squares" or "triangles" in terms of the critical features shared by all members works satisfactorily but categories such as "mental illness" or "dictatorships" have instances whose properties are not so easily defined. After all, even experienced commentators have been known to disagree on the meanings of such terms. Furthermore, adopting this approach implies that all exemplars that pass the test for category membership will be equally "good" class members; there should be no gradations in how well different instances fit into the category and there should be a clear division between members and non-members of the category. Neither implication can be easily squared with the bulk of psychological evidence.

In a series of studies, Rosch and her colleagues (e.g. Rosch, 1973; Rosch & Mervis, 1975) have demonstrated that when people are timed as they assign instances to particular categories, certain cases are processed faster than others. It is as though there is a graded variation in class membership where some class members are being treated as typical of the class while others are being treated as atypical entries. For example, are "theft" and "begging" both crimes; are "birdsong" and "plainchant" both instance of music; are "light switches" and "chairs" both instances of room furniture? Confronted by such questions, we find certain candidates seem to be obvious instances of a class but others give us cause to stop and pause for thought. In deciding their fate it seems we are doing rather more than conducting a pass/fail comparison of candidate instances against some set definition.

In order to determine how the typicality of an instance related to the properties of a class, Rosch and Mervis (1975) asked different subjects to think about typical and atypical members drawn from a variety of classes and to write down the features associated with each example. Thus, a subject might be faced with listing the attributes of five typical and five atypical instances drawn from the categories of fruits, weapons, and clothing. They predicted that the degree of typicality of an item would relate to the number of features it shared with most other class members. This aspect, therefore, was measured by counting the number of features that were listed in common for typical and for atypical class members. The resulting scores confirmed the prediction; typical class members shared more features in common than did atypical ones, implying, in contrast to the classical view, that categories can be "fuzzy" or ill-defined.

These data have been taken to suggest a probabilistic model for the internal structure of categories. Rather than the class properties being criterial for membership they are only characteristic of membership. The category prototype represents the maximal number of features that can be shared with other members of the class while at the same time sharing the fewest features with non class members. Under this interpretation, the typicality effects found in verification tasks arise because a candidate instance is being judged in terms of its similarity to the class prototype. If the match is a good one, categorisation proceeds quickly but if the match is only partial the response slows down as additional tests are made.

Categorial hierarchies

Much of the power of categorisation in the cognitive economy derives from the potential of categories to combine to form taxonomic hierarchies. Consequently, we have more than one level for classifying events when evaluating our experiences. In principle, we could as easily refer a particular object to a superordinate-level category (e.g. vehicle), as to a basic-level category (car) or to a subordinate-level category (Porsche). In practice, free variation in choice of level is not normally found and it is basic-level references that are most commonly applied. When describing the traffic violation that forced us to make an emergency stop on the way to work, we are most likely to refer to the offending "car" that got in the way. This basic-level reference gets the balance between discrimination and informativeness about right. A subordinate-level reference to the offending "Porsche" seems too specific (unless we wish to make a point about the make itself), while a superordinate-level reference to an offending "vehicle" seems overgeneralised and uninformative.

The primary purpose of categorisation is to provide access to specific information about the object in question. Reference to "car" enables us to draw distinctions with other types of vehicle while preserving information about the salient properties of cars such as their shape and function. At the subordinate level, many of these critical distinctions will be lost because other makes of car will exist that possess similar properties. This will be even more so at the superordinate level because now the different category members can vary widely in their shape and function—compare cars and bicycles as instances of vehicle. The best compromise, it seems, is to be found at the basic level which combines maximum distinctiveness with maximum informativeness.

Rosch and colleagues (1976) have illustrated the nature of these trade-offs in a variety of ways. In one of their experiments, different subjects were asked to list attributes for objects drawn from different levels of abstraction such as "kitchen chair", "chair", and "furniture". Operating at the superordinate level, subjects listed around three attributes on average, consequently many potential distinctions were not being made. Moving to the basic level led to a significant increase in the number of features being mentioned (around nine on average) but a further move to the subordinate level resulted in very few extra features being added over and beyond the basic average. Thus, the minimal gain in distinctiveness at the subordinate level failed to compensate for the increased overlap with other, related categories that also accompanied the shift.

CONCEPTS

Although categories and concepts tend to be treated synonymously, there is a case to be made for distinguishing between them (Barsalou, 1992). Concepts are implicated when we employ categorial information for purposes over and above deciding simple category membership. For example, we can employ the knowledge associated with the category "burglary" to decide whether this crime is on the increase and whether more stringent punishments should be introduced to bring it under control. Concepts depend on the information held within a category but they also allow for additional interpretations to be made according to the context in which the information is being used.

It is often assumed that concepts retain their core meanings as they re-occur in different contexts—it was this assumption that informed Fodor and Pylyshyn's treatment of systematicity as described in the previous chapter. However, matters may not be this simple. Words (and their related concepts) may not be tied to a fixed meaning but, instead, may undergo shifts in meaning as the sentential context alters. While a typical bird may be a robin in the absence of further information, given "The bird walked across the farmyard" this assumption need no longer hold. It is quite plausible that in the rural context we are more likely to invoke "chicken" as a typical exemplar than robin. Although, initially, the experimental evidence appeared to go against this argument, (e.g. Garrod & Sanford, 1977) further studies have found in favour of conceptual lability.

Roth and Shoben (1983) report an experiment in which typical or atypical exemplars from a class were preceded by sentences that were either contextually neutral or introduced a bias towards the given exemplar as a likely referent. They found that although the typicality effect held under the neutral condition, the effect disappeared when the prior context was biased in favour of the atypical case. Consequently, Roth and Shoben concluded that typicality, as determined in the absence of context, does not necessarily predict what will happen when contextual constraints are present. Our conceptual structure has a degree of flexibility which typicality measures largely fail to take into account. Similar conclusions have been reached from studies of conceptual combinations where categories are productively combined to form more restricted concepts—as when we refer to "predatory birds" or to "song birds" rather than "birds" in general. If subjects are called upon to judge the typicality of instances drawn from concept combinations, it is not possible to predict their judgements from the internal structure of the noun concept alone (Medin & Shoben, 1988). Rather, it is necessary to go beyond subjects' knowledge of the feature lists associated with the class members to include their theoretical knowledge bearing on how the features themselves are thought to be interrelated.

As set out earlier, the gist of the prototypic account is that acts of categorisation critically rest upon judgements of similarity; candidate instances are compared against the category prototype and, if they are sufficiently similar, they are accepted into the category. Once accepted, the category members will then be judged as being more similar to each other than they are to non-category items. Sadly, this neat and orderly account runs into difficulties on those occasions where categorisation and similarity judgements can be shown to diverge. If we are asked about membership of categories based on particular goals—say, things to give as birthday presents—then item similarity does not seem an important determinant of typicality. Although flowers and jewellery may be typical birthday presents, it is not because they have a high average similarity to each other or to other exemplars in the class (Barsalou, 1985).

Rips and Collins (1993) suggest that similarity judgements may underlie an act of categorisation on those occasions when subjects know little about the domain in question. On those occasions where subjects do have considerable background information (as with birthday presents) they bring this additional theoretical knowledge into play when deciding whether an instance should be accepted as a category member or not. Hence, a deeper understanding of conceptual structure requires that we look beyond listings of the features associated with particular concepts to take account of their differential salience for the category in question. But, if we are to take this extra step, we will then need some non-circular way of determining which features are to be treated as salient and which are not. As Medin and Shoben (1988) have pointed out, subjects are likely to treat people with white hair and grey hair as being more similar to each other than people with grey hair and black hair. This is because of the status of these features in their theory of ageing. In other domains, such as judgements of cloud formations, another theory prevails and different similarity pairings are likely to be made. Our intuitive theory of weather patterns implies that grey clouds are more similar to black clouds because both are portents of bad weather. In other words, the act of categorisation calls for rather more than the compilation of a discrete list of the features associated with particular classes, it also calls for registration of the manner in which particular features co-vary within their referent domain.

A number of investigators have remarked how once a list of categorial features has been drawn up, it can become evident that certain features tend to go together. The observed propensities of birds for laying eggs; making nests in trees; using wings; having feathers; and flying are all interconnected and form the glimmerings of a theory of "birdness". In fact, abstracting such structural patterns can set in train a progressive cycle of change where new concepts arise out of older versions, as Goldstone (1994, p.147) points out

> Previously developed concepts provide properties that serve as a basis for similarity. Similarity, in turn, provides a heuristic for developing new concepts. Once a new concept is developed, more sophisticated communalities between the concept's members are likely to be discovered.

We can expect, therefore, conceptual representation to undergo a process of differentiation both as cross dependencies are registered within a particular conceptual scheme and as new relationships are formed between related schemes held in memory. Exactly how this might be achieved is a central issue in understanding the nature of accumulative memory and we will have more to say about this in the following sections. For the moment, we can note that feature lists, by definition, are not suitable vehicles for representing detailed patterns of cross dependencies of this kind and more complex representational formats are needed to fill the gap.

In fact, there is a substantial body of evidence to the effect that our general knowledge is constructed as concepts are combined to form propositional representations which, in turn, can combine to form the higher-order knowledge schemas that determine our levels of expertise in particular domains.

PROPOSITIONAL ENCODING

Propositional structures were initially deployed by Fillmore (1968) as a tool for analysing the grammatical structure of sentences. Fillmore's Case grammar assumed that different verbs can be distinguished in terms of the number of arguments they can support in a sentence. For example, the verb DIE functions as a one place verb because it can occur in a grammatical sentence with only one argument. Thus, given the sentence, "The victims died" we can abstract [DIE, VICTIMS] as the underlying proposition. Other verbs such as KILL and GIVE function as two and three place verbs respectively. Compare, "The criminal killed the victims" [KILL, CRIMINAL, VICTIMS] and "The criminal gave some food to the victims" [GIVE, CRIMINAL, FOOD, VICTIMS].

At minimum, a propositional unit consists of a relational concept (typically the main verb in an utterance), and a set of slots for holding the associated arguments. Once these slots have been filled with local values, the resulting proposition can then represent the central gist which distinguishes one transaction from another. Evidence pointing to the ubiquity of propositional encoding in human memory is now well established. For example, when we process spoken or written discourse, we do not employ its surface structure—the utterance as actually spoken or written—instead we use its underlying propositional content as a preliminary indication of its meaning.

The transient status of surface structures in memory was first demonstrated by Sachs (1967) whose experiments revealed that subjects reading continuous text soon lost sight of literal sentence forms they had only just read. After as little as 80 or so interpolated syllables, her subjects were incapable of distinguishing sentences they had actually seen from probe sentences that meant the same thing but expressed that meaning slightly differently—as when an active sentence is converted into the passive form. On the other hand, they had no difficulty in rejecting variant sentences that altered the original meaning. (Of course, if instructed, subjects can still retain surface forms; we do not go to the theatre to listen to the gist of Hamlet.)

Strictly interpreted, Sach's result only demonstrates that the surface form of discourse is soon lost, to be replaced by some other coding format in memory. Establishing that this format concurs with a propositional mode of encoding calls for different investigatory techniques.

Support for propositional encoding has utilised the argument that if the proposition serves as a representational unit in memory, then we can expect it to maintain its internal integrity at recall. Weisberg (1969) has provided an experimental test of this prediction. His subjects first memorised sets of sentences and then participated in a recall cueing task where they were given words, drawn at random from the sentences in the learning set, to which they were to free associate with another word from the same sentence. The functional unity of a proposition implies that subjects should respond to a cue word by supplying another word from the same proposition rather than some other word from the sentence. He found that subjects predominantly responded in this manner even if this meant selecting a word that was serially remote from the cue in the surface structure of the sentence.

Another means of testing for the integrity of propositional units in memory is to look for priming effects where activating part of a propositional structure leads to the remainder of the structure becoming active as well. This technique was employed by Ratcliff and McKoon (1978) in an experiment where subjects read four sets of sentences of different types and propositional make-up. After they had read a sentence set, subjects were faced with a recognition task which required them to discriminate between old test words (i.e. words they had seen) and distractors (new words). Two types of priming effect were reported under these conditions. The first (sentential) type occurred when "old" words drawn from the same sentence cropped up on consecutive trials. The second (propositional) priming effect arose when the "old" test words on consecutive trials not only came from the same sentence but were also drawn from the same proposition. Thus, if the subject had seen the sentence:

The mausoleum that enshrined the czar overlooked the square

and the test word "czar" was followed on the next trial by "square", the time to respond should be facilitated as a result of sentential priming. However, a greater degree of facilitation could be expected in the case of propositional priming, as when the subject responded to "square" having previously responded to "mausoleum". Sentential priming effects (which averaged at 91msec) were significantly less than propositional priming effects (averaging at 111msec).

A more stringent test of propositional priming has been reported by Dell, McKoon, and Ratcliff (1983). In this experiment it was shown that when subjects searched for an anaphoric reference while reading continuous prose, they not only reactivated the appropriate antecedent concept but they also reactivated other arguments from the same proposition. Subjects who read *A burglar surveyed the garage set back from the street* and then, some sentences later, read about *The criminal*, could be expected to reactivate *burglar* as they registered the anaphoric link. Introducing "burglar" as a probe item just before and after the anaphor had been read demonstrated that it was recognised more quickly as being "old" just after the anaphoric link had been made. And the same outcome also applied when "garage" was used as a test probe—the companion argument from the same proposition.

We shall have cause to refer to the propositional encoding of information on a number of later occasions, especially when we come to consider text comprehension in Chapter 9. An important part of text comprehension is to arrive at a memory encoding that captures the gist of what is being described. One means of doing this is to combine the individual propositions in the text to create an overall macrostructure—a large-scale, schematic structure that represents how the main topic has been elaborated in the course of the text. Similar large-scale schematic structures are also created in the course of everyday understanding and they serve as a framework through which recurrent regularities in external events come to be registered on many levels simultaneously.

KNOWLEDGE SCHEMAS

If we are asked, unexpectedly, to comment on the latest item of news, we find that our ideas tend to take shape in a relatively structured way without any great struggle on our part to ensure their relevance. To be sure, there are exceptions; we may know little about the topic or we may be so aroused that we become incoherent but, by and large, we cope remarkably well. Schema theory aims to explain this fluency in retrieval by postulating the presence of multiple schematic frameworks in memory which serve to summarise the details shared in common by past experiences as they extend over space and time. As individual knowledge schemas can also embed within higher-order schemas, we have the situation where large amounts of knowledge can be readily assembled, as needed, for the task in hand. And the more the schematic knowledge we have at our disposal, the more expert we become at working in a particular domain.

The functional utility of schematically organised knowledge can be graphically demonstrated if we compare the performance of subjects with different levels of expertise in their chosen field. De Groot (1965, 1966) has shown that less skilled chess players remember far less of the current game state than do expert players. He allowed highly skilled and less expert players a limited (2–15 seconds) exposure to a board arrangement and then, after clearing the board, asked his subjects to replace the chess pieces on their original squares. The differences in recall accuracy associated with the different skill levels were striking.

The two subjects at or above master level scored over 90% accuracy whereas their less able counterparts performed significantly worse.

The source of the experts' advantage arose from the way in which they encoded the board details. Experts used their (schematic) knowledge of chess strategy to combine the individual pieces to form larger-scale encodings which then served both as a memory representation for the state of the board and as a retrieval guide when the pieces were replaced. Expertise, it seems, resides in the possession of a repertoire of relevant schematic structures which can enter into large-scale encoding operations. Ignorance resides either in the lack of schematic knowledge structures or their inappropriateness for the domain in question. Thus, the simple device of placing chess pieces at random on the chess board is sufficient to wipe out the expert's advantage over the less skilled player (Chase & Simon, 1973). Similar differences between knowledgeable followers of baseball and naive spectators have been reported by Chiesi, Spilich, and Voss (1979).

The modern version of the cognitive schema can be traced back to the writings of Bartlett (1932), although Piaget was working with similar ideas at about the same time (Piaget, 1926). Prior to both of these, the neurologist Head (1920) had used the "schema" to account for "the organised effects of past responses on current behaviour" and earlier still, in the eighteenth century, Kant had employed similar ideas for linking perception and experience with the process of understanding. Arguments in favour of knowledge schemas may have come and gone over the years, but it was predominantly Bartlett's work on remembering that brought the idea of the schema to the attention of most cognitive psychologists. In his book *Remembering*, Bartlett (1932) reported the results from a series of studies based on subjects' recall of geometrical figures and short texts which had been learned under different conditions. This data indicated that subjects frequently omitted peripheral and unexpected content, introduced new material in order to resolve textual incongruities, and transformed atypical event orders into something closer to the norm. Faced with this constellation of errors, Bartlett suggested that remembering was not the mere revival of the traces of earlier experience but a process of active reconstruction in which the original event was pieced together from fragmentary cues held in memory. The schema provided the framework within which this reconstruction took place.

Bartlett (1932, p.201) defined the schema as "an active organisation of past reactions, or of past experiences, which must always be supposed to be operating in any well adapted organic response". It is not an ideal definition but, in essence, it conceives of the schema as a generic structure which captures the regularities that are present in a series of related experiences. Once a schema has been laid down in memory, it can be reactivated in the appropriate circumstances and, once reactivated, it makes available a framework onto which the details of an event can be mapped as part of our "search after meaning".

A strong interpretation of Bartlett's position would hold that we have no specific episodic detail in memory at all. Once an event has been understood by assimilating it to a schema only the generic information is retained and atypical detail is lost. At recall "we turn around on our schemata" and reconstruct the original details from this generic representation by inferring the probable components of the experience. Although this strong interpretation can easily account for the types of error Bartlett had observed, if taken literally, it would have real difficulty in accounting for the presence of any unique (non-prototypic) detail that was also reproduced. And, if that difficulty is finessed, we are then faced with explaining how it is that individual schemas come to be induced from experience in the first place. Consequently, Bartlett often adopted the less extreme position of arguing that recall can be based both on a generic schematic representation and on additional episodic detail (Brewer & Nakamura, 1983).

In 1971, Zangwill used the opportunity provided by the Third Bartlett Memorial Lecture to reflect critically on the then diminished status of Bartlett's arguments. Zangwill cited as reasons for this decline the presence of two basic flaws in the original studies; (1) the vagueness associated with the idea of the schema which formed the core of Bartlett's theoretical approach, and (2) the dubious reliability of the recall data on which the schema model rested. Referring to work in his own laboratory, Zangwill stressed that the distortions observed when people freely recalled event detail were not evident when they were tested on their ability to recognise original detail. Clearly, if subjects could recognise details they had failed to recall, this was hardly consistent with a memory record that had been filtered in the course of schema instantiation. Furthermore, where Bartlett had typically found reconstructive error in free recall, Zangwill and his students typically found only errors of omission, supporting the conclusion, contrary to Bartlett, that memory entailed abstractive rather than reconstructive processes (Gauld & Stephenson, 1967; Gomulicki, 1956; Zangwill, 1972).

We can accept Zangwill's strictures up to a point—learning conditions can certainly be found which favour rote recall—but it remains the case that when subjects are encouraged to link what they read with their prior knowledge, we find the resulting protocols shift once more towards Bartlett's reconstructive mode. Thus, Spiro (1980) demonstrated that where learners have to do some accommodatory work during learning, as when the experimental passages contain information inconsistent with their background knowledge, the resulting protocols are quite in line with Bartlett's claims. Under these conditions, Spiro found that the incidence of reconstructive errors at recall not only increased with delay, but his subjects reached a point where they expressed more confidence in the accuracy of their accommodative errors than they did in the accuracy of their genuine recall of the core story content. It seems, therefore, that both Bartlett and Zangwill were partly right in what they had to say. Experimental instructions may set accommodatory processes in motion (favouring reconstructive recall) or they may hardly be triggered at all (favouring reproductive recall). Equally, both were wrong in taking their own learning conditions as defining the general case.

In the 1930s it was relatively unusual to conduct research on complex materials like prose passages—most laboratories at the time were grappling with much simpler tasks such as the serial learning of symbol strings. However, as more complex linguistic tasks became an accepted part of the cognitive research programme, Bartlett's arguments took on a new relevance. Neisser's highly influential book *Cognitive psychology* (1967), reintroduced the traditional idea of the schema as a "a non-specific but organised representation of prior experiences" and it was soon to move up the cognitive agenda to become the main item of business.

Minsky (1975) removed some of the ambiguity inherent in earlier schema accounts by introducing the concept of the "frame" which consisted of a set of slots representing the stereotypic features of an object or event. Each slot within the frame could be filled by some actual value supplied from perception, otherwise a prototypic value was supplied by default from within the frame itself. Furthermore, large tracts of information could now be co-ordinated in memory by the inclusion of pointers to other (related) frames at certain slot positions. Bartlett's admittedly vague concept of a schema was starting to achieve a concrete identity and belated recognition as a central cognitive tool for comprehending the world (see also Rumelhart, 1975, and Schank & Abelson, 1977).

These pioneering efforts have led to the received interpretation of schemas as symbolic representations that serve to encode our generic knowledge concerning objects, scenes, and action sequences. In each case, we induce the appropriate schemas from the regularities accompanying multiple exposures to the events in question. As an example, Figure 2.2 reproduces the schematic framework associated with a prototypical kitchen.

The schema consists of a set of labelled slots for the different appliances, likely users, and common activities to be found in a typical kitchen where each slot contains a particular default value (e.g. stove

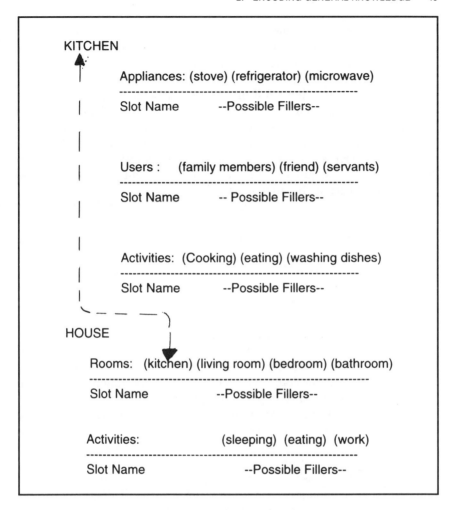

KITCHEN

Appliances: (stove) (refrigerator) (microwave)

Slot Name   --Possible Fillers--

Users :   (family members) (friend) (servants)

Slot Name   -- Possible Fillers--

Activities: (Cooking) (eating) (washing dishes)

Slot Name   --Possible Fillers--

HOUSE

Rooms: (kitchen) (living room) (bedroom) (bathroom)

Slot Name   --Possible Fillers--

Activities: (sleeping) (eating) (work)

Slot Name   --Possible Fillers--

FIG. 2.2. Kitchen schema. (Adapted from Just & Carpenter, 1987.)

or refrigerator as likely appliances). These default values can be displaced by the local values that are present when we are confronted by some specific kitchen. Otherwise, they are always there to fill out our understanding should this local information be lacking. Figure 2.2 also indicates how individual schemas can enter as constituents into higher-order schemas to form larger-scale hierarchical structures as "kitchen" reappears as one of the room values in the superordinate "house" schema. A similar embedding can also apply at a subordinate level as when "refrigerator" is unpacked revealing a subschema with its own feature slots (e.g. door, shelves, contents etc). All of which is to argue that a significant component of our general knowledge comes in the form of numerous, bespoke schematic structures tailored to the nuances of different subject domains.

Although nothing like a full inventory of schema types has yet been attempted, certain basic formats have been identified. Object schemas encode the feature sets associated with physical objects; spatial schemas encode information about the orientation of objects with respect to each other; and "scripts" serve to encode episodic details associated with recurrent action sequences. In reality, it is difficult to sustain these clear-cut distinctions because most of the situations we encounter will override these artificial divisions by activating a variety of different schemas simultaneously.

Advocates of schematic encoding have argued that knowledge schemas play an ubiquitous role in cognitive processing and they can point to an impressive body of work in suppport of this claim: Rumelhart (1980) provides an extensive review of schemas as the "building blocks of cognition". A schema can either be activated by external inputs from perception or it may be triggered as a result of internal processing. Once active, a schema makes available all of the default information it contains as well as providing slots in which the features of structural descriptions can be deposited. When the schema has been instantiated, i.e. when the available slots have been filled with the salient values from the input situation, at that point the input can be said to have been understood. Nonetheless, we can never be certain that the meaning we assign to an input is the best possible interpretation. It is always possible that other schemas that have remained inactive for some reason might have served us better.

In the course of assigning meaning to an input, the hierarchical embedding of schema structures allows for a valuable degree of control over the amounts of prior knowledge we bring into play. It would not be much use if everything we know had to be activated before a situation could be understood, because understanding would be delayed long after a response had ceased to be relevant. Hierarchical embedding effectively solves this problem. Fine-grain detail can be accessed at a subschematic level in the hierarchy while an increasingly synoptic view can be adopted by moving to higher levels in the hierarchy. This arrangement enables us to delimit the scope of activated knowledge to whatever grain size fits best with the immediate task requirements.

All told, at least five different cognitive functions have been commonly attributed to active schemas as they participate in the processing of information. Schemas are said (1) to provide for the interpretation of events, (2) to make available a mnemonic framework for organising incoming information, (3) to assist in abstracting gist from peripheral detail, (4) to allow for prediction ahead of what is to come, and (5) to serve as a guide for reconstructive recall. We will look at evidence taken to support all of these functional claims and then return to the reservations, cited earlier, concerning the extent to which schemas may actually filter, and hence distort, incoming information.

Interpretation

Once a schema has been activated, its internal organisation and default entries can be put to work in order to supplement the literal content made available by an input. Consider this short passage (Sanford & Garrod, 1981, p.10):

> John had got up late and as he hurried to school he worried about the first lesson, which was Maths. Last week he had been unable to control the class. It was unfair of the Maths teacher to leave him in charge. It was not part of the Janitor's duties.

On hearing the first sentence the listener is provided with a body of cues sufficient to activate a "school attendance" schema and this then makes available a host of prepackaged information—likely participants (teachers; pupils ...), typical buildings (staff rooms; class rooms ...) and probable times (weekday; 9.00a.m. ...). As the mapping to the schema gets underway, John is automatically assigned to a pupil slot—this is the best fit given the information available at the end of the first sentence. This fit breaks down when "controlling the class" is encountered and accordingly John is now reassigned as teacher, which is the best fit given the new set of constraints. This assignment is again altered when the text explicitly states the true nature of John's role.

Clearly, the act of assigning meaning to the passage consists of much more than passively registering the content as given. But additional interpretation will only arise provided an appropriate schema is activated at the right time. Knowledge schemas that remain inactive during comprehension are as much use as non-voters during an election—they have the power to influence the outcome but they will only do so if they have been stirred into action at the appropriate moment.

In the light of these arguments, the device of assigning two different titles to the same passage of text can be expected to have the effect of activating different assimilatory schemas in each case. As such, we should find that subjects given one or other title end up producing qualitatively different protocols at recall. Kozminsky (1977) employed this procedure with a text dealing with a trainee nurse being consulted by a patient about her excess weight. Under the condition where it was titled "Betty's Weight Problem", around 41% of the propositions judged to be central to this theme were recalled along with around 34% of the propositions related to the secondary (nursing) theme. Subjects who read the same passage under the heading "My Nursing Assignment" effectively reversed this balance. These subjects averaged around 32% recall for the nursing content compared with 30% recall for the weight content. The gross effects of dual titling may not be overwhelming, but the predicted recall biases can be observed and they are reliable.

In a similar study, Pichert and Anderson (1977) asked their subjects to adopt one of two perspectives while reading a text about two boys who have chosen to stay at home instead of attending school. Certain statements in the text dealt with the state of the house and its level of repair (e.g. "The basement had been damp and musty ever since the new plumbing had been installed") while other statements referred to the house contents and its remote location (e.g. "Tall hedges hid the house from the road"). Half of the subjects were required to read while adopting a "potential housebuyer" perspective and the other half were called upon to adopt the perspective of a "prospective burglar". At recall, subjects duly reproduced those propositions that were consistent with their adopted perspective. State-of-repair information predominated under the buyer perspective and details about potential gains and risks predominated under the burglar perspective.

Additional evidence that active schemas add default information to an interpretation is to be found in a study reported by Bower, Black, and Turner (1979). Their subjects read a series of script-based stories (such as "a visit to the doctor") which left out some typical script entries (e.g. "arrive at the surgery"). When these subjects participated in a subsequent recognition test, where they had to indicate precisely which details they had actually seen, they not only falsely recognised the default information, they also assigned it the same degree of confidence as the genuine content. (Incidentally, this tendency to add information by default has also been observed in citations of the scientific literature. For example, the control procedure of placing the chess pieces at random mentioned with regard to the De Groot studies of chess expertise, is often—incorrectly—attributed to this investigator. This and other reconstructive errors in the scientific literature have been reviewed by Vicente & Brewer, 1993.)

Although laboratory demonstrations of schema effects may not appear overly dramatic, there are circumstances where the effects of interpreting the same event under different schemas can be catastrophic. Perrow (Hutchins, 1991) described how two vessels sighted one another and, it being night-time, one of the captains erroneously concluded that the other ship was proceeding in the same direction as his own craft. This was in opposition to the view of his lookout who (correctly) saw the same ship as proceeding towards them. Perrow (Hutchins, 1991, p.289) described how, since closing came very fast:

> ... the captain decided that it must be a very slow fishing boat that he was about to overtake. This reinforced his incorrect interpretation. The lookout knew the captain was aware of the ship, so did not comment further as it got quite close and seemed to be nearly on a collision course. ... The other ship, a large cargo ship, did not establish any bridge-to-bridge communication, because the passing was routine. But at the last moment, the captain of the *Cuyahoga* realised that in overtaking the supposed fishing boat which he assumed was on a near parallel course, he would cut off that boat's ability to turn as both of them approached the Potomac River. So he ordered a turn to port [and the two ships collided].

Mnemonic functioning

The second function depends on an activated knowledge schema providing a bespoke framework onto which new information can be mapped, facilitating both learning and recall in the process. In fact, the benefits arising from mnemonic frameworks have been recognised since classical times and Yates (1966) has described how the mnemonic skills displayed by the Roman rhetoricians relied on the creation of special schemas designed for use in situations where the material to be learned lacked intrinsic structure or where it was important that the serial order of a sequence be precisely reproduced. One such classical technique, the Method of Loci, required the learner to imagine the to-be-learned content in conjunction with the features of a well known building or the landmarks associated with a familiar route. Once this had been done, the building or route was mentally traversed at recall and, as each room or landmark was encountered, this served to reactivate their associated topics in the order required.

A particularly convincing demonstration of the power of mnemonic strategies has been provided by Chase and Ericsson (1981) who reported on the progress of an experimental subject as he extended his digit span (see Chapter 4) from the normal span of 7 items at the beginning of their project to the staggering total of 80 items a few months later. Their subject, SF, was required to listen to a serial list of digits prior to saying them back in the same order. His digit span was then defined as the maximum list length that could be recalled without error.

At the start of the project, SF was an unexceptional performer but he soon hit on the idea of recoding the digit strings using his extensive (schematic) knowledge of athletic records such as Olympic records for the marathon and other distances. With this strategy in play, he recoded sections of an incoming string as a sequence of running times. This resulted in a significant expansion in his digit span which only came to a halt when the number of imposed chunks started to exceed his short-memory capacity. This obstacle was itself overcome when SF started to group chunks into "superchunks" by nesting a whole series of Olympic records within a larger representational unit. Once SF had firmly mastered this technique, just one hearing was sufficient for him to be able to repeat back, without error, a list of 80 or so digits. The advantages that can accrue from schematically organised learning are clearly considerable but they can also be highly context-specific. At the time when SF was at the peak of his form with digit strings, his span for letter strings was precisely seven items.

Abstraction

It was argued earlier that the process of comprehension normally entails going for the gist or basic meaning of an event. When listening to a conversation or when reading, we discard surface detail in favour of a more abstract, propositional representation. We also tend to drop low-level (unimportant) content in favour of high-level content—see the discussion of the "levels effect" in text recall in Chapter 9. However, laboratory studies of gist recall probably underestimate the degree to which it occurs because experimental subjects are rarely pushed to the limits of their processing abilities. Mindful of this limitation, Neisser (1982) took the opportunity presented by John Dean's testimony to the Watergate hearings to investigate the matter under more natural if somewhat unusual conditions. The discovery of the tapes relating to meetings in the White House which Dean had covered in his testimony meant that his claim to provide detailed transcripts of his conversations from memory could be empirically assessed.

When Neisser consulted these sources, he found that despite Dean's apparently sincere attempts to provide truthful accounts of what took place during particular sessions, he often failed to distinguish between meetings that had been held on separate occasions. His testimony represented the gist of a number of separate, albeit related meetings; cognate details from different conversations were grouped together and treated as having occured in a single meeting. Such an outcome is to be expected where, on different occasions, the same assimilatory schemas have been actively involved, leading to a generic, schematic representation for the events in question.

Prediction

Once aroused, schematic knowledge can be used to predict ahead. This confers distinct advantages when processing the flow of events. If our predictions are confirmed we are already prepared for what is to come. If the unexpected happens, we are alerted to the presence of novelty and its potential significance. The predictive role of knowledge schemas in cognitive processing has been investigated by focusing on the fate of atypical schema detail at recall, i.e. detail that fails to find an appropriate slot in the assimilatory framework. Graesser, Woll, Kowalski, and Smith (1980) compared the fate of typical and atypical script actions both at recall and at recognition. On immediate testing, they found that atypical content was both better recalled and better recognised than typical content. However, after a delay of one week, this pattern changed. Recall of atypical material now turned out to be worse than recall of typical content—a consequence, it seems, of the schema prototype reasserting itself. Similarly, Wilkes and Alred (1978) have shown that schematic content can be used to identify when deviations from an expected path have occurred and this has the effect of making the deviant information more memorable, at least in the short term.

Retrieval guidance

The influence of an assimilatory schema on the subsequent retrieval of information has been demonstrated by Brewer and Treyens (1981). These experimenters required their subjects, on arrival at the appointed time, to wait in a sideroom under the impression that they would then be called when the experiment was ready. In fact, when they left this room shortly afterwards, their experimental task was to recall the contents of the room.

The room had been deliberately furnished to fit the schema for a post-graduate office except that certain highly typical features (such as books) had been left out, while some atypical objects (such as a skull) had been added. The content subjects included in their recall protocols was much as would be predicted from the contents of an office schema. Typical detail was well recalled, if present, and inferred, if absent. Atypical content, on the other hand, was poorly recalled. All of which is consistent with the office schema being used as a retrieval guide.

The poor recall of atypical detail reported by Brewer and Treyens apparently contradicts the previous claim that inconsistent schema detail is likely to be favoured at recall. This difficulty can be resolved if we distinguish between schema irrelevance and schema inconsistency.

Salient information that conflicts with schema predictions is likely to be well recalled; schema-irrelevant information or inconsistent information of low salience need not be processed to the same depth.

Additional evidence of schemas serving as retrieval plans has also come from the dual perspective procedure. In a subsequent study conducted by Anderson and Pichert (1978) subjects were asked to recall the house passage (described earlier) twice in succession; first, using the perspective adopted during reading, then again when adopting the other perspective. Following the switch, subjects were able to recall passage content they had previously omitted. Subjects who switched to a "burglar" perspective after "housebuyer", now reproduced details relevant to the new theme that they had previously omitted. Conversely, they also omitted some of the details they had included on their first recall attempt; details that, following the switch, were no longer schema-relevant.

Schematic filtering at encoding and recall

Taken overall, these studies into schematic processing appear to support the weak version of Bartlett's arguments; inputs are selectively encoded to produce a filtered memory record for the experienced event but idiosyncratic detail is not necessarily lost. However, most of the studies cited have relied on free recall as a guide to the memory record for the event in question and, as the perspective-switching experiment indicates, this measure can be misleading. Content that cannot be immediately recalled may nonetheless still form part of the memory record.

Following a review of the relevant literature, Alba and Hasher (1983) concluded that although there is good evidence for schema effects at retrieval, the same is not true for encoding where recognition measures point to the formation of a memory record that is largely faithful to the details of the actual experience. When Alba, Alexander, Hasher, and Caniglia (1981) contrasted free recall data with data based on recognition testing they were able to show that although schema effects were evident under free recall, they were absent from the recognition data. Similarly, when Hasher and Griffin (1978) employed a variant of the dual title procedure in which, prior to recall, the subjects were suddenly informed that the title they had been given when reading a passage was wrong and another title was substituted, this had the effect of eliminating schematic distortions from the data. Under a consistent title condition, the usual schematic distortions were found but the subjects who experienced a title change not only made fewer title-related intrusions, they actually recalled more of the original passage. This outcome is attributed to their need to make special efforts to recall once they realised that their original retrieval plan was no longer valid. That they could then access detail that would otherwise have remained inaccessible is incompatible with a memory record based on selective filtering.

In many ways, this exchange marks yet another round in the debate initiated some 20 years ago by Zangwill. Now, as then, the dispute centres on the dangers of taking the features of free recall protocols as a faithful reflection of the properties of the underlying memory record. Adopting a more cautious approach to the available data implies that whereas schematic processing need not necessarily lead to filtered and distorted memory records being laid down, it can exert a significant influence on how we organise this information and how we access this information later. Such an imbalance between encoding accuracy and retrieval bias can be seen as an effective trade-off between "being right" and "being relevant". We have to rely on our internal memory records for conveying information about the external world and it is important that they do so without too much distortion. Nonetheless, when we need to get to the gist of a situation, it is important that the same records make this information available selectively—favouring salient over peripheral detail as defined by the typical case. If it then happens that the current circumstances are atypical in some way, the adoption of more strategic retrieval methods means that additional information can still be brought to mind.

AMODAL AND MODALITY-SPECIFIC CODES IN MEMORY

In the course of this chapter we have reviewed the significance of categorisation in the cognitive economy along with evidence implicating propositions and schemas as symbolic tools for representing our general knowledge of the external world. The overall picture that has emerged has been one in which "amodal" codes predominate—that is, codes that have been stripped of the sensory details that accompanied the initial experiences. Yet, our subjective experiences tell a different story. It is next to impossible to recall a script of a beach scene without some accompanying visual, auditory, olfactory, and tactile imagery also coming to mind—indicating that our general knowledge contains information on the manner in which external objects and scenes can impinge upon the different sensory modalities. In the next chapter, therefore, we will consider where modality-specific representations fit into the picture. As we will see, if amodal codes are to work as intended they need to make contact at some point with their referent states in the external world. Allowing for both propositional and imaginal coding in memory provides a means of overcoming this difficulty. It also allows us to look beyond human comprehension as a process of schema instantiation by capitalising on the computational properties associated with the "mental models" that can be formed from these dual encoding resources.

CHAPTER THREE

Dual encoding and imagery

At first glance, it may seem that propositional coding would not provide a suitable medium for handling such information as the spatial arrangements of visual scenes. In fact, appearances apart, this need not be the case. Our memory, say, for the spatial locations of British counties need not call upon a visual image of a map of the UK—it could take the form of the propositional format depicted in Fig. 3.1, albeit in a less abbreviated version.

Such an hierarchically organised, propositional structure could handle a range of spatial information. It could be used to access directly the spatial relationship between Scotland and England and, indirectly, to infer information concerning other relationships that are not explicitly represented—for example, that Cornwall lies to the south of Sutherland. In principle, therefore, spatial and other forms of non-verbal information could be represented in memory using a common propositional code that is independent of any specific sensory modality.

Such an arrangement could carry significant advantages. If all that we know is stored in a common format then any part of that knowledge can potentially be used in conjunction with any other part. In contrast, a mixture of modality-specific codes would significantly restrict the scope of knowledge "portability" because special arrangements would need to be made before knowledge stored in different formats could be shared. Hence, there is a strong *a priori* case to be made in favour of a unified coding system that overrides modality differences. Nonetheless,

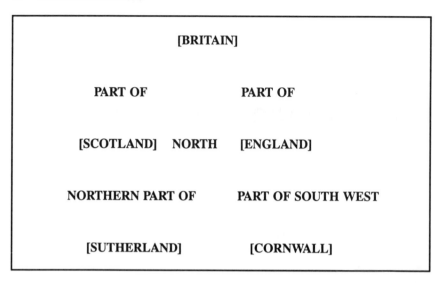

FIG. 3.1. An hierarchical propositional encoding of a spatial display.

this would be to run in the face of our subjective experience of mental imagery which seems to imply a dual coding in memory implicating both amodal (descriptive) and modality-specific (depictive) representations.

Obtaining the evidence that would enable us to decide between these alternatives has not turned out to be easy and over the years the ensuing debate has aroused a great deal of heat as well as ingenuity. The problem resides in the fact that, as with mental maps, the same information could be mentally represented in either format and, as we are dealing with internalised as opposed to public codes, we have no privileged means of deciding one way or the other. Consequently, the arguments for and against mental imagery as a component of the cognitive architecture have waxed and waned from the very beginnings of experimental psychology, generating an extended and apparently unending debate in the processs. A debate, it might be added, that has been continually refuelled by the chronic inability of the participants to give clear definitions to the issues at stake.

At one extreme we find theorists, such as Pylyshyn (1973), who treat imagery as a derivative from an abstract propositional encoding in memory. At the other extreme, are theorists such as Kosslyn (1980), who claim that different codes are used for verbal and for visual information. Somewhere in between these two positions we find yet other theorists, such as Tye (1991) and Intons-Peterson (1992), who claim that mental images can display both descriptive and depictive properties—neither form alone quite does justice to their elusive nature. We will look at the arguments emanating from all of these positions as well as some of the counter-arguments they have provoked.

MODALITY-SPECIFIC CODES

A little introspection quickly establishes that for most of us mental imagery is an everyday event. When asked to list the contents of a room in their house or to describe their place of work, most people report invoking visual imagery to assist their deliberations. Nonetheless, reliance on visual imagery is not always forthcoming and its presence seems to be especially associated with tasks that require the recall of information from an unfamiliar perspective. Recalling the most valuable coin in circulation is less likely to elicit visual imagery than deciding the direction the Queen's head is facing on the British coinage. Similarly, if asked whether the British Prime Minister's voice is higher in pitch than the American President's, whether wet sandpaper feels less rough than dry, or what a combination of salt and sugar would taste like, our answers are likely to be informed by mental images generated in each of the relevant modalities.

To take an extreme case, Helen Keller, who was deaf and blind from early infancy, describes how, haptic (touch) imagery permeated her representations of her world. In her autobiography (Keller, 1908, p.7) she states:

> My world is built of touch sensations, devoid of physical colour and sound; but without colour and sound it breathes and throbs with life. Every object is associated in my mind with tactual qualities which, combined in countless ways, gives me a sense of power, of beauty, or of incongruity; for with my hands I can feel the comic as well as the beautiful in the outward appearance of things.

Helen Keller's subjective world was obviously full of subtle shades and her reference to countless combinations of touch sensations implies a productivity to this mode of coding that could be used to support a variety of cognitive computations. Indeed, even olfactory images have been recruited into the service of arithmetical computation.

In his autobiography, *Memories of my life*, Francis Galton refers to an experiment in which he trained himself to do mental arithmetic using imagined smells as the constituent symbols. He remarks (1908, p.284) that in order to achieve this skill:

I taught myself to associate two whiffs of peppermint with one of camphor, three of peppermint with one of carbolic acid and so on. Next I practiced small sums in addition with the scents themselves, afterwards with the mere imagination of them ... I fully convinced myself of the possibility of doing sums in simple addition with considerable speed and accuracy, solely by imagined scents.

It was a typical Galtonian project—generate an interesting (and preferably provocative) hypothesis then put it to a practical test. Although it is improbable that Galton had really succeeded in bringing his eccentric quest to fruition, once again, we can see how, in principle, a system of modality-specific representations under the appropriate processing rules could aspire to the productivity necessary for sustaining a range of cognitive operations.

IMAGES AS MENTAL PICTURES

A superficially plausible (and long-standing) argument holds that visual memory images serve as internal pictures in the head. We have already met with some of the profound difficulties thrown up by this stance but even on its own terms it does not work. The equation of imagery with internalised pictures has a seductive appeal because it "explains" the interpretation of the relevant image by equating it with the supposedly simpler process of picture interpretation. But is it true that picture interpretation is a simple cognitive process?

Wade (1990) has argued that pictures, far from being transparent, call for subtle applications of the rules of iconic representation before we can arrive at an interpretation. A picture is a material object in its own right but this property normally has to be ignored when interpreting its meaning. Wade draws our attention to a variety of subtleties of this kind and, not surprisingly, we find that children do not always observe the conventions. Bornens (1990, p.193) cites an investigation, initially reported by de Schonen, in which young children were asked to categorise pictures of bears as "broken" or "not broken", i.e. as physically disabled or as physically whole. In the event:

... young children classified the pictures of bears with an arm, leg or ear missing as "not broken" and a torn card with the picture of an undamaged bear as "broken".

Referring memory image interpretation to the interpretation of pictorial stimuli, therefore, is to do little more than exchange one obscure process for another. Equally, there is no future in positing inner eyes for reading inner pictures—this strategem merely postpones when and how they are to be interpreted. As Flanagan (1984, note 17, p.386) has pointed out, because memory images are not self-interpreting:

> ... we will still need quasi-linguistic "stage directions" in order to interpret them and pick out salient features, for example to get to grandmother's blue eyes as opposed to her hair or short stature. A unified system of quasi-linguistic representations, however, will need no other mode to assist it in the job of representation; it can be self interpreting in the sense that it can simply fetch the uniquely encoded quasi proposition that states that "grandmother had blue eyes," without also fetching all the other information about her, as a picture would.

The current revival of interest in mental imagery has come about as introspective methods have been replaced by more controlled procedures for investigating the properties of memory images. Techniques such as timing subjects as they "scan" their mental images or as they "rotate" them to set positions have generated data that suggest that strong analogies exist between the properties of memory images and the properties of perceptual states. Dual coding, therefore, would appear to furnish us with new computational tools that could add significantly to the flexibility of cognitive processing. However, once we start to address the empirical evidence for dual coding in memory, a number of problems begin to crowd in.

PAIVIO'S DUAL CODING THEORY

Paivio (1971, 1986), a long-term proponent of dual coding, has argued that mental imaging has evolved for the purpose of handling different kinds of information to that represented through language. He postulates the presence of a verbal system in memory designed for the encoding of linguistic inputs (which employs an hierarchical code) along with a non-verbal system (which employs a spatial and holistic code). Each system is designed to support different kinds of cognitive operations. The verbal system is characterised by sequential processing whereas parallel processing occurs within the non-verbal system.

Such an arrangement would make sense of the robust observation that lists made up from concrete words are learned faster than lists comprising abstract words (e.g. Paivio, 1986). As concrete words, more so than abstract words, have a high probability of eliciting accompanying imagery, their advantage could emanate from their dual representational potential. Whereas abstract words are likely to have only one (verbal) representation in LTM, concrete words are likely to have two representational forms, either of which can be used at retrieval. Nonetheless, arguments relating the advantages of concrete word lists to dual coding are hardly conclusive; the same advantages can also be explained without recourse to dual memory codes.

In a critical review of the evidence linking word concreteness to comprehension, Schawenflugel and Shoben (1983) concluded that two interpretations of its effects are possible. One based on dual representation, as discussed earlier, the other eschewing imagery in favour of the greater depth of processing concrete materials are likely to receive during encoding. According to this latter argument, concrete words are more easily learned because they are more likely to recruit support from the learner's general knowledge at the time of learning.

Schawenflugel and Shoben tested between the dual coding and context availability explanations using abstract or concrete sentences which were read with or without explicit prior context. They reasoned that if the presence of explicit context acts to lift the comprehension level for abstract sentences to the concrete level, then this would support the context availability account. On the other hand, if no improvement in comprehension level is brought about by contextual manipulation then this would support the dual coding hypothesis. They found that in the absence of prior context, concrete sentences were comprehended faster than abstract versions, replicating the usual finding. However, in the presence of prior context this time advantage was significantly diminished, consistent with the context availability interpretation.

Schawenflugel and Shoben interpreted their results as reflecting the spread of activation within a propositional network instigated by the experimental materials. In the absence of explicit context, information relating to abstract concepts is likely to be difficult to retrieve because abstract concepts support a larger amount of weakly associated links in the network compared with concrete words. In consequence, when abstract inputs activate nodes within the network, proportionately less activation is available for traversing the network's links. For concrete concepts, where the degree of branching is significantly less, there will be a "deeper" spread of activation through the network and retrieval benefits accordingly. The presence of explicit context, however, served to prime a subset of the nodes associated with particular inputs and this enhanced access compensated for the source deficiency normally associated with abstract nodes.

In other words, the facilitation associated with the learning of concrete words can be explained without recourse to mental imagery at all. Nevertheless, if the evidence linking concrete words and dual coding is somewhat equivocal, there are still other lines of enquiry which appear to be more promising.

MENTAL IMAGERY AND PERCEPTUAL PROCESSES

There are obvious parallels to be drawn between the visual images generated from memory and the visual images generated through perception, implying that the two phenomena are closely related. Indeed, Finke (1989, p.2) explicitly defines mental imagery as:

... the mental invention or creation of an experience that in at least some respects resembles the experience of actually perceiving an object or event, either in conjunction with or in the absence of, direct sensory stimulation.

Under this interpretation, the imagined act of scanning or rotating a memory image depends on the imager simulating the sequence of perceptual states that normally accompany the physical acts of scanning or rotating a concrete scene or object. If so, we could expect to find close links between the generative processes employed in mental imagery and those employed in perception, including the possibility that both operations rely on the same underlying mechanisms. If the latter holds, then it should be possible to find situations where the two operations interfere with each other. Subjects who try to combine, say, a visual mental imaging task with a concurrent task that draws on visual perception, should soon run into difficulty as the two tasks compete for the same resources.

Brooks (1967) set out to create such a situation by arranging for subjects to encode information about the contents of a 4 × 4 matrix, either in the form of a mental visual image or as a verbal description. Starting with one of the squares in the matrix, a subject either listened to or read a series of statements which, under one condition, could be mentally imaged as a meandering path through the matrix. Thus, a subject might be told:

In the starting square put a 1.
In the next square to the right put a 2.
In the next square up put a 3.

Other subjects were discouraged from forming a mental visual image to the instructions by the device of replacing relational terms like "right" or "up" with adjectives like "good" or "weak". Hence, these subjects heard or read a sequence such as:

In the starting square put a 1.
In the next square to the good put a 2.
In the next square to the weak put a 3.

To retain information in this form, these subjects had to rely on rote rehearsal rather than associated imagery. The performance of the imagery and rehearsal groups critically depended on whether they had been listening to or reading the descriptive sentences. Subjects who read the descriptive sentences in the spatial condition performed less well than those who had listened to them and the reverse pattern applied for the verbal rehearsal group.

Similar results have been reported by Segall and Fusella (1970) who investigated the level of interference produced when subjects combined the detection of auditory or visual signals with the generation of unrelated mental visual or auditory images. Here too it was found that highly specific interference patterns ensued. Although the detection of visual signals was impaired by concurrent visual imaging, this was not true for concurrent auditory images and conversely for detection in the auditory mode.

Both sets of results are compatible with the perceptual system serving as a medium in which external objects can be registered directly via perception or indirectly via mental imagery. In the latter case, our memory records for physical objects and scenes are being manipulated to generate transient "copies" in the appropriate sensory buffer. Creating a mental image of an object would entail accessing its parts from the memory records based on previous perceptual parsings of the object. These parts are then assembled according to further memory records dealing with the part–whole relationships. For example, when mentally imaging a car, specific visual information about the bonnet, wheels, and body is combined according to information about their part–whole relationships prior to arriving at the composite image (see Kosslyn, 1980).

Once the mental image has been formed, we then have access to an internal representation which appears to possess analogous properties to the visual image. Consequently, the resulting memory images can be manipulated in ways that propositional representations would handle less effectively or, perhaps, not at all. A scan operation allows us to traverse the mental image from one location to another; a zoom operation allows us to change its size, and a rotation operation allows us to alter its orientation. The essential point is that an organism that has access to both propositional and depictive codes will be better placed to adapt to its world than one for which only a single type of internal representation is available.

Suppose we wish to compare the relative sizes of two objects—as, say, when deciding which is bigger, a mouse or a shrew. If we are restricted to propositional information then, unless this information has been specifically encoded, a direct judgement of relative size is not possible—although there may be circumstances in which it could be inferred. Access to mental images of the two animals, however, offers us a direct route to the required answer—the two entities could "simply" be compared. As there will be many occasions when we may wish to make comparisons of this kind (which were not relevant at the time of initial encoding), the ability to generate the required information via mental imagery would offer a potential means of transcending an otherwise significant restriction. Whether mental images really can be reinterpreted in this manner is a key question in the imagery debate. On current evidence, the answer would appear to be a resounding "maybe".

Implicit encoding

When information about the salient details of objects and their interrelationships has been verbally encoded, mental imagery on its own will not add anything new. However, if the critical information has not been verbally registered, generating a mental image could point us towards the information we need. Parts of the object previously attended to but not explicitly labelled could be brought back via mental imagery for further assessment and reinterpretation.

However, if we contrast object descriptions based on mental images with the same descriptions as elicited by pictorial stimuli, we find that they are not the same—qualitatively different reports are produced under the two conditions. This, at least, was the outcome of a study reported by Reed and Johnsen (1975). They asked subjects to study pictorial patterns and then to pass judgement on their component parts, either when they were shown, or when they were imagined (see Fig. 3.2).

Subjects in both conditions were likely to interpret the stimulus pattern as "two overlapping triangles" or "two overlapping parallelograms" and this was the description that was stored. Consequently, in the mental image condition, when subjects were asked to identify different parts of the pattern, the parts that coincided with their interpretation could be identified without difficulty but the parts that did not feature in the description were spotted only with difficulty or not

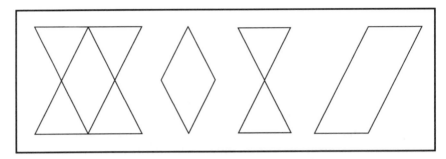

FIG. 3.2. Test patterns. (From Reed & Johnsen, 1975.)

at all. The authors report a 72% failure rate when subjects tried to identify these critical parts in the imagery condition compared with a 14% failure rate when they could consult the picture directly.

Chambers and Reisberg (1985) have also reported findings consistent with mental images as pre-interpreted information. Not one of their subjects was able to obtain the usual reversals when imaging the ambiguous figures depicted in Fig. 3.3, although all could do so when they made a drawing of their image.

The conclusion seems unavoidable; a mental image is not an uninterpreted visual pattern and, consequently, it cannot serve as a source of new information in the same way as scanning the actual referent.

Reinterpreting mental images

The aforementioned conclusion may be justified but it may be too all-embracing. Mental images may be interpreted entities but perhaps they can also be reinterpreted. After all, in Reed and Johnsen's imagery condition, a minority of subjects could detect the critical target shape and, in Chambers and Reisberg's experiment, the failure of subjects to reverse imagined, ambiguous figures may have arisen from the way in which the local ambiguities of their parts have to be resolved. The two global interpretations of the Necker cube are likely to be mutually inhibiting, so that any reversals require the imager to carry through a set of simultaneous and mutually consistent changes. Ambiguous figures that make these demands may just be too difficult to reinterpret.

A study by Finke, Pinker, and Farah (1989) indicates that there are circumstances in which subjects can reinterpret imaged information. Their subjects were instructed to superimpose mental images upon each other and then to describe any new patterns they could detect in the resulting composite image. For example, after imagining an H-shaped figure and then imagining an X superimposed upon it, a subject was

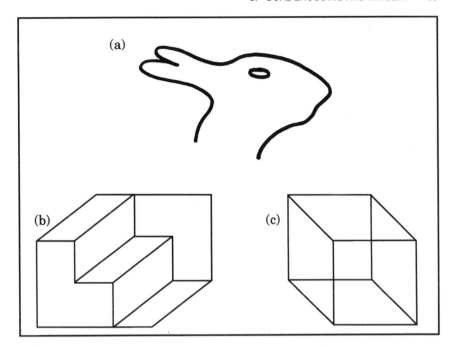

FIG. 3.3. Ambiguous test stimuli. (a) The Jastrow duck/rabbit; (b) the Schroeder staircase; (c) The Necker cube. (From Chambers & Reisberg, 1985.)

called upon to describe the result. The combination of the two figures gives something resembling a bow tie and the investigators were interested in whether or not subjects could report this pattern, or any other newly formed combinations. They found that all of their subjects reported the presence of at least one legitimate novel form in the course of the experiment and, summing across twelve subjects and six composite figures, a total of 160 new forms was recorded.

In further experiments, Finke et al. showed that other, more holistic reinterpretations could also be driven in this way. When instructed to "imagine a capital D (and then) to rotate the figure 90 degrees to the left (and then) to place a capital letter J at the bottom", subjects spontaneously reported the presence of an umbrella. Finke et al. (1989, p.67) concluded that the occurrence of these successful identifications revealed that:

> ... the kind of object a mental image corresponds to need not be assigned during an act of perception, but can also be discovered in the act of transforming and inspecting an image. If so, images must contain enough information about

the geometry of a pattern that its category can be assigned after the image is formed, ... in much the same way that categorial or symbolic descriptions are assigned to visually perceived patterns.

Hence, these authors take issue, not so much with the claim that a mental image is an interpreted entity, as with the implicit, additional claim that once interpreted it cannot be reinterpreted. With regard to the same point, Chambers and Reisberg (1992) have subsequently conceded that reinterpretation could be possible provided the target and image geometry are mutually compatible. In which case, the reason why their earlier subjects failed to find alternative ways of construing the Jastrow figure of the duck/rabbit (where both construals share the same shape, top, and figure/ground organisation) was because each version was being understood under one particular aspect—an aspect that may have left out details important for the other interpretation. In effect, subjects mentally imaging the stimulus display as a rabbit had a different image to subjects imaging the display as a duck.

Mental images as analogue structures

The assumption that a memory image makes information available in analogue form suggests that the image is capable of being manipulated in ways that mimic equivalent perceptual operations on the physical object. For example, if we mentally scan a complex memory image of a map, the internal scan could mimic the physical act of visually scanning an actual map and scan time should increase as the points attended to get further apart.

Kosslyn, Ball, and Reiser (1978) investigated this possibility by showing their subjects a map on which were marked various locations such as a beach and a lake. The subject's task was to study the layout and then to imagine the scene while answering questions about its content. On being given a named location, the subject was to focus at this point on the image. Then, some seconds later when a second object was named, subjects had to indicate when they had refocused on the new location. As the time taken for subjects to move between two locations on the imaged map was a linear function of the distance between them, this result was compatible with the memory image being construed as a spatially continuous entity. And there are other studies of subjects transforming mental images which also point towards the same conclusion.

In an experiment reported by Cooper and Shepard (1973), subjects were asked to form a mental image of a letter or number and to rotate it through a series of 45 degree angles in response to verbal instructions.

Then, while the subject held the image in a particular orientation, a test stimulus was physically presented which the subject had to identify as being an identical or a backward version of the target. Under these test conditions, it was found that subjects' reaction times increased progressively with the difference in orientation between the mental image and test stimulus—as though when making the match, subjects manipulated the memory image so as to mimic it being rotated back into the target position.

Taken together, the findings relating to scanning and rotating memory images strongly imply that they can take the form of spatially continuous representations. Whether these data really do constitute definitive evidence in favour of dual coding continues to remain a matter of intense debate.

Cognitive penetrability

The experimental outcomes described earlier could arise for reasons to do with the subject's tacit knowledge of the task demands. Subjects take longer to mentally scan between two distant points because they know from experience that that is what normally happens. If so, mental imaging is no longer an encapsulated process drawing upon the computations of a perceptual module operating at the implementational level, rather it shows all the characteristics of cognitive penetrability that is found at the algorithmic level.

Intons-Peterson and Roskos-Ewaldson (1989) have presented evidence that scanning operations over mental images can depend on rather more than their spatial organisation. In one experiment subjects were asked to imagine carrying a 3oz balloon, a 3lb ball, or a 30lb cannon ball while mentally traversing a route between two locations on a known site. This manipulation resulted in the observed mental transport times not only increasing with the distance traversed but also increasing as a function of the object's weight. Intons-Peterson and Roskos-Ewaldson took this result to mean that operations upon mental images are not simply reducible to perceptual representations and processes but draw instead upon more general knowledge. If so, mental scanning times cannot be treated as reliable and unequivocal indices of the spatial properties of the memory images involved.

Susceptibility to "cognitive penetration" confounds both the interpretation of the results obtained from mental scanning and those from mental rotation. We cannot be certain just what it is that these experiments are telling us about the properties of memory images and their role in the cognitive architecture. If we can instruct ourselves to perform in ways that mimic the analogy under test, this destroys the whole point of the demonstration (see Pylyshyn, 1984).

Although the thrust of Pylyshyn's argument is well aimed, it is not without local ambiguities of its own. Counter-criticisms have focused on his appeal to tacit knowledge as an alternative explanation of mental scanning operations. Pylyshyn's argument assumes that subjects possess the relevant tacit knowledge and can apply it appropriately to the task in hand. Some defence against the penetrability criticism is provided, therefore, if it can be shown that subjects lack the appropriate tacit knowledge that would guide the mental simulation. When Denis and Carfantan (1985) asked their subjects to predict the outcome for the map location study, they found that the resulting predictions were not as penetrating as Pylyshyn's criticisms implied. Of course it is always possible to mount the counter-claim that tacit knowledge, by definition, is not easily verbalised and the inadequate verbal predictions produced by experimental subjects may simply reflect this limitation. One can readily sympathise with theorists such as Anderson (1978) who are inclined to dismiss the whole issue as terminally intractable. However, we will continue to persevere.

Non-visual imagery

It is an empirical matter (although often assumed by default) whether the perceptual equivalence attributed to visual images generated from memory also holds for imaging in other modalities. Unfortunately, all of the ambiguities associated with the specification of the structure of visual memory images also apply when we consider other types of memory images with the added complication that far less work has been conducted in these areas. Although language is fundamentally rooted in the processing of auditory information, research into auditory imagery has come a poor second best behind research into visual imagery.

Halpern (1992), is one of the few experimentalists to have conducted research into auditory memory images along the lines discussed earlier and she has argued that, like their visual counterparts, they do exhibit perceptual equivalences. However, there are intrinsic differences between these two modalities that according to Halpern (1992, p.3):

> ... prevent a simple extension of methods from one to the other. The most obvious difference is that visual stimuli are extended in space, and we think that visual images represent that extension. Auditory stimuli are extended in time, and we may hypothesize that auditory images represent this corresponding extension.

Halpern studied the temporal extent of auditory memory images for tunes by modelling her experiments on the visual scanning procedures used by Kosslyn, Ball, and Reiser (1978). In place of visual scenes, she employed familiar song lyrics and, for each song, subjects were given starting points on particular beats followed by snatches from lyrics (that could be up to eight beats away) which were to be identified as coming from the same song or not. Subjects told to employ auditory imagery when performing the task took longer to respond than subjects in a non-imagery group, implying that they were using an auditory scanning process analogous to visual scanning (or, more prosaically, her subjects hummed the tune in their head).

Other experimental manipulations have been intended to produce an auditory analogy to the visual rotation tasks reported by Cooper and Shepard (1973). Developing an auditory equivalent for rotation is complicated by the fact that, whereas two visual displays can be presented simultaneously, this is not realistic for two sound inputs. This difficulty was finessed by giving subjects a song title and a lyric which was followed 500msec later by a second lyric. The subjects task was to decide whether the pitch of the second lyric was "higher" or "lower" than the pitch of the first. Once again parallels with the visual imagery data were found in that subjects' reaction times were a function of both step size and starting point.

So far as the generation of auditory memory images is concerned, Hubbard and Stoeckig (1992) suggest that Kosslyn's model of visual image generation could be adapted to this purpose. Now, instead of depicting properties like the size and orientation of an object in a visual mental image, an auditory mental image is generated which codes characteristics like pitch and temporal sequence.

Obviously, there has been a fruitful, if one-sided exchange, between the visual and auditory research programmes. Viewed over the longer term, there is room for the balance to tilt the other way by focusing on potential differences between different types of mental image rather than their similarities—a distinction that becomes more evident once mental images in sensory modes other than vision and audition are made the topic of investigation.

Haptic and olfactory imagery

Haptic information deals with inputs from cutaneous receptors and kinaesthetic receptors in the joints and muscles and, according to Klatzky, Lederman, and Reed (1987), the haptic system serves not only to encode object properties such as their contour and size but also their surface texture and thermal state. Klatzky and Lederman (1988, p.428) also suggest that as haptic information is best adapted to the perception of the substance of objects rather than their structure, interpreting haptic imagery solely from a visual perspective tends to undervalue its utility. It leads to a metaphor of a hand that functions like:

... a roving eye that is badly in need of glasses. The exploring effector is assumed to produce a spatial image that is essentially equivalent to one derived using vision, within limitations imposed by the low resolution of haptic sensors, and the memory demands imposed by exploring over time. The resulting image is passed to image interpreters within the visual system, and the result is as if the original display had been examined visually (albeit by a very myopic individual).

A more plausible interpretation, they submit, is that the haptic system has its own utilities revolving around such properties of objects as their surface texture or hardness.

So far as olfactory memory images are concerned, Lyman and McDaniel (1986) have argued that "odours are ordinarily represented in an olfactory component of the non verbal imagery system" (p.761). On the other hand, some commentators have expressed doubts as to whether people can mentally image odours at all, see the review of odour memory by Schab (1991). More recently, however, Carrasco and Ridout (1993) have conducted an analysis of subjects' similarity ratings of different odours, both when the stimuli were physically present and when the comparison had to be imagined. They found that the psychological space was partitioned in much the same way under both conditions, suggesting the existence of an independent olfactory imaging system paralleling those that have been identified for other sensory modalities.

MENTAL MODELS

As matters stand the evidence for mental images as modality-based representations remains contentious and Intons-Peterson (1992, p.67) captures the fluidity of the situation when she suggests that:

... the processes contributing to imagery may overlap with, or even be the same as, processes contributing to perception and cognition. That is, imagery, perception and cognition may not be defined distinctively, separately and uniquely but, rather, may recruit the similar processes to different extents, depending on the circumstances. Thus, certain imaginal tasks may require perceptual like distinctions, whereas others demand more cognitive approaches.

Taking this stance implies that it would be more productive to shift the analytic emphasis away from the structural properties of mental images as viewed in relative isolation towards their functional role in different kinds of cognitive tasks. For instance, the ability to mentally rotate a visual memory image would be useful in navigation where the opportunity to mentally retrace one's steps could compensate for a variety of errors. Similarly, the ability to anticipate the outcome of some ongoing event would be considerably enhanced by the capacity to progressively transform a mental image over time. In this way we could project ahead from some current state to possible states occurring "upstream" in the future. Any organism capable of building mental models of its world that incorporated these dynamic qualities would be at a distinct advantage as it adjusted to a constantly changing physical world.

Although the contrast between a mental model and an instantiated schema is not always clear, the distinction depends both on the greater transience attributed to the states created within mental models and the recruitment of imagery as part of the model's internal structure. The resultant mix of descriptive and depictive codes allows for the creation of an internalised dynamic representation capable of tracking the changing values of an event over time.

Arguments in favour of mental models were advanced some time ago by Kenneth Craik (1943) but their current advocacy in cognitive science is relatively recent. Some 40 years later, Johnson-Laird (1983) has argued that mental models serve as important tools for tackling a wide range of cognitive activities such as discourse processing, problem solving, and reasoning—activities where a range of situational features have to be combined if the input is to be understood. Once these have been brought together within a relevant mental model, comprehension can be facilitated as the model is used to highlight particular conjunctions of information that might otherwise have been missed.

Consider a reader attempting to comprehend a descriptive text that continually reorients its narrator in the fictional space. The "here-now" point in the text serves to locate the narrator at a particular point while setting details enable the reader to infer the immediate surroundings of the narrator in terms of the objects that furnish this space. Each time the here-now point changes, it seems the reader must update the contents of the mental model to accommodate this new information. If so, it is far from evident how this might be done. Franklin and Tversky (1990) identify three possible ways in which readers might accomplish this task.

Applying an "equi-availability" strategy would mean the reader having the same degree of access to information about objects that are equidistant from the observer. This would lead to updating being equally effective in all directions. On the other hand, if the reader's access to directional information is biased, this would mean that some directions would be more accessible than others. Thus, a "mental transformation" strategy would hold that objects in front of the observer will be most accessible, with the accessibility of other objects diminishing progressively as they fell outside this frontal region. Yet another strategy would give rise to a "spatial framework model" where updating is biased in terms of the location of objects with regard to axes defined by reference to the body of the observer.

Franklin and Tversky attempted to differentiate between these options by getting readers to adopt the role of the central story character in their mind and then measuring their response times as they verified information about objects in different directions to their imagined self. Subjects were told that they faced particular objects and, having adopted this position mentally, they were then asked about objects at their feet, near their head, in front of them, and so on.

The text continually reoriented the reader to different objects in the imagined surroundings and the subjects' response times indicated that not all directions were equally accessible to the reader. This outcome effectively ruled the equi-availability theory out of court. Subjects neither performed as though they were scanning a picture nor as though they were randomly scanning a propositional list of direction–object pairs.

The reaction times also failed to conform to an updating strategy whereby the reader mentally turned to "face" a named object before making a judgement. As such, the transformational account also received little support. Having ruled out two of the three options, this left the spatial framework model to be assessed and this model did provide a good match to the reaction times that were recorded. That is, according to Franklin and Tversky (1990, p.74) subjects behaved as though they:

> ... constructed and used a spatial framework [which] rendered certain directions more accessible than others, depending on the natural axes of the body and the position of the body with respect to the natural world. ... For the upright observer, identification times were fastest for the head/feet axis, slower for the front/back axis and slowest for the right/left axis.

It seems, therefore, that we can extrapolate from the experience of the axes of our own body when co-ordinating locations in an imagined space. This conclusion is also consistent with the work of

Intons-Peterson and Roskos-Edwaldson (1989) cited earlier, which located mental imagery neither solely within the perceptual system nor within the cognitive system, but at their interface. Thus, so far as the analogical, perceptual nature of the reader's mental representation was concerned, Franklin and Tversky concluded that the evidence was against "a perception of space" but favoured instead "a conception of space". Evidentally, the properties assigned to mental images taken in isolation are not necessarily a reliable guide to their functional role when they are recruited in the service of more complex cognitive tasks.

Computational properties of mental models

Once a mental model representing the referential meaning of a text has been formed, it can be used to extract information that the reader might have missed based on a response to the text taken on its own. It is for precisely this reason that authors introduce supplementary illustrations into their text aimed at guiding their readers towards an appropriate mental model. The resulting mix of descriptive and depictive information means that readers can then be nudged towards a level of understanding that otherwise is likely to elude them. In this respect, Glenberg and Langston (1992) have shown that supplementary diagrams in a text work their effects by focusing the reader's attention on conjunctions of information that the linear text taken alone tends to conceal.

We have seen that as a text introduces new information, elements need to be added to or deleted from the accompanying mental model. In the course of this process, the reader's attention may be caught not only by the element in question, but also by whatever other elements happen to be in the same spatial vicinity within the mental model. As a result, Glenberg and Langston, (1992, pp.130–131) state:

> ... the relationship between the updated element and those noticed is encoded and stored (propositionally) along with other propositions from the text. In this way, the mental model acts as an *infererence generator* to assist in the encoding of relationships that are implicit in the text, as well as recoding and reinforcing some relationships that are explicit in the text [italics added].

In other words, diagrams (and the attendant mental models) act to bring new arrangements of representational elements into the current mental work space and this adds appreciably to the reader's command of the text by extending the range over which relevant inferences are likely to be drawn.

As a test of their hypothesis, Glenberg and Langston conducted a series of experiments designed to measure whether the provision of supplementary diagrams did indeed facilitate the noticing of information that had been left implicit in the written text. Consider the text reproduced in Fig. 3.4 which describes a procedure in which step 1 occurs first, then steps 2 and 3 occur together, and then the procedure ends with step 4. The linear nature of this text necessitates that one of the co-temporaneous steps must be described before the other, thus obscuring their temporal properties. However, by introducing an accompanying diagram, this limitation can be overcome.

It was predicted that subjects who saw the text alone would establish a representation in which the connection between the first step ("write a first draft") and the second step ("consider the structure") would be stronger than that between the first step and the third step ("address the audience"). On the other hand, subjects who saw a diagram of the intended procedure were expected to generate a mental model in which

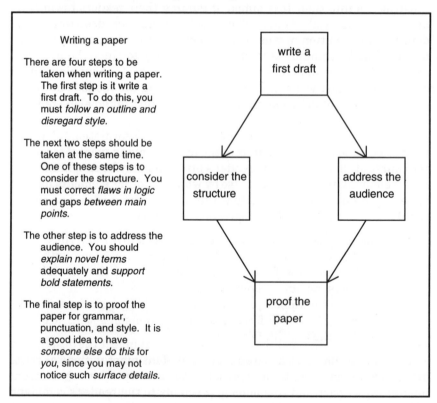

FIG. 3.4. Sequential text and accompanying diagram. (From Glenberg & Langston, 1992.)

the second and third steps are both equally related to the first and fourth steps.

Having read the text under one or other of the two presentation conditions, subjects were then tested on their understanding of the intended procedure. Paired step labels were shown, one step label printed above the other, and subjects had to decide whether the label on top referred to a step that preceded the one below at the time the procedure was performed. The results revealed that subjects in the no picture control made more errors on distant pairs of step labels (e.g. 1–3), as compared with near pairs (e.g. 1–2). Subjects who saw the diagrams, on the other hand, formed equally strong relationships for both types of pairs.

Thus, the device of incorporating depictive information into a mental model (whether via diagrams or via mental imagery) can lead to an increase in the depth of inferencing for the task in hand. This outcome will be particularly important for tasks where comprehension depends on the simultaneous activation of multiple representational elements. In these cases, ready access to a diagram and/or a mental model, by reducing the load on working memory, acts to increase the mental resources that can be assigned to inference generation.

SINGLE AND DUAL CODES

Parsimony may cast its vote in favour of a single propositional code but, on balance, the evidence suggests that we are not so single-minded. It may be more parsimonious to postulate one deep representational system into which all information is ultimately encoded but it should be noted that this position is not without difficulties of its own. As a number of commentators have pointed out (e.g. Barsalou, 1993; Lakoff, 1987), if all internal representations take the form of quasi-linguistic symbols, we find ourselves eventually being faced by a "symbol grounding" problem. Amodal representations that bear arbitrary relationships to their referents must at some point be grounded with reference to perceptual experience. Otherwise, as with dictionary definitions, we can be shunted from this quasi-linguistic description to that, without ever getting to grips with the links to the referent that invest the description with meaning. Linguistic symbols must make contact with perceptual information if they are to do their job satisfactorily. Allowing for cross referencing to occur between a body of linguistic symbols and a further body of perceptual symbols would significantly alleviate this problem (see Barsalou, 1993).

But in choosing to go down this route, there is a cost to be paid, as it serves to undermine the functionalist arguments as outlined in Chapter 1. There it was assumed that cognition derives from symbol manipulations that are indifferent to the medium in which they are exercised. Now, it seems that this indifference can only be sustained by ignoring a significant component of the symbol–referent equation.

CATEGORISING EMBODIED

The work of Franklin and Tversky (1990) pointed to an imager constructing a mental space by using the natural axes of the body, implying that the process of imaging is deeply affected by the imager's bodily interactions with the physical world. This is not a line of argument that sits at all comfortably within the functionalist position and it has been taken a great deal further by Lakoff (1987), especially as it relates to the acts of categorisation that support all forms of cognition. Lakoff's prime objection to the functionalist stance rests on its signal failure to look beyond a self-contained system of symbol manipulation to the intrinsic characteristics of the agent who is doing the categorising. For Lakoff, the internal structure of categories is critically informed by the human agent's attempts at producing cognitive models of the world. This modelling can certainly entail propositional models or schemas as discussed in the previous chapter, but it can also make use of imaginal models in which analogies are formed between aspects of the human body and aspects of the external world. This is to reject functionalism with a vengeance and it leads Lakoff to espouse an "experiential" view which holds that human reasoning is deeply affected by the morphology of the human form as we extrapolate from the properties of our own bodies in order to understand the properties of the external world.

For example, "in" and "out" are categorial distinctions that pervade many of our transactions with the external world. For Lakoff, both of these categorial distinctions rest on the presence of "a schema consisting of a boundary distinguishing an interior from an exterior" (1987, p.271) and this, in turn, is derived from our understanding of our own body as a container. And, if "in" and "out" can be derived by metaphorical extension from our own bodies, similar accounts can also be given for other categorial distinctions. "Part–whole" schemas arise from our experiences of ourselves as whole beings made up from parts; "link" schemas derive from the ties we have to other people; "centre–periphery" schemas arise because our bodies have central and peripheral parts and "source–path–goal" schemas are grounded in our ability to move from place to place. All of these bodily grounded schemas can thus serve as a metaphorical base for creating basic categories through which to partition our world. They would license, for example, a conception of the average citizen as a *part* of the state, who has *links* to other members, who is normally at the *periphery* of power and who is unlikely to find a *way round* this restriction.

In other words, the categories we construct and employ to structure the world can be construed as entities deeply imbued with our own experiences as human agents; sometimes they may be heavily constrained by the properties of the real world, at other times the correspondence may be highly metaphorical. As we have not been afforded a privileged or God-like insight into the properties of the real world, we have no independent means of knowing exactly which is which.

PUTTING THE CODES TO WORK

To this point, we have addressed how information relating to the properties of the external world might be stored and organised in long-term memory but we have largely avoided the issue of how this extensive body of information might be strategically accessed when needed. As such, we are a long way from describing a cognitive architecture that is capable of deploying knowledge in accordance with the actor's current goals and plans. Over the next two chapters, therefore, we will consider two sets of proposals bearing upon how this aim might be achieved. The first set concerns the production architectures that have been derived from classical symbol theory. The second set of proposals concerns the neural network models as espoused by proponents of connectionist architectures.

CHAPTER FOUR

Symbol processing architectures: Production systems

There is little to be gained from storing information about the properties of the world around us if it cannot be accessed when needed or, once accessed, if it cannot be exploited to further our own interests. Yet, given the sheer scale of the storage systems involved, what sort of mechanisms could sift through everything we have learned and pull out exactly those entries that are appropriate at just the right time?

Classical and connectionist models provide different answers to this question and in this chapter we will let classical theorists have their say. We will start by sketching an account of the organisation of human memory, as viewed from the general perspective of information processing, and then see how production systems such as ACT* (Anderson, 1983) and SOAR (Newell, 1990), aim to bring the various components together within a single functional architecture. Both of these models seek to provide a general-purpose account of cognition in proposing that activities as diverse as speaking, writing, problem solving, and reasoning all depend on a common set of mechanisms being put to use in these different contexts. Furthermore, both models assume that their component mechanisms have potential access to all the information that has been acquired from previous experience. It is a view that accords well with intuition and common sense and, although questioned from time to time, it has occupied a prominent position in psychological and educational theory for most of their history

TYPES OF MEMORY STORE

Since the late 1960s the dominant models of human memory organisation have envisaged a dual storage system where a memory trace could either be in some short-term store (of limited capacity and prone to rapid decay) or in a long-term store (of indefinite capacity and duration). As will become evident, this is something of an oversimplification, but the distinction between information that is currently active and a remainder set of dormant information will play an important role in what is to come. The capacity of the short-term store in the normal adult has been placed around seven items (Miller, 1956). Given one reading of a list of seven independent items (e.g. digits or letters) the normal subject can be expected to say them back in the same order without error. Going above this number is likely to induce errors, unless the subject has recourse to the types of strategies described in Chapter 2.

Measures of immediate memory span reify a phenomenon that we have all experienced—there is a definite and rapidly reached limit to the amount of information we can entertain in mind at any one go. In mental arithmetic where fairly large numbers are involved, there soon comes a point where we either reach for pencil and paper to record the intermediate steps of a calculation or we risk losing track of what we are doing. When listening to route directions, we are easily confused once the "right" and "left" turnings build up to a point where no more information can be absorbed without something else being lost. Digit span is not an optimal measure of immediate memory capacity because it can draw upon a mixture of information held in both the short-term and long-term stores. More stringent measures, such as running memory span, aim to exclude the long-term memory component, and they estimate the capacity at around three or four items (Broadbent, 1975). Which is just enough capacity to register the content of two arguments and their relationship in the form of a propositional encoding.

Building upon these observations, Atkinson and Shiffrin (1968) put forward an influential model of memory organisation which proposed that information first enters short-term memory (STM) and is transferred from there into long-term memory (LTM) via rehearsal. Subsequently, as evidence concerning the properties of the different memory stores continued to accumulate, it became clear that STM was not a simple way-station, as first thought, but constituted a more complex system in its own right.

Working memory

As the original evidence in favour of dual memory systems came under critical scrutiny—due to evidence relating to primacy and recency effects in free recall and clinical case histories indicating differential impairment of the short- and long-term memory stores—the arguments for a homogeneous short-term store no longer seemed as convincing as had once been supposed, (see Baddeley, 1990, 1992). If STM functioned as a finite workspace where information was held temporarily while it participated in various cognitive operations, we would expect the efficiency of these processes to be impaired as the capacity of the available workspace was reduced. Subjects who carried out mental arithmetic or attempted to solve problems while occupied on some other secondary task, should be placed at a distinct disadvantage compared with subjects not burdened in this way.

Thus commenced a series of experiments in which subjects were typically required to keep in mind a sequence of digits for later recall while performing another task. A concurrent digit load could vary from zero to nine items and it could be combined with some other task such as verifying the truth of test sentences differing in syntactic complexity. Subjects performing under these conditions stood up remarkably well. Although their reasoning time tended to increase with concurrent load this was not true of error rates, where no effect of concurrent load was to be found—for a review of this work, see Baddeley (1990).

An increase in reasoning time with concurrent load might seem to support the claim that both tasks were in competition for the same storage space (even then it only increased by about 30% at the maximum load) but a stable error rate under these conditions does not fit in with this assertion at all. A sequence of nine digits should be more than sufficient to occupy the total capacity of the short-term store leaving no "room" for the execution of the primary reasoning task. As similar results were obtained when other cognitive tasks were overloaded in the same way something had to give and the assumption concerning the unitary nature of the short-term store was singled out as the weak link. The experimental data could be accommodated if there was not one but a number of possible workspaces. Consequently, Baddeley and his co-workers have put forward an alternative model of "working memory" where instead of a single homogeneous store we now have a central executive of limited attentional capacity exerting control over at least two slave systems—a visuo-spatial sketch pad that is used for holding and manipulating visuo-spatial information and an articulatory loop serving in the same capacity for speech-based material.

Long-term memory (LTM)

Although common sense may not have come up with the idea of a short-term store, it would certainly make room for a long-term or permanent memory store. For all practical purposes the capacity of this long-term store must be unlimited and the sheer amount and heterogeneity of its contents has been something of an embarrassment to the cognitive theorist. Despite over 100 years of research into human memory there is still no agreed taxonomy of the content held in LTM although various suggestions have been put forward. In particular, Tulving's proposals (1983, 1985) relating to the existence of three basic storage systems in LTM—procedural, semantic, and episodic—have received considerable attention.

Procedural memory is concerned with knowledge of how to act appropriately in different circumstances; semantic (or declarative) memory refers to general knowledge of the world, and the episodic memory system incorporates our knowledge of those events we have personally experienced. Tulving suggests that these memory systems are arranged hierarchically with procedural memory providing the foundation on which the other two systems rest. Procedural memory acts as the immediate support for declarative memory which in turn supports the episodic memory system. We will look briefly at the characteristics of each of these systems and then consider how they might be merged within a general architecture capable of supporting the whole range of cognitive functions.

Episodic and autobiographical memory

Tulving refers to episodic memory as providing a record of our personal experiences by storing details about their content, chronological order, and personal significance. We rely on this memory store when answering such questions as "Where did you go to college?" or "What is your first memory?" and, by virtue of storing the cumulative details of our past history, it underpins our autobiographical sense of who we are and who we have been. Although they are obviously closely related, episodic memory and autobiographical memory are not exactly synonymous— not all episodic experiences are incorporated into our sense of self; many events are too trivial to qualify.

The first empirical investigation into autobiographical memory was conducted by Galton (1880) who tried to cue a number of his colleagues into recalling the detail of events from their daily lives. After lying fallow for most of this century, it has now become an active topic of investigation once more (see Linton, 1975; Wagenaar, 1986). We will take Wagenaar's study as a paradigm case. This exercise took no less than four years to bring to completion and throughout this time

Wagenaar kept a record of the most important event that had occurred each day, detailing what had happened, who was involved, and when and where it had taken place. The episodic inventory that resulted from this heroic dedication was then recruited into a test programme designed to reveal the characteristics of the memory storage system in which the records were held.

Wagenaar assessed his ability to recall the events on record, at delays of up to five years, by employing a standardised cueing procedure. First of all, the specific cues of "Who", "What", "When", and "Where" were recruited as individual prompts for opening up a record and, if these were unsuccessful, they were then systematically combined until either the event was finally brought to mind or the attempt was deemed to have failed. With regard to the general accuracy of his recall, Wagenaar reports that he achieved around 70% accuracy for event details after an interval of six months but this fell away to around 30% accuracy after five years. He found no evidence that any incident was completely forgotten. Although it certainly happened that after using all possible cues he still failed to recall certain events, on those occasions where it was possible to solicit the help of others who had also been involved, he found that he could be prompted into successful recall.

The individual cues differered considerably in their efficacy. "What" was the most effective cue for retrieving incident detail whereas "When" was the least effective cue. "Who" and "Where" fell between these extremes. Wagenaar (1986, p.241) accounted for these cueing variations by proposing that autobiographical records are stored in the form of "headed records" where:

> ... there is a clear distinction between information on tags, which is used to select cards from the file, and information read from the cards after they have been selected.

"What" as a cue was particularly valuable in retrieving other event detail because few cards in the file are likely to share the same heading content. What happened is likely to be unique to each event and its use as a retrieval cue is likely to open the file allowing direct access to other features of the event, such as "Who" was there, even though this detail may be shared by many other records. This implies, of course, that "Who" as a retrieval cue will be rather less effective, which is evidently the case.

The fact that "When" serves as a particularly poor retrieval prompt requires additional explanation because this detail should serve as a unique marker for each record. Accordingly, it is proposed that within a record header, "When" information is tagged using a coarse time marker.

There is nothing as specific as, say, "October 5th 1995", but something more in the order of "Autumn 1995". Once a record has been successfully entered from its heading, more specific time information can then become available. We shall encounter "headed records" again in the context of explaining the accumulative growth of information in long-term memory (Chapter 7) and there, as here, it can be contrasted against alternative accounts of memory organisation that rely on a system of cross indexing to tie related records together.

Declarative memory

When called upon to answer such questions as "What is the meaning of traduce?" or "What is the capital city of Monaco?", i.e. questions dealing with general information, we are faced with accessing the factual knowledge that is held in declarative memory. We have already discussed how this kind of information might be represented in memory in the two previous chapters, the point at issue now is how these representations can be converted into a functional system that makes its contents available as required. Network models aimed at answering this question have been gradually evolving over the last three decades, (Anderson & Bower, 1973; Collins & Loftus, 1975; Collins & Quillian, 1969; Kintsch, 1988) and they are based on the assumption that the declarative store is structured in the form of an associative network. Within the network, categorial knowledge is represented through the links between the component nodes which are typically taken to represent particular concepts or propositions.

Operations upon the network as, say, when verifying whether a given sentence is true or false, entail a search procedure which terminates once a direct link has been found between the critical nodes. Thus, if we are called upon to verify the sentence "A robin is a bird" as true or false, the perceptual input activates the nodes for "robin" and "bird" in the network and activation then spreads from these source nodes along the network's links. If the activation paths traced from each source node eventually intersect then the sentence can be verified as true.

Associative network models of this kind are well placed to handle priming effects such as those reported by Meyer and Schvaneveldt (1971). These experimenters demonstrated that in a "non-word" judgement task (i.e. deciding whether a pair of words contained a non-word), a subject's responses could be facilitated if the test items within a pair were semantically related. In the course of the experiment, a subject was shown one member of a pair and then, shortly afterwards, the second member appeared which was to be judged as a word or a non-word. Thus, the sequence might consist of a word/non-word pair ("wine" followed by "plame"), or a word/word pair. In the latter case the two words could be unrelated ("nurse" followed by "butter") or they could be semantically related ("bread" followed by "butter"). Comparison of the mean reaction times for these different pair combinations indicated substantial priming effects when the two words were semantically related. Here, a subject's response time to "butter" (the second item in the pair) has benefited from the spread of activation from the node for "bread" (the first item of the pair). When "butter" is presented as a test item, the relevant node reaches its threshold value more quickly than if it had started from its resting level.

Propositional and schematic structures. By imposing an hierarchical organisation on the associative network we can represent increasingly complex information, including propositions and schemas. In the network shown in Fig. 4.1, we can locate the knowledge schema associated with "bird", as well as various subschemas such as "poultry", and particular exemplars from these subschemas.

The "bird" schema can be derived from the default values on salient attributes such as "brown" and "straight beak" and a subschema such as "poultry" can be represented through the combination of other features such as "white" and "curved beaks".

Representing declarative knowledge in the form of an associative network which can be interrogated via search procedures based on spreading activation, takes us some of the way towards specifying a

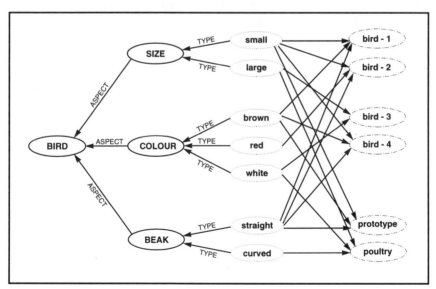

FIG. 4.1. Representing schemas, prototypes, and exemplars. (From Barsalou, 1992.)

general cognitive architecture. Nonetheless, it is apparent that a number of important aspects are being glossed over. An hierarchically structured network has something to say about how our general knowledge is organised and represented but it manifestly fails to explain how this information could be co-ordinated in the performance of complex tasks. When reading or doing mental arithmetic, we not only need to access specific items of information, we must do so in a highly systematic and ordered manner if the task is to be completed successfully.

Procedural memory

It is a matter of everyday observation that although new facts can be readily added to declarative memory, the same is not true of the intellectual or motor skills that make up our procedural memory. To become an expert in any subject, be it chess, medicine, or science, takes many years of practice. No one becomes a proficient surgeon by reading the technical manuals alone, nor by simply watching someone else perform. Acquisition of cognitive skills, while drawing upon declarative knowledge, specifically calls for repeated practice and it is during this time that new additions are made to our stock of procedural knowledge.

Procedural knowledge encodes the "how" of particular skills and it provides for the sequencing, planning, and co-ordination that is essential if intricate cognitive skills are to be successfully executed. "Knowledge how", as opposed to "knowledge that", refers to a form of knowledge that is often difficult to put into words. When explaining how we managed to drive a car in a straight line or keep a bicycle upright we may have to run a simulation of the actions involved before even beginning to find the words to convey what we have been doing.

Although Bartlett is widely credited with the initial formulation of schema models, as evidenced in *Remembering* (1932), few commentators go on to refer to his later deliberations as set out in his book *Thinking* in 1958. Here, Bartlett dispenses with the concept of the schema altogether, choosing instead to employ the idea of a "skill" as the optimal framework for analysing active thinking. Bartlett argues that the different forms of thinking—which he terms artistic, scientific, and everyday thinking—all reveal in their sequencing, timing, and control, interesting correspondences to the properties of prototypic skilled behaviour. Through this shift in emphasis, Bartlett aimed to overcome the major weakness that is immediately evident when schema theory is applied to other than the simplest of cognitive tasks. Namely, the absence of any mechanisms capable of orchestrating the multiple components of an extended cognitive task which would enable them to work together as a whole.

For example, when adding two numbers together, it is not enough just to access the meaning of the component terms, rather a whole series of intermediate operations must intervene before the final answer is reached. If carrying operations are necessary they must be executed in exactly the right sequence if the answer is to be correct. To meet this requirement, as well as a declarative knowledge base, we also need a body of procedural knowledge that determines precisely when we should do what. Cognitive models that aim to interweave declarative and procedural knowledge as a means of explaining cognitive operations are known as "production systems" and we will devote the remainder of this chapter to two influential examples from this family of cognitive architectures.

PRODUCTION SYSTEMS

Production systems have their origins in formal computational theory (Post, 1943) but their applications within psychology have largely stemmed from the work of Miller, Galanter, and Pribram, (1960) on mental planning and, more especially, from the work of Newell and Simon (1972) on modelling human problem solving.

Within a production system, procedural knowledge is represented in the form of production rules, where each production contains a condition component (that determines when the rule can apply) and an action component (that specifies what will happen when the condition has been met). A prototypic rule thus takes the form:

IF ... [condition]
THEN ... [action].

By systematically coupling a repertoire of such rules with a declarative network, we can proceed towards specifying a mental architecture that is capable of getting the cognitive enterprise off the ground.

As "production systems" refer to a family of architectures, not to a monolithic system, we will consider two distinct models which make somewhat different architectural assumptions. Their mode of operation is not that far removed from the Chinese Room situation envisaged by Searle (see Chapter 1) although the procedures adopted by commercial banks are perhaps closer to the mark. As cheques are presented over the counter, they are redeemed by matching their contents to the currency held in the bank's vaults. By the same token, as representational elements enter into working memory, they too can be redeemed as they match to the conditions associated with particular production rules.

ACT* (Adaptive control of thought)

ACT*, as initially proposed by Anderson (1983), assumes that the contents of two separate memory stores (declarative and procedural) work together to sustain the planning and sequencing that is necessary if our actions are to fulfil our current goals. Cognitive processing is initiated and maintained as the content of working memory is matched to the conditions of stored production rules. Whenever a match to a production occurs, the production is triggered and its action component may then introduce new content into working memory. This allows for another round of matching to occur and so the process continues until the main goal of the activity has been met. In this manner, declarative knowledge can be continually deployed within a procedural framework that determines exactly how and when it should be used.

ACT* postulates the existence of three types of memory system: a long-term declarative memory, where factual information is held in a semantic network; a long-term procedural memory which contains an indefinitely large number of production rules, and a working memory, which is not actually a separate storage system but refers to whatever parts of the declarative system are currently active. Activation within declarative memory can be due to the application of productions or it can arise as a consequence of perceptual activity. Cognition proceeds as the transient contents of working memory trigger a series of production rules which bring about various effects including setting up task-related goals, activating new memory content, or initiating overt behaviour. The overall ACT* architecture is depicted in Fig. 4.2.

Figure 4.2 identifies five types of operation which bear upon the contents of the different storage systems. *Encoding* operations serve to instal information from perceptual processing in working memory and this content may then be *matched* to the conditions of production rules in procedural memory. If a match is made, the action component of the rule concerned can be deposited in working memory through an *execution* operation. The *application* of a production (i.e. matching and executing a rule) works to determine its current strength. Successful application increases the strength of a rule while the negative feedback contingent on an unsuccessful application decreases rule strength.

A *retrieval* operation serves to activate part of declarative memory bringing this content into working memory. A *storage* operation works in the other direction by depositing the current content of working memory in declarative memory, thus adding new items of information to the declarative store or increasing the strength of existing records. The link to behaviour is handled by *performance* processes which serve to convert commands in working memory into sequences of overt actions.

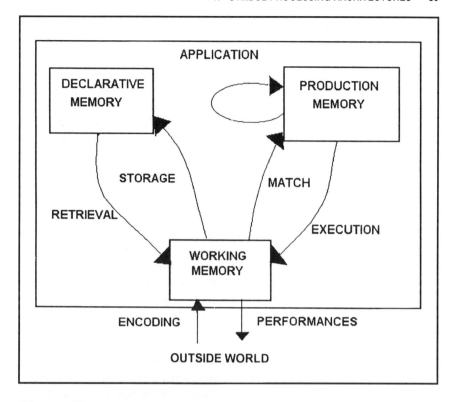

FIG. 4.2. ACT* cognitive architecture. (From Anderson, 1983.)

ACT* and the organisation of declarative memory

The data structures contained in declarative memory fall into three types, each of which can undergo different kinds of transformation. Temporal strings encode sequences of events in time (in effect representing what comes next in a sequence) and these structures can participate in only a restricted set of transformations such as the insertion or deletion of elements.

Spatial images are also stored in declarative memory (although Anderson has little to say about how this is done) and their function is to represent the spatial arrangement of scenes and their component parts. Unlike temporal strings, spatial images can undergo continuous transformations such as rotation and scanning and they are used as a basis for computing orientations and distances. The third type of declarative content (symbolic structures) encodes semantic relationships in the form of propositions.

Taken together, these representational elements comprise a general network in which currently active (source) nodes feed out activation through the network's connections to related nodes which then become activated in their turn. The strength of a source node determines the amount of activation it can transmit and receive. In the general case, source nodes decay after a certain time has elapsed but special goal units can serve as less transient sources of activation—an important consideration if the current task may take some time. Once source nodes have been established, the subsequent spread of activation determines which declarative content will feature in working memory and hence which content will engage with the productions held in the procedural memory store.

Rule matching

As all productions are candidates for matching to working memory content there will inevitably be occasions when more than one rule can apply, forcing a choice to be made between them. The resulting conflict can be resolved in a variety of ways; resolution can depend on the strength of the rules concerned (stronger rules are given preference), or on their specificity (more specific rules win out over more general versions). Alternatively, the degree of match between the active content and production conditions can be used to determine which rule will apply and, so too, the agent's current goals can be consulted when determining an outcome. If partial matching to a production occurs then whichever rule provides the greatest degree of match is favoured. The agent's current goals are incorporated into the matching process by giving precedence to those rules that relate to a current goal. And by employing productions to set up a series of subgoals it is possible to accommodate the complex planning that accompanies all but the most mundane tasks.

Goals are created by the execution of special productions and it may well be necessary to set up a series of subgoals before a task can be completed. If we wish to add two numbers together then, following Anderson (1983), the main goal (of adding the numbers) will be set by a production such as:

> P1. IF there is a problem involving a plus sign and two numbers
> THEN set up a goal to ADD with instances of the two numbers as its inputs and mark the goal as ACTIVE.

Subsequent steps in the addition process can then feature as subgoals which are created by other productions:

P2. IF the goal is to do an addition problem
THEN the subgoal is to iterate through the columns of the problem.
P3. IF the goal is to iterate through the columns of an addition problem and the rightmost column has not been processed
THEN the subgoal is to iterate through the rows of that rightmost column and set the running total to zero.

As each subgoal is set up, the solver moves closer to the point where a given goal can be directly satisfied. At this point, the goal is despatched, leaving the remaining goals to be despatched in the same way until eventually the main goal of addition has been satisfied. Thus, declarative and procedural knowledge are effectively being interwoven to produce a planned sequence of actions that is adapted both to the agent's needs and to the constraints of the immediate physical situation.

Knowledge compilation
So far, it has been assumed that productions are already present in procedural memory but, clearly, ACT* also needs to address how the repertoire of productions comes to be established and expanded. Where a task is unfamiliar, it is assumed that performance depends on general knowledge held in declarative memory which is operated upon by very general production rules. With practice, however, these general productions come to be supplemented by newly minted productions which are more finely tuned to the task demands. It is through this process of "knowledge compilation" that new and more specific rules come into existence.

To exemplify more precisely what is said to be happening during knowledge compilation, we will take as an illustrative case, a simple probe recognition task. The subject is given a string of letters to learn and is then asked to respond to a series of probe letters by deciding whether it forms part of the previously learned string, (see Neves & Anderson, 1981). At the beginning, we can expect a subject to be relatively slow and hesitant but, as practice builds up, the subject should become faster and more confident as knowledge compilation gets under way.

Suppose a subject has been given the letter string (AQRT) to hold in memory. The subject is to respond to the probe letters by saying "yes" if the probe is a member of this set and by saying "no" if it is not. At the outset when the subject is relatively unpractised, a response will be generated by drawing separately on the relevant declarative and procedural knowledge. The declarative store contains tokens for each of the component letters in the string and the procedural store contains productions capable of evaluating the status of the probe items.

In Fig. 4.3a, we have the situation as it applies during the initial phase of the experiment. The letters forming the comparison set are held in declarative memory and general productions are being matched and executed. Because the relevant information is held in two different stores, performance on the probe task is, at first, slow and prone to error.

As practice continues "proceduralisation" begins to occur as new productions are formed which incorporate declarative information as part of their conditions, as in Fig. 4.3b. The availability of these new rules serves to reduce search in declarative memory and, consequently, the time to reach a judgement speeds up. "Composition" occurs when separate productions are combined to form a new rule. For example, in Fig. 4.3c, productions previously formed in the course of proceduralisation have been collapsed to produce a single composite version. As this rule is more specific than any of the others it is more likely to be matched when a probe letter is presented and response times benefit accordingly.

We can now see why, compared with adding new information to declarative memory, setting up new production rules is relatively slow. A task has to be repeatedly practised before knowledge compilation can occur because compilation will only happen when the relevant elements

---

	Declarative memory	Procedural memory
(a)	AQRT	P1. IF considering an element in the list and the probe equals that element THEN say YES
		P2. IF considering an element in the list and it is not equal to the probe and the element is before another element THEN consider the next element
(b)		P1′. IF considering A and probe is not A THEN consider Q
		P2′. IF considering Q and probe is not Q THEN consider R etc.
(c)		P1″. IF considering AQRT and probe is not AQRT THEN respond NO

FIG. 4.3. Stages in knowledge compilation: (a) Initial phase; (b) Proceduralisation; (c) Composition. (From Neves & Anderson, 1981.)

of information are jointly active in working memory. If this condition does not hold then knowledge compilation cannot proceed and the repertoire of productions will remain unchanged.

Following knowledge compilation, the general procedures that applied at the beginning of the probe recognition task will have been supplemented by new productions more attuned to the actual test situation. Old productions are not lost but continue to remain in the subject's repertoire, and the same applies to any intermediate productions that are formed in the course of proceduralisation and composition. However, the strength of these intermediate rules will gradually decrease as they lose out in competition with rules that are stronger and more specific.

If we look at the actual practice curves associated with many different skills e.g., geometrical problem solving (Neves & Anderson, 1981), lexical decision times (Kirsner & Speelman, 1993), and even rolling cigars (Crossman, 1959), then we find that a characteristic pattern emerges which is the same for each task. Initially, performance is slow, it then speeds up as practice continues but eventually the rate of gain slows down as the practice proceeds. The systematic nature of these procedural gains can easily be overlooked as practice accumulates over many thousands of trials but this difficulty can be overcome by the use of log scales—where 10, 100, and 1000 trials translate into 1, 2, and 3 log units, respectively. If the data in the cited studies are re-expressed in terms of the log of time to perform the particular task against the log of practice trials, the result is a downward-sloping straight line. Evidentally, given the disparity of the examples cited, this "power law of learning" has very general applicability. Indeed, it has even been detected in the cumulative literary output of at least one prolific author.

Isaac Asimov produced no less than 500 books over a period of 40 years and Ohlsson (1992) treats this output as an extended exercise in "learning how to write a book". Grouping Asimov's output into five successive blocks of 100 trials (books) reveals that the first 100 titles took about 20 years to complete whereas the last 100 titles took only three to four years to write. Although these time periods were not entirely clear (the last two data points had to be estimated from the partial records available) when converted to a log–log plot, we find a close fit to the power law. A distinctly sceptical view of this exercise has been expressed by Asimov's brother (1993). He comes up with a mischievous estimation that assumes the collected works had run to 700 titles. Extrapolation from the log–log plot not only decreases the time required, it also changes the sign on the time axis. This indicates that Asimov's final work should have been completed some two years in advance of the time when he was completing his 500th title!

Putting this caveat to one side, the generality of the power law implies that common mechanisms are at work within very different situations that on the surface seem to impose quite different demands on the learner (compare cigar rolling and lexical decision). Knowledge compilation provides us with the means of explaining this catholicity. The compilation of new productions gives us the early gains in performance speed but, as new productions can only be formed when their components are currently active in working memory, the more compilation that has occurred the fewer the occasions that will be left that can give rise to new rules. Consequently, we cannot expect the initial rate of gain to be maintained as practice proceeds.

ACT* as a general-purpose architecture

The working details of ACT* include specific parameters dealing with the number of nodes that can be active at any one time, the rates of decay of activation, and the rates at which the strengths of entries in declarative and procedural memory are to be altered. Consequently, the model can be used to simulate different cognitive tasks and the results compared against the empirical data obtained from human subjects. In this respect, ACT* has been applied across the range of cognitive processes from memory retrieval to problem solving and from cognitive development to social cognition. However, as it is always possible to adjust the parameters to accommodate new data, empirical studies are unlikely to disprove the model in formal terms. Rather, the main significance of this work derives from the way in which ACT* can serve as a general framework for interpreting a variety of otherwise disparate cognitive phenomena. Nonetheless, it is not the only way of proceeding. There are other production architectures which, while having similar aspirations to ACT*, assemble the cognitive architecture along somewhat different lines.

Anderson (1993) has recently proposed a new version, ACT-R, designed around a "rational analysis" of the adaptive properties of cognitive processes. Because, as noted in Chapter 1, quite different mechanisms at the implementational level can lead to equivalent outcomes, (e.g. rule matching could proceed via parallel or serial processes), putative mechanisms cannot ultimately be distinguished on the basis of simulating observed patterns of behaviour. Rational analysis aims to address this identifiability problem by evaluating cognitive operations against the joint constraints set by the agent's resources and the external environment in which they must work their effects. In other words, according to Anderson (1993, p.14), the choice between candidate mechanisms for implementing memory, categorisation, and other related aspects of cognition can be narrowed down by favouring those that:

... maximise achievement of information processing goals within the constraint of minimising computational costs.

Thus, the conversion of ACT* into ACT-R is predicated on bringing computational costs and processing efficiency into the picture. It also aims to bring the component mechanisms into a closer match to the known properties of neural networks by allowing rules not only to be matched by the spread of activation in the declarative network but also to compete with each other via the activation of inhibitory links.

The distinction between the declarative and procedural stores is carried through into ACT-R but the new version places its emphasis on the role of the chunk as the basic unit for encoding general knowledge. Triplet groupings (see Chapter 2) are used to convert structural descriptions into chunks where the component elements can be assigned specific relational roles. The declarative knowledge base is then assembled as these same chunks combine to form higher-order encodings.

We will return to some of the issues contingent on setting cognitive processes within an evolutionary context in the final section. In the meantime, the advent of ACT-R is a useful reminder that there is more than one way of tailoring a production system to the vagaries of human cognition. Production systems may have the power to handle all computable functions but the fact that universal systems exist that can all simulate each other, does not preclude significant differences in how they assemble their mechanisms at the implementational level. Anderson has chosen to navigate this route by looking for unifying principles across the implementational, algorithmic, and knowledge levels. Newell (1990) has taken this unification exercise yet further by aiming for a cognitive architecture capable of integrating data from the biological level up through and including the knowledge level and, possibly beyond, into the social level.

SOAR as a general-purpose model of cognition
The SOAR architecture aims to specify a single set of mechanisms potentially capable of simulating cognition in all its forms—problem solving, decision making, routine action, memory, learning, skill, perception, motor activity, language, motivation, emotion, imagining, dreaming, to name but a few. SOAR may not do all these things equally well but, in principle, it is intended that none of them should lie beyond its reach.

If the *modus operandi* of ACT* can be caricatured through the procedures of the traditional bank, SOAR can be similarly caricatured in terms of the procedures adopted at auction sales. An item is put up for sale and this results in a flurry of bidding which is allowed to continue until all interested parties have made an offer. The item then goes to whoever made the highest bid. Similarly, within SOAR, as items of information enter working memory, they are allowed to match up with as many productions as they can. Once the value of these offers is out in the open, the decision is then made as to which rules provide the best bets on where to proceed next. This state of affairs is not as hit or miss as it may sound; SOAR can learn from its own mistakes as it goes along. We will look first at some of the design features that differentiate SOAR from ACT*. Then, we will consider how SOAR is designed to reflect on its own knowledge in order to create new versions that are better attuned to the demands of the environment.

SOAR architecture

Within the SOAR framework all cognitive tasks, whatever their nature, are interpreted as a form of problem solving. Each particular task is assigned a problem space in the course of comprehension and it is within this space that the relevant knowledge is assembled and the degree of progress towards a solution is assessed. A task has been completed when the initial (given) space state has been converted into the goal state through the use of operators that permit movement through the problem space in the desired direction. At minimum, therefore, executing a task requires (1) the formulation of an appropriate problem space, (2) the selection of a particular starting state, and (3) the selection of operators for moving around within the problem space. All of this activity depends on production rules being triggered as new content flows into working memory from perceptual activity and from the residue of prior solution attempts.

Viewed on a global level, cognitive activity in SOAR is oriented around a series of decision cycles. On each cycle, information is first assembled and it is then evaluated in order to decide what to do next. If the task is a familiar one, it will be accomplished within the initial problem space as the appropriate operators are selected and applied one after the other. However, when there is insufficient information to decide what to do next, SOAR automatically creates a subgoal to resolve the impasse. It then continues creating subgoals until the impasse is broken or it cannot proceed further. In order to get the flavour of how all this fits together we will consider first of all how SOAR proceeds in the context of a simple block-stacking task.

Example application: Block-stacking task
Suppose the task is one of stacking three blocks on top of each other according to a set order (see Newell, 1990). In Fig. 4.4 we have the state at the start where block A is on top of block B and block C is lying on the table. At the extreme right hand side of the figure, we have the desired arrangement where A is stacked on top of B which is on top of C.

With regard to this task, SOAR is equipped with operators for moving around the relevant problem space and it is further equipped with some simple heuristics such as "do not select an operator that undoes what has just been done", or "do not propose altering a state if it is already a part of the desired state".

To begin with SOAR proposes three operators all of which are acceptable in the circumstances (see Fig. 4.4). The options available are:

1. Move A to the table (A → T)
2. Move A on top of C (A → C)
3. Move C on top of A (C → A)

This immediately results in a tie impasse because there is no knowledge as to which operator is best. Consequently, a subgoal is set up to select one of these operators. A new selection space is created and an evaluator operator (E) checks each move in turn. If the move (A → C) is selected, the operator is tried in order to "look ahead" and to see what happens and what can follow. In fact, only one further move is possible—assuming the previous move is not simply reversed—which is (B → A) and this does not produce the desired state.

Next, the operator (C → A) may be selected for evaluation. If so, this gives the state where C is on top of the stack, not A, so this is rejected in turn. At this point the tie has been broken because two of the three alternatives have accumulated "reject" preferences in this context. This just leaves (A → T) and it is implemented in the top problem space, not the evaluation space. After (A → T), an heuristic recognises B on C as part of the final state, leaving just the move (A → B) which gives the required end state.

Even from this abbreviated account of SOAR in action, it can be seen that it differs from ACT* on a number of fronts. Within SOAR, there is no separation between a declarative memory store and a procedural store, rather these are merged to form one storage system and then combined with a working memory that now features as a distinct store in its own right. Another difference is that SOAR decides which productions should apply, not through the strengths of the elements being matched, but via preferences as determined during the elaboration phase. Consequently, knowledge compilation no longer

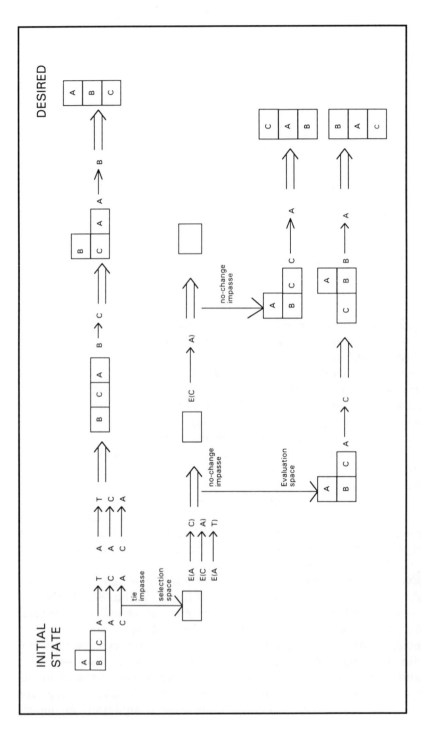

FIG. 4.4. Behaviour of SOAR on blocks task. (From Newell, 1990.)

involves transferring information from declarative to production memory, it relies instead on the different mechanism of "chunking" (see later).

Production memory in SOAR

Accessing knowledge in ACT* entailed both production matching and spreading activation in declarative memory but in SOAR only one process—production matching—needs to be invoked. SOAR proposes a single long-term memory—a production system—that is used for both declarative and procedural knowledge. Thus all of SOAR's permanent memory comes in the form of production rules where the action component of a production provides content and its conditions serve as retrieval cues. As Newell points out, although this seems to present a major break with the assumptions behind ACT* this is more apparent than real because the manner in which activation relates to production matching is similar to the manner in which it "spreads through the declarative network". The symbols in SOAR provide access to memory structures that are not currently being used in processing and, when accessed, these enter into working memory as elements carrying descriptions of the objects concerned in the form of attribute/value pairings, e.g. an object's shape or location. In other words, unlike ACT* which allowed for different types of declarative content (temporal strings, spatial images, and propositions), SOAR specifies a single, common code for all forms of knowledge.

Whereas ACT* assigned strengths to each element in declarative and procedural memory, SOAR's single memory does not differentiate its contents through their strengths. Instead, SOAR executes all satisfied instantiations and, as a result, all matched productions are allowed to fire in parallel. This defines the elaboration phase of a decision cycle and it does away with the need to decide which rules should be triggered. Following elaboration, a decision phase ensues where particular rules are selected and hence what action is to be taken. As SOAR allows for a wide range of information to get involved in problem solving—current goals, perceptual information, motor commands, and preferences for actions to be taken—this calls for a working memory whose capacity extends well beyond the limits typically considered.

Elaboration and decision phase

During the elaboration phase of any decision cycle, knowledge is being recruited concerning the current situation. This is done by triggering all productions whose conditions are satisfied and all of these recruited productions add new working memory elements. As there is no conflict resolution, everything is free to flow in and this process continues until a state of quiescence is reached where no further matches are possible. At this point, the preferences attached to various options are used to decide which of the available actions are to be taken. Preference values can range from "acceptable" to "reject" and the decision procedure singles out which action offers the best way foward. Provided a decision is reached and the action is taken, a new decision cycle then ensues and so on.

Where a decision cannot be taken at the end of a decision cycle about the best way of proceeding, an impasse arises which is resolved by setting up a goal to overcome the difficulty. Thus, ACT* and SOAR also differ in their mechanisms for creating goal hierarchies and this leads to a significant divergence in how they account for the coinage of new productions.

Impasses and chunking

SOAR creates goals only on those occasions when a decision cannot be made about how to proceed. These are the occasions when an impasse has been reached because there are no clear preferences favouring one course of action over another. When this happens, the system creates a new subgoal to resolve the situation by searching for further information that will get it out of difficulty. This processs continues as and when further impasses arise until it bottoms out at a point where the knowledge immediately available in a space enables an action to be taken. At the point where an impasse has been successfully resolved, the conditions immediately preceding the impasse and the dependent actions that cleared the hurdle are automatically chunked together to form a new production. The newly coined production is added to permanent memory and it is available for use immediately thereafter.

The critical elements for forming the chunk are identified by a process of backtracking that picks out which elements were causally linked to the desired outcome. Elements that are part of this causal chain are selected while other, uninvolved elements are discarded. Once chunking has taken place, should the same situation arise in the future, the newly formed production will be available to fire and the impasse can thus be avoided. Transfer of learning will be possible because the new production will continue to be triggered even if its condition elements are accompanied by totally new content. Consequently, the distinction between episodic memory and declarative memory now becomes one of degree not kind; chunks will encode episodic memory details but they can also encode abstract details that can have relevance for many different contexts.

Total cognitive system

The central cognitive structure of SOAR, as described here, is itself embedded within a larger system incorporating perceptual and motor components. Taken together, these components constitute the Total Cognitive system. This arrangement marks a further difference between ACT* and SOAR. In ACT*, input and output functions are assigned to systems outside the main cognitive architecture. SOAR, on the other hand, locates its central architecture as part of a larger structure which contains additional productions that deal with encoding and decoding processes. As these productions lie outside the decision cycles of central cognition, they can "run free" in response to the features of the external situation. Nonetheless, overall control remains with central cognition and its serial decision mechanism.

To grasp how all of this activity fits together as a whole we need a somewhat more demanding task than the block-stacking task described earlier. Accordingly, we will consider a relatively complex case drawn from developmental psychology; the development of the child's gradual understanding of the principles behind the beam balance. As we will see in Chapter 7, the principles underlying cognitive growth constitute a difficult and problematic issue within developmental psychology. Consequently, to the extent that Newell is able to apply the SOAR architecture to throw light on such matters this constitutes a strong argument in support of its claims as a general-purpose architecture.

Understanding the principles of the beam balance

Numerous developmental studies have confirmed that when children of different ages are asked to predict the behaviour of a balance under different loads, (which arm will go down), they pass through distinct levels of understanding before arriving at the principle of torque (e.g. Inhelder & Piaget, 1958). Consequently, any satisfactory account of this developmental sequence must be capable of explaining how the gradual progression from simple guessing to informed insight comes about.

Various ways of accounting for the observed developmental progression have been suggested including the possibility that the child's predictions arise and change as different production rules become available through experience. Thus, Siegler (1981) has proposed that children start off by using general rules to guide their predictions which are then replaced by the more specific rules that are created as their experience with the apparatus increases (see Fig. 4.5).

Siegler argued that a sequential progression through four simple rules would suffice to explain the typical developmental pattern. As each rule comes into play, the child is led into making characteristic errors when predicting the behaviour of the beam until, with the advent of the

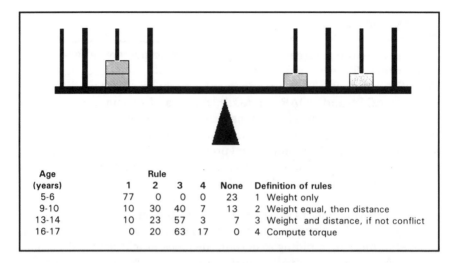

Age (years)	Rule 1	2	3	4	None	Definition of rules
5-6	77	0	0	0	23	1 Weight only
9-10	10	30	40	7	13	2 Weight equal, then distance
13-14	10	23	57	3	7	3 Weight and distance, if not conflict
16-17	0	20	63	17	0	4 Compute torque

FIG. 4.5. Balance beam task and percentage fitting rule by age. (From Newell, 1990.)

fourth rule dealing with torque, the child is finally brought to the position where correct predictions can be sustained for all possible combinations of weights and distances.

At first, the child may simply guess at what is likely to happen but, with a little practice, the child begins to respond in terms of the weights on each arm while ignoring their distance from the fulcrum. At this point, the child predicts that the side with the heaviest weight will go down or, if there are the same weights on both arms, the child predicts that the beam will balance. Somewhat more sophisticated predictions become possible when the child starts to take distances into account. Under rule 2, predictions are made according to weight, if the totals on each side are different, but, if the weights are equal, some distance information can now be taken into account. With the advent of rule 3, information concerning both weights and distances can be registered, at least for those combinations where they are not in conflict. This final restriction is removed when the child can compute the torque on each arm, at which point correct predictions can be generated for all stimulus combinations.

Although children normally take some years to progress through the rules in the order listed, their rate of progress can be accelerated by training programmes designed to focus attention on the rule-generated errors. The training procedure and its consequences can be simulated within SOAR which uses its chunking mechanism to account for process of developmental change.

SOAR simulation: Chunking and rule changes
Viewed from SOAR's perspective, the developmental sequence comes about as the child creates new productions via the chunking mechanism which is invoked by earlier mistakes. Mistakes will occur, either because the relevant productions are lacking, or because they are not in the correct form and need to be relearned. As this distinction will crop up again elsewhere we will try to be clear about exactly what Newell has in mind. How SOAR should react when it becomes evident that the information it has available is wrong differs from how it should react when the relevant information is simply lacking. According to Newell (1990, p.466) the latter situation occurs:

> ... when a system does not know something and acquires that knowledge for the first time. The [former] occurs when it does know something but has it wrong and must relearn it correctly. ... The balance-beam developmental situation is that the child learns to predict the tilt of the balance beam according (say) to rule 1. It has behaved this way for a while. Then, one day it finds out that the rule is wrong (the experimenter arranges the world so that the conflicting facts cannot be ignored). The child's problem is to change its behaviour.

Rule correction, as opposed to rule acquisition, calls for a recovery mechanism that can override and isolate "rogue" productions (inadequate rules). Newell considers various ways in which the continued existence of rogue productions could be handled. One possibility is to allow for the extirpation of "bad structure" altogether. This option, however, is rejected as too dangerous—we may not know all of its ramifications and deleting part of the control structure could not only throw out the good with the bad it could also disrupt the functioning of the remaining productions. Alternatively, as in ACT*, learning could be modulated by using feedback to alter the strengths of productions. Rogue rules could lose strength and the likelihood of their being triggered would be reduced accordingly. However, to go down this road would mean altering the basic architecture of the model, so this option too is rejected.

The third possibility, the one actually adopted by Newell, is to build a discrimination mechanism so that "bad structure" is unlikely to be evoked once it has been identified. If it can be arranged that the system never goes down the path that leads to working memory containing the elements that match to the rogue production's conditions then it will not fire and it will have been effectively quarantined. This outcome is achieved by forcing an impasse whenever there is feedback that a response is incorrect and it works its corrective effects by exploiting the properties provided by nested problem spaces. As all activity, good or bad, occurs in a specific problem space, moving to a new problem space makes it possible to leave a contaminated space behind while saving whatever good activity it has supported. In effect, this means creating a new, clean problem space by selective transfer from the old problem space. Hence, developmental progression is predicated on new problem spaces being created following a reflective analysis of the inadequacies associated with a current problem space.

Problem solving starts in a prediction space (P) and it is here that prediction operators predict tilt. Consequently, all other spaces arise out of impasses that originate in the P space. Now consider three separate trials on the beam task when feedback about errors is available each time. On trial 1, nothing is known and a production for making a prediction has to be created, say, the child guesses. To simulate this outcome, SOAR moves from the P space into a new (G) space where it attempts to generate an appropriate operator. This prediction operator must encode the particular beam balance situation, then compare the encoding of the left-hand side against the encoding of the right-hand side in order to select between the responses "left down", "right down", and "balance". The relevant encoding is handled by perceptual operators in yet other spaces that deal with the comparison of the two sides of the balance and that serve to link this information to a prediction response. At this preliminary stage, the result is a tie impasse because all the options (right, left, balance) seem possible. Hence this leads into a selection space where a response is picked at random which is then made in the P space. As there is no feedback at this point, it doesn't know whether it is right or wrong but at least it does respond.

On trial 2 a new test situation is arranged so that there is feedback that the prediction from this operator is wrong. This calls for the operator to be replaced by another, say rule 1. With the new test arrangement in place, SOAR applies its previous guess, only to get feedback that it is incorrect. It consequently rejects this operator only to end up in another impasse—what to do next. The resolution lies in building a new problem space (P2) that can support a new prediction. SOAR works in the new prediction space (P2) as long as it can but returns to the earlier space P when impasses need to be tackled. In fact, as P2 is an empty space at this point, all problem solving is in P whereas all impasses are in P2. Consequently, when an impasse is solved in P, the resulting chunk transfers the solution into P2. Because only that knowledge in P that contributes to solving the current impasse gets transferred across, this cleans up the space by leaving bad knowledge behind. In this manner, a new P2 space is built out of P through the filtering introduced by impasses and chunking.

Suppose the new prediction operator created on trial 2 encodes the weights on each arm, and the more heavily laden arm is predicted to go down. On trial 3, it is again arranged that the predictions from this new rule are disconfirmed and this negative feedback leads to a yet another problem space being set up, P3, which is backed up by P2. Because at this point, only weight is being encoded, a new impasse arises and this prompts SOAR into a reanalysis of its encoding of the balance situation.

In a new encoding space, E, operators are used for taking measurements and for noting the features present in the actual situation. This could lead the child to attend to the colour of the discs on each arm, or their texture, or whatever, but distance is always there as a candidate feature. If distance gets encoded then rule 2 is constructed and so matters continue as earlier rules are disconfirmed and replaced by new versions, at least up to rule 3. (Newell suggests that the fourth [torque] rule is qualitatively different from the others and is probably acquired through formal teaching.)

In short, it is being proposed that chunking, driven by feedback from failed predictions, acts as the transition mechanism that takes the child from one stage to another. It is also being proposed that as this same reflective mechanism applies in other developmental contexts besides the beam balance, it is conflict between predictions and outcomes that serves as the principal determinant of cognitive reorganisation and growth. This constitutes a major theoretical claim and in Section Two we will look at the matter again in the light of additional data and rather different theoretical perspectives.

SOAR as a unified model of cognition

The representational elements and mechanisms specified within SOAR's architecture all fall within the algorithmic and implementational levels of description as described earlier. However, this architectural framework is also intended to have implications both for operations taking place at the biological level and for the transactions that occur at the knowledge level and beyond. Because it has these properties, Newell presents SOAR as an exemplar of a unified theory of cognition. Its validity can be assessed through its capacity for handling the cumulative processing constraints created as higher-order cognitive operations are assembled from the workings of submechanisms on lower levels.

If higher-order operations are built out of processes occurring on lower levels then they must respect whatever time constraints have been set by their component elements. Consequently, a stringent test of the validity of the SOAR architecture becomes possible by taking these additive constraints seriously. The architecture should be capable of adjusting to such demands without the need for *post hoc* adjustments. If it cannot meet these standards, this will count as evidence against it. On the other hand, where it does meet these time constraints this should count as evidence in its favour.

Newell shows that when SOAR is put through its paces and applied to a variety of cognitive processes at varying levels of complexity, it fares remarkably well. It can handle the temporal properties of immediate behaviour which is close to the level at which the architecture is defined (behaviours such as simple and choice reaction times) and it can scale up to meet the temporal requirements of other forms of behaviour that are composed from these basic operations, such as sentence verification and skill acquisition.

Although most critics have expressed their admiration for the sheer scale and bravado of this exercise this has not stopped them from objecting to its lightweight treatment of specific issues such as the interface between perception and central cognition or the influence, say, of affective processes on cognitive operations. Equally, where the model has been applied to specific cognitive tasks such as text comprehension and problem solving, it is open to the further criticism that too much of the microdetail has been strategically ignored (see the critical comments accompanying Newell, 1990). Similarly, Cooper and Shallice (1995) have criticised SOAR's claims to provide a unified theory of general intelligence on the grounds that:

(a) it is not clear which of its components are intended as psychological principles and which are merely *ad hoc* mechanisms that are needed to get the program to work;
(b) the changes it has undergone have not necessarily been psychologically motivated, but have also been made in order to cope with local difficulties in application;
(c) The evidence adduced from additive time constraints has been selectively assembled at the expense of time estimates that do not conform with SOAR's predictions.

We will address some of this experimental detail later on but, for the present, it will be useful to make some general comments on the theoretical status of general-purpose models of cognition.

Both ACT* and SOAR illustrate how knowledge-level processes can be grounded in mechanisms at lower levels of description. This is no mean achievement and provides a rebuttal to critics such as Fodor (1983) who have argued that central cognition is not amenable to explanation outside the knowledge level. The source of Fodor's scepticism derives from a set of ideas first formulated in the late eighteenth and early nineteenth centuries. Ideas that emphasised the differences between kinds of knowing rather than their sameness.

INPUT MODULES AND CENTRAL COGNITION

In the early part of the nineteenth century, Franz Joseph Gall (1758–1828) mounted a direct attack on the traditional unified view of mind by proposing the existence of cognitive faculties which specialised in handling particular types of information. Memory for faces was different from memory for melodies, which was different again from memory for language. On this view, there is no general faculty of memory, rather it is to be divided into distinct memory faculties each dealing with its own kind of information. Gall's espousal of phrenology (the belief that the presence or absence of individual mental faculties could be assessed from the contours of the skull) brought immediate and justified criticisms from physiologists of the time. Nonetheless, as Fodor was to conclude some 200 years later, Gall's views differentiating dedicated input modules from central processes could not be dismissed so easily.

The principal characteristic of input modules is that they are specialised for dealing with certain kinds of information in a highly restricted manner. As Fodor expresses it, they are "computationally encapsulated"—an arrangement that carries distinct processing advantages. An organism equipped in this way can reach its decisions quickly. If an oncoming cloud of dust is processed by an computationally encapsulated module, it may be identified as a potential threat without referring to everything the organism knows about possible predators. As the output from this (and other) modules can be passed on to a central mechanism, it still remains open to the organism to ponder the significance of the fact that it was about to be eaten, but by then a flight response will have ensured that it was around to benefit from a bout of reflection.

Fodor proposed that a modular system can be identified by the co-occurrence of a number of operating properties: (1) mandatory operation (we cannot control whether to apply the mechanism or not); (2) fast processing; (3) shallow computation (it gives only a preliminary characterisation of an input); (4) a fixed neural architecture; (5) a characteristic pathology; and (6) a characteristic developmental sequence. Possible candidates for modular processing are colour perception; the analysis of shape and face recognition; sentence parsing;

and the detection of melody—where each module processes its characteristic input to produce an output in a form that is suitable for domain-general, central processing.

The function of the input modules, therefore, is to take external inputs, process them in some restricted and encapsulated manner, and to convert them to a form where they can be of use to central mechanisms, such as thinking and problem solving. Obviously, there needs to be some point in the processing cycle where the outputs from individual modules can be checked against the products of other modules and against the person's store of general knowledge, otherwise we would never be able to form such a store in the first place. It is only at this central level that everything known by the organism can be potentially recruited to influence the outcome.

Fodor expresses deep scepticism that central cognitive processes can be approached at other than the knowledge level precisely because they are cognitively penetrable. This means that there is no way of experimentally prising the processes apart as can be done with cognitively encapsulated input modules. It is on this critical point, of course, that both Anderson and Newell disagree. The whole point of their production system architectures is to translate central cognition into constituent operations at lower levels.

On the other hand, there is some weight to the criticism that, in formulating the mechanisms of ACT* and SOAR, neither Anderson nor Newell have concentrated on the functional properties of the neural networks that comprise the biological level. These properties suggest there are other ways than production systems for modelling human cognition. Skinner (1985) has captured the crux of this divergence rather well when he contrasts the classical metaphor of "mind as encyclopaedia", with the rival metaphor of "mind as electrical battery". Under the former metaphor we may speak of knowledge being stored and then retrieved as needed. Adopting the battery metaphor permits us to talk of knowledge being generated as needed and to forget about its storage in symbolic form. It is this type of distinction that informs the connectionist architectures for cognition that feature in the next chapter.

CHAPTER FIVE

Non-symbolic architectures: Connectionism

THE ROOTS OF CONNECTIONISM

Although claims for the neurological sophistication of the cognitive models subsumed under the banner of connectionism can be overplayed—some of these models show all the neural inspiration of a phrenological bust—theoretical deference to the neural organisation of the brain has been seen as the main factor in promoting subsymbolic models of cognition. Accompanying this shift to a subsymbolic level, we find a number of operating characteristics that are markedly different from those we have considered so far.

Table 5.1 lists examples of the characteristics of neural organisation which for connectionists set significant constraints on attempts to model the human cognitive architecture (Rumelhart & McClelland, 1986).

The nature of these properties will become clearer once we have described example connectionist networks (also known as parallel distributed processing and neural networks) in more detail. For now, we can note that responding to these constraints shifts the emphasis away from the macrocognitive (symbolic) level to a microcognitive (subsymbolic) level where a large number of simple processing units co-operate in parallel to generate particular input–output relationships. The function that relates the computed output to the input is determined by the strengths on the links between the component units in the network and by dint of changing these connection strengths, the

TABLE 5.1
Properties of neural networks

1. Neurons exhibit slower processing than conventional computational components
2. There is a very large number of other neurons
3. Neurons receive inputs from many other neurons
4. Learning involves modifying connections between neurons
5. Neurons communicate by sending activation or inhibition through their connections
6. Information is continuously available
7. Neural networks show graceful degradation with damage and information overload
8. There is distributed not central control
9. Relaxation is the dominant mode of computation

Adapted from Rumelhart and McClelland, 1986.

network can be steered towards different input-output computations. Although these ideas have led to the opening up of important new territories, they are not entirely original.

Connectionism has its main historical roots in an associationist psychology which has surfaced, sunk, and resurfaced many times in the history of psychological explanation. The enduring appeal of associationism lies in its unremitting simplicity. Ideas become linked together in the mind if and when they are contiguous; the more frequent their association, the stronger their mutual link. Whole theories of mind have been built around this basic principle and, despite many putdowns, it has never quite gone away (Anderson & Bower, 1973; Warren, 1921).

In the eighteenth century, David Hartley (1705–1757) had speculated that the arguments introduced in Newton's *Principia* could be extended to address the neurophysiological basis of thought. In his *Observations on Man* (1749/1791), Hartley proposed that sensations enter into the nervous system as vibrations (matter in motion) giving rise to localised vibrations in the brain. As these vibrations can persist after the external object has been removed, Hartley further supposed they go on to function as the physical substrate for our ideas. Thus, memory images are to be interpreted as smaller-scale vibrations (vibratiuncles) in the same regions of the brain as the original experience and, as they become associated by contiguity, they serve as the physical basis for the stream of consciousness.

In fact, associationist models of cognition can proceed perfectly well with or without an accompanying mapping onto the brain. Nonetheless, as Hartley had realised, there is a compelling link to be made between physical activity in the brain and the flow of subjective experience. At the time, Hartley could do little more than ground the material basis for thought and memory in the vibratory motions of brain particles, but when Alexander Bain (1818–1903) started to address these same issues in the following century he was in the position to exploit a better understanding of the physiology of the nervous system (Wilkes & Wade, in press).

For Bain, the phenomena of memory were best understood, not as entailing a repertoire of prestored memories, but via constructive operations capable of putting together whatever output was required on line. As Bain's contributions to the connectionist canon have largely been neglected in the available histories (e.g. Valentine, 1989; Walker, 1990) we will look at what he had to say in some detail.

It was the problem of trying to match quantitative estimates of the number of associations held in memory to the neural structure of the brain that first drew Bain into this area although it was this same problem that eventually led him to abandon this line of theorising. In his book *Mind and body. The theories of their relation* (1873), Bain proposed that the act of recollecting an item from memory implicates the neural connections involved in the original experience and, by extension, the mechanism of retention resided in the internal structure of the neural groupings that happened to have been activated at the time. Associations between ideas were formed as modifications occurred within these neural groupings. Specific inputs led to "special growths" occurring at the cell junctions which, in turn, led to specific associative pathways being favoured.

Having formulated these hypotheses, Bain proceeded to raise two fundamental questions about the manner in which nerve groupings could come to sustain the known flexibilities associated with human thought: (1) how could the internal organisation of a neural network come to support different responses under different conditions of stimulation? and (2) how would a neural network come to possess such an internal organisation in the first place?

On the first issue, Bain noted that the same neural grouping could support different responses to different patterns of stimulation because of the way in which nerves could combine together to channel activation along different associative pathways. As an example of what he had in mind, Bain instanced the network shown in Fig. 5.1. Here, the joint stimulation of a with b gives x; of b with c gives y; and of a with c gives z.

Thus, Bain conceived of a neural network as made up from nerves carrying excitatory links to selected parts of the network which summated the degree of stimulation they were receiving from the network as a whole. Under this arrangement the same network could come to compute different responses according to the inputs it received

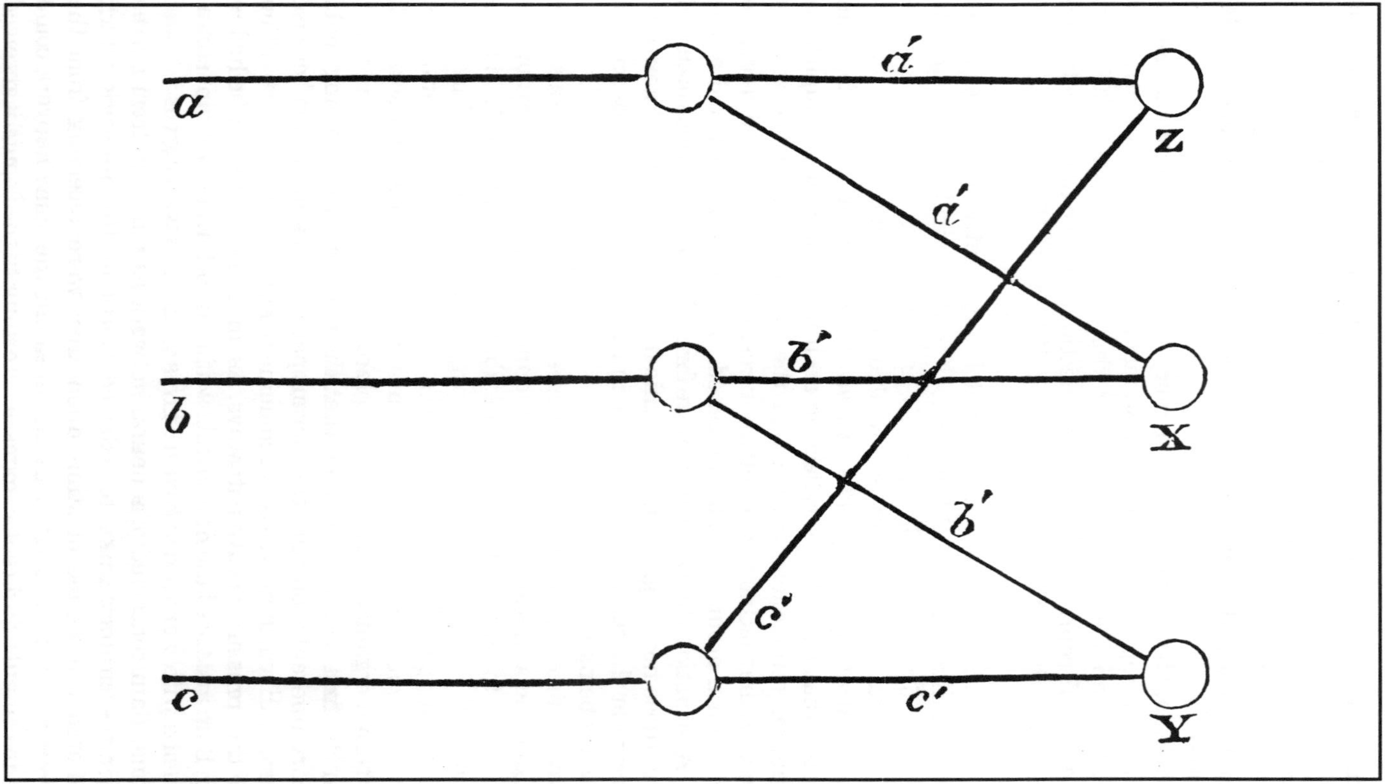

FIG. 5.1. Joint stimulation within a neural grouping. (From Bain, 1873.)

on different occasions. Futhermore, given the complex neurological structure of the brain, such networks could, in principle, be scaled up to cope with the degrees of flexibility that would be required to handle human cognition.

On the second issue of how a network's connections came to be established in the first place, Bain (1873, p.117) pointed to the consequences that would arise when its elements were active together:

> ... when two impressions concur, or closely succeed one another, the nerve currents find some bridge or place of continuity, better or worse, according to the abundance of nerve matter available for the transition. In the cells or corpuscles where the currents meet and join, there is, in consequence of the meeting, a strengthened connexion or diminished obstruction—a preference track for that line over lines where no continuity has been established.

In short, as experiences reoccur, we can expect the relevant neural groupings to come to reflect the mutual dependencies between their component parts, and *pari passu* so too for the ideas that they sustain.

By virtue of raising both of these questions together, Bain emerges as the first theorist to move beyond generalised statements aimed at linking neural activity to mental phenomena to providing detailed examples of how this could be achieved in practice. Nevertheless, a decade later (Bain, 1904, p.313), he was having second thoughts, mainly because the sheer number of memory associations seemed likely to outstrip the neural resources of the brain:

> The hypothesis was a legitimate one; but subsequent reflection led to the belief that the number of psychical elements, although run up to hundreds of thousands, was still inadequate.

Having been disowned by their orginator, it is not surprising that Bain's arguments had little impact at the time or since. Even so, they were remarkably prescient in foreshadowing some of the central concerns addressed by modern connectionist writers.

In the present century, another major (and sustained) advance occured when McCulloch and Pitts (1943) drew attention to the parallels that exist between the logical circuits of digital computers and information processing by neurons. In particular, they noted how the "all or none" properties of conduction could be used to simulate different forms of logical processing. Subsequent work in this area has aimed at exploiting this computational potential in less idealised forms that are intended to provide a closer match to the neurophysiological data.

The main historical figure to pave the way for this new connectionism was Donald Hebb who, in his book *The organisation of behavior* (1949), discussed the potential role of "cell assemblies" in the processes of perception and memory. Hebb reasoned that structural changes are likely to occur in the brain when nerve cells are repeatedly active together at the same time. Under these conditions, an assembly of association area cells comes to be formed which "can act briefly as a closed system after stimulation has ceased". In other words, once a cell assembly has been established as a result of contiguity, activity in some of the cells will give rise to activity in the other cells in the assembly.

These arguments provide the core of Hebb's neurophysiological postulate which states (Hebb, 1949, p.62):

> When an axon of cell A is near enough to excite a cell B and repeatedly or persistently takes part in firing it, some growth process or metabolic change takes place in one or both cells such that A's efficiency, as one of the cells firing B, is increased.

From the operation of this simple mechanism, different cell assemblies can be formed which can chain together giving rise to patterns of activation that mirror the regularities holding between stimuli in the external world. The resulting phase sequences would come to play an important role in perceptual organisation and, by extension, in the sequencing of thought as one idea follows on the heels of another.

The new connectionism that builds upon these ideas is rather more than a revitalised form of associationism because it also allows for emergent properties that are not evident when the component parts of cognitive processes are viewed separately. In this respect, both Hebb and the new connectionists draw upon Gestalt theory which, in the earlier part of this century, produced many examples where the "whole is more than the sum of its parts". The merging of these influential ideas from associationist and Gestalt psychology combined with the recent advances in computing technology have resulted in a new family of cognitive models which deny that cognitive activity must necessarily be equated with symbol manipulation.

NEURAL COMPUTATION

Connectionist models treat cognitive activity as deriving from the ebb and flow of activation in neural networks as it is channelled by associative constraints laid down from past experience. At their simplest, such models employ a network of units where each unit serves in either an input or an output role. External stimulation sets up patterns of activation over the input units and whatever the network can compute in response to the input is expressed through patterns of activation over the network's output units. The form this computation actually takes will depend on the way in which previous inputs to the network have acted to modify the weights on its connections.

A unit that possesses a positive activation value will transmit *excitation* to other units in the network with which it shares connections carrying positive weights. Similarly, it will transmit *inhibition* to those units with which it has connections carrying negative weights. External inputs (say from the sensory receptors) are encoded in the network by setting up activation values over the input units and these then start to propagate activation over the whole network. This will continue to occur until eventually the network relaxes into a stable state which provides the best compromise between the input constraints and the constraints present in the network's connections. At this point, the activation pattern set up over the output units represents the network's response to the input. Changing the weights on the network's connections can lead to a new output being computed and for this reason we can speak of the knowledge underlying a mental computation as residing in the connection strengths in the network taken as a whole. This relatively elementary architecture can be used to model a wide variety of cognitive activities and training procedures also exist which enable neural networks to set the connection strengths necessary for carrying out particular computational tasks.

In the 1960s, theoretical positions were not so entrenched as they have become since. The classical symbol model had yet to achieve its position of theoretical dominance and it was in direct competition with cognitive models that looked to neurophysiology for their inspiration. Papert (1988, p.3) takes a wry pleasure in describing this period of flux:

> Once upon a time two daughter sciences were born to the new science of cybernetics. One sister was natural, with features inherited from the study of the brain, from the way nature does things. The other was artificial, related from the beginning to the use of computers. Each of the sister sciences tried to build models of intelligence, but from very different materials. The natural sister built models (called neural networks) out of mathematically purified neurones. The artificial sister built her models out of computer programs.

Papert could afford to be generous in contrasting the "artificiality" of the classical approach with the "naturalness" of neural networks because he was jointly responsible with Minsky for the judgement that neural networks suffered from serious theoretical limitations (Minsky & Papert, 1969). When Minsky and Papert delivered their verdict they had in mind early versions of neural networks, such as the perceptron (Rosenblatt, 1962).

The perceptron was a device that could be trained to classify sets of patterns as alike or distinct, not by reference to some stored copy or template, but via the computations of a neural network built out of Pitts and McCullough type units. Two possible versions are illustrated in Fig. 5.2a and b.

In Fig. 5.2a, the network consists of two input units which are connected to the single output unit that should respond whenever "1" or "0" or both patterns are present at input. This is accomplished by setting each input unit the task of responding to a particular pattern. At any moment, it assesses its total input and adjusts its output to the response unit accordingly. While the input units have negligible thresholds, the output unit only fires when its net input exceeds 0.5, and this will occur each time an input unit is triggered.

The perceptron can be taught to perform this particular function from scratch using feedback from its detection errors. Failure to detect a pattern should result in an increase in connection strength on the relevant input–output link and by a decrease in the threshold assigned to the output unit. Conversely, false recognition should prompt a reduction in connection strength and an increase in threshold. Following such training, the device will eventually come to respond whenever one or both input units are active, i.e. it can carry out an "inclusive or" task (respond to 1 or 0 or both).

On the other hand, an "exclusive or" task (respond to 1 or 0 but not both) cannot be handled by this device although the addition of "hidden units" to the network will overcome this difficulty. Hidden units do not themselves receive direct inputs from the environment nor do they output directly to the environment, rather they serve as an intermediate stage in the analysis of the input (see Fig. 5.2b). Now, it can be seen that when both 1 and 0 are present, the output unit is inhibited, thus registering the distinction that is required.

At the time these models were being developed the utility of hidden units had been recognised but little progress had been made on the appropriate training procedures. Solving these problems set in train the recent resurgence of interest in the potential of connectionist networks for cognitive modelling. As a result, as well as modelling pattern recognition, neural networks have now been applied to higher-level cognitive activity such as concept formation, schema instantiation, and (more contentiously) problem solving and planning—see Rumelhart,

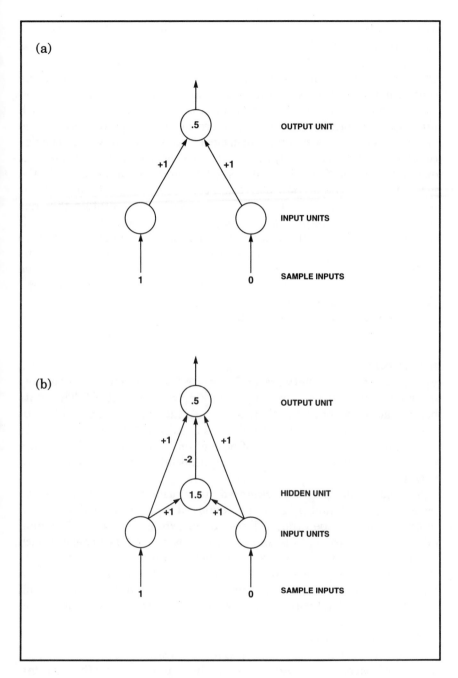

FIG. 5.2. (a) Perceptron and the inclusive "or" task; (b) Perceptron and the exclusive "or" task. (From Johnson-Laird, 1988.)

McClelland and the PDP Research Group (1986); McClelland, Rumelhart and the PDP Research Group, (1986) for an extensive review.

It is worth reiterating at this point that the knowledge employed when a network computes a response to an input resides in the connection strengths on the network links. It is these strengths that control how activation spreads around the network and which ultimately determine whatever pattern of activation appears on the output layer of units as a response. Consequently, whatever knowledge concerning the correct output the network may be said to possess, it exists, not in the form of encoded symbols and productions, but in the form of constraints on how activation can spread from the input layer to the output layer. It is this shift in conceptual orientation that has prompted a major rethink of how cognitive activities might proceed. If it is connection strengths that determine how activation will propagate from the input to the output layer, this means that the computations underlying cognition do not have to be based on structure-sensitive operations over symbol tokens, as envisaged in the previous chapters. To clarify what this means in practice we will look at two types of connectionist network in more detail.

Autoassociator

Figure 5.3 depicts a network of five units (1–5) which are completely interconnected, except for weights linking a unit to itself. The units become active according to their net input; turning "on" if the net input is excitatory and turning "off" if the net input is inhibitory. Its function is to map an imposed pattern of activation over the units into a new pattern at some later time, including associating an imposed pattern with itself.

This particular network has stored the information for computing two patterns, (1, 2, 3) and (1, 4, 5). If an external input is allowed to turn on units 1, 2, and 3, then they will remain on while units 4 and 5 remain off. This is because units within the stored pattern mutually excite each other and collectively they propagate more inhibition than excitation to the rival units. Similarly, when units 1, 4, and 5 are activated by an input, they remain on and this time it is units 2 and 3 that remain off. In each case, the network computes the same pattern at output as that provided at input.

Although the performance of an autoassociator may not appear particularly exciting, consider what happens when, at input, only part of a stored pattern is provided. If we activate units 1 and 5 (but not unit 4) then, as activation spreads around the network, it comes to turn on unit 4, the missing element from the input pattern. The same outcome

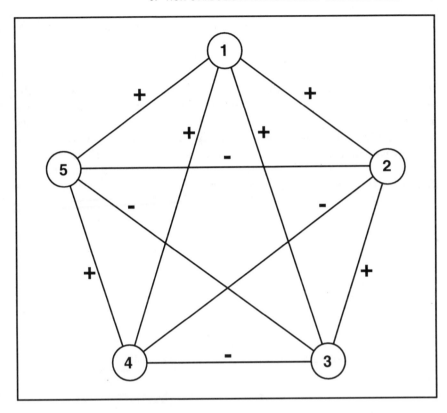

FIG. 5.3. An autoassociator. (Adapted from Levy, 1988.)

would also apply given a partial input of the other pattern—in both cases the network functions to restore the full pattern. This functional property is termed "content addressability" and it is highly characteristic of human memory. Prompted to come up with a musical instrument beginning with a letter "v" and ending with "n" we have little trouble in retrieving "violin". When prompted with partial information about an autobiographical episode, e.g. "what happened", we are quite good at retrieving information about who was there and where the event took place. The target information comes to mind more or less automatically even though we may only start out with a few pieces of the target pattern.

For classical models the address at which information is stored in memory can be quite arbitrary and locating information calls for pointers to particular addresses before the required content can be retrieved. Content addressability, therefore, is handled by these models using somewhat "*ad hoc*" procedures whereas with connectionist systems it is said to emerge as an automatic consequence of their mode of computing.

Paired associator

The autoassociator is a special case of a more general system—the paired associator—which functions to pair an input with an arbitrary response. Everyday instances would be recalling the name of the face we have just seen, reading a word at sight, or remembering the title of a tune we have just heard. Table 5.2a shows a network taken from McClelland, Rumelhart, and Hinton (1986) which acts to associate a (hypothetical) visual input (e.g. a rose) with its characteristic aroma as the response.

The network consists of eight units, four units acting as visual units, (A), and four acting as olfactory units, (B). Any two units may be connected so that they excite each other or so that they inhibit each other and these excitatory or inhibitory links each carry a particular strength or weight which modulates the signal being transmitted. By adjusting these connection weights we can produce different activation patterns within the network. As before, each unit carries out the same elementary

TABLE 5.2
(a) Paired associator: Rose–aroma association

A units	+1	−1	−1	+1	
					−1
					−1
					+1
					+1
					B Units

(b) Matrix representation with weights

+1	−1	−1	+1	
−0.25	+0.25	+0.25	−0.25	−1
−0.25	+0.25	+0.25	−0.25	−1
+0.25	−0.25	−0.25	+0.25	+1
+0.25	−0.25	−0.25	+0.25	+1

From McClelland et al., 1986

computation of working out how much excitatory and inhibitory activation it is receiving from the other nodes to which it is connected. The outcome of this computation sets the unit's current activation level.

In Table 5.2b, the network has been converted into a matrix form in order to emphasise these functional properties. The input (visual) activation values are given along the top, and output values (for the aroma) are given down the right-hand column. Weights on the connections are given in the body of the matrix. In this realisation, when a given pattern of activation occurs over the visual units, (say, +1, -1, -1, +1) it eventually causes another, pattern of activation to appear over the olfactory units (say, -1, -1, +1, +1).

To see why this happens, consider the effect of each A unit on each B unit. This is determined by multiplying the activation of the A unit by the strength on its connection with the B unit. The final activation value set up in a B unit depends on summating the excitatory and inhibitory inputs it is receiving from all A units. For example, the first output unit (B1) is receiving inputs from A1–A4 which are respectively:

$$A1 (+1 \times -0.25) + A2 (-1 \times +0.25) + A3 (-1 \times +0.25) + A4 (+1 \times -0.25)$$

Consequently, the net input to the first B unit (B1) sets its activation value to -1 and, in the same manner, the activation values for B2, B3, and B4 are set at -1, +1, and +1, respectively. As a result, once the visual input pattern (+1; -1; -1; +1) has been set up over the A units, the network computes the olfactory pattern (-1; -1; +1; +1) as the output. In effect, the network remembers the response paired with the stimulus, not by looking up some symbolic token, but by generating the appropriate code,

We do not need a perfect copy of the input pattern before we can get the required output. If we disable unit A3 (producing the pattern +1, -1, 0, and +1 over the A units), "graceful degradation" ensures that, despite the degraded input, we get an output over the B units that is close to the desired output pattern—the B units are all activated in the right direction although their response is now somewhat weaker.

Local and distributed representation

The robustness of computations in the face of degraded inputs arises from the distributed nature of the information held in the network. Activation values computed for each of the B units is not dependent on any individual A unit but on all of the A units acting in unison. This arrangement ensures that the loss of certain input information does not result in the complete breakdown of the system. Had the critical information been localised in a particular A unit, the effect would have been far more catastrophic; degraded inputs in *local* networks can lead to the loss of the representational function altogether. With *distributed* networks it may merely lead to a fuzzier but still recognisable response.

A distributed memory representation applies when the input and output nodes in the network all contribute in parallel to the representational process. Consequently, the registration of a particular representation will call upon many nodes simultaneously and any given node can participate in the activation patterns for different representations. This means that distributed and local networks display rather different representational properties. A meteorological analogy employed by Estes (1988) will help to illustrate what is at stake. Reports of the weather conditions in different cities can either be made by placing an observer in each city that is to be monitored (localised representation) or by using a combination of observers for the same purpose (distributed representation). In the local model, rain in a particular city is signified through the activity of the person assigned to that location. In the distributed model, rain in that area is signified through the joint activity of whichever combination of observers has been given that target. If we decide to cover the weather conditions in more cities, the local version requires that we add more nodes (observers) to the network. In the distributed case, however, we can accommodate more cities than there are observers because each node contributes to the representation of more than one weather state. But nothing comes for free. Local networks can signal rain in one or more places simultaneously whereas distributed networks can only indicate the weather in one place at a time.

Expressed more formally, local models with a population of N units provide us with codes for N different things where up to N representations can be active at a time. In distributed representations, as the population of N units can all feature in different activation patterns, we have codes for 2^N different things but only one of them can be active at a time. Later on, we will see that these operational differences have an important bearing on how successfully each type of system can handle the representation of part–whole relations.

LEARNING IN CONNECTIONIST NETWORKS

In Table 5.2b, the connection strengths required to compute the response over the B units were already present in the network and it is reasonable to enquire how they got there. In fact, they were arrived at by arranging for each A unit to excite (+) each B unit that takes on a compatible activation value in the desired aroma pattern and for each A unit to inhibit (-) each B unit that takes on an incompatible value in this response pattern. The actual connection strengths on the A to B links were then set by making each strength proportional to the product of the two units' activation values. For example, applying this principle to the four A units connected to B1 we get:

$$A1B1\ (+1 \times -1)/4 = -0.25$$
$$A2B1\ (-1 \times -1)/4 = +0.25$$
$$A3B1\ (-1 \times -1)/4 = +0.25$$
$$A4B1\ (+1 \times -1)/4 = -0.25$$

Other weights have been calculated in the same way. More to the point is that it is possible to use this rule to train a network to learn the appropriate weights from scratch.

In his discussion of the properties of cell assemblies, Hebb codified rules that would allow neural networks to store information about input regularities. Hebb reasoned that as an input will activate certain units but not others, the connection strengths between units that tend to be on together should be increased while units that are incompatible should have their connection strengths decreased. This principle can be expressed as the formal learning rule (McClelland, Rumelhart, & Hinton, 1986, p.36):

Adjust the strength of the connection between units A and B in proportion to the product of their simultaneous activation.

This formulation covers both excitatory and inhibitory links. When the product is positive, (both units have the same sign, positive or negative) the dependent change in connection strength makes the connection strength more excitatory. When the product is negative, (both units have different signs) the change makes the connection more inhibitory. By following this principle (since termed the Hebb rule) we can train a network so that input/output regularities come to be reflected in the weights on its connections.

Applying these ideas to the paired associator, we can start out with the situation where there are no weights on the network connections and then commence training by presenting the A and B patterns together, using the Hebb rule to alter the connection strengths. Eventually, the network will acquire the appropriate weights for carrying out the required function.

As matters stand, a network capable of storing only one paired associate would not be much use however adept it might be at learning to set its own connection strengths. On the other hand, trying to store multiple association patterns within a single set of connection strengths seems to lead to a quandary. Once the weights for computing a given response are present, further training to represent a new association may introduce adjustments in connection strengths that put at risk the initial learning. How then can it be arranged for the same network to handle multiple associations so that the whole enterprise is not ridiculously circumscribed?

It turns out that under certain circumstances, interference between new and old learning is not inevitable. There are learning circumstances where a network can be trained to adjust its connection strengths so that it comes to "resonate" in different ways to different inputs, computing the appropriate response in each case. In these cases, if we superimpose one associative pattern on another, in effect add together their respective connection strengths, we can arrive at composite weights that preserve the component associative pathways.

Consider the network previously used to represent the rose–aroma association and suppose we want it to represent a further association, say, apple–aroma. A network containing the new input values, connection strengths, and output values that would be necessary for the second association is shown in Table 5.3a.

The network has been set up using the principles described earlier. With these new weights in place, imposing the apple input pattern (-1; +1; -1; +1) means that activation will propagate through the network resulting in the desired output pattern (-1; +1; +1; -1) being computed. If we want the same network to handle both kinds of association (rose/aroma; apple/aroma) we must add the two sets of connection strengths together, as applies in Table 5.3b.

In this composite matrix, no entry has been recorded if the combined weights are incompatible but a double weighting has been entered where the weights are compatible. This new set of connection strengths will now compute the aroma pattern for the rose input and the (different) aroma pattern for the apple input. These examples were chosen by McClelland et al. so that the associative memories would not interfere with each other and the Hebb rule could be applied directly. Once we move to more complex networks rather different training methods are required.

LEARNING IN MULTILAYER NETWORKS

Pattern associators employ an input layer of units, an output layer of units, and one layer of modifiable connections between them and they can be trained using the Hebb rule. However, as we create more complex networks by adding one or more layers of hidden units to a network (as with the exclusive or EXOR example earlier) and by employing non-linear units (units whose output increases with their net input but

TABLE 5.3
(a) Apple–aroma association

-1	$+1$	-1	$+1$	
+0.25	−0.25	+0.25	−0.25	−1
−0.25	+0.25	−0.25	+0.25	+1
−0.25	+0.25	−0.25	+0.25	+1
+0.25	−0.25	+0.25	−0.25	−1

(b) Composite matrix

A1	A2	A3	A4	
		+0.5	−0.5	B1
−0.5	+0.5			B2
		−0.5	+0.5	B3
+0.5	−0.5			B4

From McClelland et al., 1986

in a non-linear fashion) we find that matters become distinctly more complicated. Although the Hebb rule is no longer adequate as a training method, the method of "backward error propagation" can be used to overcome this hurdle (see Rumelhart, Hinton, & Williams, 1986).

Suppose we have a network of non-linear units designed to operate in a bottom-up mode so that activation spreads from the bottom to the top layer. This could involve a layer of input units connected to an intermediate layer of hidden units which in turn is connected to a top layer of output units. Using whatever connection strengths are currently in place, the network can be tested by setting up an input over the bottom layer and allowing it to propagate upwards to set activations over the top, output layer. This output can now be compared with the required output in the usual way. If there is a discrepancy, the error measure can be used as a guide for adjusting the network's connection strengths. First, the strength on each connection from a hidden unit to an output unit is altered in the direction of reducing the discrepancy. Then a similar adjustment is made for the connections at the next layer down—in this case, the connections from the input layer to the hidden units in the intermediate layer. Repeated application of the method of backward error propagation thus serves to move the computed output in the direction of the desired target pattern by making contingent weight adjustments at all levels in a multilayered network.

Once this training technique became available, the stage was set for a dramatic resurgence of interest in connectionism that has surprised even its most ardent proponents. Consequently, rather than attempting to provide a representative survey of an area that is changing too fast to be summarised adequately, we will put the emphasis on the use of connectionist networks as tools for simulating a variety of cognitive phenomena. We have already seen how classical symbol models can be used to interpret concept formation, schema instantiation, mental models, and conceptual development. Now we will consider, albeit briefly, how these same issues may be interpreted from the subsymbolic perspective.

CONCEPTUAL REPRESENTATION

The gist of the earlier discussion concerning distributed models of memory representation was to the effect that episodic experiences could be superimposed and stored in a network in a composite form. In this respect, distributed models of memory are consistent with Bartlett's view of episodic memory as reconstructed from some underlying schematic record that has abstracted the details underlying multiple related events. Children encountering different dogs, build up their concept of "dog" by abstracting the microfeatures common to the different instances. Each dog is slightly different from the others but there is a typical dog pattern which can be detected and stored in the network's weights. Concept formation, therefore, depends on the subject acquiring the dog prototype and this will happen whether or not actual prototypic instances form part of the training programme.

For example, McClelland and Rumelhart (1985) refer to a network of 24 units being exposed to multiple instances of "dogs" as well as instances from other categories. Presenting a particular dog pattern led to a "visual" activation pattern being imposed over units 9–24 in the network and presenting the name of the dog produced another activation pattern over the first eight units. Training proceeded by exposing the network to multiple instances of "dogs" which consisted of random variations around the prototypic dog pattern. As each new name and visual pattern pair was presented, the weights in the network were re-adjusted to take account of this new information and the process continued until the module had learned a set of weights that was close to the underlying dog prototype. At this point, therefore, the module came to respond more strongly to a prototypic input (not employed during training) than it did to the actual variants that had been introduced during the training period. The presentation of the category label served to turn on the prototypic visual pattern and vice versa. Furthermore, as noted earlier, the same set of weights could also be used to store the prototypes for other categories introduced during training.

In this respect, this exercise simulates the process of normal concept formation but it does so at the expense of some oversimplification. As Schyns (1991) has pointed out, a training procedure where instances come ready-labelled is hardly typical of everyday experience. On the other hand, when we come to consider how the process of schema instantiation might be simulated using neural networks we find that they can accommodate certain critical issues rather better than their classical competitors.

CONSTRAINT-SATISFACTION NETWORKS AND KNOWLEDGE SCHEMAS

One of the most ardent advocates of the new connectionism has been David Rumelhart who originally started out as a strong proponent of schema processing models (Rumelhart, 1980). It was the subsequent struggle to find ways of making preformed schemas match up to their central role as the "building blocks of cognition" that eventually forced Rumelhart into making his shift in theoretical allegiance. The problem that he faced is easy to state and demonstrate although the same cannot be said for its solution at the macrocognitive level. It boils down to the fact that preformed schemas of the kind described in Chapter 2 are too inflexible to cope with all but the simplest instantiations.

When we considered the "John attending school" vignette earlier, we found that at first John was mapped onto the role slot for "pupil" but, as more information came in, that role slot needed to change to "teacher" in order to achieve a better fit with the input and the schema constraints. This change in role is not insignificant as John's default age must now alter as well. Construed as pupil, John's likely age will not exceed 18 years but, construed as teacher, his age will occupy a different range altogether. And we can expect similar constraints to apply to the entries for other slots in the schema which will set up their own dependencies in turn.

In other words, rather complex cross dependencies can be created as the slots in a schema are occupied by specific entries. These are not easily handled if schemas are treated as prestored, symbolic structures because each feature is mapped onto the frame independently of the others. The problem of their cross dependencies then has to be left to the adjudications of some, largely unspecified, monitoring mechanism. This same problem, however, can be handled quite easily if we interpret schema instantiation as a process of constraint satisfaction occurring within a local connectionist network.

In this type of network, the units can be conceived as representing hypotheses about features in the external world, say, the presence of particular shapes or objects. In which case, a unit's activation level will reflect the extent to which its particular hypothesis is being confirmed by the input. A high activation on a particular unit means there is strong evidence supporting the hypothesis it represents and a low level of activation indicates only weak support. As the connections between the units can reflect the extent to which different hypotheses are mutually compatible, external inputs to the network can be evaluated against these constraints taken as a whole.

Suppose we represent a school schema in the form of a local network whose individual nodes stand for hypotheses about different roles (pupil, teacher ...), for hypotheses about different age ranges, and so on for any additional hypotheses that have a bearing on this situation. Features that tend to go together—such as pupil and age range 5–18 years—will share excitatory links while features that are not mutually compatible—such as teacher and age range 5–18 years—will share inhibitory links. A network that is organised in this manner will respond collectively as the external information is being assimilated and mapped. When we read about John at the outset of the passage, the node representing "pupil" becomes active and serves to turn on the other nodes in the network with which it has excitatory links. However, once the new information starts to come in which favours the "John as teacher" hypothesis, the activation pattern now changes. The new input now serves to damp down associations from the "pupil" node while supporting a different aura of associations emanating from the "teacher" node. As all this activity will be occurring in parallel, when the network relaxes into a stable state this will represent the best fit both to the input constraints and the internal constraints based on the network's weights. In other words, instantiating a schema via a constraint-satisfaction mechanism automatically maximises the number of mutually consistent hypotheses that can be supported under the circumstances.

Adopting this perspective on schema instantiation means that we can now clear up a number of the difficulties that accompanied the macrocognitive stance. First, the interdependencies between the values inserted into different slots in the schema can be handled with a flexibility that would be very difficult to achieve at the macrocognitive level. Second, the decision of when to form a schema is resolved, as schemas will emerge quite naturally as input regularities impinge upon the connection strengths in the network. Third, the vexed question of mixed schematic processing is resolved. It is rarely the case that an event activates one schema or script at a time, yet we experience no more difficulty in understanding these mixed cases than we do in the supposedly purer cases. Consider listening to an account of a birthday party held on 5 November, in an expensive restaurant that burns down at the height of the celebrations. Clearly we have a number of separate schemas or scripts all active here which, while specifying their own default values (candles; fireworks; ice buckets; firemen), will require an extremely subtle blending process as they combine to form a larger whole. It is very difficult to see how this outcome could be reached by welding together preformed macroschemas. At the microcognitive level, however, the contrast between mixed schemas and pure schemas makes little sense. By allowing each of the story features to resonate both within its own subnetwork and the larger network as a whole we can arrive at a final relaxation state that gives us precisely the kind of blend that seems to be required.

To expand upon these ideas in a more concrete form, consider how a constraint-satisfaction network would handle our prior example of a "house" schema and its subschemas for different rooms. If we take the units in the network as corresponding to hypotheses about the features of different rooms, such as their size and likely furnishings, then it is possible to simulate the process of instantiating different room schemas using a single set of weights on the network's connections (Rumelhart, Smolensky, McClelland, & Hinton, 1986).

At the outset, prior to building the network, the experimenters provided two subjects with a series of 40 room descriptors referring to the possible sizes and furnishings likely to be associated with different rooms. Then, the subjects were asked to bear in mind a kitchen and to say which of the room features listed were likely to be present in various kinds of kitchens. The same exercise was also carried out with four other types of room: living room, bedroom, bathroom, and study.

In the light of the subjects' responses, a network was created consisting of 40 nodes (one node for each of the descriptors) and connection weights that reflected the interdependencies between the nodes. For example, the units representing "fridge" and "stove" were linked by a positive connection (they tend to co-occur) whereas "fridge" and "toilet" were linked by a negative connection (when one is present the other is absent). The overall effect of translating these (and other) conditional probabilities into excitatory or inhibitory links between the network's units meant that the network could be steered towards different relaxation states according to the inputs it received. These different settlement states corresponded to each of the room schemas in question; kitchen, living room, bedroom, bathroom, and study.

The process of instantiating one of these schemas was simulated by clamping a node on (setting its activation value at 1 and not allowing it to be turned off) and then updating other nodes in the network, one at a time, until the network reached a stable state where the activations of its component nodes remained unchanged. When "oven" was clamped on in this way, the system relaxed into a state where the nodes for other kitchen descriptors were also turned on but not the nodes relating to the remaining rooms. Similarly, clamping on "bed" led to the bedroom features becoming active and so on for the remaining rooms. Hence the network came to represent each of the room schemas, not so much through its connection strengths, as through the relaxation states it was likely to adopt.

Focusing on the relaxation states a network can adopt calls for viewing the network as a whole and keeping track of these state changes can be confusing. Consequently, the analogy of tracking a ball as it rolls over hilly terrain has frequently been used to clarify what is involved. When activation in the network reaches a stable state this is analogous to the ball ending up in a hollow. Arranging for a network to store some preset schema (as with the kitchen example) is then equivalent to landscaping the terrain and so steering the ball towards a predetermined resting place.

Attributing schema instantiation to constraint-satisfaction mechanisms at a microcognitive level clearly enables us to deal with a number of difficulties that were left unresolved at the symbolic level. Even so, all of this activity is assumed to occur in parallel beyond conscious awareness and in this respect it fails to account for the serial nature of understanding that characterises our conscious experience. This gap can be bridged, however, if we assume that once a network has relaxed into a stable state, it is this state that can be consciously accessed. As a network can only settle into one relaxation state at a time, at the macrolevel it will appear to move serially from state to state. Nonetheless, these serial states will arise out of extended sequences of parallel processing occurring outside of consciousness at a micro-cognitive level.

As constraint-satisfaction systems are very effective tools for modelling schema instantiation, it is worthwhile pausing to consider which other types of cognitive operations might yield to the same approach. According to Holyoak and Thagard (1989, pp.306–307) these operations will be those where multiple constraints need to be satisfied but there is little guidance on the order in which the decisions are to be made:

A co-operative algorithm for parallel constraint satisfaction is preferable to any serial decision procedure when (a) a global decision is composed of a number of constituent decisions, (b) each constituent decision should be based upon multiple constraints, (c) the outcome of the global decision could vary depending on the order in which constraints are applied and constituent decisions are made, and (d) there is no principled justification for preferring any particular ordering of constraints or of constituent decisions.

These are precisely the kinds of circumstance that attend many aspects of discourse comprehension and problem solving and we will return to these arguments when we discuss these topics in later chapters.

RECURSIVE CONNECTIONIST ARCHITECTURES AND MENTAL MODELS

In Chapter 3, the significance of mental models for comprehension and mental planning was outlined along with some discussion of their properties on the macrocognitive level. Viewed from a microlevel, Rumelhart, Smolensky, McClelland, and Hinton (1986) have shown how the ability to preview the consequences of an action (by imagining that it has been carried out) could be simulated using a relaxation network which takes as its input the output from another network which computes how a sequence of actions will impact on the environment.

Rumelhart et al. cite as an example the situation where two players compete over a board game. As each player makes a move, this changes the state of the board and thus constrains how the opponent will respond and the whole process will be repeated when the counter-move has been made. A network capable of such sequential interpretation is depicted in Fig. 5.4.

It takes the current state of the board as input and its response to this situation is given by its relaxation state. This changes the environment and the new state is fed back as a new input requiring a further interpretation. Thus, the network can simulate a sequence of moves. If this network is then linked to a second relaxation network which takes as its input a certain subset of the actions that could be carried out, its outputs will be an interpretation of what this would mean in the context of the game. That is, it can predict how the world would change if particular courses of actions were followed and we have the equivalent of running a mental model of the game in play.

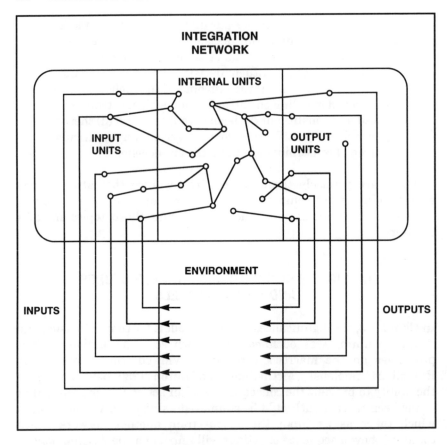

FIG. 5.4. Mental models and recursive networks. (From Rumelhart et al., 1986.)

CONNECTIONISM AND COGNITIVE DEVELOPMENT

Bates and Elman (1992, p.15) refer to the design features of neural networks as being particularly appropriate for handling the emergent stages typically reported within the developmental literature. This is because:

> In trying to achieve stability across a large number of superimposed distributed patterns, the network may hit on a solution that was "hidden" in bits and pieces of the data; that solution may be transformed and generalised across the system as a whole, resulting in what must be viewed as as a qualitative shift.

We will illustrate the thrust of this argument by looking again at the developmental progression in children's understanding of the principles of the beam balance, this time from a connectionist standpoint. Previously, when adopting the SOAR framework, the changes in the child's level of understanding were attributed to the formation of new production rules as the chunking mechanism was invoked by mistaken predictions. On the subsymbolic level, growing understanding is also predicated on the mismatch between what is predicted and what actually happens. However, negative feedback does not lead to the formulation and revision of underlying rules, rather it allows for new emergent computational properties to arise as the network adjusts its internal weights in the direction of the correct outcomes.

McClelland and Jenkins (1991) have simulated this developmental sequence using back propagation procedures in conjunction with a multilayered network designed to respond to weight and distance information. As before, the task is to predict what will happen when the balance is allowed to swing freely under different weight and distance combinations, as indicated in Fig. 5.5.

The input layer in the network consists of two groups of 10 units where one group is assigned to encoding distance information and the other group to encoding information about weight. Activation feeds forward from this layer to a layer of four hidden units which in turn are connected to two units in an output layer. The various balance problems are represented as patterns of activation over the input units and, once the network is allowed to relax, a pattern of activation is set up over the output units which represents the prediction for the problems as posed.

The input units have been arranged in rows, one for weight and one for distance, and within a row they proceed from left to right in order of increasing value. The arrangement of the rows also allows for weight and distance information to be distinguished for each side of the balance (left or right).

The four hidden units have been deployed so that one pair of units is connected to the weight input units while the other pair is connected to the distance input units. Each of these hidden units also projects to each of the two output units where (L) corresponds to the prediction "left side down" and (R) corresponds to the prediction "right side down". The overall aim is to train the network on the various balance problems so that the output unit corresponding to the side with greater torque becomes activated and, for states that balance, so that both output units become turned on half-way.

At the outset, the strengths on the various connections were all set at random between the limits, +0.5 and -0.5. Training then proceeded by presenting a particular beam arrangement as input and comparing

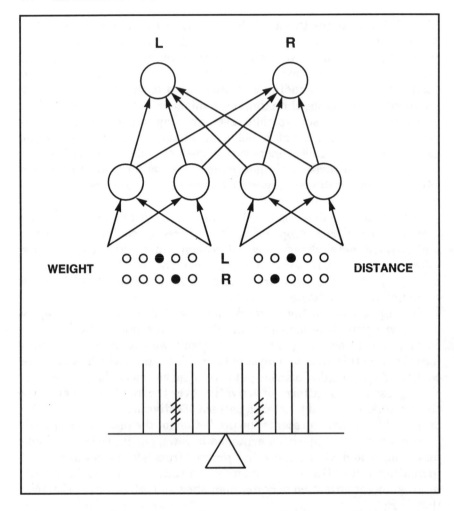

FIG. 5.5. Connectionist modelling of balance beam problem. (From McClelland & Jenkins, 1991.)

the computed output against the correct answer. The discrepancy between each output unit and its target activation value was then used in a back propagation procedure to determine how each connection strength in the network should be adjusted to reduce the discrepancy. As training proceeded, the predictions computed by the network became increasingly accurate while mimicking the rule sequence initially described by Siegler (1981). In other words, stage-like properties emerged in the behaviour of the network despite the use of a training procedure that entailed gradual and continuous weight changes to the network's connections.

The fact that connectionist models can dispense with stored rules yet still reproduce the stepped advances that are normally associated with the advent of new rules is eloquent testimony to their explanatory powers. However, explanatory power is not the whole story. We also need to be reassured that the explanations on offer are psychologically valid. As noted in Section 2, an important aspect of developmental advance depends on knowledge becoming increasingly accessible outside its initial context of acquisition. At present, it is unclear how this aspect of developmental change could be explained solely by reference to subsymbolic processes.

CLASSICAL AND CONNECTIONIST MODELS

It should now be evident the extent to which connectionism espouses a different approach to cognitive phenomena compared with classical symbol models. Physical symbol systems compute over structured representations following explicit rules. Connectionist systems employ computations that can be described in algorithmic terms but they are not dependent on the deployment of symbol tokens and combinatorial rules.

Strong support for the classical symbol position was adduced in Chapter 1 based on the argument that it alone could provide the resources to sustain the productivity and systematicity of thought. At that time it was argued that the principles of productivity and systematicity arise when cognitive processes are able to call upon symbol transformations which are sensitive to the constituent make-up of the data structures involved. Judged against these same criteria, fully distributed connectionist networks can be shown to run into problems. In choosing to represent psychological states through activation patterns that are distributed across the units in a network, these models have relinquished the means of representing the explicit tokening of part–whole relationships that are crucial for differentiating one psychological state from another.

An essential feature of distributed networks is that only one representation can be active in the network at a time. It is this limitation that now leads to problems if we try to use these networks to represent complex ideas. To entertain the molecular thought "Paul teaches John" requires that we understand that Paul occupies the role of teacher and John that of pupil. Distributed models run into difficulty at precisely this point. Although they can arrange for clusters of nodes relating to

"Paul", "Teach", and "John" to all be active together this is to fall significantly short of what is required. This same activation pattern could just as well apply to the thought "John teaches Paul". In other words, the crucial distinction between the two interpretations of teacher and taught resides in the constituent relations of their component arguments. As Fodor and Pylyshyn (1988, p.27) have remarked:

> There are two questions that you need to specify the content of a mental state; which concepts are active and which of the active concepts are in construction with others. Identifying mental states with sets of active nodes provides resources to answer the first of these questions but not the second. That's why the version of network theory that acknowledges sets of atomic representations but no complex representations fails in indefinitely many cases to distinguish many mental states that are in fact distinct.

If this point is conceded, it confers a major victory on the classical camp. If the counter-response is to attempt to meet these strictures by adding explicit constituent structure to the distributed representations, then this leaves connectionism as the means for implementing a classical architecture. This, in itself, would be no small gain but connectionists had greater territorial gains than this in mind.

A possible counter-response is to deny Fodor and Pylyshyn's claim that atomic representations cannot token propositional content (Butler, 1991), or again, to point to the attempts currently being made to represent constituent structure within distributed representations (e.g. Hinton, 1991). Alternatively, hybrid cognitive models can be sought that aim to capitalise on the strengths of both camps.

Hybrid models: Symbolic connectionism

One fork of this compromise route is represented by symbolic connectionist models which aim to combine the computational strengths of both approaches. Holyoak (1991) refers to such hybrid models as constituting a third generation of cognitive models which, by separating representational and processing issues, offer a form of "symbolic connectionism". Within this paradigm, the units in a network can represent complex hypotheses whose constituent relations can be analysed in symbolic terms. For processing purposes, however, the computational dynamics of neural networks can be used—as when manipulating this information for the purpose of knowledge retrieval or decision making. According to Holyoak (1991, pp.316–317) the gain from this form of hybridisation is significant because:

Symbolic connectionist models can make inferences that standard symbolic systems are often too brittle to derive; using knowledge that diffuse connectionist systems cannot readily represent.

Such hybridisation could be achieved by using a production system architecture to generate a series of unconstrained inferences to an input eventuating in a rich but incoherent set of hypotheses about its possible meaning. The task of deciding which subset of this pool of possible hypotheses is the most appropriate in the given circumstances is then referred to a constraint-satisfaction network to settle. Models based on these ideas will be discussed elsewhere—see Kintsch's use of the Construction–Integration model to simulate text comprehension (Chapter 9) and Thagard's use of ECHO to simulate complex problem solving (Chapters 10 and 13).

Hybrid models: Internalised (individual) and externalised (collective) representations

Another fork along the road to supplementing the representational powers of connectionist networks is more subtle. In this case, the hybridisation comes from recognising that all individual acts of cognition are culturally situated. Computations that may be difficult or impossible for the individual alone may be made less intractable by the device of shifting a large part of the load outwards onto the external world. At its simplest, this may mean little more than using pencil and paper to help out with the mental arithmetic but, in its more sophisticated forms, it means exploiting a whole range of social networks and cultural artefacts. Some of the implications of this argument will be explored in later sections of the book. For present purposes, it will suffice to sketch out the general argument as it applies to the problem of deriving adaptive, intelligent outputs from cognitive structures that by their nature "settle" into solutions to problems rather than employing logical operations for this purpose.

Addressing this problem, Rumelhart, Smolensky, McClelland, and Hinton (1986, p.42) point to our ability:

> ... to create physical representations that we can manipulate in simple ways to get answers to very difficult and abstract problems ... we succeed in solving logical problems, not so much through the use of logic, but by making the problems we wish to solve conform to problems we are good at solving.

They note that what people are good at solving, in the sense of arriving at solutions by non-logical means, is pattern matching; forming mental models and manipulating their environment by imbuing physical artefacts with representational meaning. Thus, while we may not be able to perceive directly the answer to many of the problems that confront us, we may, given sufficient experience, be able to convert them into a form where pattern matching will do the work required. In this respect, external symbol systems can serve as important cognitive tools. The act of writing down an arithmetical sum that is too difficult to do in our heads (say, 18,764 + 17,355), is effective because it converts a difficult calculation into a series of simpler calculations. Now each step may be answered via a pattern match, as when we recognise that 4 + 5 is 9. Once this has been written down, we can go on to tackle the next step in the same way.

Manipulative skills employing external symbols can take many forms; we may extend our mathematical powers by means of the slide rule or log tables, we may check the quality of our logical reasoning by means of Truth Tables or Venn diagrams and we may bolster our arguments by providing tables or graphs. Of course, we do not have to invent these ancillary devices from scratch, these are tools that (certain) cultures make available to their members. Repeated use may then lead to their becoming internalised as components of mental models which can take over the role of guiding thinking in particular directions. In the process, we (or others) may then discover new external devices that can support more extended patterns of reasoning, thus giving rise to a dialectical exchange in which the external environment plays a key role in shaping the depth and scope of cognitive activity. For Rumelhart et al. (1986, p.44), the behaviour supported by this process:

> ... is *real* symbol processing and, we are beginning to think, the primary symbol processing that we are able to do. Indeed, on this view, the external environment becomes a key extension of our mind [original italics].

This argument contains a number of important insights, not least in referring individual human cognition to its social, cultural, and historical contexts. However, this is to get well ahead of a story that will be developed in later sections. Before then, we need to elaborate on certain troublesome aspects of memory and cognition that have been strategically neglected by classicists and connectionists alike.

To this point, we have considered in some detail how knowledge of the world can be laid down in the human mind, whether in the form of symbolic representations or in the form of associative weights.

Evidentally, both approaches can claim their legitimate successes. Nonetheless, both accounts of knowledge in mind will be rendered ineffectual to the extent that they fail to recognise and address the problems that accompany the relentless, cumulative nature of day-to-day cognitive activity. Each and every one of us has the capacity for creating extensive and systematic bodies of domain-relevant knowledge which we piece together over time. In the process this means weighing the significance of newly acquired information for other things that we already know. When we do this, we may then find it necessary to discard information that has turned out to be unreliable or incorrect. Exactly how this is done—how we cope with updating our knowledge—is not only unclear, it also has the potential to be extremely disruptive to the cognitive economy as a whole. Reorganising our knowledge systems as we go along has something in common with asking a builder busy on the construction of the upper floors of a building to go back and rebuild the ground floor at the same time. The whole exercise is fraught with difficulties.

In the next section, therefore, we will look at some of the issues attending the accumulation of knowledge that arise over the short and the long term. Over the short term, this means confronting topics such as interference effects in memory and the updating of individual memory records in the light of newly acquired information. Over the long term, it means trying to understand how the often haphazard accretions of discrete items of information somehow manage to get transformed into the systematic bodies of knowledge that enable us to adapt successfully to our world.

SECTION TWO

Memory dynamics and the accumulation of knowledge

CHAPTER SIX

Accumulative memory

Despite universal agreement that the cardinal feature of human memory is its ability to accumulate information about the world, cognitive research has been rather timid in pursuing the implications of this remarkable capacity. Of course, production models and connectionist models address some of these issues, albeit in different ways. Knowledge compilation in ACT* and chunking in SOAR create new entries in procedural memory without expunging earlier entries. Entries that are incorrect are either left to decay or become marooned in unvisited niches of a problem space. Within the connectionist paradigm, matters are much more fluid. New experiences are continually forcing adjustments in connection strengths and it makes little sense to contrast new against old forms of knowledge. New entries are not addded into the repertoire so much as blended with what existed before.

Maintaining control over an open-ended and constantly changing inventory of memory records requires that a variety of housekeeping demands be met. The demands associated with minimising levels of interference between competing memory records have been well documented. Somewhat less well documented is how we utilise our metamemorial skills to keep our bearings within a memory system that is constantly changing. Least understood of all, is how we respond to the demands associated with revising what we already know in the light of new information. This neglect is not exactly surprising; as we reflect upon the issue of knowledge updating we soon find ourselves beset by a host of baffling conundrums.

THE FRAME PROBLEM

McCarthy and Hayes (1969), first drew attention to the "frame problem" when they concluded that it was well nigh impossible to specify a formalised procedure that would keep track of all the consequences that would arise as we acted upon the environment. The nub of the frame problem lies in deciding precisely what should be taken into account; some features of the current situation will change as an action takes place but which are they? On the surface, what looks like a straightforward problem in deduction has so far turned out defy any translation into an appropriate algorithm. Hayes (1987, p.125) sets out the frustrating nature of this predicament:

> When I go through a door, my position changes. But the color of my hair and the position of the cars in the streets and the place where my Granny is sitting don't change. In fact, most of the world carries on in just the same way as it did before ... One feels that there should be some economical and principled way of succinctly saying what changes an action makes without having to explicitly list all of the things it doesn't change as well; yet there doesn't seem to be any other way to do it.

Dennett (1987) makes the same point in the form of a poignant fable intended to drive home the full enormity of this dilemma. It involves three generations of robots who all come to summary ends because of their failure to solve the frame problem. The first-generation robot is created by its designers to be capable of planning its actions and adjusting them to its current goals. But, although it is programmed to consider the intended implications of its actions, it is not capable of going further to assess the significance of other implications which were not intended. This defect turns out to be an unfortunate omission.

Dennett introduces his robots when they are in the throes of trying to replace their dwindling power supply by getting a new battery from a room that happens to contain a bomb on the point of exploding. The Mark 1 version reasons that as the battery is (conveniently) placed on a wagon within the room, then pulling the wagon out of the room will do the trick. It does this and is promptly blown up by the bomb which was also on the wagon. Mark 1 knew the bomb was on the wagon alongside the battery, but it failed to draw the obvious implication.

A Mark 2 version is duly equipped to consider the full implications of its actions and then despatched to tackle the same task. This time the bomb goes off just as the robot has finished deducing that pulling the wagon out of the room will not alter the colour of the walls. The Mark 3 version, therefore, is given the additional refinement of being able to sort relevant implications from irrelevant ones, and we meet it tackling the same situation. Its creators, clearly hoping for better things, were frustrated (Dennett, 1987, p.42):

> ... to see it sitting, Hamlet like, outside the room containing the ticking bomb. ... "Do something" they yelled at it. "I am", it retorted, "I'm busily ignoring some thousands of implications I have determined to be irrelevant. Just as soon as I find an irrelevant implication, I put it on the list of those I must ignore and ... [the bomb went off].

A variant of the frame problem resurfaces when we need to make dependent changes in our memory records consequent upon a new item of information being added to the cumulative store. Learning any new fact can have implications for any part of the existing store. How then should we decide on the relevant readjustments to be made and on the readjustments dependent on these changes? In practice, unlike Dennett's robots, human beings experience little difficulty when executing planned actions or when learning new things about the world. Indeed, it is quite the opposite; we get better at doing these things as we acquire more and more knowledge—or so it seems.

FORGETTING AND INTERFERENCE

Since Ebbinghaus published his monograph on *Memory* in 1885, it has been known that the forgetting curve for learned material characteristically entails a drop in accessibility that is most marked just after learning but then diminishes as the delay increases. Numerous experiments have been conducted to try to identify the possible causes of forgetting and quite early on it was established that the process of interference makes a major contribution to our propensity to misplace what we have learned. Interference occurs when learned responses to stimulus events are forced to compete with different responses to the same or similar stimuli that have been acquired subsequent to the original learning. As a result, earlier learning can impinge on the recall of content learned subsequently (Proactive Interference or PI) and later learning can impair the recall of earlier learned content (Retroactive

Interference or RI). In each case, the degree of interference depends on the similarity between the content of prior and subsequent learning.

As the majority of the early studies into interference effects employed word lists, it was an open question whether or not the same findings would generalise from learning lists to the learning of prose passages. At first, the evidence seemed to indicate that prose materials were indeed different but defining their degree of similarity called for something more than counting the number of words they had in common and more sophisticated comparisons have revealed the expected interference effects. When Bower (1974) used passages describing the actions of fictional characters as learning materials and measured inter-passage similarity in terms of their shared propositional content, he duly found that the more we learn about similar people doing similar things the more confused we become as the level of interference builds up.

Yet in arriving at this conclusion we again seem to be faced with a paradox. Bower's results imply, contrary to our everyday experience, that the more we come to know about some central topic the harder it becomes to access particular details. Far from additional knowledge serving to improve our performance, which is what common sense would predict, it actually slows us down. As one of Tom Sharpe's characters observes: "If a little learning is a dangerous thing just think what a lot of it can do".

Fan effects in memory

A study conducted by Anderson (1974) confirmed that the more facts his subjects learned about a particular concept the slower they became when recognising any one of them as having been previously studied. The phenomenon has since been termed the "fan effect" due to the way in which the learned information is said to be represented in declarative memory. As extra facts are acquired relating to some person or object, so they fan out in the form of arcs in the associative network where each arc supplies the link between the person or object node and each of the new predicates.

In the original experiment, Anderson's subjects were asked to commit to memory sentences like "A lawyer is in the park" and the experimental design manipulated the number of times a person or a location appeared in different sentences. After learning many such statements, subjects were then timed to judge whether probe sentences had previously been learned or not. For every additional sentence a subject learned that repeated a concept—whether person or location—recognition times were found to be retarded by about 100 milliseconds. Anderson's explanation for this result assumed that when subjects recognised a test sentence as old (studied), they searched for a link between the node for the person mentioned in the probe sentence and the node for the mentioned location. As the search process involved the spread of a limited amount of activation from each target node along connecting arcs, the more arcs that fanned out from either node source, the slower the search proceeded.

Fan effects became something more than a remote laboratory phenomenon when Lewis and Anderson (1976) demonstrated the equivalent spread of interference into a subject's factual knowledge base following the learning of fantasy facts about a real person. Presenting such fictions as "Napoleon Bonaparte was from India" should increase the fan of "facts" linked to this character node and it was shown that introducing this manipulation had a measurable effect on the subject's ability to retrieve the relevant information—whether real or fantasy.

Once again, therefore, we are presented with the situation where fan effects and expertise seem to be entirely at odds. The laboratory results appear to be saying that extending our knowledge about a topic will create increasing interference, yet common sense observation states the opposite—the more we learn, the better we are at deploying this knowledge. There must be something else going on under normal learning conditions that protects the accumulating knowledge against increasingly debilitating interference effects.

Fan effects and thematic integration

Studies conducted by Smith, Adams, and Schorr (1978) and Reder and Anderson (1980) have shown that one form of protection against interference effects comes from using our general world knowledge to organise new information under thematic headings. Subjects who learned a number of different facts about "Marty" such as that he "warmed up by jogging", "ran five miles", "heard the conductor", and "arrived at Grand Central Station" could organise these items of information around two thematic subnodes, one based on running and the other based on taking a train. This results in the network representation depicted in Fig. 6.1.

Representing the information in this form could facilitate the probe judgements in at least two ways; (1) by bringing schematic knowledge to bear on the judgement process, and (2) by streamlining the verification procedure. Both interpretations have received experimental support.

Smith et al. compared the recognition times of subjects who thematically integrated their learning with the recognition times of subjects who learned without this opportunity. As expected, the fan effect was significantly reduced in the presence of thematic integration.

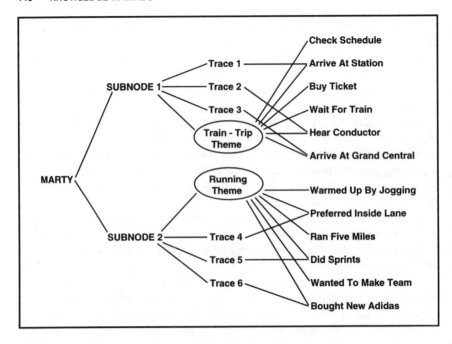

FIG. 6.1. Thematic grouping and fan effects. (From Anderson, 1983.)

In explanation, they suggest that the presence of a thematic statement served to invoke an appropriate script and, once this script was active, the studied statements were mapped onto the appropriate slots. When faced with distinguishing old statements from test foils, subjects in this condition reactivated the script as a unit with the consequence that the number of studied facts became irrelevant.

Reder and Anderson (1980) obtained similar results but chose to base their explanation on the way in which thematic integration acted to alter the subject's judgement strategy. Adding a thematic label to a group of statements allowed for the creation of a thematic subnode in the memory representation from which the relevant facts fanned out. Consequently, when subjects were faced with distinguishing studied facts from theme-irrelevant foils they could now treat the recognition task as one of consistency rather than direct verification. Was it plausible that the probe proposition was consistent with the theme?

With this strategy in play, search stops at the thematic subnode and, as the fan spreads out from this node and not the subject node, the fan effect will disappear. It should return in full force, however, if the test probes are also theme-related, because this will force the judge to activate the full record in order to be more precise about old and new examples. In a series of experiments, Reder and Anderson showed not only that both of these predictions held up, but also that a thematic fan effect could be demonstrated—as additional themes fan out from the subject node so interference starts to build up once again.

The fact that fan effects can be mitigated by thematic integration provides the learner with some degree of strategic control over the course of cumulative learning; levels of interference can be kept under control provided the learner takes steps to adopt the appropriate encoding strategies. This strategic aspect to learning has been well illustrated by Ericsson and Polson (1988) through an investigation into the skills of a professional waiter (JC) who was capable of taking up to "twenty complete dinner orders without taking notes". They arranged for JC to be tested under controlled conditions and found that as the orders accumulated, JC grouped together all food items from the same category, using a specialised code in each case. For example, cooking times were encoded along an imagined spatial dimension from least to most cooking time while a further code for entrees was adapted to include an associative link to the diner placing the order. Using these encoding rules, JC could handle the course choices of up to four different diners. If the number of diners exceeded four, he simply started again on a parallel record. Thus, JC had devised an effective set of strategies for dealing with a situation where most of us would soon be floundering under the press of detail.

Elaborative rehearsal strategies of this kind, while acting to reduce interference between the content of different memory records, can also create additional management problems for their users. The more we reflect upon the details of an original experience the more likely we are to create additional memory records that are *internally* rather than *externally* sourced. These two types of memory record are unlikely to contain identical details and, *in extremis*, certain records may never have occurred outside our imagination. Consequently, assigning the appropriate source to a record is a necessary metacognitive skill for any accumulative memory system that is seeking to navigate safely between the realms of fact and fantasy.

REALITY MONITORING

Johnson and Raye (1981) refer to the process of distinguishing memories based on perceptual processing from memories produced by reasoning or imagination as "reality monitoring". They suggest that in making this distinction, we use the internal properties of each type of record to trace it to its source.

Consider a subject who experiences a list of words, some of which are read aloud by an experimenter and some of which the subject only imagines being read aloud. In this situation, the two classes of memory trace, (internally and externally sourced), are likely to possess different attributes. Table 6.1 lists some of these distinctive attributes and their likely role in the monitoring procedure.

Externally generated traces are typically associated with a rich set of attributes linked to the sensory properties of the event and its spatio-temporal context along with the presence of considerable semantic detail. Internally generated memories are typically associated with memory traces that are less well endowed in these respects. However, with regard to the cognitive operations that produced the traces, the internally generated memories can be expected to be accompanied by the richer set of operational attributes. Imagined states depend on strategic processes whereas perceived states depend on relatively automatic processing activities. The net outcome is that subjects can make use of these characteristic trace signatures when assigning records to their probable source.

Source allocation proceeds via subjects making a weighted comparison of the target trace against the prototypic pattern for its

TABLE 6.1
A framework for reality monitoring

	Memory trace	
	Externally generated	*Internally generated*
Attributes		
Contextual	+ +	+
Sensory	+ +	+
Semantic	+ +	+
Cognitive operations	+	+ +

Monitoring decision
1. Compare target trace attributes to external and internal trace criteria
2. Use inferences from trace content and associated traces

Sources of error
1. Target trace atypical
2. Interference
3. Inference error

After Johnson and Raye, 1981.

supposed source. If a match is returned, all well and good, the source can be identified. If not, (the comparison turns out to be ambiguous), then further detail relating to associated cognitive operations must be sought in order for a choice to be made. If that exercise also fails, an additional round of inferencing may be initiated based on the content of the record. To take an extreme case, a fantasy record of winning a large sum of money may be identified as internally generated, (1) because the sensory detail is sparse and there is little or no episodic context leading to or from the record, (2) because there is some awareness of the wish fulfillment that accompanied the fantasy, or (3) because there is absolutely no evidence for the change in lifestyle that would go with it. Monitoring will proceed quite adequately along these lines under most conditions but there will be occasions when the tests fail to fulfil their purpose. These conditions arise when a target trace is atypical of its class or when a target gets drawn into faulty inference patterns. Manipulating the original learning conditions to create these anomalous conditions has allowed for the monitoring claims to be put to empirical test.

In one study (Johnson, Foley, Suengas, & Raye, 1988), subjects were asked to remember either a perceived or an imagined autobiographical event, e.g. to remember a previous trip to the dentist or some dream or fantasy. When they had done this, the subjects then filled out a Memory Characteristics Questionnaire in which they rated their two types of memory for their sensory detail, emotional tone, and contextual support. Comparison of the ratings assigned to perceived versus imagined events demonstrated that the former records carried greater detail about their sensory features such as visual appearance, setting, spatial arrangement, and temporal organisation. They were also more positive in tone and included more supporting memories from before and after the target event.

Having established that the two types of record carried distinguishing signatures, the experimenters next set out to demonstrate that subjects actually used this information when determining source. Accordingly, subjects were asked to remember one perceived and one imagined event and then to explain how they knew which was which. The resulting justification protocols were scored for details mentioning the qualities of the target memory, for details concerning supporting memories, and for any additional reasoning that served to discriminate memory type. It was found that when subjects were dealing with memories for perceived events, they relied most heavily on the properties of the target memories and their supporting background and less heavily on reasoning about their content. The reverse situation applied for memories based on imagined events.

In a further study (Johnson, Foley, & Leach, 1988), subjects had to imagine saying some words to themselves while listening to other words being spoken by the experimenter. They then had to judge which words were which. The ensuing judgements were significantly impaired if the subjects had imagined the words in the experimenter's voice—as would be predicted by the reality monitoring model. Under this condition the differences between the trace signatures for the imagined and experienced words were reduced, thus eroding the main basis for discriminating their source. Other manipulations known to impair the quality of source monitoring include making imagined events more automatic (Finke, Johnson, & Shyi, 1988) and making imagined events more vivid by encouraging rehearsal modes that stressed either their sensory detail or their feeling tone, (Johnson & Suengas, 1989). The boundary between memory records based on external events and records based on internalised activities is more permeable than perhaps we would like to think.

METAMEMORY

Reality monitoring is but one of a number of metamemorial strategies we have at our disposal which work to facilitate learning and recall by drawing upon knowledge relating to the functioning of our own memory system. Another instance arises when we decide which of the mnemonic aids in our repertoire is best suited to the current learning context. For example, we may decide to use an external aid, such as note taking, or to use an internal aid, such as mental rehearsal. Each type of aid is most suited to a particular learning context and competent learners can register these differences (Intons-Peterson & Fournier, 1986).

In many respects, the metamemorial literature paints a picture of the average subject as being quite finely attuned to the fit between the working characteristics of memory and the demands of different learning situations. Nonetheless, it would be wrong to rely too much on this general picture; the information derived from metamemorial processes may be perceived as helpful but it is not necessarily reliable. This note of caution is prompted by the findings relating to another set of metamemorial operations which deal with our "feelings of knowing" (FOK)—as when we decide the point at which our efforts after learning should cease. In the course of rehearsing to-be-learned material, we use FOK to decide when further rehearsal is unnecessary. If no such feedback were available, learning could go completely awry; either we would stop learning too early or we would waste time continuing with our learning attempts long after we have overshot the task requirements. "Knowledge of our own knowledge" is clearly important in identifying which of these circumstances applies in a given situation but its promptings can be misleading.

Durso and Shore (1991) report that subjects who had rated words as familiar, vaguely familiar, or unknown could, when forced, distinguish those occasions when an "unknown" word was being used in a context that respected some aspect of the word's general meaning. Consequently, although the individual is likely to rely on FOK as an important indicator of the status of what has been learned, it need not be well calibrated in this respect. This is hardly surprising. Each nuance and ramification of all that we know is unlikely to be equally available to introspection and what is available need not be in a form that can be readily condensed into one index. In fact, there are certain occasions when we acquire new knowledge without realising that we have done so.

IMPLICIT VERSUS EXPLICIT LEARNING

Explicit learning has occurred when the acquired knowledge is consciously accessible and amenable to verbal report. Implicit learning is said to occur when knowledge is acquired without any awareness of learning or any intention to do so (e.g. Reber, 1989), although these claims have been disputed (e.g. Dulaney, Carlson, & Dewey, 1985). The formation of these two types of knowledge, explicit and implicit, has been linked to the operation of distinct learning systems designed to handle different types of stimulus information.

Hayes and Broadbent (1988) employed this functional distinction to account for the different patterns of learning they observed when subjects were called upon to interact with a computer in order to control its outputs. As presented to the subjects, their task was to get the computer to respond in a "friendly" manner in the course of an exchange. Subjects could input from a keyboard any one of 12 responses varying from 1 (defined as very unfriendly) through 8 (friendly) to 12 (loving) and, once a specific numerical response had been entered, the computer replied with another numerical response from the same scale. The subject's task was to steer the computer's response towards position 8 (friendly) and hold it there.

Subjects were run under two different experimental conditions depending on the time lag that ensued between a subject's response and the computer's reply. For the "no-lag" condition, the computer's response was primarily determined by the *current* numerical input from the subject. For the "lag" condition, the computer responded primarily in terms of the subject's *next to last* input from the keyboard. The two experimental conditions, therefore, differed in the transparency of the relationship between the subject's actions and the computer's response. The introduction of the lag made it more difficult for a subject to detect the fact that the computer always responded two degrees less friendly than their chosen input.

For the "no-lag" group, the formula controlling the interaction was:

$$O_t = I_t - 2 + r.$$

Where O_t refers to the computer response, I_t refers to the input attitude keyed in by the subject and r refers to a random variable between -1, 0, and $+1$. Hence, for this group, the computer's response was always two attitudes less friendly than the subject's current choice plus a degree of noise. For the "lag" group, the response equation was:

$$O_t = I_{t-1} - 2 + r.$$

The computer responded in the same way as before, not to the subject's current response, but to the next to last input.

After a period of training based on these equations, the factor (-2) in each formula was replaced by a new value of $(+2)$. At this point, therefore, the computer now started to respond two degrees more friendly than before. Subjects were not informed that this would happen and they were given further training under this new regime. It was during this second learning phase that the performance of the lag and no-lag groups was found to diverge. Performance was significantly worse under the lag condition.

In subsequent experiments, subjects carried out the same task under the lag and no-lag conditions but this time they also performed a concurrent task in which they generated a series of letters or digits. Now, after the equation change, it was the "no-lag" group who performed worst.

Hayes and Broadbent explained this experimental outcome by assuming that subjects in the no-lag group were able to formulate a rule that captured the stimulus contingencies. That is, their learning took on a conscious and intentional form. In contrast, for the lag group, learning followed the implicit route. These subjects adopted a more passive approach resulting in a non-verbalisable impression of the stimulus contingencies. In the first experiment, when the equation change took place, subjects with access to an explicit rule could "easily" reformulate the rule to take account of the new circumstances. Hence the better performance of the "no-lag" group after the formula adjustment.

In the later experiments, introducing the concurrent task served to interfere with the explicit learning mode by impairing the capacity of these subjects to identify the rule change. As the lag group were not using an explicit rule, they were not disadvantaged in the same way. The resulting double dissociation thus comes down strongly in favour of implicit and explicit learning relying upon two distinct learning systems. A similar distinction has also been applied to the learning of artificial grammars (Reber, 1989) and sequential pattern acquisition (Cleeremans, 1993).

However, Green and Shanks (1993) have failed to replicate Hayes and Broadbent's results which as they point out require the strong assumption that a single task can elicit the exclusive activity of one or the other learning system. Furthermore, although Hayes and Broadbent imply the presence of a strict dichotomy between implicit and explicit knowledge, this formulation may be too simple. Acquired knowledge could be represented on a number of representational levels ranging from implicit to explicit with intermediate levels falling between these extremes. We will discuss the developmental significance of such an arrangement at some length in the next chapter. For now, there is another aspect of Broadbent and Hayes's design that warrants further comment. These experimenters placed their subjects in a situation where they had to revise their prior understanding of the target's behaviour to take account of a change in circumstances. Arguably, it is the exercise of this facility, above all, that is needed if a cumulative memory system is to sustain its operations within a world that is constantly changing. There can be no cumulative gains from experience if old beliefs cannot be revised and updated in the light of new experiences.

MEMORY UPDATING

Demands for updating an explicit knowledge base can, ultimately, be reduced to two basic modes—the "addition" of new content and the "disaccreditation" of old content. We are constantly enjoined to add new names to our list of acquaintances and, for various reasons, we also find ourselves deleting other names as time goes by. Although adding to or deleting from a discrete list of names may be relatively straightforward, assimilating new information to an *interconnected* knowledge base can be far more complex and demanding. In this case, the changes may well lead to ripple effects spreading throughout the knowledge base as a whole. Exactly how all this might be managed is far from clear. Nonetheless, it defines a vital design feature of cumulative memory and we will devote the remainder of this chapter to sketching out what appears to be involved.

When adding information to memory, the simplest case arises when a new item of information is tagged on to an existing data base. Meeting a new acquaintance and subsequently learning his or her name establishes a relatively straightforward updating demand. Learning one paired associate need impinge hardly at all on the other paired associates we have previously learned, although according to Bower, Thompson-Schill, and Tulving (1994), even this case may not be entirely straightforward.

There will be other circumstances, however, where the act of acquiring new information leads to indirect effects as the knowledge base becomes amplified through whatever ripple effects have been set in train. Learning that someone has gone abroad and then learning that they are in "France" may lead us to alter our inferences about what they are likely to see and do.

In the second category, disaccreditation, the attendant updating demands are directed not so much towards expanding the data base as reappraising its contents. These demands arise when the new information questions the veridical status of old information in some way. The extent to which the old information is discredited can be a matter of degree. At one extreme, the target information may simply need to be "discounted"; it is to be held in temporary abeyance but not necessarily rejected out of hand. For example, a jury may be instructed to ignore some prior testimony without necessarily being told that it was incorrect. At the other extreme, old information may be specifically singled out because it is wrong, as when new information serves as a correction. In this case, earlier information is singled out as being incorrect; possibly someone was lying or, perhaps, they were genuinely mistaken in what they had to say. Whatever the reason, information previously taken in good faith is now found to be unequivocally false and, in principle, should be expunged from the record.

Somewhere in between discounting and contradiction, there is the case of "misinformation"; having learned item X, we are subsequently misled into believing that it was really Y. This state of affairs can arise when leading questions are used to plant a false idea in the mind of a witness. Having seen a red car jump the lights, the witness is asked about the blue car involved in the traffic violation. Although detail X has not been explicitly targeted for discrediting, both entries, X and Y, can now compete with each other as conflicting details relating to the same event property. Here too, indirect ripple effects are also likely to be invoked. If the targeted information has generated a series of dependent inferences in an episodic record, any subsequent correction should extend to include these ramifications as well. Not only should the discredited item be expunged from the record, so too should all the dependent inferences it may have supported. Similar indirect effects will also apply to discounting and delayed correction.

Hence, when responding to the cumulative press of new information, one or another of these editing modes is likely to be deployed at some time or other. Of course, mixed cases will often occur. Thus, contradiction and amplification can be expected to occur together, as when we are told "The year in question was not 1980 but 1981". At this stage, it is not clear whether the various editing modes are psychologically distinct. Nonetheless, we will look at the factors that appear to differentiate one mode from another and the cognitive strategies each is likely to call into play.

Amplification of information in memory

Addition to memory occurs when existing content is supplemented by later inputs. In its simplest form (accretion), we have the kind of situation that has been extensively studied in the guise of verbal learning (e.g. paired associate learning) and I shall not even attempt to summarise this extensive literature (see Postman, 1975). Rather more characteristic of everyday experience is the process that typically accompanies discourse comprehension. As a conversation or text unfolds, the central topics become increasingly elaborated through the explicit information that is being provided and via the ripple effects created as related items of information are brought together. For the moment, we will keep matters simple by considering only the tip of this iceberg. In Chapter 9 we will venture below the waterline.

As we read a book or listen to someone speaking, token representations for the events described are created which are then updated as the discourse proceeds. Although we tend to think of such updating as occurring "on line" at the time, the reality is somewhat more complex. Should we be questioned afterwards about what we have read or heard, the act of questioning itself may serve to update some detail in the memory record. This point may not be immediately obvious but work on the simulation of text comprehension strongly suggests that memory search during comprehension and memory search elicited by subsequent questioning are functionally equivalent (Lehnert, 1984).

To see why this is so, consider one of Lehnert's examples (1984, p. 37). Suppose we read:

> John and Bill went to a restaurant to discuss a business deal. When the meal was over, John left a very large tip and apologised to Bill for wasting his time. Bill thanked John for dinner, and they went their separate ways.

Here, the last sentence in the text replaces the less informative entry "meal" by the more informative entry "dinner". So far so good, we have the normal process of text comprehension taking place. Now suppose, that the text had omitted the final sentence (leaving "meal" in the record at the end of the acquisition phase) and the reader is then asked "Was the dinner a success?". Clearly, the subject who understands the question is just as likely to update "meal" into "dinner" as the subject who read the explicit text. There is no principled difference between amplification during acquisition and amplification resulting from questioning—provided search for the target content has been successful. This latter proviso is an important qualification as we often fail to make connections even under what appear to be propitious circumstances.

The constraints set by target accessibility on the scope of amplification can often be severe. In a study conducted by Schustack and Anderson (1979) subjects learned a number of short biographies and then, in a later test phase, described which statements had previously been paired with which name. In some cases the biographies were close parallels to a famous name and, provided subjects registered the link, this should have facilitated any subsequent recall. In fact, there were very clear limits on whether or not such facilitation occurred.

Subjects were informed of the parallels in different ways; some were told at the time the passage was studied and again at the time of testing; others were told at study only, at testing only, or, in the control condition, not told at all. Only in the first condition, where the link was repeated, were any benefits observed. Being told in any other way only served to depress performance below the control level. The moral, it seems, is that the mere existence of potential semantic links between old information and new information is no guarantee that they will be activated.

The probability that a subject will fail to link potentially related items of information is significantly increased if the learner adopts strategies that lead to new information being compartmentalised rather than integrated into the general knowledge base. There are advantages as well as disadvantages associated with compartmentalisation. If retrieval of the critical content is sought in a context similar to that at acquisition, compartmentalisation makes it easier to access the information as a unitary whole. The disadvantage comes in the form of poorer access to the compartmentalised content when retrieval is attempted in new contexts.

Potts, St John, and Kirson (1989) reasoned that although it was likely that subjects would incorporate information they knew to be true into their general knowledge base, it was unlikely that subjects would do the same for information they knew to be "artificial". If so, subjects told that the materials they were about to learn had been specially created for the experiment could well be led into compartmentalising their learning. When actually placed under these conditions, subjects did indeed perform on later questioning as though they had created a localised entry in memory with few links to other, related things that they knew. But there again, as professional teachers know only too well, learners hardly need to be encouraged to keep their ideas compartmentalised. They do pretty well of their own volition.

Studies of subjects attempting to solve analogical problems have vividly demonstrated just how hard it can be to nudge subjects into making "spontaneous" links between new and old information, even when the critical items of information have featured as part of the same learning situation. This situation applied in a study reported by Gick and Holyoak (1983) where students had been given a problem taken from Duncker's (1945) monograph on problem solving. The problem is relatively difficult, and only around 10% of a student population are likely to come up with a solution unaided (see Table 6.2).

The aim of the study was to investigate the extent to which solution rates could be increased by making the solution available in analogical form just before the problem was tackled. It had been found previously (Gick & Holyoak, 1980) that the solution rate could be raised to 75% if subjects were given an explicit but non-specific hint that the analogy might be relevant to the problem. The present study was designed to specify the conditions under which subjects could spontaneously make the link for themselves.

The usual solution to the problem is to use multiple weak rays coming in from different directions that converge on the tumour site where they summate to the required intensity. This solution, therefore, was dressed up in the form of the story about a general attacking a fortress surrounded by mined roads; his troops approached the target from different directions before mounting a simultaneous attack.

TABLE 6.2
Content of ray problem

Suppose you are a doctor faced with a patient who has a malignant tumour in his stomach. It is impossible to operate on the patient, but unless the tumour is destroyed the patient will die. There is a kind of ray that can be used to destroy the tumour. If the rays reach the tumour all at once at a sufficiently high intensity, the tumour will be destroyed. Unfortunately, at this intensity the healthy tissue that the rays pass through on the way to the tumour will also be destroyed. At lower intensities the rays are harmless to healthy tissue, but they will not affect the tumour either. What type of procedure might be used to destroy the tumour with the rays and at the same time avoid destroying the healthy tissue?

From Gick and Holyoak, 1983.

Prior to tackling the ray problem, different groups of subjects read the military story and then recalled it; read the story when it was accompanied by a verbal summary reiterating its main point, or read the verbal summary on its own. A control group tackled the problem without seeing the story or the summary. Only 10% of control subjects successfully solved the ray problem and, measured against this baseline, it was evident that providing the analogical solution beforehand in the form of the story or its summary was nowhere near as helpful as might have been supposed. Of those who read the summary alone, only 28% went on to solve the problem. This success rate was raised to 32% when the story was read as a whole but providing the story and the summary together led to no further gain.

Although the figures for the experimental groups all show a significant increase over and above the control level, it remains the case that the majority of subjects supplied with the analogical solution failed to see any connection. Further manipulations, such as accompanying the story with a diagram of the general's solution, did little to improve matters. In fact, subjects shown the diagram alone actually fell somewhat below the control level (7%), while subjects shown the story plus the diagram could do no better than a 23% success rate.

The only manipulation that boosted performance on the ray problem significantly beyond these levels was when two analogical stories were supplied which illustrated the solution in different contexts. Whereas subjects experiencing two stories drawn from the same domain (military strategy) managed a 39% solution rate, the success rate rose to slightly more than half (52%) for subjects who read two stories drawn from different domains (military and firefighting strategy). It seems that subjects who read two different versions of the same principle created a more abstract, schematic representation of the solution in which the irrelevant contextual details had been pared away. Only when this schematic version had been formed was it more likely than not to engage with the target problem.

Even so, it took a remarkably heavyhanded procedure before a bare majority of subjects could be brought to the state of "spontaneously" seeing the analogy. And if amplification can be so limited in scope under relatively favourable circumstances, this does not augur well for the quality of updating likely to be achieved when the status of old information has to be revised in the light of new information.

Discounting information in memory

Direct discounting applies when the learner is called upon to put to one side prior information. In its simplest form this could mean no more than being asked to "forget" a list of words that has just been learned—a procedure that has been termed "directed forgetting." This procedure was employed in a study by Bjork, Bjork, and Glenberg, 1973, (cited in Bjork, 1978) in which subjects were given word lists to learn, only to be told to forget the earlier lists they had seen. The point at issue was whether the instruction to forget prior material would reduce or even remove its potential for interfering with subsequent learned material.

In the Forget group, (FR), subjects saw 16 words, one at a time, and then received a signal to forget this set and to go on to learn another set of 16 words. Another group of subjects (RR) experienced the same procedure but the signal after the first word set indicated that they were to remember this set while tackling the second set. Subjects in a control group, (-R), were not given the first set of 16 words (they carried out a visual judgement task instead) but they did go on to learn the second set. We would not expect to find proactive interference (PI) occurring under (-R) and we would expect it to be present under (RR), but what of (FR)? Would this follow the (RR) or the (-R) pattern?

After learning, recall was tested in one of two ways, (1) immediately after a forced recognition task (which could take two different forms) and, (2) after a delay involving an interpolated arithmetic task. The dependent measure in each case was the accuracy of recall of the content in the second list. Taking immediate recall first, it was evident that the forget instruction could eliminate PI under certain conditions. (FR) subjects who, prior to recall, experienced as part of the forced choice task some of the words from list two (targets to be recognised as old) and new words as distractors, went on to recall the remaining words from list two at a level similar to (-R) subjects. Furthermore, subjects in both of these groups performed significantly better than subjects in the (RR) condition.

However, when recall followed a forced choice task that used as distractors some of the words from the first (to-be-forgotten list), the position reversed. Now the effects of the forget instruction were completely over-ridden and this subset of (FR) subjects matched the performance of (RR) rather than (-R) subjects. With delay, although the overall levels of recall were reduced, the forget instruction still ensured that the subjects performed as though no first list had been presented, provided it had not been reactivated in the meantime.

Evidently, directed forgetting can be beneficial and to-be-forgotten content can be quarantined from later learning. But the resulting memory state is unstable. Reactivating just part of the quarantined content can be sufficient to reinstate the full PI effect. This result will be important when we come to consider the updating of structured material, as the routes for reinstating to-be-forgotten content are obviously more numerous.

Indirect discounting effects

The indirect consequences of discounting information have been investigated by Robinson and Hastie (1985). They found that their subjects showed little, if any, revision of their dependent beliefs after discounting previously learned target information. The experimental task entailed subjects comprehending a short detective story and at different stages in their reading they were asked to estimate the probability of guilt of the various suspects involved. As some of the clues supplied at different points in the narrative served to eliminate particular suspects, we could expect on logical grounds that the presumed guilt of the remainder set of suspects would be adjusted accordingly. This did not happen. Subjects totally failed to adjust their estimates of probable guilt in any way that was consistent with the available clues. Instead, Robinson and Hastie (1985, p.454) reported that the subjects acted:

> ... like jurors trying several defendants charged with the same crime; each defendant is given a separate trial in a separate courtroom, and the juror hears evidence against all defendants but is unable to use evidence gathered in one courtroom to aid a decision in any other court.

This outcome implies that for these subjects, maintaining the internal consistency of their beliefs in the light of new evidence was not set as a psychological priority. If so, some rather damaging consequences are appearing over the horizon. Most of our knowledge is acquired piecemeal at different times and, if we are not disposed to work at maintaining its internal consistency, it is difficult to see how we could aspire to employ our beliefs in a rational manner. Obviously, it would be premature to reach such a conclusion on the basis of just one experiment. Perhaps there are other circumstances where we manage our affairs better.

On being misinformed

Misinformation occurs when we have been misled on some point of detail. Having originally experienced say, a "blue book", we may be misled if it is later implied that it had a different colour. Once again, the consequences of misinformation could be directly limited to a target item of information, or they could involve indirect, knock-on effects as the implications of the change are followed up. Unfortunately, despite numerous studies having been conducted into the dynamics of misinformation effects since they were first reported, there has been little in the way of cumulative insight into what might be happening.

In a study reported by Loftus, Miller, and Burns (1978), subjects saw 30 colour slides illustrating the sequence of events leading up to an accident. The slides depicted a car travelling along a side street toward an intersection, turning right, and then running into a pedestrian crossing the road. One of the slides in the series depicted the car as it was stationary next to a road sign. For half of the subjects this was shown to be a stop sign but the other half saw the car next to a yield sign. This variation apart, the slide sequence was identical for both groups.

Immediately after viewing the slides, all subjects answered 20 questions on what they had seen including a critical question that either presupposed a different sign to the one they had been shown or the same sign. A 20-minute filler task then ensued before half of the subjects participated in a forced choice recognition test relating to the sequence of events leading up to the accident—the remainder took the recognition task one week later. In the course of the recognition test, pairs of slides were presented and subjects had to choose which slide had appeared in the original sequence, including the critical pairing of the car with the stop sign or the yield sign. On this critical pair, subjects in the misled group chose the actual slide significantly less often than the subjects in the consistent group: misled subjects averaged 41% accuracy whereas consistent subjects averaged 75%. Clearly, the provision of misleading information resulted in poorer recognition accuracy.

If we focus for the moment on a subject's memory record for the experienced event rather than on the recognition response, then we can speculate on what might give rise to such a misinformation effect. Basing our analysis on Bjork's data, cited earlier, we could argue that the misled subjects were working with a memory record in which the actual and planted detail simply coexisted; both the stop sign and the yield sign were present in the record. When the critical recognition choice was made, the two versions were placed in competition and the most recent won out. This explanation would cover the findings and would be consistent with other work outside the misinformation field. However, this was not the interpretation put forward by Loftus. Her explanation assumed that the post-perceptual information served to alter the memory record. In some way the original detail of the road sign was overwritten by the planted sign resulting in the loss of the old information—variously termed erasure or destructive updating.

Given these competing explanations, coexistence or erasure, it would seem a straightforward matter to test between them by probing for the continued presence of the old information. Demonstrating that there are conditions under which the old information could be retrieved would settle the matter in favour of coexistence. Yet, after more than 100 studies focusing on this effect, this apparently straightforward issue has still not been adequately resolved.

Loftus et al. duly ran a series of experiments to check on the availability of old information for misled subjects and concluded that try as they might, they could find no means of accessing it. Experimental manipulations such as telling subjects that some of them had experienced the misinformation procedure; payment for accuracy or (using new materials) introducing a second guess procedure, all failed to move the subjects beyond chance level in their response to the old information. For all practical purposes, it seemed, the old information had disappeared and this was taken as strong presumptive evidence for the erasure claim. But the fact remains that even where many different methods of probing have failed to elicit the old information, the next attempt might succeed where the others had not. Loftus acknowledged this dilemma but countered by adopting a pragmatic line of argument—for all practical purposes the old information had been lost as result of the misinformation.

As it is a matter of considerable theoretical and practical importance whether or not detail in a memory record can be erased as part of an editing strategy, we will review the case for alternative interpretations of misinformation effects. These can be classified under four headings, (1) contextual cueing, (2) response bias, (3) source monitoring, and (4) test sensitivity.

Contextual cueing

Bekerian and Bowers (1983) rejected the erasure explanation in favour of the hypothesis that failure to access the old information following misinformation was solely due to the testing procedure Loftus had employed. In the original experiment the test pairs of slides had been presented in random order, but Bekerian and Bowers argued (for reasons we will consider later) that a more stringent test would have been to present the slide pairs in the order in which the original slide sequence occurred. When they ran the experiment in this form and compared random versus narrative test orders, only the random condition gave rise to misinformation effects. This finding would seem to put matters to rest but there is another, more serious, methodological critique of Loftus's procedure that applies equally to the Bekerian and Bowers modification.

Response bias

The design criticism stems from McCloskey and Zaragoza (1985) who, after reviewing the studies described earlier and after running some studies of their own, concluded that misleading post-event information neither erased old information nor rendered it inaccessible; the reported effects are artefacts created by shortcomings in the logic of the design. The argument hinges on the likelihood that the misled subjects will perform worse than the controls on the recognition test because of the response biases built into their experiences. If the misled subjects do not remember which road sign they originally saw but do remember the planted version then they will choose this detail on the recognition test at above chance level. Control subjects in the same state of uncertainty will only choose the new item at chance level. This factor alone would act to depress the misled level of accuracy below that for the control. But it is not the only factor in the design contributing to response bias. Yet other misled subjects may recall both the old and the new information but they may not trust their own recall, perhaps reasoning that the post-event information supplied by the experimenter is more reliable. Such induced compliance would also serve to lower recognition accuracy in the misled group while having no counterpart in the controls.

It was necessary, therefore, to find an experimental procedure that removed these biases altogether. Under the modified condition recommended by McCloskey and Zaragoza, instead of presenting the old and the planted detail together as part of the recognition test, the old information was presented along with totally new information. For example, where the standard procedure would require a subject to choose between a stop and a yield sign, the modified version employed a stop and a no parking sign. A series of experiments comparing both procedures showed that whereas the standard form confirmed the misinformation effect, the modified version wiped it out altogether. Clearly this is a powerful critique and Kroll, Ogawa, and Nieters (1988) have presented further supporting evidence along the same lines.

Source monitoring

An alternative account of misinformation effects can also be sought in the context of reality monitoring. Misinformation procedures just happen to establish ideal conditions for the creation of source monitoring errors. A subject takes in information from the original slide sequence and then, prompted by later questioning, creates a new record of the event when responding to the misleading questioning. Consequently, there is a strong possibility that misinformation effects arise due to retrieval errors based on faulty source monitoring. In testing for the validity of this argument, Lindsay and Johnson (1989) introduced yet another modification of the standard procedure, this time by giving the misinformation beforehand!

Their subjects first heard a narrative describing a scene and only afterwards was a slide of the actual scene displayed. Misled subjects heard items mentioned in the narrative that were not on the slide and, as this misinformation preceded viewing the scene, there was no visual memory to update. Consequently any misinformation effects found under this condition would arise, not from memory editing, but from a retrieval error based on source monitoring. Subjects tested with the reverse procedure did exhibit misinformation effects, much as a breakdown in source monitoring would predict. Misinformed subjects, unlike consistent subjects, were no longer sure which point of detail was in the narrative and which related to the slide.

Test sensitivity
Evidence of failure to access old information after misinformation is significant only to the extent that the tests used are sufficiently sensitive to detect the critical detail. Another possible explanation for misinformation effects, therefore, is that the standard tests of recall and recognition do not meet this criterion. Accordingly, Dodson and Reisberg (1991) have suggested that monitoring for priming effects would be a more sensitive procedure for detecting the presence of old detail. They showed that although tests based on recognition measures were consistent with erasure, tests employing priming measures did not support this conclusion. According to Dodson and Reisberg (1991, p.333), when the test took the form of a lexical decision task, where priming from passage detail could occur:

> ... [the] decision latencies were shorter for words naming items seen in the original presentation, in comparison with baseline words; misinformation had no impact on this reaction time advantage.

Clearly, misinformation effects tap into a number of different memory operations and the full picture has yet to emerge.

Memory blends
At first, faced with the growing body of criticisms, Loftus sought to bolster her arguments for erasure by attacking the evidence in favour of the permanence of records held in LTM (Loftus & Loftus, 1980). With permanence out of the way there was no good reason why erasure could not occur. Then, over time, the erasure argument itself underwent modification. First, it was argued that coexistence could occur as well as erasure but there were circumstances where erasure would win out. Finally, under continuing critical pressure, this line of argument gave way in favour of a compromise proposal in the shape of a memory blend.

If the alterations arising from misinformation took the form not of erasures but of blends—where the new information is integrated with the old to produce some compromise entry—this could explain much of the critical data.

As an example of a blend, Loftus, Schooler, and Wagenaar (1985) cite data from a study by Weinberg, Wadsworth, and Baron (1983) in which subjects were misinformed that a yellow yield sign had been a red stop sign. Testing misled subjects for recognition accuracy using the standard procedure (yellow yield/ red stop) or a modified procedure (yellow yield/ red yield) showed that they performed worse than controls in both conditions. Consequently it was argued (Loftus et al., 1985, p.378) that the misinformation effect cannot be due to response bias because in the modified version, the red yield sign:

> ... contains features of both the original information (the shape of the yield sign) and the misleading post event information (the colour of the stop sign).

Nonetheless, evidence for the occurrence of blends in a memory record rests on a rather slim body of results and, as Schooler and Tanaka (1991, p.97) caution, different usages of the term "blend" call for distinctions:

> ... between "recollection blends" which correspond to subjects' memory report and "representation blends" which refer to a specific hypothesis about the relationship of the underlying memory traces ... with respect to recollection blends we think it is critical to distinguish between two general classes; composite recollections and compromise recollections.

Composite recollection refers to a response where the features of the original and post-event sources are brought together in a purely additive manner leaving them unchanged, as when a car is (incorrectly) recalled next to a yield sign planted as a result of a leading question. A compromise recollection is involved if some additional detail is mentioned, detail that "emerges" from combining the original and post-event sources, as happens with colour blends. It is the evidence for blends as compromise recollections that is rather scanty although, theoretically, they are the most interesting. The blending of two inputs is precisely what would be predicted by distributed models of memory as different input vectors are superimposed on each other (see Metcalfe, 1990).

Indirect effects of misinformation

So far, we have concentrated on the fate of items directly targeted by misinformation but we can also enquire if misinformation effects ripple out to influence dependent information. There has been very little investigation into this matter but one study by Lehnert, Robertson, and Black (1984) is directly relevant. They arranged for subjects to read a series of five short stories following which they were given two sets of questions dealing with each narrative. The first set contained misleading questions about part of the story content and came immediately after the stories had been read. The second set of questions was intended to check whether alterations in the memory record had indeed been brought about by the misinformation.

The misinformation supplied could either concern an action contained in the story line or a descriptive state. Thus a subject might read:

(Actual State Description) Shelley noticed that her lamps were too high.

and then be questioned on this detail in a misleading manner:

(Misleading Question) Was it on the first or second day that Shelley noticed that her lamps were too low?

A similar manipulation was conducted with targeted actions, e.g. raising or lowering the lights. Subjects' answers to the second set of questions showed that state information was susceptible to direct modification from misleading questions whereas actions were much less open to change.

The study also included measures dealing with the extent of the indirect consequences elicited by misinformation. As the materials were narratives, it follows that if the subjects had been successfully misled then there should be knock-on effects for other text details. If the lamps were actually described as being too high, the appropriate action would be to lower them. Changing the state from too low to too high by judicious questioning should change the dependent action from lowering to raising the lamps in order to maintain consistency. Similarly, any actions directly modified by misleading questions should carry equivalent ripple effects for their related state detail. It was found that ripple effects of this kind were minimal and consisted largely in subjects becoming confused by what they had read and heard. There was no evidence that misled subjects embarked upon making *specific* changes designed to remove inconsistency.

I have spent time on these studies of misinformation effects because not only do they address important practical aspects of memory, they also touch upon one of the issues at the centre of how cumulative memory might proceed. Assume, for the moment, that we really do have the power to erase some of our memories. When should it be exercised? To which we might reply "when we know that an item is wrong". But how can we be sure of this? The correction itself may be wrong. If we erase details too soon, can we repair the damage? If so, how is this done? Do we undertake yet another erasure, and so on? On reflection, there appears to be something deeply suspect about the whole idea of memory erasure. If exercised at all, we would be at risk of unthreading our own past.

In any case, a memory system relying on erasure as an updating technique makes little evolutionary sense. It is important that we register mistakes in order to learn from them. If mismatches and contradictions can be wiped from a memory record, or perhaps obscured by blends, then it seems precious little retrospective understanding will be possible. Conflict is an important source of new understanding about the world; "Blendings and Conjectures" does not have the right Popperian ring to it at all. A critical next step, therefore, is to look at what happens when we are confronted with unequivocal evidence relating to the presence of an error in one of our memory records. Is the record purged of the erroneous detail or not?

Contradiction of information held in memory

Direct contradiction, unlike misinformation, explicitly singles out a target item for correction. Having learned item X, we then encounter item Y which informs us that X was wrong. If the target information has been used to interpret other (reliable) information then responding to the correction may also mean embarking on the alteration of a whole chain of dependent inferences. Note that even if the suspect information can be relocated and erased, the individual may be unaware of the extent to which it has been used to create additional inferred information. And assuming the inference range is known and all of the contaminated material is deleted, this could then result in an incoherent knowledge base whose causal links have been severed as a result of editing.

The more we look into this problem the less easy it is to decide what is the right thing to do. Not responding to the correction will mean the knowledge base is misleading. Responding to the call for correction may turn a coherent record into an incoherent one. Once again we come up against the central issue in dynamic memory; how is a coherent knowledge base to be edited and updated in line with new information without at the same time destroying its utility in the process?

Wilkes and Leatherbarrow (1988) investigated memory updating driven by correction by placing subjects in a situation where they had to integrate a series of messages to create a coherent memory record dealing with an ongoing event. For one group of subjects it was the progress of a fire that was being reported, for another group it was the events that led up to a road accident. In each case, as the messages came in, the subject could eventually piece together what might have happened—much as in any extended investigation. Extracts from the Fire sequence, as seen by control subjects, are given in Table 6.3.

After reading each message in sequence, control subjects were called upon to write down their account of what was known about the fire and then to answer 20 questions about the fire's features. Some of these answers had to be inferred (e.g. what caused the explosions?) because this information was not provided explicitly. For control subjects, only a "stationery subtheme" was available for this purpose; somehow, the paper and photocopying equipment caused the explosions and other features of the fire.

In the "edit" condition, subjects were first given another subtheme (careless storage of gas and paint) which was subsequently corrected. These subjects read exactly the same message sequence as the controls except for message 5 and 12. Message 5 now stated that:

> 5. Police message received to say that they have reports that inflammable materials including gas and paint have been carelessly stored in the side room.

The availability of this item of information introduced a second subtheme ("inflammable materials") which accounted rather well for the spread of the fire and its consequences. However, this piece of information was corrected at message 12 which read:

TABLE 6.3
Sample message sequence, fire text for control condition

1.	Alarm call received from warehouse premises
2.	Serious fire in storage hall
4.	Started by short circuit in wiring of a side room
5.	Message from police—side room was empty before the fire
7.	Explosions occurred during the blaze
10.	Storage hall contained paper and photocopying equipment
12.	Second message from police—asking how investigation progressing
	[Sequence ended after message 13]

From Wilkes and Leatherbarrow, 1988.

12. A second message received from the police ... stating that no storage of inflammable materials had occurred and the side room had been empty before the fire.

At this point, therefore, the subjects were faced with the task of updating their memory record in order to discard the wrong subtheme (along with its implications) and to replace it by the stationery subtheme which now had to do the same inferential work. Ideally, after updating, these subjects should arrive at an episodic record equivalent to that for the controls where only the stationery subtheme is used when answering the inference questions. Consequently, subjects' answers to the inference questions were scored in terms of the thematic information employed. As is evident from Table 6.4, edit subjects continued to use the discredited information as an inference source.

Information that had clearly been labelled as wrong had nonetheless been retained and used during the comprehension phase of the experiment.

It is not that the correction was missed. Over 90% of the direct edit subjects accurately referred to the correction during free recall or at some point during the comprehension questioning. Even so, far from pursuing ripple effects throughout the knowledge base, they apparently tolerated or did not register the contradictions—much as Robinson and Hastie's subjects failed to register the consequences of reducing the pool of suspects.

TABLE 6.4
Percent inferences based on correct/wrong themes, fire and accident sequence

	Fire	Accident	Combined
Controls			
Correct	61.5	69.6	65.6
Wrong*	3.0	8.9	5.9
Other	35.6	21.5	28.5
Direct edit			
Correct	45.2	47.4	46.3
Wrong	32.6	31.1	31.9
Other	22.2	21.5	21.9

[*For the Control condition, although there was never any exposure to the wrong theme, certain kinds of inference could (rarely) be interpreted in this way]

From Wilkes and Leatherbarrow, 1988.

Despite this striking failure to update following a correction, there are conditions where what is required does take place quite effectively. A second experiment reversed the updating demands by first giving the wrong information that the side room was empty, and then correcting this by stating that it contained inflammable materials. With this new format there was no difference in the deployment of the new, volatile materials subtheme in the control and correction conditions. It seems then that the difficulty in updating lies not with the delayed introduction of the new information, but in keeping the old information suppressed. Suppression is not a problem when the target is peripheral to the main topic (as in the second experiment) but when it is highly salient to the text as a whole it can continue to exert a major effect. This echoes Bjork's findings for directed forgetting discussed earlier. Provided the suppressed information is not subsequently reactivated, its potential for proactive interference is removed but if it is reactivated the quarantine effect is lost.

Johnson and Seifert (1994) have replicated the persistence of corrected information under more extreme conditions where the correction was placed *immediately* after the wrong information in the message sequence. They also report that if a corrected subtheme is not simply negated but is replaced by an alternative theme capable of playing an equivalent causal role in the message sequence, then this mode of correction goes some way towards attentuating the perseverance effects. It seems then that subjects faced with correcting an episodic record of some complexity do not necessarily go in for a systematic purge at the time the error is identified. That is, we avoid getting caught up in the frame problem by the device of simply consulting the most recent version of a correction at the time of questioning. Provided the new information can supply the answers required it will be used. If not, the older, incorrect version is brought in to do the job.

GENERAL THEORIES OF ACCUMULATIVE MEMORY

We have arrived at an account of accumulative memory in which, (1) memory records can be organised to avoid interference (not always very successfully), (2) records may be integrated over time (not always very exhaustively), and (3) records may be updated (not always very extensively). We may do all of these things some of the time but there are many occasions when our efforts are, at best, perfunctory. Such limitations appear to reflect a trade-off in which the scope and consistency of a record are balanced against each other. The resulting compromises may not be logically perfect but they do work. Accumulative memory has evolved to make information available when needed, not to put it on trial. There are other ways and times for doing this.

Although all theories of memory address some aspects of knowledge accumulation, the processes involved in adding new nodes to an associative network or creating new schemas do not take us much below the surface. A somewhat deeper understanding of what is at stake can be found in the way in which SOAR "cleans up" a contaminated problem space (see the discussion of the beam balance in Chapter 4) and from the way in which connectionist models imply the presence of blends. More specifically, according to proposals made by Morton, Hammersley, and Bekerian, (1985), knowledge accumulation is a purely accretive exercise where discrete "Headed Records" are formed which are independent of each other. Schank's (1982) theory of "Dynamic Memory", on the other hand, proposes that memory updating is occurring all the time as new inputs trigger reminders to parallel events that have occurred in the past.

Headed records

Morton et al. (1985) assume that all experienced events give rise to isolated memory records, each of which must be consulted separately. No record cross refers to any other and each record requires its own key before it can be opened up and the details within consulted. An experienced event leaves a representation in memory which has two component features—a heading for the representation and a record containing a detailed set of contents. The information held in the heading may or may not be reproduced within the record itself but before any internal content can be accessed the appropriate heading must be found.

The theory assumes that when we are searching memory for the features of some past event, we first of all form a description from the information available. Armed with this description we search through the record headings until a match is found. Once the record has been opened, if its contents meet our requirements, the search ceases. If not, a new description is formulated (perhaps recruiting additional cues from the recently accessed record) and search proceeds as before. Any cross linking between records has to come from the content of an accessed record providing a new basis for formulating a new descriptive heading.

Although there are many difficulties with this approach—e.g. how are the headings created?; how might a complex and extended event be parsed into subrecords?—in some respects it does fit with a number of the studies we have discussed. Essentially, it argues that once a memory record has been established it cannot be altered, although an experienced event can be represented in memory via multiple records created internally by reflection. Sometimes a specific point of detail will be present in one of these records, sometimes it will not. What is recalled will thus depend on which record is opened up and consequently particular items of information can be expected to vary in their accessibility.

Applied to misinformation effects, headed records can explain the effects by assuming that they arise because the recognition test favours the formation of a description that will match to the heading for the most recent record, i.e. that containing the planted information. This was the point behind the Bekerian and Bowers (1983) study cited earlier. Presenting the slide pairs in their original order at the time of recognition testing favoured the formation of a description that would match to the heading for the original record. But, as noted at the time, the design flaws listed by McCloskey and Zaragoza (1985) apply just as much to this design as to standard procedure used by Loftus. This leaves a question mark over the reliability and the validity of the results.

Applied to the explicit correction studies, the theory could account for the insinuation of wrong information into the answers to the inference questions by assuming that the questions provide cues to the old record heading. However, such an explanation would require a number of *ad hoc* adjustments to cope with the circumstances where the correction is effective. In any case, by treating accumulative memory purely as a matter of accretion the theory pays little heed to what might be learned from their communalities. By denying any systematic cross referencing, the potentially emergent properties of a dynamic memory system seem to have been ruled out of court from the outset.

The nature of these emergent properties has been addressed in an alternative account of accumulative memory which goes to the opposite extreme of employing extensive cross referencing between related records. According to this approach (*Dynamic memory*, Schank, 1982) long-term memory organisation is continually being updated as a result of analysing its own failures.

Dynamic memory

In 1983, Kolodner described a computer model (CYRUS) which was designed to update its knowledge of the movements of the (then) US Secretary of State, Cyrus Vance. As it learned about each new round of engagements, it sorted out and stored together those episodes in Vance's career that shared similar meanings. In this manner, it created new knowledge structures as it went along which could be consulted when answering questions about Vance's movements. If an answer was not directly stored, CYRUS could infer a response by progressively transforming the question into a version that could be answered. Thus if asked "Has Vance's wife ever met Mrs Begin?" it progressively translated the question into a form that could be answered, e.g. "Under what circumstances do diplomats meet?" and it continued in the same vein until a satisfactory reply was generated.

Question transformation was made possible by allowing CYRUS to capitalise on extensive cross indexing between episodic records that had been established at the time of storage. This work was carried out by EMOPS (Episodic Memory Organisation Packets) which kept track of event similarity and generated indices for linking related events together. The normative component of an EMOP provided typical information about the event itself and an indexing component held pointers to prior events that had previously been processed at this level. Hence, as each new event in Vance's career was encoded (say a meeting with another politician) the features that differentiated this event from similar events in the past were extracted and then used for the indexing.

New EMOPS could be created when more than one event had been indexed in the same way. Under these circumstances, when a new event was processed at this level, it was likely to prompt a reminder of the earlier event. As a result, the two episodes could be compared and their similarities extracted, leading to a new EMOP being formed with its own normative information and indexing potential. By elaborating on these basic ideas, Schank (1982) has proposed a more general model intended to apply to memory updating *tout court*.

If we are to come up with an appropriate explanation for an unexpected event, long-term memory needs to be organised so that the relevant items of knowledge come to mind just when they are needed. One way of doing this is to make the cross indexing in the system dependent on expectation failures. Where pointers to different memory addresses are made dependent on prediction failure, experiencing an unexpected event will activate pointers to past episodic records that involved a similar surprise. These will be the records that are most likely to clarify our current difficulty. When we experience one type of prediction failure for the first time, the event is indexed through the knowledge structure that generated the inadequate prediction. The next time a similar predictive failure comes around, because of this indexing we are then likely to be reminded of the previous failure. This means we can benefit from the way in which the problem was handled previously. Furthermore, as both episodes will now be active together, it also provides an opportunity to learn from their combined properties. Schank's dynamic memory, therefore, achieves its ends by proposing that episodic memory is organised around exceptional events which are tagged in terms of the predictions they happen to have violated.

Failed expectations play a critical role in the resulting cross indexing but other modes of processing may also be implicated. Speculating how an event might turn out may remind us of other memories sharing the same outcome. In these cases, the episodes involved may have very little in common beyond their shared outcome. In fact, Schank suggests that a variety of structures can participate in indexing, ranging from MOPS (that handle the details of specific events), through EMOPs, to higher-order structures such as Thematic Organisation Packets (TOPS) which can look beyond specific event detail to abstract the underlying theme. Thus while *Romeo and Juliet* and *West Side Story* differ on many specifics we can appreciate that they match very well at a thematic level.

When we comprehend an event, each of these memory structures can serve as a predictive source for its own level of abstraction and each structure will carry pointers to past instances where it has failed to work. If a reminder then helps to resolve the problem, the current mismatch is itself stored with a pointer from the memory structure used in its interpretation and it joins the pool of potential reminders. As more and more episodes get stored at the same level of anomaly, they serve as the basis for a new processing structure with greater predictive powers. The net outcome is a memory system that updates itself by analysing its own failures. It is both open-ended and permanently evolving, while at the same time being tightly organised so as to provide critical information when needed. In this regard, dynamic memory is one of the few theories to address itself seriously to the question of how an accumulative memory could serve to sustain its internal organisation, coherence, and utility.

Schank provides little more than anecdotal evidence for his model although some support has come from Read and Cesa (1991) who report that subjects could use previously read stories as analogical explanations for new story outcomes when expectation failures were present. When subjects were faced with a story with an unexpected outcome, they were often reminded of previous stories they had just read which involved the same type of violation although they differed in surface detail. Even so, when set against the body of empirical data reported throughout this chapter, dynamic memory presumes a level of updating efficiency well beyond what is typically found. For example, whenever an unexpected event provokes a reminder of some previous event, it has activated an analogy to the current case. Yet, as we saw from the work of Gick and Holyoak (1983), their subjects frequently failed to register analogies even after a series of heavyhanded hints. Similarly, when set against the main body of empirical data on memory updating, Schank's theoretical account fails to recognise how often updating falls short of what is required. At best, dynamic memory provides us with a blueprint of how we might proceed under optimal conditions.

To arrive at some deeper understanding we need to track the way in which multiple related items of information acquired at different times come to be fashioned into a coherent body of domain-relevant knowledge. However, to find commentaries with this degree of scope we need to turn to developmental psychology for theories capable of addressing the course of knowledge accumulation over the long term. In fact, this shift in orientation need not to be too great, as it is improbable that totally different principles are operating over the short and long term. Indeed, when Schank singled out predictive failure as the principal factor behind knowledge reorganisation, he touched upon a central issue in the developmental literature where conflict based on predictive failure has also been cast as the primary factor leading to cognitive reorganisation and growth.

CHAPTER SEVEN

Accumulative memory: Developmental perspectives

The contrast between learning and cognitive development rests not so much on their different time signatures as on the extent to which numerous localised changes in a knowledge base come to be co-ordinated as a whole. The child acquiring the notations and algorithms of arithmetic is not just on course towards making fewer errors and solving problems more quickly, he or she is also beginning to co-ordinate a set of component skills into a larger, integrated system. Addition and subtraction can be learned in isolation but they can also be understood as inverse operations within a larger representational system. If this progressive reorganisation does not occur, then a child may be able to provide the correct answers to particular problems but the necessity behind these answers will be missed—that they really could not be otherwise. Murray (1987, p.43) puts the point succinctly:

> It is not just that 15 from 91 is 76, true as that is, but that it has to be 76, that it cannot be anything else however notated. Moreover, if it were anything else an entire mental system of other known things would have to be changed. The development of necessity requires the invention of a system in which otherwise separate events are connected together on some common dimension.

This gradual organisation of particulate knowledge into co-ordinated systems provides us with the means for distinguishing development from "mere" cognitive change; development proceeds as higher-order knowledge structures are created out of lower-order antecedent versions. Clearly, if we are to make use of this distinction we need some metric on which we can distinguish "higher" from "lower" levels of knowledge organisation. How exactly all this might be done has been a key issue in developmental theory and, as one of the principal theoreticians in this area, Piaget devoted his entire professional life to the search for a satisfactory answer.

For Piaget, the critical feature that distinguishes higher from lower levels of knowledge organisation resides in the extent to which the systems in question are in "equilibrium", i.e. can function effectively in a variety of different contexts. We will defer discussion of the details of Piaget's theory of equilibration and its role in explaining the dynamics of accumulative memory until later in this chapter. First, we need to set the scene by considering how the basic mnemonic functions are thought to develop in the growing child.

DEVELOPMENT OF MNEMONIC FUNCTIONS

Establishing whether recognition responses are present in early infancy is an important first step in this developmental exercise because there can be no learning if the infant fails to recognise when a stimulus has occurred before. In fact, recognition has been demonstrated at very early ages, as shown in a study reported by DeCasper and Fifer (1980). They arranged for the sucking activity of newborn infants to switch on a tape recording which reproduced either the mother's voice or that of a female stranger. Whichever voice was broadcast was made contingent on the infant's rate of sucking and hence the experimenters could monitor whether the infant could make the distinction and go on to choose the mother's voice over that of a stranger. Most of the infants tested in this way did adjust their rate of sucking to select the maternal voice— indicating the difference between the voices had been recognised despite the infants having as little as 12 hours prior contact with their mothers since birth.

Habituation studies offer independent support for the early onset of recognition as well as providing more information about its developmental course. Under this procedure, infants are confronted with the same stimuli over a number of trials while being monitored for the amount of time they spend looking at the display on each occasion.

If the time they spend looking at the displays diminishes with practice, this implies that they have recognised that the same stimuli are recurring across the experimental trials. Using this procedure, Martin (1975) compared the time infants spent attending to geometrical figures when they were presented on two consecutive days. It transpired that all of the subjects tested, (from 2 to 5 months old), showed a decline in interest on the second presentation.

Recall develops after recognition, making its appearance in the second half of the first year. As the child gets older, levels of recall for to-be-remembered items will then depend on whatever mnemonic strategy the child chooses to use. At first this may entail little more than touching the items concerned but, over time, more sophisticated strategies appear which rely less on the features of the physical setting and more upon the mental representations the child elects to create.

DEVELOPMENT OF MNEMONIC STRATEGIES

Preschool children respond to instructions to memorise groups of items by invoking low-level mnemonic strategies such as touching the items involved or subjecting them to close visual scrutiny. Verbal rehearsal is not used spontaneously until typically around 7 years. Flavell, Beach, and Chinsky (1966) report that whereas only around 10% of 5-year-olds employed rehearsal, this level increased to 60% at 7 years and had reached 85% at 10 years. Children who did not spontaneously rehearse were capable of doing so if explicitly instructed and their recall improved as a result. But these gains were short-lived. Once the external requirement to rehearse was lifted these children simply resorted to their earlier, more passive mode of memorising.

Post 7 years, different styles of rehearsal begin to emerge where older children tend to employ more active forms of rehearsal than their younger counterparts (e.g. Ornstein, Naus, & Liberty, 1975). In this study, children around 8, 11, and 13 years were tape-recorded as they rehearsed aloud while learning a list of 18 unrelated words. Although the gross amount of rehearsal employed did not differ by age, there were clear strategic differences. The youngest children tended to rehearse each item as it was presented and they did so in minimal combination with other list items. Older children adopted a more active rehearsal strategy by intermixing several different words within each rehearsal set. Higher levels of recall were associated with the more active rehearsal technique.

Rehearsal strategies that organise the items to be learned according to their meaning also show changes with age. Adults learning a list of words such as "table; chair; car; desk; boat..." typically show clustering at recall where items from the same semantic category are recalled together. With younger children the semantic links between items are only employed spasmodically, if they are used at all, and it is not until around 10 years that semantic clustering is used systematically (see Moely, Olson, Halwes, & Flavell, 1969).

Elaborative encoding strategies (adding information to the material to be learned in order to make it more memorable) show a similar developmental progression. Paris and Lindauer (1976) tested children of 5, 7, and 9 years on their memory for sentences that described an action but failed to specify the instrument employed. Thus, on reading "The man unlocked the door", it is up to the reader to infer that a key was implicated in the action. Sentence recall was tested either using cues taken from the sentence or using the implied instrument. Whereas the oldest subjects could make use of both types of cue (explicit and implicit) when retrieving a target sentence, the 5-year-olds fared less well with implicit cues than they did with explicit ones. It was as though the youngest children had failed to draw the appropriate instrumental inference.

Although an expanding repertoire of mnemonic strategies increases the older child's cognitive flexibility it also brings new demands in its wake. Flexibility presupposes that the child can select the most suitable strategy for the task in hand—after all, there is little to be gained from an expanded strategic repertoire if the mnemonic tools are then selected at random. If children are to reap any benefit, they need to be aware of the various alternatives on offer and appreciative of the circumstances in which they can best be deployed. Furthermore, having adopted a particular strategy, they need to know when it has accomplished its purpose. Arriving at this flexibility, therefore, presupposes the presence of metamemorial processes which, by virtue of being attuned to the functioning of the memory system itself, can act as a guide to strategy selection and application.

Interrogating children of 5 years and older on their awareness of their own memory functions reveals that their insight in this respect is distinctly patchy although even the youngest children show a degree of acumen. They understand that relearning is easier than learning and that presenting information in story form helps recall (Kreutzer, Leonard, & Flavell, 1975). Nonetheless, there are other aspects where they appear to go wildly wrong.

Flavell, Friedrichs, and Hoyt (1970) arranged for young subjects to estimate their own memory spans and found that the preschool estimates were optimistic in the extreme. At a time when their measured span was little more than three items the same children provided estimates averaging about eight items. Predicted and measured spans did not converge until around 9 years of age. Similarly, probing the young child's awareness of the degree of success associated with the use of a mnemonic strategy can also expose major deficiencies. According to Masur, McIntyre, and Flavell (1973), their youngest subjects did not appreciate that items they had recalled badly on one trial should be given special attention on the next trial. First-grade children were as likely to go on to rehearse items they could recall as items they could not.

Studies of reality monitoring in children indicate that 6–7-year-olds can match adult levels of performance under certain conditions. When discriminating words they have said themselves from words they heard someone else say, young subjects perform quite well. But younger children are more apt to become confused when the discrimination is between words they have spoken aloud and words they have only imagined themselves saying (see Foley, Johnson, & Raye, 1983). Subsequently, Foley, Santini, and Sopasakis (1989) confirmed and extended this finding using a broader age range. Subjects in this experiment had to say some words aloud and to imagine other words being spoken by themselves, by a friend, or by a parent. Once this had been accomplished, they were given a list of words, including distractors, and asked to identify their source as spoken or imagined. The youngest children (7 years) fared worse overall but all age groups experienced the most confusion when asked to use themselves as the imagined actor.

It was stated in the previous chapter that adults distinguish between internally and externally sourced memory records through the degree of cognitive elaboration involved. Similar cues, it seems, are also used by young children. When asked to explain how they had discriminated one source from another, even the youngest children referred to the elaborations selectively associated with the imagined words. This claim received further support from a second experiment which demonstrated that reducing these sources of information led to an increase in source confusion at all ages—consistent with the subjects' claims that they monitored elaboration as part of the source signature.

Between the ages of 6 to 10 years, therefore, we find an apparently straightforward progression from mnemonic incompetence to a degree of mnemonic sophistication. But the experiments on which this conclusion is based may have overstated the degree of early incompetence. Faced with the artificial and unfamiliar circumstances typical of most laboratory studies, it is possible that the younger children had been placed at an undue disadvantage.

If 7-year-old subjects can exploit the presence of spontaneous elaboration when monitoring the source of their memory records this contradicts the claims made earlier that elaboration does not normally appear until 10 or 11 years of age. The age gap is a substantial one but it could arise if the elicitation of spontaneous elaboration is as much task-dependent as it is age-dependent. Possibly, instructing children to learn a set of experimental materials only serves to inhibit their idiosyncratic elaborations which, if they are to appear, require less formal circumstances to apply—such as creating imaginary responses. In which case, formal learning tasks are unlikely to provide the optimal basis for estimating the extent to which younger children can make use of mnemonic strategies.

Consider once more the reported disparity between self-estimates of memory span and actual measured capacity, this time in the light of the demands being made by the experimental task. Cunningham and Weaver (1989) point out that a young child asked to make such a prediction has to carry out a number of computations. First, to imagine learning a list, second, to imagine what a certain number of words sounds like, and third, to imagine how many will be remembered. All of which has to be done within the confines of a task that is bound to be unfamiliar. Looked at in this way, it is not surprising that young children are not very good at it. On the other hand, less demanding procedures for eliciting self-estimates of memory span could well present the young child in a more favourable light.

This prediction was tested by Cunningham and Weaver by replacing the prospective measure of memory span with a concurrent measure. Under the revised procedure, rather than getting children to make an estimate before they performed the task, it was arranged for them to base their estimate on feedback from the task itself—the child stopped a tape playing a list of words when he or she thought recall was just possible. Self-reports obtained in this manner were more accurate and realistic than those derived from prospective techniques.

The tendency for standard laboratory procedures to conceal cognitive abilities that become evident when the child performs under more natural conditions has not exactly gone unremarked in the developmental literature (e.g. Donaldson, 1978) but it continues to bedevil estimates of when particular cognitive skills make their first appearance on the scene. As Donaldson has made amply clear, if we are to discount this potential bias, we must be willing to replace the arbitrary memory tasks typical of the laboratory with everyday events that are more likely to carry meaning for the child.

REPRESENTING EVENT SEQUENCES AND SCRIPTS

Although children as young as 3 years of age are reported as recalling everyday events in much the same fashion as older children, the origins of this skill in still younger children have gone relatively unstudied. Bauer and Mandler (1989) set out to remedy this situation by investigating the extent to which children between 16 to 20 months were capable of representing the details involved in a sequence of related events. In particular, they were interested in whether their subjects could, (1) encode temporal order information, (2) use this order information to organise their recall of newly experienced events, and (3) organise their recall around causal relationships.

Subjects were shown various three-element event sequences which were either familiar or novel occurrences for the child. In the latter case, the component elements of the event were either causally related or arbitrarily assembled. Examples of the three event types are given in Table 7.1.

The children were encouraged to imitate the given sequence after they had watched the experimenters' demonstration. It transpired that even subjects as young as 16 months could encode and retain information about the temporal order of familar events and, for subjects of 20 months, the same was also true for the unfamiliar events.

The presence of a causal relationship served to facilitate recall of both novel and familiar event sequences for both age levels. Thus, the youngest subjects were capable of using causal information to organise their first experience of an event sequence and, as a second experiment demonstrated, disrupting this causal chain led to a deterioration in recall. When an irrelevant action was inserted into the novel causal and the novel arbitrary sequences (e.g. placing a sticker on one of the cups or on the doll) the effect on recall was greater in the former case. For

TABLE 7.1
Familiar and novel event sequences

Familiar event sequence
"Bath sequence": (1) undress toy bear; (2) place in bath; (3) wash

Novel causal sequence
"Rattle sequence": (1) place ball in small cup; (2) invert and nest small cup in larger one; (3) shake the cups

Novel arbitrary sequence
"Train sequence": (1) link two carriages; (2) put on track; (3) put doll in one of carriages

---

From Bauer and Mandler, 1989.

both age groups, interrupting the causal sequence led to more displacements or omissions of the irrelevant event than the equivalent interruption of the arbitrary event. These findings are significant because they suggest that scriptal knowledge structures are being laid down in memory as early as 16 months of age. Consequently, the regularities in everyday experience that are encoded in these early scripts could serve as one of the sources feeding into the child's later categorisation behaviour.

THE DEVELOPMENT OF CATEGORISATION

It has long been held that "true" conceptual categories are not found until around 7 years. Prior to this age it was thought that the child formed pre-concepts rather than organised categories. Pre-concepts are heavily dependent on contingent perceptual factors and, for this reason, they are likely to change from one context of application to another (Inhelder & Piaget, 1964; Vygotsky, 1962). However, the early work in this area has suffered from the same bias as was noted for mnemonic skills; it tended to stress the young child's weaknesses while ignoring the constraints introduced by the standard modes of testing. In the light of more recent work where investigators have moved away from testing childrens' classificatory attempts using arbitrary materials (such as coloured shapes or beads) to testing based on natural kind categories that correspond to the child's own experiences, somewhat different answers have been forthcoming.

Natural kind categories refer to classes of objects and substances that occur in nature as opposed to being man-made. The distinction may not be an absolute one but it can be readily applied in the general run of cases. Although natural categories cannot be defined by simply listing required features, there are underlying featural patterns that are shared by their members. As a result, adults use class membership to infer that new instances of a class are likely to possess features in common with other instances. In principle, young children could also use the act of categorisation as a basis for inferring similar information. Although such behaviour would conflict with the traditional view, studies conducted by Gelman and Markman (1986) suggest that young children, far from being incapable of inductive inference, appear to be rather good at it.

Gelman and Markman employed an experimental procedure in which their subjects were first taught a new fact about each of two objects. They were then asked to infer which of the two new facts applied to a third object which injected an element of conflict into the choice. It was labelled in the same way as one of the pair but looked like the other. Adults tested in this manner predominantly based their inferences on class membership and they were highly confident about their choice. The same test procedure can also be used with young children to see which kind of inferential route they prefer.

Gelman and Markman arranged for subjects of 4–5 years to view a pair of pictures depicting a tropical fish and a dolphin and they were told new facts about each instance. For the tropical fish, they were told "This fish stays under water to breathe" and for the dolphin they were told "This dolphin pops above water to breathe". The children were then confronted with the target picture of a shark and told:

"See this fish—does it breathe under water like this fish or above like this dolphin"?

Consequently, although the target looked like the dolphin it had been labelled along with the tropical fish.

Altogether the experimental design employed three treatment conditions. The "Conflict" condition, as just described, pitted category membership of the test item against its physical similarity to another stimulus and thus provided the means for testing whether young children would follow class membership or perceptual similarity when forming their inferences. A "No Conflict Control" arranged for the physical appearance and category membership of the test item to be congruent with a target picture, and an "Attributes Control" employed the test item on its own in order to obtain a measure for guessing.

Testing was carried out using biological and non-biological categories and in both the non-conflict and conflict situations the children preferred class membership over appearance as a basis for their inference. However, there is an obvious confound in this experimental design. The same label "fish" has been used for both the test object and the category exemplar. This was removed by running additional controls where synonyms were used instead of a single label (e.g. rock and stone). As the results remained unchanged, it was concluded that the observed selections were not experimental artefacts, rather the children were basing their inferences on common class membership.

In the light of these results, the traditional conclusion that young children form loosely structured categories based on transient perceptual information seems unwarranted and we are faced with yet another example of the way task constraints can lead experimenters into making premature generalisations. Traditional classification procedures require children to sort objects into categories which have been (arbitrarily) predefined by the experimenter. There are few constraints on how the sorting should be done and it is not surprising that in the absence of anything else to go on, the child turns to physical appearance *in lieu*. The modified testing procedure of "new fact plus inference" proceeds rather differently. It provides the child with a class label at the outset and only then probes for the generalisations the child can generate. This procedural difference is quite sufficient to cast a different light on the young child's classification abilities.

It is not, of course, being claimed that the 4-year-old fully understands the test materials. What is being claimed is that preschool children use class membership to generate new inferences in a principled manner. Far from making all sorts of promiscuous and false generalisations, the young subjects showed themselves to be sensitive to the distinction between illegitimate and legitimate inferencing. They recognised that while it is legitimate to expect members of the same species to share the same methods of reproduction, respiration, and locomotion, they will not necessarily share everything in common. Children who predicted that the shark would share the same respiration patterns as found with other fish did not go on to conclude that the shark would weigh the same as the fish. Rather, when confronted by this question their choices between the two options were distributed at chance level. Although the data indicated no difference between biological and non-biological categories in their support for class-based inferencing, for older children (7 years) the difference does become important (see Gelman, 1989).

To take stock, it seems there is good evidence that children as young as 4 years can use category membership rather than physical appearance as a basis for inference. Furthermore, it seems that they can adjust the range of their inferencing to take into account property type and, eventually, the difference between category types. The next question is how do children bring classes into construction with each other to form class hierarchies?

Basic and superordinate classes

For adults, superordinate categories serve as powerful inductive tools and they readily generalise novel properties from one basic category to another within the scope of the same superordinate. Gelman and O'Reilly (1988) have used the new fact plus inference procedure to compare childrens' inferencing from membership of basic and superordinate categories both with regard to natural kind classification systems and artifacts. Their subjects were drawn from preschool or second grade and each child was taught a new fact about the internal structure of an object. The question was then raised whether this fact was true of four further items. For example, having been told a fact about a "wooden chair", the child was then tested on an item from the same level (soft chair); an item from the same superordinate (bed); an atypical item from the same superordinate (crib); and an unrelated item (a picture of a fly).

Analysis of the inferences made as a function of category level showed that all children drew more inferences at the basic level than at the superordinate level, although the older children drew more inferences than the younger ones when operating at the superordinate level. That said, even the youngest subjects managed to draw more inferences to the superordinate category pictures than they did to the unrelated items.

Vocabulary growth and categorisation

Whereas basic-level categories can be said to be present in the external world (at least they can be pointed to) the same is not true of superordinates, which appear to be as much part of the natural language system as part of the physical world. As Nelson (1988, p.4) states:

> The taxonomic relation is a relation among words, not among things. There is no animal that includes "dogs", "cats" and "tigers"; there is only a term "animal" that stands in an abstract hierarchical inclusive relation to the terms "dog", "cat" etc. The hierarchy creates the taxonomy (... and) the taxonomies in a language are constructed by the language community and have to be acquired anew by each child.

This is to imply that the developmental route towards the representation of superordinate information is to be found in the young child's communicative experiences, especially those involving event memories and their associated scripts.

A script, by virtue of its slots for holding different instantiations of an event sequence, can be applied in a variety of different contexts. In this respect it demonstrates some of the important properties of superordinates. The child who has established a script for "getting dressed", has a framework with slots for "putting on X", where X can take on local values such as sweater, shirt, shoes, and so forth. In other words, the script shares some of the properties of "clothes" as a superordinate category and it can serve as a potential starting point for building the more abstract levels of a class hierarchy. Further refinements will of course be needed but these can arise out of the child's attempts to communicate with others.

It is unlikely, however, that the child's progress in forming class hierarchies follows a single route. Markman and Wachtel (1988), while agreeing with Nelson that language usage is important, further suggest that young children are steered towards the formation of taxonomies by virtue of innate constraints that are operative during vocabulary acquisition.

Labelling constraints

It is a striking feature of early word learning that it takes place very rapidly. This is rather odd because the meaning of a novel term is often grossly underdetermined by the information available at the time of learning. Hence, it is something of an enigma how different children learning under different conditions nonetheless manage to converge on similar meanings for the same terms. For Markman and Wachtel, this convergence is made possible because there are definite constraints on the potential meanings the child is likely to attribute to new words. All children, when confronted by a new word, will tend to consider the same (limited) set of possible meanings due to the presence of two heuristics which are called into play whenever they acquire new terms.

On those occasions when a child perceives say, a dog, and hears it labelled as "dog", if there were no constraints at all, the label could easily be taken to refer to a wide variety of features such as the dog's colour, size, or bark. It is rarely evident from the actual situation precisely which features are being singled out by the label. However, if we introduce the constraint that the child assumes that "dog" is to be treated as a category label—i.e. as referring to dog as an instance of a category and not as referring to some specific property—the underdetermination of the label meaning would present far less of a problem. Markman and Wachtel refer to this constraint as the "taxonomic principle" and its presence frees the child from entertaining a variety of redundant hypotheses about the meaning of category terms.

If, in addition to the bias towards treating names as category terms, the child were also to treat category labels as mutually exclusive, this would further delimit the set of features treated as related to the word meaning. Once an object had been given a label the child would not be predisposed to assign new labels to it. There will be occasions where this cannot be avoided but it will occur under "protest". The first heuristic serves to link labels to whole objects as opposed to internal detail (the taxonomic constraint) and the second heuristic imposes constraints on their willingness to accept more than one label being applied at the same level within a hierarchy (the mutual exclusivity constraint).

Markman and Wachtel report a series of experiments intended to explore situations where these two principles would be likely to hold. In one study, children were shown two objects (one familiar and the other novel) and given a new label applicable to one of the objects. The mutual exclusivity constraint suggests that under these circumstances the children will be unwilling to assign this new label to the familiar object. Hence, the child should select the unfamiliar object as the referent of the new label. Children from 3–4 years, tested in this manner directed their choices as predicted.

Less obvious is what will happen when the child is given a new label for a familar object and there is no unfamilar companion object for the child to select. Here the child faced with the question "where is the X?" cannot treat it as yet another category label for the familiar object without violating the mutual exclusivity rule. What happens next, therefore, is both interesting and instructive. The child compromises by treating the new label as referring to some part of the familiar whole; almost three times as many part responses occurred under this condition than when the exclusivity rule was not being violated. Thus, while young children prefer to follow the principle of mutual exclusivity if they can, they will override its requirements where necessary. This means there is a potential for "creative tension" between the two heuristics. When they are set in conflict, a joint constraint emerges which forces the child to explore an object's properties in search of an appropriate part response.

Children operating under the mutual exclusivity assumption would be well equipped for acquiring basic-level terms (the same object cannot be both a "cow" and a "bird") but this would not on its own help them to acquire superordinate terms where the same object can be both a "cow" and an "animal". Nonetheless, as children come to experience more than one label applying to a single object, this aspect could prepare the ground for the special dual labelling that is characteristic of more abstract levels in the class hierarchy.

Remembering and understanding

Ultimately, the function of categorisation is to support the conceptual systems through which the child comes to understand the world and its properties. In the course of this process, the child's burgeoning theories may then serve to refine and reorganise the original categorical distinctions that prompted theory construction in the first place. Thus, Carey (1988) has shown how changes in the quality of childrens' biological reasoning can occur, not only through the accumulation of new facts, but also as a result of the children restructuring their extant knowledge. To come to grips with this aspect of cognitive development, we need to consider, not only the individual categories the child is laboriously putting into place, but also the different modes of understanding they license at different points in the developmental cycle. For example, the mnemonic strategies available to the child can be expected to change not only as a function of localised practice but also in step with the child's growing expertise in understanding its world. Insight into the reasons why natural events unfold as they do provides a powerful mnemonic tool and this can only mean that remembering and understanding must be closely related processes.

The interdependence of memory and knowledge has played a central role in Piaget's developmental research, (Piaget & Inhelder, 1973), where the distinction is drawn between "figurative" and "operative" memory functions. Figurative functions apply in cases where no transformation of the input information is involved, as with the perceptual component in recognition. Operative functions apply in cases where the input is transformed in some way at encoding or at retrieval through the assignation of additional structure to the content of a memory record. A case in point would be remembering the numerical aspects of a display. Numerical features are not literally present in the input (in the way that shape or colour can be said to be present) but rather they arise through strategic cognitive transformations.

Precisely which encoding strategies a child can apply to an experienced event must depend on the cognitive structures available at the time. Equally, as these cognitive structures develop, so the memory functions they service should improve. Which brings us to a non-obvious conclusion; younger children experiencing cognitive reorganisation may well recall the features of a stimulus array more successfully after a delay than they do at the time of its presentation. Provided new cognitive structures have made an appearance in the interval between seeing the stimulus and recalling its content they can license transformations that were previously unavailable to the child.

To illustrate, suppose that a 5-year-old has been shown and told to remember a display of 10 unequally sized sticks arranged in order of their size from smallest to largest. If at the time the figure is first presented, the child cannot encode the display as a co-ordinated whole, but only as two or more partial seriations, the recall attempts will reflect this limitation. However, should recall be delayed sufficiently to allow the cognitive structures for constructing an overall seriation to emerge, the recall performance may well reflect this change. If so, the reproduction of the stimulus array will be more accurate after the delay than when it was tested immediately.

Piaget and Inhelder report finding qualitative improvements of this kind when children were tested under the appropriate circumstances. Of their sample of 24 subjects exposed to a seriated display, no less than 22 showed improved recall after a delay of 6–8 months. Testing using more complex displays confirmed the generality of the phenomenon although there were definite limits to the complexities of the displays that could be transformed in this manner.

It would seem then that there is a dialectical aspect to cognitive development whereby new advances in understanding come about as underlying knowledge structures are revised. These changes in understanding can then initiate a further round of revisions in the knowledge structures concerned. Unfortunately, explaining how this balancing act is actually achieved has confronted developmental theorists with a major conundrum. Advances in the child's understanding certainly occur over time but how is the change managed so that the whole cognitive enterprise does not fall apart? Why, during development, do later knowledge structures show an advance on earlier forms, as opposed say, to remaining at the same level?

PIAGET AND COGNITIVE DEVELOPMENT

If we focus on the end point of cognitive development—the mature adult mind—we find a rich diversity of conceptual knowledge and reasoning skills. The normal adult can be expected to comprehend basic physical concepts such as time, space, motion, causality, and probability which allow for the abstraction of subtle continuities from a welter of surface differences. According to the Piagetian model of cognitive development, this impressive cognitive flexibility derives from a rich and structured knowledge base coupled with a complex set of logical reasoning skills. Through the exercise of these logical skills, categorised experiences can be combined to form a coherent system which can be interrogated in ways that would be impossible if they had remained as discrete cognitive representations. It is one thing to be able to label objects as instances of subordinate or superordinate categories. It is quite another achievement to be able to use these classification hierarchies as a tool for reasoning about the properties of content domains using logical class addition or class multiplication.

Piaget conceived of the progression from childish incompetence to adult competence as a stepped series of cognitive stages where each new stage inherited the capabilities of its predecessor while adding new properties of its own. At the outset of the journey from cognitive immaturity to maturity, the only means of understanding the world available to the infant is through direct action on the immediate surroundings. Whatever knowledge is present at this stage resides in the *sensori-motor* schemas the infant uses when manipulating external objects. The sensori-motor stage terminates when, by the end of the second year, these action sequences begin to internalise as mental representations. There then follows a long period, referred to as the *pre-operational* stage, during which further development centres around the elaboration of mental representations and their coordination one with another. Around 7 years, the benefits of this intercoordination become evident as the first logical skills start to appear in the form of class and seriation logic. This marks the third *concrete-operational* stage of cognitive development. Finally, during early adolescence, following additional cognitive reorganisation, higher levels of reasoning become possible during the *formal operational* stage when mental structures supporting propositional reasoning skills will have been assembled (see Piaget & Inhelder, 1969).

This summary of Piaget's ideas is brutally abrupt. But rather than get caught up in a detailed exposition of Piaget's stage theory, our primary concern is with how the theory explains the process of cognitive growth. As knowledge accumulates in the growing mind, what is it that triggers the new forms of organisation associated with each stage and why are these new versions developmentally superior to their precursors?

Equilibration and the dynamics of stage progression

If we ask what drives intellectual growth within the Piagetian model then we find not one but four factors are implicated. Maturation certainly contributes but is not in itself a sufficient cause. Interaction with the physical world and formal teaching play their part as well but they too are not the whole story. The critical, fourth factor that supplies an overall direction to cumulative change is "equilibration" and it is intimately linked to the innate organisational processes said to be operating at all stages of development. Piaget assumed (there is now ample evidence to the contrary) that the infant has no innate knowledge relating to the physical properties of the world, rather these properties have to be constructed in the course of the child's development. What is innate, (which is consistent with more recent work) is a set of primitive operations which allow the whole developmental enterprise to get going.

At all stages of intellectual growth, whenever an event is experienced and given meaning, two processes are jointly involved—assimilation and accommodation. An event is invested with meaning by assimilating it to some relevant knowledge schema, and, whenever assimilation occurs, accommodation must also occur. The activated schema must accommodate to any unique features of the input and it may undergo change to make the fit possible. The degree of balance between these two processes determines just how successful the child's quest for meaning will be. If neither process dominates, an adaptive transaction with the world has occurred in the form of an intelligent response.

Whenever assimilation and accommodation move out of balance, the child's responses become less adaptive—tending towards fantasy if assimilation is dominant and towards rote imitation if accommodation is paramount. When a transaction with the world results in an adaptive response the cognitive structure that mediated the response is said to be in a state of equilibrium. Prior to intellectual maturity, by definition, the content domains over which the child can maintain adaptive responses will be limited. The direction of cognitive growth, therefore, is in the direction of extending the scope of adaptive responding and "equilibration" refers to the process by which these higher levels of equilibrium are attained.

As the child's adaptive range expands, so the child gets drawn into increasingly varied and novel circumstances which step up the demands being made on the cognitive structures that are available. Eventually (and inevitably) a situation will arise where, although the cognitive structure is sufficiently elaborated to support predictions about the properties of the situation, the predictions turn out to be wrong. What the child expects to happen fails to occur. The resulting disequilibrium creates the conditions under which cognitive reorganisation can take place. Self-regulatory processes are said to be invoked which remove the conflict by creating new cognitive structures that are capable of maintaining their equilibrium under the new conditions and, once this has been done, a further step along the developmental route will have been achieved.

With the advent of logical reasoning, the child comes to possess a body of cognitive structures whose internal organisation can compensate for most forms of induced disequilibrium. At the concrete operational stage, the child can cope with a variety of problem situations provided they present themselves in a tangible form. With the advent of formal operations, cognitive equilibrium can be further maintained in the context of hypothetical problems—as when the adolescent reasons about how things might be as opposed to how they actually are. Thus, Piaget's theory of equilibration, like Schank's theory of dynamic memory, casts predictive failure as the main cause of cognitive change. However, for Piaget, conflict is not only implicated in the formation of new knowledge structures, it can also bring about a transition from a lower to a higher form of understanding. It is this additional claim that has troubled and confused many critics.

Many otherwise sympathetic observers have condemned the concept of equilibration as circular and vacuous, complaining that it is not an explanation of cognitive growth at all but at best a redescription of the process it tries to explain—see Boden (1982); Bruner (1959); Bryant

(1986). Their principal objection is that equilibration is opaque at precisely the point where it should be clear. Namely, why should any change in cognitive organisation dependent on failed predictions necessarily come in the form of a higher-level cognitive structure? Disequilibrium resulting from predictive failure may well signal that extant knowledge needs to be revised but that on its own cannot tell the child what needs to be done to remove the problem. Consequently, equilibration totally fails to explain how the move from lower to higher cognitive structures actually takes place.

To make this objection clear, consider how equilibration would apply in a particular situation, say one in which the child has to reason about the conservation of continuous amount. Typically, the experimental subjects are faced with two identical beakers of water, which they agree at the outset contain the same amount of liquid. They are then asked to watch as the contents of one of the beakers is poured into another container of different shape, perhaps one that is taller and thinner. If now asked whether the two amounts are still the same, pre-operational subjects answer that they are not—perhaps arguing that there is more water in the thinner container. The error comes about because they focus initially on the difference in the height of the containers while ignoring the commensurate difference in their width. Eventually, however, an occasion will arise where the subjects attend not to the height difference but to the difference in width. At this point a major disturbance in equilibrium for the assimilatory cognitive structure is established, as there is now a state of direct conflict between a judgement of "more" based on height differences and a judgement of "less" based on the dimension of width. A resolution is found when the child understands that changes in the one dimension compensate for changes in the other. In consequence, the child moves from a state of limited equilibrium to a more advanced form once a new cognitive structure is formed which encodes the reciprocal relationships between height and width.

It should be evident that this "explanation" does little more than describe what should happen. It offers nothing new for our understanding of cognitive change beyond the claim that it is conflict (and not something else) that prompts the change. Obviously, if disequilibration is to serve as the driving force behind cognitive reorganisation these ambiguities will have to be resolved. One way of doing this is to look more closely at what happens when subjects find themselves trapped into adopting contradictory cognitive states.

COGNITIVE CONFLICT

In his book *Experiments in contradiction* (1980), Piaget described an experiment in which children were asked to look at a series of seven metal discs (A–G) and to comment on the relationships between them. On the surface, the discs all appeared to be of the same diameter but in fact they increased in size by a small amount (0.2mm) from one disc to the next so that although adjacent discs looked the same, the first and last disc were visibly different. Consequently, it was possible for the child to generate conflicting descriptions of the same display. On the basis of local comparisons, the child could argue that the discs making up the series were all equal. Alternatively, the child could conclude that the discs were unequal if the two end discs were being compared. The point at issue is how did children of different ages (5 to 12 years) make sense of this situation?

The pre-operational children (around 5 to 7 years) were not particularly disturbed when they upheld contradictory statements in this situation. Claims such as "A is equal to the remainder items", "G is equal to the remainder items", and "A is not equal to G" were freely proffered without any apparent concern for the contradictions that were building up. Slightly older children, just entering the concrete-operational stage (around 7 and 8 years), were somewhat less sanguine about the situation and showed signs of registering the contradictory implications of what they were saying. Some of these subjects tried to resolve the difficulty by partitioning the series into subgroups. If the end points A and G were not equal, then this was because the series was made up from small discs, say, ABC and from bigger discs, say DEFG. Although this strategy coped with some of the local comparisons and with the discrepant size of the end items, it did not, of course, remove the problem. The child was still left with the apparent equality of the boundary items C and D despite their assignment to different subgroups on the basis of their size. Shifting to other subgroupings merely displaced the boundary contradiction to another part of the series.

The induced conflict started to be resolved at around 10 years, when the child began to harbour the suspicion of imperceptible size differences, and it was fully resolved at around 12 years when the additivity of imperceptible differences across the series was used to account both for the apparent local equalities and for the perceptible difference in size between A and G.

Evidentally, the subjects who experienced conflict in this experimental task could respond by questioning their initial assumptions and by reformulating what they believed to be the case. But it remains unclear why this enforced reflection should have provided sufficient impetus for them to arrive at an understanding. Induced conflict also occurred with the younger subjects without necessarily bringing about an advance in their understanding of the situation.

Conflicting representional systems

A more explicit example of conflict-induced conceptual gain has been provided by Strauss (1987). He observed children between the ages of 7 and 11 years, working on a problem that could engage either of two independent representational systems; one based on their everyday experiences and the other based on formal teaching. The task entailed predicting the temperature of a beaker of water after it had been filled by mixing water from two other beakers each at 10 degrees centigrade. When predicting the temperature of the mix, the child could either draw upon everyday experience of similar situations, or upon ideas derived from formal schooling. Which of these two strategies was likely to be engaged depended on how the task was described and presented and, for this age range, they were likely to deliver different answers despite the problem remaining the same in each case.

Presenting the task in the form of pouring cold water from cup A and cold water from cup B into cup C, could be expected to engage the child's personal experience of similar situations in everyday life. Hence the question "Is the water in C the same temperature as in A and B?" should present the children with little difficulty in coming up with the answer that it will be the same. Presenting the same task so as to engage a numerical strategy rather than a qualitative one, is far less straightforward because to arrive at a correct answer the child must distinguish extensive from intensive properties. When told that "The water in cup A is at 10°C" and "The water in cup B is at 10°C" and then questioned about the temperature of the mix, the temptation is to add the two temperatures. If so, the child is treating temperature (incorrectly) as an extensive quantity. The two tasks, therefore, provide the children with plenty of scope for coming up with conflicting answers.

As suspected, Strauss found that children who arrived at the correct answer using their everyday knowledge were likely to get it wrong when the numerical version was presented. Here, they promptly added 10°C and 10°C to get 20°C and concluded it would be hotter than either of the two constituents. How this conflict between "same" on one occasion and "hotter" on another was handled varied with the age of the child. The youngest children, 7–8 years, were not bothered by the fact that they answered differently on the two occasions. As one subject is said to have remarked "It's different when you have numbers".

Around 8–9 years, there was a tendency to respond to the induced conflict by altering one of the answers. Unfortunately it was often the correct response that was sacrificed. Faced with the contradiction, these children dropped the correct qualititative judgement of "same" in favour of "colder". This was subsequently justified on the grounds that there were double amounts of cold involved. This hardly helped, because their answer in the numerical form was a mix at 20°C which left them with the diametrically opposed conclusions of hotter and colder. Thus, compared with the younger children, these children experienced a deterioration as they tried to co-ordinate the two representational systems. A year or so later, the difficulty was overcome; 10-year-olds experiencing conflict between their two answers simply dropped the 20°C claim in favour of the mix remaining the same.

Strauss's study is particularly interesting because it reveals children, probably for the first time, explicitly reflecting on their reasoning strategies while trying to arrive at a co-ordinated solution. As with Piaget's study of contradiction, the improvement in understanding was contingent upon the induced conflict but, this time, we are provided with some clues as to why conflict should act as a catalyst for change.

Strauss's experimental design ensured that two potentially incompatible representational stategies were both currently active within the same problem space. Thus the solver was presented with a unique opportunity for cross mapping one representational system onto the other. In other words, the agency for change is not conflict *per se* but the cross mapping that can follow when contradictory beliefs happen to capture the same input simultaneously. The subjective experience of conflict is only a contingent sign that an appropriate mental configuration favouring change has been brought about. Conflict is not so much the cause as the occasion for cognitive change.

Although there can be no guarantee that the new representational structures will resolve the current difficulty on any given occasion, this outcome will be more likely than if these discrete elements had been left dormant. And, if this interpretation is correct, conflict should not be the only indicator of when a productive cross mapping is possible. Any situation in which two hitherto separate representational systems are brought into the same work space will present similar opportunities for cognitive advance. Conflict may signal the presence of such an opportunity but so too may the experience of unexpected agreement—as when two hitherto independent reasoning strategies are unexpectedly found to generate outputs that agree with each other.

Strategic agreement and cognitive change

Arguments in favour of strategic agreement (but not conflict) as the initiator of cognitive change have been put forward by Bryant (1982, 1986). They arose out of a reinterpretation of Piaget's finding that children of 5–6 years do not spontaneously make use of a measuring instrument when judging lengths. Bryant and Kopytynska (1976) replicated this result but they also showed that children could be induced to use measurement if their preferred strategy of visual comparison was blocked. If children were given the task of comparing the depth of two holes bored in a block of wood, they were likely to use a stick when making the comparison.

Bryant (1982) went on to ask how and when a child would realise that measurement and not visual comparison was the more reliable method. According to equilibration theory this will come about when the child finds that the answers based on visual comparison are in conflict with the answers based on measurement. According to Bryant, on the contrary, it is when both sets of answers are in agreement that such change is most likely to occur. As a means of testing between these alternatives, Bryant devised situations where the two types of measurement were likely to agree or disagree with each other and then monitored what happened next. As Bryant had predicted, the presence of strategic agreement did work to bring about a significant increase in the number of subjects using spontaneous measurement. On the other hand, various forms of judgemental conflict did not lead to any significant shift from visual comparison to spontaneous measurement.

There are, therefore, occasions when agreement rather than conflict between the products of different representational systems sets the scene for cognitive reorganisation. Even so, proponents of strategic agreement as the agency for cognitive change are open to similar criticisms to those that were levelled at Piaget's account based on conflict. Agreement between the outputs of two strategies only implies that both are likely to be correct. It does not reveal why, as here, measurement should be given preference over visual comparison in the future. Championing the one factor over the other still leaves the basic question concerning cognitive advance unanswered—why should the eventual outcome entail an advance from a lower to a higher level of understanding? This question will continue to haunt us so long as the crucial strand in the argument remains unaddressed. It can be exorcised provided we treat both conflict and agreement as signalling the opportunity for some deeper process to get to work which is the real agent for change.

The factors common to both the Bryant and Strauss demonstrations are, (1) the solver starts with two cognate representational systems which are relatively independent of each other, and (2) training ensures that both of these representational systems are currently active and working on the same problem. When this happens it appears the scene is set for new responses to be generated which neither representational system could support on their own. Unfortunately, the Bryant and Strauss studies fall short of indicating how all this might occur; how the the cross mapping might take place and how the end product could license more advanced forms of reasoning. Fortunately, a study reported by Lawler (1981) does provide us with some crucial insights into what is going on.

MICROVIEWS AND THEIR FUSION

Lawler (1981) recorded the progress of his daughter, Miriam, as she acquired the rudiments of arithmetic over a period of six months following her sixth birthday. At the beginning of the study, Miriam had isolated islands of understanding which dealt with different aspects of number. By the end of the study this strategic isolation was breaking down as the separate representational systems (or *microviews* to use Lawler's term) started to coalesce to form more generalised modes of understanding.

At the beginning of the investigation, if Miriam was asked to add two numbers and then, immediately afterwards, to carry out the same addition using monetary values, she was not capable of registering the equivalence of the two numerical operations. At this stage she relied on one representational system for adding numbers and quite a different representational system for dealing with coin denominations. In fact, for most of the period under study, Miriam continued to use different representational systems for different tasks and she remained unaware of their correspondences.

When the study began, Lawler identified the presence of four discrete microviews: COUNT, DECADAL, MONEY, and PAPER SUM. Taking these in turn, COUNT depended upon one-to-one correspondence and resorted to finger counting at critical stages in addition e.g.:

5 + 6 = 6, 7, 8, 9, 10, 11 (on fingers)

The second microview, DECADAL, was adapted to Miriam's experiences with the computer language Logo and, in particular, to its use in drawing pictures on a VDU. This is a somewhat unusual skill in a 6-year-old but she had had many opportunities to play with a computer under her father's guidance. In consequence, she was used to typing instructions such as "Right Turn 90 plus Right Turn 90" which she employed to reproduce particular geometrical patterns on the screen. Similarly, through playing another computer game, "Shoot", Miriam had used equivalent instructions to aim and fire at a target on the screen. DECADAL had developed out of these rather specialised experiences, and it handled the addition of large numbers by converting them into multiples of 10. For example, the procedure for adding Right Turn 55 + Right Turn 22 would be:

$$(50) + (20) + (5 + 2) =$$
$$5 + 2 \ [0] + (5 + 2) =$$
$$7[0] + 7 =$$
$$70 + 7 = 77$$

In effect, the procedure consists of (1) stripping off the zeros from 50 and 20, (2) referring the result to COUNT, (3) restoring the zero when an answer is returned, and (4) handling the residuum by COUNT once more.

The third microview, MONEY, also drew upon COUNT but was adapted to Miriam's every day dealings with her pocket money and handled such transactions as—"75 cents plus 25 cents = $1".

Whereas COUNT, DECADAL, and MONEY all deal with some aspect of mental calculation, the fourth microview, PAPER SUM, was solely concerned with problems in written addition. It would be invoked when a sum was written down and it arrived at a solution by adding from right to left across columns.

Each microview, therefore, dealt with a different aspect of the number system and, as Strauss had noted in the context of heat and temperature, which strategy would be activated depended on how a task was presented. It is assumed that all of the microviews compete to process a particular problem but, as they parse situations in different ways, each has its own preferred sphere of application. COUNT was based in the external world and its objects; DECADAL in the control of movements of a cursor on a VDU; PAPER SUM in the world of written arithmetic; and MONEY in the sphere of coin transactions. This then defines the repertoire of microviews available to Miriam at the beginning of the study.

Subsequently, some development occurred within COUNT as Miriam started to decompose numbers. This meant she could now represent 12 as 10 + 2. However, while progress in carrying numbers had been made within COUNT, it still presented something of a problem in the other systems. Carrying could not be done in PAPER SUM and, it had only been partially solved in DECADAL. Working in DECADAL, Miriam would correctly arrive at 77 as the answer to 55 plus 22, but she would calculate 55 + 26 as:

$$55 + 26 = (50 + 20) + (5 + 6) = 70 \text{ and } 11$$

Eventually, Miriam came to solve the problem of carrying in DECADAL and Lawler makes the strong claim that he actually observed the moment when this occurred as a consequence of the cross mapping of one microview onto another, albeit he did not realise the full significance of the observation until afterwards.

At the time when Miriam had started to decompose number in COUNT, she was asked to work out 37 + 12. Normally she would have done this in DECADAL:

$$37 + 12 = (30 + 10) + (7 + 2) = 49$$

but at the time of the request she had been working in COUNT. Table 7.2 sets out how Lawler describes the scene and what happened next.

Lawler's subsequent interpretation of the episode was that because COUNT was currently active, it (unusually) captured the harder problem that Miriam had requested. Following the recent decomposition advance, the sum was tackled as:

$$37 + 12 = (37 + 10) = 47, 48, 49 \text{ (the finish involving finger counting).}$$

TABLE 7.2
Concurrent activation of two microviews

Bob	Miriam do you remember when you used to count on your fingers all the time? How would you do a sum like seven plus two?
Miriam	Nine
Bob	I know you know the answer—but can you tell me how you used to figure it out before you knew?
Miriam	(counting on her fingers): Seven; eight; nine
Bob	Think back even further to long ago last year
Miriam	(counted to nine with both addends on her fingers—leaving the middle finger of her right hand depressed): But I don't do that any more. Why don't you give me a harder problem?
Bob	Thirty-seven plus twelve
Miriam	(with a shocked look on her face): That's forty-nine

[Something about this problem and result surprised Miriam. I recorded this situation and her reaction in a vignette; I did not appreciate it as especially significant at that time.]

From Lawler, 1981, pp.25–26.

Normally, Miriam would have done this sum in DECADAL as:

$$37 + 12 = (30 + 10) + (7 + 2) = 49$$

and her shock came from registering that the two microviews converged on the same answer.

Obviously, Lawler's claims are somewhat speculative but there are three lines of argument to be made in its support. First, following this episode, Miriam's behaviour suggested the presence of a new microview, SERIAL. Second, the new SERIAL microview was based on a combination of COUNT and DECADAL. Third, the circumstances surrounding this cognitive advance are precisely those where we would expect concurrent activation to lead to this type of cross mapping.

Count + Decadal = Serial

It is being suggested that the new microview, SERIAL, emerged from the union of COUNT and DECADAL and the outcome was a new representational system that not only retained the functions that each ancestor system had served in the past but also added new functions on top. Using SERIAL, Miriam could now, for the first time, actually test the veracity of her answers because she could derive the same answer by taking different routes. For example, within DECADAL, she had known for a long time that $90 + 90 = 180$. Now, using SERIAL, she could arrive at the same answer in a different way:

$$(90 + 90) = (90 + 80) \text{ then (on fingers) } 170, 171....180.$$

In effect, SERIAL allowed for operations not only on elements in the real world but also on the products of the microviews themselves.

When SERIAL was put in place, Miriam had still not solved carrying in PAPER SUM. This critical insight came when she linked an element in SERIAL (tens) with an element in PAPER SUM (column position). At this point, therefore, we find a further advance as PAPER SUM begins to merge with SERIAL. The consequence of this cross mapping was a new structure, CONFORMAL, which served to underpin a deeper understanding of number than had been possible before it made its appearance.

Overall, Lawler's study shows very clearly how small changes in a representational system can lead to quite radical changes in understanding. The presence of different representational systems, each tuned to a special microdomain, ensured that equivalent events were parsed differently. The context of a task thus determined which particular microview would be invoked. But there was always the possibility that more than one microview would capture a given problem, activating their individual features in parallel. At this point the opportunity arose of producing a hybrid version that not only retained the repertoire of prior skills but also brought new versions onto the scene.

Subjective states of conflict and agreement, therefore, are not so much the cause of change as signs that the child's reflective attention is being engaged and a new turn of dialectical spiral is getting underway. Lawler, like Piaget, interprets the growth of knowledge as a constructive activity on the part of the child. Unlike Piaget, he views the course of cognitive growth as being much more susceptible to environmental influence. Exactly which fusions of microviews occur will depend on the vagaries of the child's physical and social interactions.

SUBSYMBOLIC PROCESSES IN COGNITIVE DEVELOPMENT

Piaget's account of adaptive behaviour arising from a balance between assimilation and accommodation could be interpreted as another way of describing a constraint satisfaction network in action. That is to say, assimilation can be translated into the process of mapping the input features from a situation into activation values over the input layer of a network (schema) and the subsequent spread of activation to related nodes in the network. Accommodation, on the other hand, resides in the adjustments that are made to the network's weights that register the unique properties of the situation concerned. In which case, adaptation, (where assimilation and accommodation are in balance), will reside in the best fit the network can compute to a current input when all of the operative constraints (internal and external) have been satisfied. And, to continue the analogy, if assimilation is allowed to predominate, this is equivalent to damping down the impact of the external constraints on the final settlement state. If accommodation is allowed to predominate, this is equivalent to damping down the impact of internal constraints on the final settlement state. Ideally, as Piaget had well understood, both sets of constraints should be allowed to work together in guiding the system towards an appropriate response.

A network that has been inadequately trained to compute the appropriate outputs for a given content domain is equivalent to an unequilibrated knowledge structure. Training based on error analysis (i.e. based on conflict between the computed output and the target output) serves to move the network in the direction of greater equilibrium. After training, neural networks come to retain their computational stability in many different contexts of application and generate predictions that are more likely than before to be confirmed. And, as we saw in Chapter 5, a connectionist network is capable of deriving stepped stages in the child's understanding of the beam balance using continuous and gradual alterations to the network's weights.

Given this degree of theoretical convergence it is hardly surprising that connectionist models have been hailed as concrete implementations of the kind of developmental mechanism Piaget appeared to have in mind. Bates and Elman (1992, p.17) point to the fact that as neural networks can produce unexpected outputs as a consequence of their non-linear dynamics they are likely to prompt:

> ... a return to ... Piaget's program of genetic epistemology, instantiating his principles of equilibration and adaptation in concrete systems that really work—and really change.

We seem, therefore, to have reached a point where the much criticised equilibration model may be on the verge of translation into concrete and explicit forms which will allow us to understand, far more clearly than before, what is at stake as a knowledge structure moves towards a higher level of equilibration. If so, we have a singularly encouraging example of theoretical convergence taking place between developmental and mainstream cognitive models. Nonetheless, it is also possible that we are being faced with another example of premature theoretical closure.

The examples of cognitive advance cited earlier from the work of Piaget, Strauss, Bryant, and Lawler, largely resist direct translation into a process of knowledge reorganisation that is occurring at the subsymbolic level. Simply equating the updating of explicit knowledge with an automatic process of weight adjustment (where all the weights in a relevant network are open to change) is to ignore the serious limitations that can attend this updating process. Ironically, if we are pretty good at handling partial information, we are markedly less good at handling the full implications of detailed information. Possibly, these limitations could be accommodated by varying the rates at which the weights in a network are adjusted or by introducing a modular architecture where different networks handle different content domains. Perhaps so, but it is also possible that the most important characteristics of the cognitive advances described earlier are occurring beyond the microstructural level at the symbolic level.

REFLECTION AND KNOWLEDGE REDESCRIPTION

One of the consequences of the changes that Lawler recorded in Miriam's arithmetical knowledge was that her arithmetical procedures ceased to be locally embedded in the contexts of specific tasks but were rendered increasingly available for use in many different contexts. This issue of "knowledge portability" is an important aspect of developmental change and it raises issues that are not easily accounted for at a microstructural level of description although they do appear to be amenable to a macrostructural analysis.

Karmiloff-Smith (1992) has proposed a Representational Redescription (RR) model that holds that all knowledge when it is first acquired has a limited degree of access. Initially, knowledge comes in a form where it is "procedurally embedded" in the context of acquisition; it can be accessed in similar contexts to that in which it was accquired but not in other, dissimilar contexts. Eventually, these contextual constraints are gradually shaken off as the knowledge in question is used and consolidated. Once it has stabilised, metareflective processes can be brought to bear which serve to rewrite the procedurally embedded format into new representational versions that are more generally accessible to the cognitive system as a whole. We will consider a developmental example taken to support this claim and then look at the workings of the Representational Redescription model in more detail.

Karmiloff-Smith (1979) has shown that there are times when children, who have been using their knowledge quite correctly, can spontaneously regress to a less mature form of behaviour, before reverting back to the correct usage again. She suggests that this regression marks the point where a process of representational redescription is underway. The outcome is the creation of a new representational format that has been freed from some of its previous constraints—as in the following example.

In French, the word "*un*" can act both as the indefinite article "a" and as the numeral "one" and Karmiloff-Smith found that children of 3–5 years interpreted and used "*un*" in both of these ways, apparently behaving quite correctly. However, she also noted that this phase could be followed by a stage when slightly different expressions were used to mark each function:

"*une voiture*" (a car)
"*une de voiture*" (one car)

and the children appeared to regress from their initial level of competence into a less mature form. This lapse was temporary and at around 7 years, the children reverted once more to the single expressive form for both versions.

Such a developmental sequence makes sense if we assume that the linguistic performance of the younger children actually concealed a limitation in their linguistic competence. That is, these children originally treated each function of *"un"* as an independent operation and there was no cross reference to the other function. The intermediate (regressive) stage marked the point where the child came to realise that the dual function existed. As a result the two functions were separately tagged until their dual properties could be merged within a new representational form which supported the single expressive version once more.

Metaprocedural reorganisation

If all knowledge starts off being procedurally bound then a major goal of cognitive development must be the creation of new representational forms which can enter into a broader range of cognitive operations. For Karmiloff-Smith, it is metareflection that provides the means for overcoming this limitation in knowledge accessibility. In the course of metareflection, internal procedures are invoked that serve to rewrite the initial representations into more accessible formats (Karmiloff-Smith, 1986, 1992).

This is to propose that individual items of knowledge can be represented in memory at different levels of abstraction. At the lowest level, implicit knowledge (I), the internal representation entails isolated elements and procedures. The knowledge may be called upon and used in specific contexts but it lacks cross linkages to other, related forms of knowledge.

Three further representational levels are envisaged (E1, E2, and E3) where the same information becomes available in an increasingly accessible format. Following the transition from I to E1, knowledge representations are becoming more abstract and less procedurally bound. At E2 it is in a form that can support conscious access and at E3 the representational format is in a form that can support verbal report.

Progression from a lower to a higher representational level requires the application of a reflective cycle where the child's attention is withdrawn from the task specifics in order to bring the procedures themselves into the problem workspace. Repeated reflective cycles then give rise to increasingly accessible versions of the knowledge involved until, ultimately, it has been rewritten in the form of a universal code which is available for use with any other forms of knowledge existing on the same level.

The role of subsymbolic processes in knowledge redescription therefore, may turn out to be a severely restricted one. According to the RR model, the point at which the weights in a network stabilise (further training results in little or no change), marks the behavioural mastery that is typical of the I level. In other words, connectionist simulations stop at precisely the point where the RR model starts and, hence, connectionist accounts leave entirely open the question of how the transition from implicit to explicit representation should proceed. Arriving at a more complete account that terminates in unencapsulated knowledge strikes into territory that has effectively been colonised by classical symbol models.

Consciousness and knowledge reorganisation

In fact, both ACT* and SOAR specify much the same sort of constraints on knowledge compilation at the macrostructural level as those proposed by the RR model. For both of these production models, new productions can only be constructed utilising the current contents of working memory. Similarly, if new groupings of knowledge elements on levels E2 and E3 are to occur, Karmiloff-Smith's analysis suggests that this will only take place when they are currently co-active in working memory, i.e. when they participate in the serial states of consciousness. Hence, it is presumably no coincidence that explicit corrections in a structured text elicit little or no *automatic* readjustments within a memory record.

Indeed, there is something deeply paradoxical about an explicit knowledge base being automatically updated outside of consciousness. Were such automatic change to be the case, we would lose a major element of cognitive control as our belief systems were continually revised under the press of each new day's events. If, following an intense argument about religion the night before, we woke up to find ourselves totally converted to the opposition view, we would also find that many other beliefs had changed at the same time. In effect, we would wake up to find that we were ignorant of our own knowledge, as each change would have to be activated before we knew what it entailed. Restricting change to items of verbally accessible knowledge that are concurrently active in working memory would set definite limits on the extent and the scope of knowledge reorganisation. Such an arrangement would favour conceptual change that is timely (circumstances require it), and circumscribed (much more that we know will be unaffected).

It would also mean that whatever changes were wrought at this level would be changes that could be given a measure of explicit justification, whether to ourselves or to interested others. This is an important consideration if we are to extend the horizons of our own knowledge by accommodating to the experiences reported by other people. This aspect of knowledge acquisition will be discussed in Section 3 with reference to the comprehension of written text. Before then, we have not yet finished with the dynamics of knowledge reorganisation.

If conceptual change is intimately related to whichever mental contents happen to be active in consciousness, any factors that influence selection for focal attention will necessarily have an important role in the construction of new knowledge. One set of factors will reside in our perceptual transactions with the external world; there are certain things we cannot afford to ignore. Another set of factors resides in the emotional valence we assign to our experiences; there are certain things we may prefer to ignore but find that we cannot. In the final chapter of this section we will look at some of the evidence indicating that emotional states can further the elaborative processing of selected informational content.

CHAPTER EIGHT

Cognition and affect

Bower (1992) has argued that if goal-seeking systems are to operate effectively in an uncertain environment, they must be capable of monitoring their internal states and deciding which states take preference. At minimum, he suggests that such cognitive vigilance calls for (1) discriminating the urgency associated with different need states, (2) using this information to decide issues of priority, (3) converting needs into action plans, and (4) resetting the planning agenda quickly whenever circumstances warrant a change. Without these abilities, a goal-seeking system will be seriously at risk in a hostile and changing environment. A system with these components will tend to experience emotion-like states as a "by-product" of converting its needs into overt behaviour.

Once present, these emotional states can then act as a metacommentary on the organism's experiences and, in certain cases, this will result in the course of new learning being steered in particular directions. According to Bower (1994, p.304) this is possible because emotions:

> ... frequently accompany failed expectations (or interruptions), and thus direct attention to accompanying events as important items to be learned. Second, emotions mobilise attention to those features of an external situation that learners judge to be significant or predictive of the cause

of the failed expectation, and in so doing cause greater learning of them. Third, the inertial persistence of the emotional arousal, and its slow decay, leads to continued recycling or rehearsal of those encoded events viewed as causally belonging to the emotional reaction.

Accordingly, we will proceed to define terms as a prelude to reviewing some of the evidence that the interactions between affective states and information processing can work to direct the course of learning in specific directions.

AFFECT, EMOTION, AND MOOD

"Affect" tends to be used as an umbrella term referring to emotional phenomena in general. It subsumes "emotion" and "mood" as more specific descriptions of internal states which can be distinguished through their effects on attentional processes.

The arousal of an emotional state leads to an interruption of ongoing thought by redirecting attention towards particular, affect-relevant stimuli. For example, negative emotions (sadness; anxiety; anger) typically occur at times when desired goals are not achieved and these states can be aroused very quickly. A state of sadness may be triggered by major failure or loss, feelings of anxiety can accompany threats to self-preservation, and anger can be produced by the frustration of our current plans. In each case, the negative affect produced by frustrated goal attempts works to bring about a change in our current preoccupations.

Moods refer to more pervasive affective states which can accompany cognitive processing without necessarily producing significant breaks in the train of thought. Their relevance to central cognition is that they too can work to increase the salience of mood-congruent information.

ORGANISATION OF EMOTIONAL KNOWLEDGE

When questioned, people in general exhibit an extensive body of personal knowledge dealing with these topics. They can talk about the differences between emotional states and their likely sequelae. They can report on the circumstances that elicit different emotional states and they can describe what it is like to be in such states. For Shaver,

Schwartz, Kirson, and O'Connor (1987) the cross-cultural similarities to be found in these reports are sufficient to suggest a basic core of emotional knowledge which is universally distributed. Although this claim has been debated—see Russell (1994) and the rejoinders by Ekman (1994) and Izard (1994)—the fact remains that subjects evaluating emotional reactions in others do not respond at random. On the contrary, they seem to have access to some primary corpus of knowledge which bears upon what it is like to be angry or afraid and which predicts how these states translate into overt behaviour. Consequently, as for any other body of knowledge, we can enquire how this emotional knowledge is organised. Is it the case that emotional terms show the distinctive arrangement into superordinate, basic, and subordinate levels that has been found with other taxonomies?

Shaver et al. addressed this issue by using a corpus of emotion names—213 terms in all—which subjects were asked to rate on a four-point scale from, 1—"definitely would not call this an emotion", to 4—"definitely would call this an emotion". This exercise enabled them to select 135 "good" examples of emotional terms which were given to different subjects to sort through by putting similar terms together. The resulting categories were then entered into an hierarchical cluster analysis which assigned each term to a particular level in the categorial hierarchy.

At the basic level, this led to five (or six) separate clusters being identified which singled out love, joy, (surprise), anger, sadness, and fear as basic emotional terms. Going above the basic level left only the distinction between positive and negative emotions in place while moving down to the subordinate level simply resulted in these basic terms being given more specialised meanings.

In a subsequent study, subjects were asked to write accounts of their personal experience of basic emotional states. These reports were then analysed for the presence of (1) the contextual antecedents of the basic emotion in question, (2) its mode of expression, associated feelings, and concurrent physiological reactions, and (3) any associated behaviours. These macrofeatures were then used to specify the individual scripts associated with each of the basic emotions.

Overall, the scripts for the five basic emotions (surprise was dropped as a doubtful case) all revealed the presence of a common macro-structure relating to likely antecedent conditions, the core experience, and associated responses. Thus, the fear prototype indicated that its antecedents consist of events interpreted as threatening to the self, the central core dealt with the phenomenal experience, and a further component dealt with response mechanisms aimed at bringing the state under control. It seems, therefore, that the basic emotions are conceptually represented in episodic form where each emotional episode has identifiable beginnings, responses, and outcomes. However, other investigations into the structure of the emotional lexicon in English have reached somewhat different conclusions which bear directly on the functional role of the emotions in the cognitive economy.

FUNCTION OF BASIC EMOTIONS

Contrary to general-purpose models of cognition, Johnson-Laird and Oatley (1989) have argued that the human cognitive architecture is constructed around a number of independent processing modules operating in parallel. The top of their modular hierarchy is occupied by a module whose function is to generate models of the self. Operating below this module are other modules that serve lower-level functions such as visual or auditory processing. Evidentally, if these modules are to work in unison, some form of signalling mechanism will be required which can reset and co-ordinate their priorities as circumstances change. It is this signalling function that Johnson-Laird and Oatley assign to the basic emotions which are seen as having evolved as a primitive means of co-ordinating a modular nervous system. At critical junctures where plan application appears to be going wrong or where one plan needs to be replaced by another with a higher priority, emotional arousal allows for a signal to be transmitted which results in all modules in the hierarchy being set to the same state.

The core assumption here is that each basic emotion provides a direct (atomic) signal to all of the modules in the cognitive architecture which ensures that readjustments are made quickly. Without this arrangement there would be inevitable delays attendant on the parsing and interpretation of molecular (propositional) signals. Unlike natural language, therefore, where meaning is conveyed via molecular signals that need to be decomposed into their constituent parts, the basic emotions communicate through atomic signals that, due to their lack of internal structure, can participate in a fast, albeit limited, mode of signalling.

Johnson-Laird and Oatley propose that only a small number of emotional terms are used to denote the emotional states that serve this signalling function. These are the terms applied to the five basic emotions—Happiness, Sadness, Anger, Fear, and Disgust. Contrary to Shaver et al, these terms are said to be capable of standing alone without the support of an associated script specifying antecedent and consequent conditions. In fact, the signalling function of the basic emotions critically depends on the way in which they can be experienced without any necessary awareness of any propositional content. Hence, with reference to a basic emotion such as happiness, it should be permissible to say "I feel happy but don't know why". Such licence should not apply to non-basic emotions and a statement such as "I feel embarrassed but don't know why" will appear deviant or odd. This is because non-basic emotional labels are derived from the basic terms by adding semantic content. It is the presence of this propositional information that converts a basic state into a complex state.

In putting their theory to the test, Johnson-Laird and Oatley worked with a corpus of 590 English emotional terms, pre-screened as referring to subjective feeling states. Various intuitive tests were then applied to the words in the corpus in order to decide whether they were basic or non-basic terms. Words referring to states that can be experienced without awareness of evaluations were seen as denoting basic emotions. All other emotional terms that denoted emotions by including propositional information about their cause or the object of the emotion were taken as referring to non-basic states. This resulted in a total of six categories made up from the basic emotion terms and a further set of categories relating to non-basic emotional terms such as emotional relations (e.g. love) and caused emotions (e.g. horror). By adding a seventh category (Generic Emotions) which combined emotions and feelings, Johnson-Laird and Oatley arrived at a taxonomy that they claimed not only sufficed to capture the full range of emotional terms in English but did so in a way that reflected their internal structure, i.e. as unanalysable qualia or as modified by additional propositional information.

Although the scope of this analysis is clearly intended to have a universal application, to date it has been applied only to the emotional lexicon in English. Consequently, the data can only provide partial evidence in favour of the general theoretical argument being mounted (see Ortony & Clore, 1989 for a critical commentary).

Of course, the terms in the emotional lexicon stand at one remove from the emotional states they describe—talking about being happy or sad is not the same as experiencing happiness or sadness. Consequently, if we are to address the interface between affect and cognition directly we need to look at studies designed to induce contrasting affective states as subjects participate in different cognitive tasks. If affect does work to reset subjects' priorities in information processing we should find that they attend to different features of their world as their affective states come and go.

MOOD STATES AND MEMORY

Mood states can persist over relatively long periods of time and their presence can determine both how we appraise the features of current events and how we recall these features later. This conclusion has been reached by getting subjects in specific mood states (variously induced by hypnosis or other forms of suggestion) to perform a range of tasks which are to be recalled later. "Mood congruent memory" is said to occur when material whose affective valence is congruent with the prevailing mood is selectively favoured either at encoding or recall.

The phenomenon of mood congruent memory was first reported by Bower and Cohen (1982). In this experiment, subjects were inducted into happy or sad frames of mind prior to reading narratives describing the activities of two central characters, one described as being happy, the other as being sad. Subjects read the text under instructions to identify the central character in the story and the same subjects went on to recall the passage content when in a neutral mood on the following day. It transpired that subjects had predominantly identified with the character matching their own mood at the time of reading and that their recall was biased towards reproducing more facts about this character.

A parallel phenomenon, "mood state dependent memory", has also been reported which depends on the presence of an interaction between mood at learning and mood at recall. In this case, subjects who have learned word lists under happy and sad states respectively show greater accuracy in free recall when they are in the same mood at the time of testing than when they are in a different mood (Bower, 1981). Subsequent research into these two phenomena has indicated that although mood congruency effects have continued to receive experimental support, the evidence favouring mood state dependent memory has been less consistent.

MOOD CONGRUENCE, EMOTIONAL NODES, AND PROPOSITIONAL NETWORKS

Mood state congruity holds that we find it easier to encode and recall positive items of information when we are happy and conversely for negative items when we are sad. Bower and Cohen's explanation of this effect was framed around the suggestion that different emotions can be represented as nodes in a semantic network. Each of the distinct emotions is assigned a particular node from which pointers fan out to other parts of the network. Mood-inducing instructions serve to activate the appropriate emotion nodes and activation then spreads to other nodes in the network congruent with the activated emotion and supplementing the spread of activation induced by coincident events. This type of model may handle mood congruence effects but it has difficulty in accommodating the mood incongruent effects that have also been reported in the literature, e.g. Rinck, Glowalla, and Schneider (1992). These experimenters induced happy or sad moods in their subjects who then rated a list of words for their emotional valence (pleasant or unpleasant) and their intensity. On the following day, each subject was faced with a surprise recall test for the list items when in a neutral mood. The recall data were then analysed both in terms of the incidence of recall for each category of word, (pleasant vs. unpleasant) and their intensity (strongly toned vs. slightly toned).

Significant interactions between mood and word characteristics were found which supported the mood congruent hypothesis in some respects but not others. Support came from the fact that strongly toned words, which were negatively valenced, were recalled more often if they had been learned in a sad mood rather than a happy mood (35% vs. 27%). Equally, it was found that the strong, positively valenced words were recalled more often if they had been learned in a happy mood, (42% vs. 30%). However, for the slightly toned words there was some evidence for a mood incongruity effect. Now subjects in a happy mood recalled the slightly unpleasant words more frequently, (24% vs. 5%), whereas the slightly pleasant words were favoured at recall if they had been learned in a sad mood, (40% vs. 19%).

Accordingly, these investigators have proposed a modification to the network model which introduced additional processing assumptions dealing with the evaluation of inputs. Mood incongruity effects come about, they suggest, because slightly mood incongruent words elicit a greater degree of elaborative rehearsal. This modification, therefore, implies that other factors can combine with the activation of emotion nodes to produce the observed experimental effects. Yet other studies have gone further in raising the question whether emotional nodes are needed for this purpose at all. In experiments conducted by Perrig and Perrig (1988), subjects who were instructed to behave "as if" in a certain mood while undertaking a verbal learning task, also demonstrated a mood congruency effect—suggesting that mood arousal may not only be an insufficient condition for congruency effects in memory to occur, it may not even be a necessary condition. Thus, while the mood state congruity effect appears to be fairly robust, it need not rest upon the mechanisms implicating emotional nodes as originally proposed.

MOOD STATE DEPENDENT MEMORY

Following Bower's initial claims for the existence of mood state dependent memory (recall is best if mood at learning matches mood at recall), his subsequent views on the matter have become more guarded (Bower & Mayer, 1985). Reviews of the experimental findings by Blaney (1986) and Ucros (1989) indicate that a number of factors contribute to whether or not the effect is found. Ucros cites the following factors as influential:

1. The valence of the affect—the effect tends to be weaker for negative than for positive mood states.
2. The intensity of the mood state—the stronger it is at encoding, the stronger the effect.
3. The degree of contrast between input and output moods—the greater the contrast, the greater the effect (e.g. a positive mood shows greater contrast against a negative mood than against a neutral mood).

Overall, mood state dependent memory seems to be a less robust phenomenon than mood congruency, although this may be a function of the weak methods normally used to establish a link between encoded content and prevailing mood (see the reference to Wenzlaff, Wegner, & Klein, 1991 later). Where it is found, the effect has been also been explained via the network model in terms of the spread of activation from the relevant emotion nodes. Reinstating a particular mood allows the appropriate node to spread additional activation through the network and to increase the activation of its associated nodes.

Unfortunately, there is a general defect with all of these experiments that casts an element of doubt on the reliability and validity of the laboratory findings. We simply cannot be sure that the methods used to induce specific mood states (methods such as hypnotic suggestion and the provision of background music) operate in the manner intended. Field studies of subjects faced with genuinely traumatic events are not plagued by this deficiency, although they too are not without difficulties of their own.

FLASHBULB MEMORIES

In 1977, Brown and Kulik advocated the existence of a special memory mechanism which could be selectively activated in extremely dramatic contexts. When triggered, it delivered a "print-now" instruction to the memory system which ensured that the contents of consciousness at the critical moment were permanently preserved in the form of a "flashbulb" memory. Taking the assassination of J.F. Kennedy as the prototypic case, Brown and Kulik were impressed by how often people seemed to be able to recall many details about the circumstances under which they received the news. When asked about the events in Dallas, most respondents could confidently come up with information about who told them, where they were, and what they had been doing at the time. As though, in fact, the memory record had preserved not only the content but the context of reception—much as a photograph records the contextual details of a family scene at the time the flash goes off. Brown and Kulik speculated that such a mechanism could have evolutionary significance; following dramatic, possibly life-threatening events, it would be an adaptive advantage for the organism involved if it had access to a detailed and permanent record of all that took place.

They proceeded to test their hunch by getting subjects to free recall the events in Dallas in 1963 as well as eight other dramatic events that had occurred in the public domain. Once subjects had recalled, they were then asked to rate each event for the degree of personal importance they attached to it. Given that the flashbulb hypothesis deals with the context of discovery, the resulting recall protocols were subsequently analysed for circumstantial detail concerning *when* the information was first received; *what* the subject was doing at the time the news came through; their *location* at the time; and the *source* of the information.

The results of this analysis indicated that as the consequentiality of an event increased, respondents did indeed provide a lot of circumstantial detail of the kind predicted, apparently supporting the initial hypothesis. Consequently, in the case of flashbulb memory we seem to have a striking example of affect-laden content entering into a qualitatively new mode of encoding where the recording of the detail surrounding the event is complete, accurate, and impervious to loss.

On closer scrutiny it soon became apparent that Brown and Kulik's data did not really support these claims. Although their subjects had reported many details concerning "who", "what", "when", and "where", the obdurate fact remained that there was no possibility within the experimental design of making an independent check on their accuracy and hence whether details had been lost during the years that followed. This necessary control was introduced by McCloskey, Wible, and Cohen (1988) who took the melancholy opportunity to look at the question again when the launch of the *Challenger* space vehicle ended in tragedy. It was a much publicised event that was undoubtedly highly traumatic to those watching or listening as the launch took place. Within three days of the disaster, these experimenters had arranged for their colleagues to be questioned about the circumstances surrounding their discovery of the news. Altogether, 29 respondents were tested within one week of the event and they were retested, in the same way, after an interval of nine months.

At first glance it seemed that the special properties attributed to a flashbulb record had been elicited because, both at immediate and delayed recall, nearly all of the subjects could provide answers to the questions raised. However, once a subject's immediate recall was compared with recall after a delay, the hypothesis turned out to be somewhat less well supported. The experimenters recorded the number of occasions over the intervening nine months where details became more specific, became more general, became inconsistent, or could not be recalled at all. Lumping these variants together led to difference scores which were not exactly those we would expect if a permanent record of the event had been formed. Subjects were able to reply to the questions on both occasions, but what they had to say was hardly immutable. In the light of these results, McCloskey et al. concluded that no special mechanism of flashbulb memory was needed to explain what was happening, as the properties of the recall protocols were entirely compatible with the events being repeatedly rehearsed. Observers may have rerun the event in their minds more often than is usual, but there was no evidence of anything over and beyond the normal mode of encoding. Christianson (1989) arrived at a similar conclusion after testing the immediate and delayed recall of Swedish subjects for the circumstances surrounding Olaf Palme's assassination.

Wagenaar and Groeneweg (1990) managed to combine the autobiographical recall of traumatic events with, if not records of the event at the time, at least with the content of an earlier recall attempt. They capitalised on the opportunity provided by the restaging of a military trial of Martinus De Rijke who, although a prisoner in a Dutch concentration camp during the Second World War, had taken on the role of controlling and terrorising other prisoners. Testimony about the camp and De Rijke's activities had been recorded from survivors just after the war and this testimony was available when the case was reopened and De Rijke was brought to trial in 1984. Comparison of what witnesses had had to say in both their earlier and later interrogations indicated that although there were consistencies for general details about the camp and its maltreatment practices, there were also some surprising inconsistencies. A small but significant proportion of subjects failed to recall the defendant's name, although they had done so in the early interrogation, and there were also failures to recognise his photograph. Most surprising of all, specific brutalities that had involved particular witnesses were not resistant to forgetting. To take two instances from the six examples provided (Wagenaar & Groeneweg, 1990, p.84):

1. Witness GHV saw how a fellow prisoner was maltreated by De Rijke and Boxmeer, till the man died. In 1984 he had forgotten both names. In 1943 he reported how another prisoner, De V was violently assaulted by Boxmeer. In 1984 he reported that De V was the perpetrator instead of the victim.
2. Witness L van der M was beaten up by De Rijke and was unable to walk for days. In 1984 he remembered only receiving an occasional kick. He also witnessed the murdering of a Jewish fellow prisoner, but had forgotten all about it in 1984.

These results indicate that intense experiences are hardly immune to forgetting. Of course, it can be argued that the initial post-war testimony was itself unreliable and, therefore, did not provide an adequate basis for assessing the accuracy of the later testimony, but this simply shifts the locus of the problem without altering the conclusion. It seems that although people may recall the main details of emotional events quite well there is room for considerable individual variation. How we interpret this data then depends on whether we focus on the consistencies in the reports or their inconsistencies.

Flashbulb memories without the flash

16 January 1991 was the day that US forces initiated their bombing of Iraq, and Weaver (1993) reports conducting a laboratory study (designed in advance) to ascertain whether instructing subjects to make special efforts at concentrating on an ordinary event (their next meeting with a friend) could lead them to encode the event in the same manner as the flashbulb examples. By the end of that day, therefore, Weaver was in the serendipitous position of being able to compare the long-term fate of memories created with and without "flash". Testing subjects' recall for both events, two days later and then again after an interval of one year, revealed there to be few differences between the two types of record. There was, however, one significant point of difference: although subjects were no more accurate in their recall of the public event, they were significantly more confident that what they recalled had actually happened.

Although the intensity of the emotion at the time of encoding an event appears to offer no guarantee against forgetting consequent details, memory for the inconsequential detail attending highly significant events does appear to be recalled later (quite often much later) with high levels of confidence. In this respect, at least, flashbulb memories do stand out in contrast with memory for more routine events where detail of this kind is lost quite quickly. The differential amounts of private and public rehearsal associated with highly significant events could contribute to this difference but the extent to which subjects are inclined hang on to background, contextual information suggests that this may not be the whole story. But this is to raise another instance where the experimental methods are open to question; distinguishing between the focal and background details accompanying an emotionally laden event is not as straightforward as it might at first seem.

ATTENTIONAL FOCUSING AND EMOTIONAL STIMULI

Whereas studies of flashbulb memory have concentrated upon the possibility of heightened accuracy in the resulting memory record, other studies have asked whether emotionally toned events may result in biases in attention at the time they are experienced. A number of these studies suggest, contrary to the flashbulb claims, that recall of the details of emotional events can turn out to be worse than recall for detail of neutral events. An outcome, it is argued, of the selective focusing that accompanies the induction of an affective state (Christianson & Loftus, 1991; Loftus & Burns, 1982).

Drawing upon the results of a series of experiments in which subjects were tested on their recognition accuracy for central and peripheral details relating to neutral, unusual, or emotional events, Christianson and Loftus concluded that reliable differences did exist between these conditions. First, subjects in the emotional condition recognised central detail better than subjects in the other two conditions. Second, peripheral detail was better recognised by subjects in the neutral condition. Third, subjects in the unusual condition acted like the emotional subjects with respect to the peripheral detail but failed to show any gain for the central detail. On this data, it seems that when perceiving affect-laden stimuli, subjects are prone to experience a degree of "attentional narrowing" that affects their subsequent recall.

Heuer and Reisberg (1990) have criticised both the technique and the theory behind these experiments. They argue that the procedure employed by Christianson and Loftus, whereby subjects were asked to focus on the slides by writing down the most distinguishing feature that was present, led to a selective set that is not typical of the genuine eyewitness. They also question the adequacy of the definition of central and peripheral detail which, as they stress, is hardly an absolute distinction. In a revised procedure adopted by Heuer and Reisberg, subjects watched as a story unfolded in the form of a sequence of slides accompanied by a taped narration. For the neutral version, subjects were told that the sequence depicted a boy and his mother on a visit to the father's workplace (a garage) and some of the slides depicted the father at work. In the arousal version, the same opening and closing sequence of slides was used but now the subjects were told that the father worked as a chief surgeon at the local hospital and certain slides depicted a patient's injuries. Thus, subjects in both groups saw equivalent opening and closing slides and differed only in the slides dealing with the father's workplace.

Subjects were told that the experiment dealt with "physiological reactions to different materials" (to encourage incidental learning rather than deliberate memorising) and they were given a surprise memory test after a delay of two weeks. Central information contained in the slides was defined as "everything directly relevant to plot and which could not be changed without changing the gist of the story", which left everything else as peripheral detail. The results of the memory test showed that arousal was associated with better recall for central information, but, far from being linked to a narrowing of attention, arousal also acted to enhance the range of detail attended to—producing a more detailed memory, at least when testing at this delay. A follow-up study using the same materials (Burke, Heuer, & Reisberg, 1992) showed that background detail can be selectively enhanced as a result of arousal if these details are spatially or temporally tied to the main action.

In many respects the problems associated with separating central from peripheral detail in slide sequences echo the confusions that have accompanied a debate relating to local and global inferencing during reading (see Chapter 9). This debate has hinged on the fact that intuitive analyses of the causal structure of a text need not match to the structural accounts derived from psycholinguistic analyses of the texts in question. Notably, none of the studies cited here offers anything other than a cursory or, at best, intuitive account of such structural detail. Thus, the conflicting findings concerning attentional narrowing could arise from attempts to define central versus peripheral content in the absence of a thoroughgoing causal analysis of the story content. Equally, to repeat an earlier criticism, we cannot be sure that the slide sequences did bring about the degree of arousal that was intended.

As before, a resolution of the last issue has been sought through studies that encouraged subjects to recall actual traumatic events they had experienced in their own lives. One such example is provided by Christianson and Loftus (1990) who asked volunteer subjects to report their "most traumatic memory" and to state, (1) how vivid it was, (2) how many central details they remembered, (3) how many peripheral details they remembered, (4) the strength of their emotional feeling at the time, (5) the strength of their feelings now, and (6) the type of event that was involved.

Subjects proceeded to report events like the death of a relative or involvement in traffic accidents and their ratings indicated that these memories were relatively vivid—the original emotional feeling at the time of the event was high compared to their present feelings about it. Subjects claimed to remember more central detail than peripheral detail for the event in question and overall the investigators found a significant positive correlation between the original intensity of feeling and the number of central details subjects actually recalled. In comparison, the equivalent correlation for peripheral details recalled was insignificant.

More detailed questioning was then undertaken using new subjects, this time covering such aspects of the trauma as, how long ago did it occur, how many times had it been mentally re-experienced, and how many times had it been discussed? One may doubt whether subjects could be very accurate when answering these questions but, from the figures provided, more than half of the subjects said they had thought about the event more than 10 times since it had occurred. Somewhat unexpectedly, there was no correlation between the rated emotion for different events and the number of times the experiencers said they had thought or talked about them. However, this may simply reflect their inability to quantify such data accurately.

With all the faults consequent on the use of individual introspection, this study at least indicated there were no substantial differences between the Christian and Loftus findings based on laboratory methods and those based on genuine experienced events. Nonetheless, to the extent that their subjects were retelling the story of an event that had happened to them it is perhaps not surprising that they favoured central over peripheral detail. The very act of narrating what had happened to them can be expected to bias subjects towards the retrieval of central gist—see the discussion of the "levels effect" in the next chapter.

Rather than narrowing our account in a determined pursuit of such procedural detail, we will instead attempt to open it out. This means shifting our attention away from the supposed permanence and accuracy of affect-laden memories towards considering how the presence of affective states can bring about strategic variations in ongoing cognitive processes which would not have occurred otherwise.

INTRUSIVE THOUGHTS AND THEIR SUPPRESSION

At an anecdotal level, we are all familiar with instances where negative emotional states result in a preoccupied state of mind—to the detriment of whatever else we might be doing at the time. According to data from Seibert and Ellis (1991) any mood state, whether positive or negative, can be expected to have a deleterious effect on cognitive processing which is brought about as emotion-specific thoughts interfere with the concurrent task demands. They based their conclusion on an experiment in which subjects experiencing happy, neutral, or sad moods participated in a verbal memory task under instructions to report any intrusive thoughts that accompanied their efforts at memorising. It revealed that, compared with performance under the neutral condition, both happy and sad states led to more irrelevant thoughts being reported and their presence resulted in a poorer performance on the memory task that followed.

Clearly, the subjects in this experiment were not at much risk of being seriously discommoded by the mood manipulation employed. But there are other circumstances where the presence of emotionally distracting thoughts may feature as a painful and distressing accompaniment to daily life. So painful, in fact, that sufferers may be forced to search for ways of suppressing them in order to bring them under control. If so, they may then find that their chosen suppression strategies contribute to making things worse rather than better.

When we are bothered by intrusive thoughts, one obvious strategy is to block them out by thinking of something else. Obvious it may be, but thought suppression may not work as expected, as suppressors can run the risk of actually boosting the incidence of the unwanted thoughts when the censorship is relaxed. The efficiency of suppression strategies was investigated by Wegner, Schneider, Carter, and White (1987) who planted the thought of a "white bear" in the minds of their subjects and then asked different groups of subjects either to suppress this idea by deliberately thinking of other things, or to express the thought freely. Both groups were then asked to switch to the complementary task, i.e. suppressors were to go on to think freely about "white bear" and conversely for the other group. Subjects indicated each time the target thought came to mind by ringing a bell. In the event, suppression turned out to be relatively ineffective, as subjects who had suppressed in the first phase of the experiment tended to experience a rebound effect later (Wegner, 1988, pp.691–692):

> These subjects rang the bell an average of 15.71 times and mentioned white bear an average of 14.35 times, a level significantly greater than that shown by the subjects in the expression period in the group that performed no initial suppression. The mere act of avoiding a thought for 5 minutes, it seems, made subjects oddly inclined to signal a relative outpouring of thought occurrences when they were subsequently allowed to express the thought.

During the first phase of the experiment, the suppression technique had worked more or less as intended, as suppressors indicated thinking of "white bear" on average 6.07 times in five minutes compared with subjects in an expression condition who averaged 11.82 tokens in the same time period. This advantage clearly dissipated when the tasks were switched.

The reason for this undesirable outcome is to be found in the way in which suppressors set about censoring their thoughts. They started off by recruiting other thoughts in order to block out the target content but, as no distractor is likely to work perfectly, they then had to come up with another distractor when the target thought returned, and another when that failed and so on. In the process, these distractors became converted into reminders for the target. Hence, the unfocused suppression technique created opportunities for new associations to be formed between many of the subject's current concerns (i.e. those thoughts likely to be recruited as distractors) and the unwanted thought. Far from achieving its intended aim of keeping certain ideas at bay, unfocused thought suppression effectively tied them in with the subject's current perceptions and preoccupations.

This explanation of the rebound effect suggests that suppression would be more effective if it employed a focused distraction technique where only one or a small set of distractors was used. This ploy would reduce the number of new associations to the unwanted thought and hence should lead to a scaling down of the rebound effect. In a second experiment, therefore, Wegner et al. compared subjects using unfocused suppression with another group of subjects who were instructed to use focused distraction. Under the new condition, subjects were told that whenever white bear came to mind they were to think of a red Volkswagen instead. The rebound effect was removed under this experimental treatment although we might question the practical utility of the cure. Oscillating between thoughts of white bears and red Volkswagens hardly sounds like an optimal recipe for mental tranquillity.

Wenzlaff, Wegner, and Klein (1991) have used the suppression/expression procedure as an alternative tool for investigating mood state dependent memory. Their experiments were concerned with whether the reintroduction of a mood state that had been active during a suppression phase could also create a rebound of thoughts about the suppressed item. Mood was manipulated by playing music either at the time of suppression or at expression, and it was found that suppressors did indeed show a greater rebound effect consistent with the mood state dependent hypothesis. They then tested the association between suppression and mood from the other direction. This time, the question at issue was whether subjects who suppressed when in a particular mood would find that mood reinstated when the target thought could be freely expressed. This prediction was also confirmed.

As Wenzlaff et al. point out, their experimental procedures offer an alternative and more disciplined way of looking at mood state dependent memory compared with the standard research methods that have tended to come up with equivocal results. Unlike the simple (and tenuous) associations created between thoughts and moods typical of the standard procedure, the technique of thought suppression (Wenzlaff et al., 1991, p.506):

> ... creates a unique integration of thought and mood, a bonding based on the frequent choice of mood related distractors and on the proneness of such distractors later to become reminders of the once-suppressed thought.

There are, of course, other ways than suppression for dealing with the intrusive thoughts generated by unpleasant experiences. Yet another strategy is to try to defuse the intensity of the experience either at the time or later. According to Freud (1905), humour can serve as an effective defence mechanism in this respect by enabling us to face a difficult situation without becoming overwhelmed by unpleasant emotions. More recent work, e.g. Lefcourt and Martin (1986); Nezu, Nezu, and Blissett (1988), suggests that Freud was probably correct when he associated humour with the mitigation of negative events.

HUMOUR

Psychological analyses of humour are not exactly thick on the ground but Wyer and Collins (1992) have argued that humour arises as a byproduct of the schematic processing accompanying comprehension. The events that we are inclined to find funny are those that require an unexpected change in the assimilatory schema. From this perspective, jokes are understood and appreciated through the same schematic processes that apply to comprehension in general. However, once the punch line of the joke has been delivered this results in a mismatch to the assimilatory schema, forcing us to seek out an alternative schema that will do a better job. The experience of humour resides in the way in which the new schema prompts a reinterpretation of the original information. Needless to say, as not all cases of schema mismatch strike us as funny, there must be other factors that are also relevant.

Drawing on earlier work by Apter (1982), Wyer and Collins identified three factors that must accompany schematic processing if the input is to be judged funny; (1) the initial and the new interpretation must continue to coexist, (2) the new interpretation must lead to a downgrading in the perceived importance of the first interpretation, and (3) the subject's primary goal is to understand and enjoy what is being said or done. They also added two more factors of their own; (4) the degree of difficulty in arriving at a reinterpretation influences the level of humour involved, and (5) the degree of elaboration that follows on from the reinterpretation also contributes to the humorous effect. According to Wyer and Collins, most forms of humour from puns to shaggy dog stories, can be readily understood within this framework.

Although Wyer and Collins have indicated how the phenomenon of humour could be brought within the scope of an information-processing framework, their analysis does not go very far towards explaining why humour should mitigate the effects of negative experiences. Downgrading the perceived importance of an event could be helpful in this respect but so too could be the way in which humour serves as a safety fuse for terminating thought patterns that have begun to spiral out of control.

METACOGNITIVE CENSORSHIP

As we are far more likely to try to suppress intrusive thoughts deriving from negative mood states than those arising from positive mood states, there is the potential here for individuals to become locked into a vicious cycle. Negative moods engender repeated suppressive attempts only to recruit more cues capable of reinstating the unwanted mental contents. An intriguing possibility, therefore, is that humour is an example of a metacognitive procedure whose purpose is to enable us to skirt around such traps and pitfalls by aborting the activities involved. In fact, abort procedures of this kind could be of general use to the cognitive system in providing a means for keeping reasoning in check by damping down potentially disruptive chains of thought.

Minsky (1984) has speculated along these lines in positing the existence of a number of (unconscious) metacognitive skills which act to disentangle the mental knots that would be caused by an unregulated application of computational algorithms. These metaskills would be useful, not only for regulating negative affective states, but also for regulating reasoning itself. If reasoning is to maintain its effectiveness, it needs to be backed up by unconscious mechanisms which can act to prevent the process going out of control—as would happen if we tried to pursue a paradoxical line of argument to its logical ends. Individuals who cannot rest until they have arrived at a definitive solution to the chicken or egg conundrum would be in need of precisely this form of restraint. More prosaically, it also bears on the exercise of our mundane common sense which presupposes that we have ways of avoiding placing too great a reliance on the uncertain and limited bodies of knowledge that are normally our lot.

Suppose, therefore, that we could mark out the potential traps and loops that bring cognitive nonsense in their wake through the activity of "intellectual censors", analogous to the Freudian censors that keep emotional traps at bay. These intellectual censors would then serve to keep common sense reasoning on target by defending us against the lure of logical paradoxes. But, if such mechanisms do exist, how might they operate? As we have seen, censorship based on suppressing thoughts after they have occurred can be a risky process. Somewhat more effective would be to prevent the suspect thoughts arising in the first place. With this arrangement, recourse to suppression would be left as a last resource because an early warning system would transmit alarm signals when it detected the precursors of meandering or circular thought patterns. And, if these censors did their job effectively, we need never notice their presence.

At this point in his argument, Minsky (rather quaintly) comes up with the suggestion that humour could have evolved for the purpose of providing a socially acceptable means of alerting others to potential bugs in their reasoning. He also suggests (more plausibly) that humour could serve as a self-regulatory mechanism capable of disrupting or aborting a line of thought that has started to go badly wrong. Thus, for Minsky (1984, p.193), humour is a serious matter intimately tied in with the maintainance of cognitive hygiene:

Jokes are not really funny at all but reflect the most serious of concerns; the pursuit of sobriety through the suppression of the absurd.

There is something not entirely right with this argument. Taken literally, it implies that all those individuals who survive, and indeed flourish, without any apparent sense of humour whatsoever should have self-destructed long before they came to work with you. Nonetheless, Minsky's recruitment of humour into the armoury of metacognitive skills contributing to cognitive balance is an interesting proposal meriting wider discussion than it has received so far.

Wegner (1994) has also reflected on the fact that mental control seems to require, not only processes that search for a desired mental state, but complementary processes that continually monitor for the presence of mental contents inconsistent with a target state. He notes (1994, p.34) that under certain circumstances, these two types of process can combine to produce "ironic consequences" as when the very opposite of what we seek occurs. The rebound effect associated with unfocused thought suppression would be a case in point and there are many others:

> We stay awake worrying that we cannot sleep and we spend all day mentally in the refrigerator when we are hoping to diet.

According to Wegner, it is no coincidence that ironic effects of this nature should occur. If monitoring mechanisms attuned to undesired mental content exist there is always the danger that resource limitations will allow them to break through into the foreground. Once this happens their output can then determine the contents of consciousness and we are left to reflect on another of life's little ironies.

Should we be faced with one of life's big ironies, on the other hand, the experience may be so traumatic that there is absolutely no way it can be laughed off. Neither the strongest sense of humour nor the most sophisticated control processes can guarantee us complete protection from the vicissitudes of life and there will always be some unfortunate victims who are faced with making sense of truly horrific life-events. Observing how they cope with the aftermath of disaster has thrown light on another facet of the interaction between affect and cognition.

TRAUMATIC LIFE-EVENTS
AND ASSUMPTIVE SCHEMAS

All of us are inclined to temper our sense of personal vulnerability to external threat by holding to particular assumptions about the world. These assumptions serve to moderate our expectations of being caught up in life-threatening events by pointing to circumstances under which they are unlikely to happen. Taken collectively, they form an "assumptive world schema" whose prime function is to bring the harsh realities of the real world into some form of alignment with our subjective probabilities (see Janoff-Bulman, 1992). If we assume that good and bad outcomes are determined by a principle of justice, (people get their just deserts), then it is the sort of person we are—decent or malign—that determines whether we are likely to be on the receiving end of negative events. Consequently, our vulnerability to physical or mental harm can be reduced by resolving to become a better person in future. If we assume that good or bad outcomes are distributed as a function, not so much of underlying character, but according to our outward behaviour then by taking the appropriate precautionary measures we can hope to control for the occurrence of negative outcomes. Even if we assume that the distribution of good and bad outcomes is purely a matter of chance, so that neither inner decency nor prudent behaviour can influence what is likely to happen to us, we may still console ourselves with the thought that we are part of the lucky few. Blind chance may deal the hand but those annointed lucky can expect to be shielded from the extreme vulnerability this would seem to imply.

Individuals who believe themselves to be good and decent people will feel less vulnerable in a just world. Individuals who take pride in their foresight will feel less vulnerable in a controllable world. The plain lucky will expect to be elsewhere when lightning strikes. But it can still happen that, despite our virtuous lifestyle, despite our careful planning, and despite our charms and talismans, our luck simply runs out. At this point, we can then be on the receiving end of events that test such assumptions about the world to breaking point.

Where negative experiences are so extreme that they threaten the whole assumptive edifice and its foundations, victims can then be put under great pressure as they try to assimilate the new information while striving to maintain the integrity of their assumptive world. Under such conditions, Janoff-Bulman suggests the symptoms of post-traumatic stress disorder (PTSD) can be expected to arise as outward signs of the assumptive schemas moving towards re-establishing their inner equilibrium. In the aftermath of a major negative event, we may thus find victims displaying inordinate levels of self-blame by taking responsibilities upon their own shoulders that the outsider would consider unreasonable. Or again, participants in such events may reinterpret what has happened to them in positive terms—even to the point of their being especially valued for the timely lessons they provide. In each case, the response can be interpreted as part of a process of assimilation in which the new information is being reworked into a form where it becomes more compatible with the content of the prior schema. By blaming their behaviour (not themselves), victims may minimise the extent to which schematic change is necessary because, in the future, whatever actions were at fault can be carefully avoided. Reinterpreting the features of a negative event in a more positive light (learning the lessons of experience) can also help by reinforcing our efforts at making the necessary repairs.

Other symptoms of victimisation such as denial and recurrent intrusive flashbacks can be seen, not so much as part of the process of assimilation, but as coping modes that give re-equilibration the "space" in which to work its effects. Denial adds to the time over which the necessary repairs can be made although, if it were total, no repair would be possible. Flashbacks are the other side of the coin, and they serve to reinstate the critical information in active memory where it can enter into new modes of interpretation as we focus upon different features each time. In other words, the often bizarre symptomatology associated with PTSD can be interpreted as the outward signs that schema reorganisation and updating are underway.

SOCIAL CONFIDING

Retelling the story of what happened to sympathetic others can also help victims accommodate to their lot as, with each retelling, the possibility of pulling an otherwise inchoate experience into a meaningful shape increases. Each time the story is constructed, the component details need to be called to mind and reintegrated as a whole. Consequently, we can expect to find social confiding acting as another route that is taken by victims in their quest to regain their mental equilibrium. When Pennebaker and O'Heeron (1984) investigated the subsequent behaviour of a sample of subjects who had suffered serious setbacks, they found a significant relationship between their degree of self-disclosure to others and the severity of their later reactions to the initiating event.

Subjects who reported talking more to others about their spouse's death were the ones who showed fewer health problems in the following year. And the more they talked and expressed their feelings, the less they ruminated about the event. Although these observations are hardly conclusive concerning the value of social confiding or why it should work, they are consistent with the iterative, piecemeal nature of knowledge updating discussed elsewhere. Assimilating the significance of a traumatic event (by definition an extensive task) cannot be accomplished overnight, not least because of the sheer amount of detail that will need to be worked through. The loss of a spouse will literally affect all aspects of the bereaved person's life and activating even part of that background in the context of the loss will inevitably take time and effort. Retelling the story of a traumatic event, whether to others or by writing up a purely personal account, allows for the concurrent activation of old and new knowledge and for the possibility of their potential resolution. Even then, it may well be necessary to renarrate an event many times before "ripple effects" have been smoothed out of the record. Viewed from this perspective, it is to be expected that the victims of calamitous events often feel compelled to tell their story and continue to experience this compulsion despite many retellings.

CODA

Despite methodological problems, the data cited in this chapter point to a number of ways in which our affective states can impact on the course of cognitive processing. Such states can influence how we attend to the world; how we are likely to recall the events we have experienced; and, in extreme cases, they can lock our cognitive resources onto discrepant information and thus increase the likelihood that it will be successfully assimilated.

The exchanges between affect and cognition may often be counter-productive but it seems we would fare even worse if they did not exist at all. As it is, they can work in tandem with cognitive mechanisms by focusing new learning on those features of our experiences that appear to be most relevant for repairing and updating significant gaps in our current states of knowledge. Nonetheless, human agents can be proactive as well as reactive. We are eminently capable of seeking out particular experiences with the aim of adding new entries to our pool of knowledge and (with rather less eminence) we can proceed to question and evaluate any of this existing content. How we set about accomplishing these particular ends furnishes us with the central topics of the next section.

SECTION THREE

Acquiring and manipulating knowledge

CHAPTER NINE

Management of text comprehension

As we become fluent at speaking and reading so we gain access to the accumulated body of learning contained within our culture. We learn from experience but our experiences need not be confined to our current circumstances; we can also learn vicariously from the experiences of others through being told about what they have seen and done. In consequence, a significant proportion of our knowledge is acquired indirectly through discourse with others, including the reading of texts whose authors may have long since left the scene.

The aim of this chapter is to explore how written text can act as a source of new information for the reader. There are many levels on which this question can be addressed (Gernsbacher, 1994, provides a good summary) but we will bypass work relating to word recognition and grammatical parsing in order to concentrate on how the reader extracts meaning from a text as a whole. Even working with this restriction in mind, we will find that keeping track of all that is going on is quite sufficient to test our our cognitive models and tools to their limits.

TEXT TYPES

Although it is possible, more or less, to get agreement on what is a letter, a word, or a grammatical sentence, the process of separating text from non-text is not so straightforward. Beyond the claim that there should be some degree of referential coherence between the component sentences, definitions are likely to diverge. Even so, we do have an intuitive sense of when we are reading connected discourse as opposed to random sentences and this intuition implies that there are structural patterns underlying the various forms that discourse can adopt.

Brewer (1980) has distinguished three types of written discourse structure (descriptive, narrative, and expository) and four types of discourse force (informative, entertaining, persuasive, and literary/ aesthetic). He proposed that each text type serves a different expressive purpose and each gives rise to its own characteristic memory representation. Descriptions are predominantly concerned with the details of stationary perceptual scenes and their primary function is to generate a visuo-spatial encoding in memory. Expositions deal mainly with logically organised information and give rise to representations that are intended to draw extensively on the products of formal reasoning. Narratives refer to a series of related events as they unfold over time. Their representation in memory is based on whatever storyline the reader has been able to construct from the causal chains linking one episode to another.

As the same basic text structure can serve different rhetorical ends, the author's communicative intentions are also relevant to a classification of text types. A narrative may set out to inform the reader (e.g. an historical narrative), to entertain (a detective story), to persuade (an advertisement), or it may lay claim to literary or aesthetic merit (a "literary novel"). Obviously, at this point, the distinctions are starting to become extremely fuzzy. However, the taxonomy is intended to be used as a rough guide not as a precise literary tool.

Applying this classificatory framework to the published work on text comprehension reveals that to date, the research endeavour has been highly selective. Most investigations have concentrated upon memory and comprehension for narratives while descriptions and expositions have been relatively neglected. Similarly, studies of discourse force also show a markedly skewed distribution where the processing of aesthetic texts has been almost completely ignored. To a large extent, these invest- igative biases reflect the very real complexities awaiting any investig- ator who dares to stray from using other than purely banal stories. But this cannnot be the only reason. After all, we do not have to look very hard to find examples of banal descriptions and expositions. Rather, over and above experimental convenience, there is an immediacy and fluency to narrative comprehension which appears to mark it out from the other textual forms. We will revert to this aspect of narrative comprehension at the end of the chapter. In the meantime, we will put textual distinctions to one side in order to examine how readers set about establishing the semantic coherence inherent in all types of text.

COHERENCE IN TEXT

In the discussion of propositional encoding outlined in Chapter 2, it was stated that a sentence may be understood and remembered by abstracting its propositional content. According to Kintsch and his associates, (Kintsch, 1974, 1988; van Dijk & Kintsch, 1983) as the reader progresses through a text, sentence by sentence, the meaning is abstracted in the form of a propositional listing. This listing is then analysed for argument overlap in order to create the "text base" that constitutes a record of the text that is laid down in memory. For example, when we read a series of sentences such as:

1. John went to London
2. He cursed the train
3. It was dirty

we come to comprehend the content by abstracting the propositions contained in the individual statements and by registering their overlap. This may require us to infer new propositions in order to maintain overlap. In this example, sentences 1 and 2 can be linked if we infer the implicit proposition [Travel, John, Train].

Having identified the relevant propositions, we can then go on to use their shared arguments in order to arrange the content in hierarchical order of importance and arrive at a macrostructure. The main topic comes in at the top level of the macrostructure and subsequent elaborations on this theme come in at lower levels. For the brief account of John's travels this gives us something like:

Level 1. [Go, John, London] (Main Topic)
Level 2. [Travel, John, Train]; [Curse, John, Train]
Level 3. [Dirty, Train]

Proposition 1 [Go, John, London] serves as the main topic at the top level of the hierarchy; other propositions, whose arguments overlap with the arguments represented on level 1, come in at the next level down, and similarly for the lower levels of the hierarchy. The resulting text base and its macrostructure then serve as a record of the text meaning in memory. Although this account leaves a number of important issues such as referential meaning unaddressed, we will elaborate on this aspect later. For now, it provides a useful framework for distinguishing between local and global processes in text comprehension.

Local coherence in text

Detecting argument overlap in a text base can be a convoluted processs but it is essential if the reader is to understand how consecutive sentences relate to each other. Quite often we find that the relevant conceptual content may not be foregrounded at the time an overlap occurs and the reader then needs to engage in search and reinstatement operations to make good the deficiency. This is especially likely when the reader comes across pronominal terms in the text. Pronominals such as "who" or "it" are common to all types of text and their presence necessitates careful and focused search if a correct antecedent is to be identified and the thread of continuity maintained.

In the example just given, the pronoun "he" in sentence 2 referred anaphorically to "John" and the device enabled the writer to streamline the transfer of information to the reader by avoiding tedious repetition. This will only work provided adequate cues are available that can guide readers to an unambiguous resolution. Even then, when locating the intended referent, readers must marshal their resources as best they can. Successful resolution can require (1) the application of general knowledge, (2) the use of surface syntactic cues such as the number and gender of pronouns, (3) cognisance of the topic that is currently foregrounded, and (4) the introduction of bridging inferences to supplement the given text. All told, it is remarkable that for many instances solutions are found at all, let alone found with the practised ease of the fluent reader.

One of the first experiments to study local coherence operations on line during reading was carried out by Haviland and Clark (1974). The experiment focused on the "given–new" distinction which assumes that a sentence can be partitioned into a component conveying given or old information and a component introducing new information. To forge a link between these items of information the reader may have to make a bridging inference, as illustrated here:

1.   Mary unpacked the picnic things
2.   The beer was warm.

The use of the definite article in "The beer" marks this information as given despite there being no previous explicit mention and it is left to the reader to bridge the gap. Haviland and Clark found that the presence of such bridging requirements resulted in longer reading times for the sentences concerned compared with other sentences where the given information had previously been made explicit.

Even when target information has been stated explicitly, subsequent reference to this content may be difficult to process if the target is no longer in conceptual focus. For example, consider a text cited in Webber (1980, p.154):

> While driving through a game reserve I passed a pregnant zebra, though I almost didn't notice her. Then on, past enormous termite nests and a river full of hippopotami, before I came to our camp. She looked like a distended Moiré pattern.

Here "zebra" is awkwardly referenced and we are likely to flounder for a while as we sort out exactly what "she" refers to. The problem arises because of the scene changes intervening between the referent and its pronoun which act to displace the target concept from working memory and to replace it with new entries. As a result the reader is forced to search through the text base in order to reinstate the critical content.

Such textual demands can be extremely subtle because different textual elements will vary in their susceptibility to displacement following a change of scene. The central character in a text (the protagonist) can move freely from one scene to another and still remain in the foreground, but scene-dependent, peripheral characters may enjoy only a brief moment at centre stage before they recede into the background when the scene changes. These comings and goings play an important part in keeping a storyline moving along and the reader needs to be alert and responsive to quite small nuances if local coherence is to be maintained (Sanford & Garrod, 1981).

Local coherence and reading span

Although establishing local coherence may seem effortless and automatic for the fluent reader, less skilled readers who have difficulty keeping relevant textual detail in conceptual focus are likely to find themselves at a significant disadvantage when confronted by other than the simplest texts. Following the discussion of immediate memory capacity, we might expect measures such as digit span to be capable of predicting the textual range within which individual readers can maintain local coherence. In fact, Daneman and Carpenter (1980) found that this measure was a poor predictor of individual differences in performance when resolving anaphoric references.

The main reason for this failure is because during reading, working memory is called upon to do rather more than just store text content. It also needs to support the search processes contributing to local coherence described earlier. Digit or word span measures address the storage component of the reading skill but they fail to incorporate a processing component. Consequently, Daneman and Carpenter have proposed a different measure, "reading span", designed to tap into the individual's storage and processing capacity at the same time.

Reading span is measured by presenting a subject with a set of, say, two sentences, that has to be read out loud. Once the first sentence has been read, the subject tries to hold in memory its last word while moving on to read the next sentence in the set whose terminal word is also added to working memory. Having completed the set the subject then recalls the two terminal words. Individual differences in reading span are assessed by gradually increasing the size of the sentence set until the subject is failing to recall the terminal words correctly. Applying this procedure to a population of college students, Daneman and Carpenter found that reading span rarely fell below two or extended beyond six terminal words.

Unlike its predecessors, reading span has turned out to be a remarkably exact predictor of the textual range over which a reader can match an anaphor to its antecedent. Subjects with a reading span of five or more were completely accurate at locating anaphoric antecedents over small, medium, and large tracts of text. Span 4 subjects showed a significant drop in accuracy for large distances and subjects with the lowest spans showed an additional deterioration over the middle distance. A similar relationship has also been found between reading span and text comprehension. Low-span subjects made by far the most errors when questioned on the text meaning. However, the overall correlation between reading span and comprehension level ($r = +.59$) was not as impressive as the reported correlation with anaphoric resolution, ($r = +.90$).

Processing text macrostructure

There is more to text comprehension than just establishing its local coherence. A competent reader will also go on to register the text's global properties or macrostructure. Should we be asked to recall a text after a delay, inevitably we will have forgotten some of the content during the interval. Which content will be lost or retained is no random matter—thematically relevant content is retained at the expense of peripheral content—and content relevance is determined by its place within the relevant macrostructure.

This highly selective pattern at recall has been demonstrated in various ways. Johnson (1970), for example, used a deletion procedure to demonstrate differential accuracy at recall for important and unimportant text content. In the first phase of his experiment, the locations of major pauses during normal reading were used to mark the occurrence of clause boundaries in the text. Next, using texts where these divisions were clearly marked, three groups of subjects were instructed to eliminate 25%, 50%, or 75% of the story content by removing the least important units. Thus, the units selected under a 25% reduction demand were likely to be those of least importance. Units dropped under the 50% and 75% demands defined the next two levels of importance and the units that survived to the end were those with the greatest structural importance. At this stage, therefore, Johnson was able to assign each phrase in the text to one of four levels of importance.

In the final phase of the experiment, the original, unsegmented texts were given to a new group of subjects under instructions to read for immediate or delayed recall. On both occasions, accuracy of recall was significantly correlated with the level originally assigned to the text content. Readers, it seems, can not only abstract propositional content during comprehension, they also determine where this content fits within the text's macrostructure.

Story macrostructures function very much like knowledge schemas. Once activated they facilitate subsequent reading by providing a framework within which the text content can be assessed. It is at this level that differences in text type can be distinguished, as each type tends towards a particular canonical form. As regular readers of scientific articles soon come to appreciate, journal articles follow a characteristic pattern that is not met elsewhere. The reader who recognises the constituents of this pattern can use the information both to "home in" on specific features of an experimental report and to arrive at a global impression of the argument as a whole. Other types of text make use of different macrostructures and we will now focus on narrative macrostructures as they participate in the processes of story comprehension and recall.

STORY GRAMMARS AND SCHEMAS

At minimum, a story could consist of just one episode; a central character attempts to reach a goal and then either succeeds or fails in the attempt. More typically, this minimal form is embellished in various ways— perhaps by supplying additional detail about the setting in which the action takes place, or by introducing obstacles that require detours on the way to the main goal. Each embellishment serves to fill out the story in a particular way and, just as the constituent structure of a grammatical sentence can be captured using generative rules, so too the macrostructure of narratives has been attributed to the application of rules for combining their constituent parts.

Thorndyke (1977) was the first to adopt this "story grammar" approach, arguing that stories are generated from basic constituents such as a theme, setting, plot, and resolution, which are combined according to the generative rules set out in Table 9.1.

The theme specifies the primary goal underlying a protagonist's actions and the plot unfolds as a series of episodes in which the protagonist takes steps towards achieving the main goal. A reader in possession of such a generic macrostructure will be primed to expect particular kinds of information at different points in the narrative. When we find ourselves embarking upon a new episode, we can expect to be informed about whatever subgoal is operative, the attempts made at reaching the goal, and how they turned out.

The case for parsing narrative macrostructures along the lines set out in Table 9.1 has attracted many critics and the status of story grammars in recent psycholinguistic theory is much diminished (e.g. Harley, 1995). Nonetheless, although the analogy between rules for generating sentences and rules for generating stories may be weak, the constituent units they employ, such as episodes and settings, have been shown to play a distinctive role in the encoding and retrieval of text content.

Episodic structures and causal chains

Haberlandt (1980) and Haberlandt, Berian, and Sanson, (1980), asked subjects to read stories based on two well formed episodes under conditions where they read each sentence at their own rate. Generally, it was found that the reading time for a sentence beginning an episode was slowed down, as compared with the reading times for other sentences and, to a lesser extent, the reading time for the concluding sentence of an episode was also relatively retarded. Surface cues in the

TABLE 9.1
Extracts from a story grammar

Story	=>	Setting + Theme + Plot + Resolution
Setting	=>	Characters + Location + Time
Theme	=>	(Event)* + Goal
Plot	=>	Episode*
Episode	=>	Subgoal + Attempt* + Outcome
( ) = Optional (*) = Repeatable		

Based on Thorndyke, 1977.

text such as "one day" enabled the reader to recognise when a new episode had begun and reading time slowed at this point in response to the additional processing demands associated with formulating the appropriate expectations. Other surface cues such as "and then" were treated as a signal that the episode had finished and at this point the reader proceeded to wrap up the whole package of information in the form of an episodic unit.

Mandler and Goodman (1982) have reported similar variations in reading times along with evidence that story episodes function as discrete encoding units in memory. Using cued sentence recall, they showed that subjects were faster at recalling the next sentence when the cue was drawn from the same episode than when it fell within another episode. Retrieval latency was about 340msec slower when the cue and the target sentence featured in separate episodes, as though readers were crossing a structural boundary created by treating the individual episodes as discrete encoding units.

As stories rarely come in the form of one or two episodes, it is encumbent on the reader not only to register when an episode has occurred, but also to register how a series of episodes are causally related to each other as the tale progresses. In formal terms, a causal link can be registered whenever two events occur and it is the case that if the first event had not occurred then, in the circumstances, the second event would not have occurred either (van den Broek, 1994). In practice, the causal links in a text may be inferred by readers employing their general knowledge of physical causality or their common-sense knowledge of psychological motivation. Following this inferential work, the reader should be in a good position to articulate the central causal chain that links the beginning episode of a story to its concluding episode.

Not all episodes in a story need be part of the main causal chain. There will be certain episodes that push the storyline along while others exist as mere spur lines leading off the main track and fluent readers are able to register this distinction during normal reading (Trabasso & Sperry, 1985). Events that participate in the narrative spine have an initiating cause and they serve to introduce consequences that are important for later events. Events that are not part of the chain are those that lack an initiating cause or that fail to move the narrative forward. As a result, each event can be indexed in terms of its centrality to the gist of the story and the extent of its connections to other events making up the causal chain. Both of these indices have been shown by Trabasso and Sperry to have a bearing on how the reader encodes the story events. They can be used to predict the content likely to be reproduced at recall and the importance ratings that readers attribute to different parts of the text.

Story settings and mental models

The setting of a narrative specifies the spatio-temporal framework within which the reported action takes place. Given this information, we can then proceed to draw spatial inferences which serve to bring the story details together in the form of a mental model. At which point, we may then find it difficult to distinguish between spatial information that was specifically stated and spatial information that had to be inferred in order to construct the model (Bransford, Barclay, & Franks, 1972). Temporal inferences may also be used in the construction of the model and when this happens they are co-ordinated with whatever spatial inferences have been made in parallel (Meringoff, 1980). Setting details, therefore, are important in enabling us to create a mental world within which the story events take place. Consequently, as these events come and go, the reader is faced with updating the model to keep in step with the story action.

Morrow, Greenspan, and Bower (1987) claim that readers engage in extensive updating of their situation models as they monitor how story characters interact and move around their fictional world. They suggest that as the "Here and Now" point changes (i.e. the current location of the protagonist), the situation model is continually adjusted to accommodate what has happened. Morrow et al. based these claims on an experiment in which subjects first memorised a ground plan of a building and then read about a protagonist moving around the building in the course of his work, where each change in location served to alter the Here/Now point in the story. Thus, subjects who had just read that "Wilbur walked from the experimental room into the reception room" experienced a shift in the Here/Now point from the Source room (Experimental) to the Goal room (Reception). The aim of the experiment was to determine the state of the subject's mental model at this point.

This was achieved by presenting subjects with probe sentences designed to compare the relative accessibility of objects in the old and new locations. Each probe sentence named two objects from the building and the subject judged whether the two objects were from the same room or from different rooms. If updating of the Here/Now point had accompanied the comprehension of the relevant sentence then reaction times to source room objects (which have moved out of focus) should be slower than the reaction times to goal room objects (which have come into focus). Using this measure, Morrow et al. found that their subjects were quickest to respond when the test probes involved objects associated with the protagonist's current location. A subsequent study (Morrow, Bower, & Greenspan, 1989), further demonstrated that even a projected mental location (as when Wilbur merely thinks about going into another room) had a significant effect on the reaction time measures.

Note that, unlike the experiments conducted by Franklin and Tversky described in Chapter 3, the subjects in the present experiments were not specifically instructed to make dependent changes in their situation model as the text moved along. That they made these changes anyway seems to imply that detailed updating of the mental model is part of the normal reading process. Later on we will have cause to question this conclusion. For now, there is another implication from the present data that needs to be considered. The situation model, it seems, can not only be constructed around setting detail, it can also be built around the protagonist's thoughts and plans.

Plans, goals, and plot units

Readers can use information about a character's thoughts to infer why a character behaved in a certain way. Stories are frequently unclear about the immediate intentions of their main characters and under these circumstances we may then seek to adopt their perspective within the story as a means of inferring their current intentions. When functioning on this level, Abbott and Black (1986) suggest that readers make use of representational units constructed around a character's intended goals. These representational units are made up from three components; the Source of the goal, the Goal itself, and the Plan chosen for reaching the goal. Once activated, SGP units assist story comprehension by directing the reader's attention to whichever text details bear upon an actor's current intentions.

The claim is based on the observation that Source, Goal, and Plan information function as an integral unit at recall. The reader who recalls that a character was motivated by a particular goal is likely to accompany this information with a reason for desiring this goal and a possible plan of action. The likelihood of a subject recalling part of an SPG unit when cued by some other part averaged around ($r = +.82$)—a correlation that was significantly higher than that obtained from the joint recall of sentences linked through argument repetition ($r = +.38$).

If SGP units participate in story comprehension, this raises the further possibility that they can combine together to form more complex encoding structures, much as episodes can combine to form causal sequences. This aspect of story comprehension has been investigated by Lehnert (1981) who isolated the typical plot lines that emerged as different characters interacted over the course of a story. Thus, one common plot structure in narrative occurs when character A's success rests on character B's failure—the staple diet of the fictional potboiler. Other plot lines will arise in a similar manner as the characters engage in different patterns of interaction. Altogether, Lehnert identified 15 basic plot lines whose presence made a significant contribution to the reader's interpretation of story coherence.

To take a genuine, literary example, Lehnert (1981, p.315) refers to a story by O. Henry (*The gift of the Magi*) which consists of:

> ... a story about a young couple who want to buy each other Christmas presents. They are both very poor. Della has long beautiful hair, and Jim has a prized pocket watch. To get money for presents, Della sells her hair and Jim sells his pocket watch. Then, she buys him a gold chain for his watch, and he buys her an expensive ornament for her hair. When they find out what they've done, they are consoled by the love behind each other's sacrifices.

This story is nicely symmetrical because the motivations of the actors and the things that they do, while appearing in conflict at the time of the exchange of the gifts, are eventually resolved through the "hidden blessing" that emerges at the end.

Using this general framework, Lehnert has been able to predict how subjects set about constructing summaries of the stories they have read. She has also demonstrated that readers are likely to detect similarities between stories that differ in surface detail but share common plot units—as found, say, between *Romeo and Juliet* and *West Side Story*. This is an observation that may have prompted a reminder in the reader of what Schank has had to say about similar matters.

Thematic abstraction units (TAUs)

It will be recalled that Schank attributed the phenomenon of reminding to different experiences being linked together as a result of activating common processing structures during comprehension. His theory of dynamic memory organisation postulated a family of knowledge structures, all available for processing experienced events, including structures operating on the abstract level occupied by Lehnert's plot units.

In Schank's terminology, TAU structures (Thematic Abstraction Units) function by registering the presence of common themes underlying different events. The theme "An eye for an eye and a tooth for a tooth" can apply equally well to interactions between individuals or to diplomatic exchanges between countries. Hence TAUs provide the reader with access to abstract knowledge structures which can be generalised across a range of different contexts. And just as Lehnert has provided evidence that readers are sensitive to the particular plot units associated with narratives, Seifert and Black (1983) have shown that readers can also register when similar thematic structures are present in different stories. Their subjects were able to create new stories serving as different exemplars of the same TAU and, when confronted by multiple stories based on different TAUs, their subjects were able to sort them into the appropriate thematic categories.

If TAU structures are active during normal reading then we can expect readers to be spontaneously reminded of an earlier story when they come across a new version constructed around the same theme. This prediction was tested by Seifert, McKoon, Abelson, and Ratcliff (1986) who presented their subjects with a sequence of discrete texts, some of which were thematically similar, while checking for evidence of priming effects. A typical experimental sequence consisted of an initial story concerning a student who transferred from one college to another because the first institute had let him down. The student's withdrawal galvanises the first college to promise better things in future, but too late, the decision had been made. In a second story that followed some time later, a girl is described as breaking off her engagement to her unenthusiastic boyfriend and becoming engaged to another boy. This action provokes the former boyfriend to promise to do better, but again, too late. Both stories share the theme of "closing the stable door after the horse has bolted" and, on the analysis just described, a subject reading the second story should experience priming of the memory record for the first story due to this common link. As matters turned out, although priming effects were obtained for sentences drawn from the same story, Seifert et al. found no evidence for spontaneous priming occurring across thematically linked stories. Thematic priming was only observed where subjects had been specifically instructed to look for this common link.

Subsequently, McKoon, Ratcliff, and Seifert (1989) suggested that the failure to obtain thematic priming may have arisen because there was too little content overlap in the stories employed. Accordingly they turned to new stories made up from the set of scenes associated with the achievement of the same goal (i.e. stories sharing the same MOP). This time one story dealt with "Linda going to the beach" and the second story dealt with Mary doing the same thing. Each story contained beach-related scenes, albeit expressed in slightly different terms. Where one story referred to "putting on lotion", its paired version referred to "splashing on oil". Altogether, subjects read in the region of 40 stories which could be paired through their common MOPs and it was arranged that members of a pair were never separated by less than eight different stories.

After reading through the full set of stories, subjects were presented with test phrases which were to be judged as true or false for the stories as read. The priming conditions of interest were (a) when two consecutive test phrases came from the same story; (b) when they were from different stories forming a pair; and (c) when they came from unconnected stories. The results indicated that priming occurred under conditions (a) and (b) but not under (c). Thus this data supported a more constrained interpretation of the reminding hypothesis.

On the surface, these findings appear similar to the results reported by Gick and Holyoak (1983) concerning the detection of analogies as described in Chapter 6. There, it was stated that the registration of underlying similarities between inputs differing in surface detail did not always occur spontaneously. For this to apply, Gick and Holyoak found it necessary to bring the underlying theme more sharply into focus by using analogical stories employing very different contexts. Only then was it more likely than not that the connection would be made. Thus, studies of remindings across thematically related stories and analogical problem solving agree on there being definite constraints on whether reminding will occur. But the constraints are quite different in the two cases. For Gick and Holyoak, facilitation in the use of an analogy was greater when the prior stories agreed at the thematic (TAU) level than when they were drawn from scenes relating to a common goal (MOP level). On Seifert and McKoon's data the link between two stories sharing a common TAU structure was less likely to be made than where they shared a common MOP.

Of course, the experimental designs were different and they could rely upon different psychological operations. Possibly, simply priming an item of information in memory during reading provides insufficient activation for its use in overt problem solving. This argument would lay one source of inconsistency to rest but it still leaves something of a puzzle. Seifert and McKoon's priming effects may have been too weak to bring information above the threshold where it could be put to practical use, but why should information that is put to use (thematically different analogical stories) fail to show any priming effects at all during the course of normal reading?

One resolution of this issue would be to acknowledge that during normal reading (as opposed to strategic problem solving) there are stringent constraints on the degree of reminding that is likely to exist. Certainly, without some constraints there would be no end to the process as reminders triggered further reminders; we need to be protected from distractions just as much as we need to be reminded of relevant information. In which case, we can draw a distinction between reading under normal conditions and reading with a special purpose in mind. But this distinction then brings into question the status of the varied encoding strategies we have met with in this discussion. Do they all form an integral part of the normal reading process or may some have been enlisted by the specialised requirements of the experimental tasks employed to demonstrate their presence?

LOCAL VERSUS GLOBAL INFERENCING

In the course of this review of narrative comprehension, we have seen a major proliferation in the processes said to be involved. Despite taking the earlier stages in comprehension such as word identification and sentence parsing for granted, we still find that the strategies associated with local and global coherence have burgeoned into Gothic proportions. Parsing stories into episodic units led on to the identification of causal chains and the postulation of SGP units prompted a similar progression towards abstract plot structures. Are we to assume, then, that all of this activity must always occur as readers proceed with their task? Perhaps not, since experiments demonstrating readers' sensitivity to textual features of this kind are not necessarily demonstrating that each and every strategy constitutes a part of the normal reading process. Realistically, there has to be some element of control over the scope and extent of inferencing that is typical during normal reading. But, that said, where should we draw the line?

In addressing this problem, McKoon and Ratcliff (1992, p.440) make the strong claim that:

> ... readers do not automatically construct inferences to fully represent the situation described by a text. In the absence of specific goal directed strategic processes, inferences of only two kinds are constructed; those that establish locally coherent representations of the parts of the text that are processed concurrently and those that rely on information that is quickly and easily available.

On purely functional grounds, without the establishment of local coherence it is difficult to see how comprehension could get off the ground. However, the case becomes less persuasive when it comes to global inferencing being made on-line. Global inferencing need not form part of the default reading repertoire although it could be on hand to serve specialised reading strategies as, say, during study or whenever we read with a particular purpose in mind. This "minimalist" stance, although consistent with our previous arguments concerning knowledge updating, is completely at odds with many of the studies reported throughout this chapter. One way of untangling this knot is to monitor whatever on-line inferencing is actually occurring during normal reading. Information that is currently involved in inferencing (whether local or global) should be detectable though its specific priming effects on test probes introduced as reading proceeds.

In the first of a number of priming experiments, McKoon and Ratcliff (1992) tested for the availability of local and global information as subjects read through a series of short texts. Each experimental text consisted of two paragraphs, an introduction which set out a general goal (e.g. an assassin aiming to kill the president by using a rifle) and a continuation paragraph that took different forms depending on whether the main goal had been achieved or not. In the control condition, the main goal is met and the text deals with the gunman's escape. In another version "try again", the first attempt fails and a second attempt is made using the rifle. In a third version, "substitution", after the attempt at shooting the president has failed, the assassin tries to use a hand grenade instead.

Probe words intended to tap into local and global inferencing were presented shortly after the final sentence of the continuation passage had been read. Thus, presenting the word "kill" as a test probe to which subjects should respond if they had seen the word earlier, was intended to tap into inferencing relating to the general goal described in the first paragraph of the text. Presenting "rifle" as a test word was intended to tap into the subordinate goal employed to achieve the main goal. As all three texts were locally coherent, the minimalist position holds that global inferencing would be unnecessary and hence, no priming of "kill" would be found. With regard to the subordinate probe, "rifle", it is relevant for local coherence in only one of the continuation passages—the "try again" version. Here, therefore, the minimalist prediction holds that priming effects will be observed. The more liberal, constructivist position would hold that while the general goal should not be reactivated under the control continuation, it should be reactivated under both the "try again" and the "substitution" versions where it continues to be relevant.

In sum, the minimalist position predicts no priming across conditions for the general goal, although it does predict priming variations for the subordinate goal. Here, both the minimalist and the constructivist arguments predict that the presentation of "rifle" as a test word should demonstrate priming in the "try again" version. The results clearly supported the minimalist stance. The general goal "kill" showed no facilitation at all in any of the continuation conditions and, while "rifle" was primed under the "try again" continuation, it was not primed in the continuations where it was not required for local coherence.

In the light of these and similar results favouring the minimalist view, McKoon and Ratcliff looked again the evidence normally cited in support of the constructivist theory and concluded that this evidence is not as strong as has been claimed. For example, the work by Morrow et al. on updating mental models can be criticised on the grounds that the subjects probably used special strategies centred on "room/object" rehearsal because they knew that they would be tested later on these item relationships. In any case, a subsequent study conducted by some of the original experimenters has cast doubt on the generality of the original findings. Wilson, Rinck, McNamara, Bower, and Morrow (1993) report a failure to replicate, at least when only the names of room items were used as probes. To obtain their previous results they found it was necessary to pair an item of room furniture with the protagonist's name. Their subjects showed the original effects only when an item of furniture coincided with Wilbur's current position and it was this association that was being tested. Otherwise, there was no evidence for the kind of detailed model updating they originally had in mind. A conclusion that is consistent with the minimalists' claims.

To the extent that the minimalist view restricts inferencing either to those items already held in working memory or to items that can be easily reinstated, this position is also consistent with the conclusions reached in Chapter 6 dealing with updating driven by corrections. However, the argument does have its local difficulties. What is meant by "easy reinstatement" is left undefined and given that McKoon and Ratcliff's conclusions depend on accepting the null hypothesis (they report what did not happen) their experiments are hardly a stringent test of the minimalist position. The latter criticism derives from Trabasso and Suh (1993) who have also objected that McKoon and Ratcliff provide no independent evidence that their test probes were located at exactly those points in the text where the critical local and global inferences could be expected to occur on line.

According to Trabasso and Suh, a more effective experimental procedure would have been one where the attack on the problem proceeded along three separate but related fronts. First, it should have recourse to a theory of textual analysis in order to establish precisely where local and global inferencing could be expected. Second, it should be demonstrated that readers actually do experience these inferences on-line during the reading process—say, by means of "talk-aloud" protocols to check on the contents of working memory at different points. Only then, with this data to hand, is it feasible to design the priming experiments that serve as the third prong in the argument. When Trabasso and Suh implemented this design strategy they found that, contrary to the minimalist case, global inferencing could be detected even when the texts were locally coherent. Further critiques of the minimalist argument have been mounted by Graesser, Singer, and Trabasso (1994) and by Singer, Graesser, and Trabasso (1994) whereas a more conciliatory stance has been adopted by Myers, O'Brien, Albrecht, and Mason (1994).

On one point, at least, all sides in this debate can agree. Strategic processing is possible and it becomes increasingly likely as we replace the trivial texts favoured by the majority of discourse researchers with more complex literary texts. This genre of text can impose very heavy demands as its readers struggle to keep abreast of what is happening.

LITERARY TEXTS

It must be evident by now that studies of narrative comprehension have rarely strayed from using stories of such tedium that no respectable editor would deign to print them. Behind the selection of these materials is the implicit assumption that the results they yield will scale up to meet the extra demands introduced by more complex literary examples. This belief may be too optimistic. Miall (1989) has argued that if we apply standard analytic techniques to one of Virginia Woolf's short stories (*Together and apart*, 1944) it soon becomes evident that an account of comprehension built around predetermined categories such as a character's goals and plans does not work. It does not work because these details may be deliberately concealed or mis-stated in order to provide the indeterminacy and ambiguity that gives the story its interest. Literary texts are generally not well formed in canonical terms and the more well formed they are, the less interesting they become as literary works. Comprehending these materials is not a matter of finding some preformed encoding units or schema onto which to map the story content but more a matter of creating from scratch an appropriate structure to do the job. Unfortunately, while we are casting around trying to find this optimal processing structure, by definition, we will lack the overall co-ordination and guidance the missing structure is supposed to provide in the first place.

As its title implies, *Together and apart* deals with the failure of two characters to communicate with each other for reasons that are left to readers to infer. To do this, they have to rely on their emotional reactions to the content as it unfolds. Thus, Miall not only places great emphasis on the reader's affective response to the story content to provide the guidelines for constructing an interpretation, he also finds it necessary to appeal to levels of inferencing which go well beyond anything we have considered hitherto (Miall, 1989, p.65):

Although the actual cause underlying the failure of communication is not described directly, the reader is able to grasp a cause at the affective level. The cause is inherent in some deficiency in Miss Anning and Mr Serle, some lack of alignment in their vision of the situation which calls into question the possibility of communication itself. This interpretative schema, which must be created by the reader, is signalled by references to the sky and setting which occur throughout the story and by perspectives on the inner self of each character ... The role played by affect is thus critical ... Whereas a schema is domain-specific, affect can transform the meaning of a schema by transference of inferences across domains, as in this case the affect induced by the sky phrases transfers to the relationship schema.

To date, there have been few investigations into how a reader's affective responses can be deployed in making sense of a series of complex events, and work on narrative comprehension still has a long way to go before anything like a satisfactory account is likely to emerge. However, for the corpus of simple to middle-range texts that make up the bulk of experimental materials, less ambitious cognitive models are on offer that aim to simulate the on-line processes involved in normal reading for comprehension.

KINTSCH'S CYCLIC MODEL OF TEXT COMPREHENSION

One example is provided by Kintsch and his colleagues who, over the years, have been working on a cyclic comprehension model that is applicable to both written and spoken discourse. The basic model has undergone various transformations in response to new experimental data since its last incarnation but, in the main, these changes have been in the direction of extending the scope of the model rather than repudiating earlier assumptions about how it should operate. In its initial version (Kintsch, 1974), the model concentrated on the operations involved in the formation of an hierarchical text base. Then a subsequent version was put forward which addressed the additional procedures needed for forming mental models. In the most recent version, the aim has been to explain how the numerous processing strategies invoked during normal reading are orchestrated as a whole. We will look at these developments in turn.

As, for all practical purposes, there appears to be no upper limit to the length of text we can understand, we must be capable of assimilating the content, section by section, in a series of discrete processing cycles. The cyclic model aims to delineate whatever operations are occurring on each processing cycle that give rise to local and global coherence. It is assumed that during each reading cycle, a manageable chunk of the text is selected and the underlying propositional content abstracted. This content is then retained in working memory as another cycle gets underway and a further propositional analysis occurs. The memory representation for the meaning of the text (the text base) is created from these cyclical inputs as local and global processes are brought into play.

On the first processing cycle, as the reader embarks on the opening sentence, propositional content is abstracted up to some limit determined jointly by the syntactic structure of the text and the capacity of the reader's working memory. This propositional content is then held in working memory while the next processing cycle gets underway. The propositional input from this cycle is added to the existing content in working memory and local coherence is then established through the patterns of argument overlap that happen to be present in this current set of propositions.

Next, a subset of these active propositions is selected for retention in working memory during the following input cycle while the remainder propositions are transferred to long-term memory. Which propositions are to be held over from cycle to cycle is determined on a "leading edge" strategy—content to be retained is selected either in terms of its importance, as defined by its height in the text base hierarchy or, other things being equal, in terms of its recency of mention. This basic process reiterates as reading proceeds. If, on a given cycle, no argument overlap can be found between the current propositional input and the content in working memory (the text is locally inconsistent) then a search is made of the text base held in long-term memory in order to reinstate the missing content. If the relevant content is found, it is reinstated in working memory and processing continues. If search is unsuccessful, the reader then has the option of drawing upon relevant background knowledge to infer the missing content in order to maintain the coherence of the text base.

The macrostructure of a text specifies details about its global organisation such as the narrative structure described earlier. According to the model, the reader can make use of reduction rules to eliminate unimportant detail and to create summaries of the remaining content in the form of macropropositions. As these reduction rules can also operate on their own output, the summarisation process can be extended until, at limit, a single macroproposition may stand for the text as whole.

Macroprocessing proceeds under the control of knowledge schemas which, when activated, allow relevant background information to be brought to bear on the reduction process. For example, on reading:

"X goes to the airport; X checks in; X waits for booking ..."

the reader can replace all of this detail by a single macroproposition "X is taking a plane" because all of the actions described are part of an air-travel script.

This version of the cyclical model has been used to simulate actual reading activity by making certain assumptions concerning the model's basic parameters such as the size of the short-term memory buffer, the number of input propositions associated with each reading cycle, and the number of cycles over which a microproposition is held in working memory. We can expect these values to vary from reader to reader, partly as a function of individual differences in reading span and partly as a function of the reader's prior knowledge of the text topic. A reader with a small reading span will be limited in the amount of information that can be held over in working memory and a reader who is unfamiliar with the subject of the text will experience similar limitations. Thus, the model can be used to throw light on the issue of text readability. Viewed from this perspective, readability is not so much an absolute property of a text as a function of how well it is written and the processing resources of the individual reader. (Further comment on text readability can be found in Chapter 12.)

The model also provides a plausible explanation of why the levels effect in story recall occurs. Information high in a text base hierarchy is likely to spend the longest time in working memory, either because it is repeatedly selected for retention across processing cycles or because it has to be repeatedly reinstated from long-term memory due to its relevance for coherence operations. The result is that important text content ends up being processed to a deeper level than more peripheral content, which will be held in working memory when it is first encountered but not thereafter.

As a general model of text comprehension, this particular version has some obvious shortcomings. Even when assessed on its own terms, the model takes for granted many of the processes it aims to deploy. The parsing of sentences into component propositions is taken as given and the "leading edge" criteria used for selecting the propositions to be retained during a cycle fail to address the causal calculations that are also involved (see Fletcher & Bloom, 1988). Similarly, the use of argument overlap to establish local coherence can, at best, provide only a coarse guide to what is required. As defined, two consecutive inputs could exhibit the same degree of local coherence both when they happen to agree with each other and when the second input contradicts the first. If we are to distinguish such cases (as we surely must) some unpacking of what is meant by argument overlap is sorely needed.

In seeking to revise the comprehension model, van Dijk and Kintsch (1983) next focused on the formation of a mental (or situation) model dealing with the text's referential meaning. Under this revision, the function of the text base was much as before (i.e. to record the explicit propositional content contained within the text) but now the situation model was made the repository of the majority of the reader's inferential elaborations on the text content. The presence of the model, therefore, allowed the reader considerable freedom to go beyond what was written in order to register what was meant, an arrangement that carries distinct processing advantages. Readers armed with this dual record are not only in a better position to grasp the author's intentions, they can also use the situation model to guide the formation of the text base as, say, when the literal text content is ambiguous or when certain information has been missed out altogether.

To make the distinction clear, consider an example input which supports the construction of a coherent text base but does not support the construction of an accompanying mental model. Suppose, following Bransford and McCarrell (1974), we read:

The haystack was important because the cloth ripped.

We can abstract a perfectly good text base from this input while still being at a loss to know what it means. On receipt of the hint "parachute", however, we can proceed to construct a situation model in which the referential meaning is clarified. Furthermore, this situation model can now be used to inform local coherence operations on subsequent sections of text. Thus, if the next sentence had been "It was a good job it was in the way", the "it" that was in the way could refer to "haystack" or to "cloth". This ambiguity is easily resolved provided the current content of the situation model can be consulted. Thus we find anaphoric resolution often proceeds more effectively via the contents of the situation model than via search through the text base (Garnham & Oakhill, 1992; Sanford & Garrod, 1981).

Although this revised version of the discourse comprehension model went some way towards rectifying the limitations of the earlier version, it did so at the expense of packing everything in that might possibly bear upon strategic understanding. The scope of the model had been broadened but only at the expense of introducing numerous processing strategies whose interactions had been asssumed but not explained. The most recent revision has been designed to redress this imbalance.

Construction–Integration model

If we stand back and view text comprehension as a whole, it is evident that so many processing activities are occurring in parallel that, as Kintsch (1988) remarks, "it borders on the miraculous" how readers are able to cope with all that is required of them. There may be arguments for doubting that normal reading invokes all of the activities that Van Dijk and Kintsch have in mind but even what remains is miraculous enough. Creating a text base and an accompanying situation model calls for interdependent decisions to be taken on many different levels simultaneously. Where syntactic parsing has not yet been completed, propositions cannot be abstracted. Where the propositional content is unclear, macropropositions cannot be formed. Where the text base remains half formed, there can be no accompanying situation model and where there is no situation model an important source of disambiguation for the text base is missing. All told, we seem to be faced with a horrendous processing tangle where what to do first is determined by decisions much further down the line that critically depend on the content of the first move. The most recent version of the comprehension model (Kintsch, 1988) attempts to untie this knot.

The Construction–Integration (C–I) model retains the representational distinctions between surface memory, text base, and situation model as envisaged earlier but it provides a different account from before of how these representations are produced. The C–I model now envisages text comprehension as comprising an iterative, two-phase process. In the first phase, *Construction*, everything is allowed to happen at once, regardless of the internal consistency of the individual decisions. During this phase, production rules fire whenever their conditions are met, creating a detailed if inchoate network of information at all levels of processing. Thus, at the level of word identification, homonyms like "bank" ("financial institution" or "side of a river") will trigger productions whose actions invoke both types of meaning. Equivalent inconsistencies will arise as other "dumb" rules identify propositions, generate macropropositions, and derive elaborative inferences. As each operation ignores what is happening on other levels in the system, redundancies and contradictions will continue to pile up as a result of this bottom-up processing. This eventuates in a mixed and varied set of elements being generated where the "right" elements are present but there is much else besides.

Once the Construction phase is over, an *Integration* phase ensues. It is during this phase that the "best" decisions are singled out and the remainder information is discarded. This is achieved by treating the informational network constructed during the first phase as a constraint-satisfaction network. In settling into a stable state, the network serves to pick out whatever body of mutually consistent elements happened to be present in the orginal chaos. In short, by deferring decisions about internal consistency to a post-construction phase, the model allows for the generation of a rich body of information within which the required patterns will exist. Only when this network of information has been produced is it feasible to identify that subset of information which best fits the prevailing sets of constraints. In other words the C–I model is an example of the hybrid models discussed in Chapter 4. It employs production rules to generate the pool of potential information during its construction phase (much as occurs during the elaboration phase in SOAR) and then it relies upon constraint-satisfaction networks to settle upon the "best fit" in the course of an integration phase.

Forming a text base

On any reading cycle, as a section of the text is read, production rules are triggered that together handle all aspects of encoding to give every plausible interpretation on every level. This process relies on general knowledge being held in long-term memory in the form of an associative network whose nodes are concepts and propositions and whose links carry positive and negative connections. The text base is constructed as inputs activate particular concepts and propositions in the network, turning them into source nodes which then direct activation to the other parts of the network with which they are related. Macropropositions formed during this stage also draw in associated knowledge in the same way and yet more information will be added to this expanding text base as a function of whatever inferencing has been deemed necessary. Consequently, by the end of the construction phase, a temporary structure will have been constructed from whatever knowledge elements were activated by the current inputs and their associations. At this point, connection strengths are assigned to the links in the resulting network which specify the degree of interconnection between the individual elements.

Propositions that are directly derived from the text are given a positive interconnection whose strength is proportional both to their proximity in the text base and their degree of relationship in the general knowledge network. At the end of the construction phase, therefore, we are left with a temporary network of information based on whatever items have been accessed in the store of general knowledge as a result of local and global production rules being triggered. As this output has been carelessly constructed, the next and final phase calls for an integration process wherein mutually consistent elements increase in activation and inconsistent elements become deactivated. It is during this phase, therefore, that the redundancies and contradictions are eliminated.

At the outset of the integration phase, the network will contain certain elements that possess few links to other elements in the network or that carry inhibitory links to other elements. Equally, there will be some elements that share excitatory links with a number of other elements and which work to support each other. Consequently, by letting the network settle into a relaxed state, we can proceed to extract just those elements that provide the best fit to the growing text base. At the end of the cycle these elements represent the text base up to that point. As more of the text is read, another C–I cycle ensues and the text base is modified in the light of the new input and so on.

Surface representations and situation models

Whereas Kintsch (1988) was concerned with applying the C–I model to the construction of a text base, Kintsch, Welsch, Schmalhofer, and Zimny (1990) consider how the model would apply to the formation of a surface representation of a text and to the associated situation model. For both of these representations their component elements are put together in much the same way as applied to the text base. Just as the elements of the text base were generated freely at first and then assigned connection strengths according to salience measures derived from the explicit text and the subject's general knowledge, so the elements comprising the surface record and the situation model are integrated along similar lines.

For the surface representation of the text, once candidate elements have been proposed during the construction phase, they are assigned connection strengths in the integration phase, based on the grammatical structure of the individual sentences involved. In the case of the elements comprising the situation model, the connection strengths assigned during the integration phase are based on the proximity of these elements within the scripts and schemas comprising the reader's general knowledge.

When Kintsch et al. used the C–I model to simulate the normal reading of sample texts, they report that its outputs provided a reasonable match to the comprehension performance of actual subjects. It predicted subjects' accuracy levels for specified text content at recall and it also predicted variations in how readers with different degrees of prior knowledge of the topic chose to answer subsequent questions tapping their level of comprehension. Readers with some prior knowledge of the topic tended to construct their responses to comprehension questions mainly around the information contained in their situation model. Readers lacking this background tended to rely more on the surface and text base detail when answering the same questions.

In presenting their account, Kintsch and his associates often have to resort to a fair amount of *ad hoc* reasoning to keep the model afloat. On the authors' own admission, the rules for constructing situation models are not well understood and the model cannot cope with much beyond the very barest of texts. In fact, the task of translating any moderately sized text into its surface, text base, and situational models through their associated connectivity matrices promises to be so complicated as to overwhelm our abilities to follow what is going on.

As productions are allowed to fire whenever they can be matched during the construction phase it is surprising that this licence is not reflected in the priming effects obtained on-line during reading. As we have seen, at least on the global level, these are somewhat less than prolific. Another problem is that it is far from clear how corrective updating would proceed within the C–I model. We might speculate on ways in which it would be possible to "damp down" the impact of a correction on an existing text base and situation model but to date the model offers little theoretical guidance on how to proceed in this critical case. In addition, this model has little to say about the microdetails of text comprehension such as the cognitive mechanisms involved in sentence parsing and in handling anaphoric reference.

All of these criticisms are well aimed but they should not be allowed to obscure the principal virtue that attends Kintsch's efforts in this area. His prime concern has been to address the way in which the multiple subtasks invoked during reading can be made to dovetail together in the service of comprehension. Accounts of the reading process that duck this issue in favour of ploughing one small corner of the field buy their integrity at the cost of leaving the overall reading process in the realms of the miraculous.

THE STATUS OF NARRATIVE UNDERSTANDING

One feature that stands out very clearly from the work on narrative comprehension is just how good at it we are. Given the complexity of the processing that is involved this fluency should not be taken for granted. The processing of expository texts is distinctly less impressive (see Chapter 12) and were we to try our hand at syllogistic reasoning using more than two or three premises at a time we would soon give up in disgust. We have a remarkable aptitude for constructing stories which seems rather profligate if its sole function is to service the reading of books.

The pre-eminence of narrative comprehension is the less surprising if we assume that it draws upon the same cognitive mechanisms that handle the currency of everyday social exchange. That is, when we set out to interpret the behaviour of those around us, we proceed by inferring their possible intentional states and cast around for a storyline in which these states and their dependent actions make sense. Viewed from this perspective, narrative text comprehension is an offshoot of a more general capacity for reasoning about a world in which human agents are striving to satisfy their personal goals. And, just as we can learn from our actual experiences, so too we can learn from the vicarious experiences created in the course of reading. Understanding how and why the characters in stories have behaved as they do can help us to understand ourselves better. Miall (1989, p.76) makes essentially this point when he argues that narratives can serve as vehicles "to explore the emotions of the self through engagement with the text".

Similarly, Bruner (1990) has noted how when we encounter an exception to the ordinary run of affairs during daily life, we tend to explain what has happened by searching for a storyline that could supply a justification for the deviation. If a friend has suddenly turned hostile, we look for a possible world where this deviation has a meaning. We try to concoct a story in explanation and, if we succeed, we are then in a position to explain what has happened. In the next chapter we will expand upon this argument by noting how the processes of rational thought can call upon narrative reasoning—both as a means of structuring the flow of external events and as a tool for drawing conclusions based on this understanding.

CHAPTER TEN

Evaluating and manipulating knowledge

Solving problems, making decisions, and engaging in reasoning are all reflective activities aimed at evaluating and manipulating the information we have at our disposal. Problem solving entails finding a way of changing a given situation into a form that is more to our liking. Decisions are made when we make comparisons between possible options and settle upon what we think to be the best choice. Reasoning occurs when we scrutinise our beliefs with the aim of producing new and more coherent versions.

Determining just how these cognitive operations are conducted has provided the staple subject matter for a variety of disciplines including philosophy, cognitive psychology, and cognitive science. Regrettably, this shared involvement has resulted in neither general agreement on the specific nature of these activities nor on the standards by which their products should be assessed. We have already broached the topic of problem solving when discussing the problem spaces employed by SOAR so we will start by linking into that account.

PROBLEM SOLVING

When we desire some goal state and the means to achieve it lie entirely to hand, the only question remaining is whether we still want it. Problem solving enters the picture when the solver wants to achieve a particular goal state but the means for doing so are not immediately evident. Following Duncker (1945) and Newell and Simon (1972), problem solving can be interpreted as a search procedure conducted in a problem space that contains the initial state (S1), the goal state (G), and numerous other states which can be reached via operators that transform one state into another. Successful problem solving consists of selecting just those operators that will trace a path through this state space that links S1 to G.

Typically a problem will call for a number of intermediate states to be generated along the way to a solution and the solver has to decide which these should be. Where a number of operators can apply to an initial state (say different equations when solving physics problems) their application will create a new set of states which, in turn, can be transformed to produce a further set of states and so on. Consequently, it is implausible to cast the solver as searching all possible states in the problem space, as search demands will increase exponentially as the depth of search increases. Rather, the solver is likely to trace out a solution path by employing heuristic procedures that avoid placing excessive demands on the solver's cognitive resources while still offering a good chance of eventual success. Should the problem domain be an unfamilar one, the solver has little choice but rely on general methods of heuristic search for getting problem solving under way.

General-purpose heuristics, by definition, can apply in many different circumstances and typical examples can be found in "forward chaining" and "means–end analysis". Forward chaining is being deployed when the solver focuses on the initial state of a problem and selects an operator that moves closer to the goal state. Under means–end analysis, the solver attempts to narrow the choice between operators by focusing on the differences between a current state and the solution state. With either of these heuristics in play, the solver has a good chance of avoiding dead ends without having to backtrack in order to repair any damage produced by an inappropriate choice of operator. Which heuristic is likely to be used depends on the solver's relative familiarity with the problem domain; more experienced problem solvers tend to use forward chaining methods whereas complete novices tend to rely on means–end analysis.

Expert and novice problem solving

In an investigation into the nature of expertise in problem solving, Chi, Feltovich, and Glaser (1981) invited physics experts and novices to go through a series of physics problems with the aim of putting together those that were similar to each other. Their novice subjects responded by grouping together problems that shared similar physical features. More experienced solvers, on the other hand, organised their sorting behaviour around principles that ignored surface appearances in favour of similarities in solution methods. Problems dealing with inclined planes were grouped with problems dealing with compressed springs because their joint solutions depended on the principle of conservation of energy. By dint of repeated practice, it seems that solvers had come to recognise the solution patterns associated with particular classes of problems and it was this schematic knowledge that licensed reasoning ahead from the problem givens.

Insight into the way in which problem schemas are formed can be gained by monitoring subjects as they practise solving an extended series of problems. Such a study has been described by Sweller, Mawer, and Ward (1983) whose subjects were required to tackle a large number of problems in kinematics, similar to the example given in Table 10.1.

A set of equations accompanied each problem and, by observing the order in which the formulae were applied, the investigators were able to track any changes in heuristic procedure that came about as practice increased. A subject employing a means–end heuristic would start by applying equation (2), the one that contains the goal term (s). In contrast, a subject employing forward chaining would work forward from the problem givens by using equation (1) to get problem solving under way. Consequently, by monitoring the order in which the equations were applied the experimenters were able to record any variations in approach that arose as subjects worked their way through the 77 problems that comprised the practice set.

For the initial problems in the series (where subjects were unpractised) the preferred method was means–end analysis. However, with increasing levels of practice, the incidence of this procedure diminished as forward chaining became the method of choice. Whereas around 80% of the first five problems were solved using a means–end procedure, this had dropped to 40% by the time the last five problems were being tackled. At this stage, solvers had progressed beyond the

TABLE 10.1
Example practice problem

A pile driver takes 3.732 seconds to fall onto a pile. It hits the pile at 30.46mps. How high was the pile driver raised?

EQUATIONS

1.	$v = 0.5V$	(v = Average velocity; V = Final velocity)
2.	$s = vt$	(s = Distance; t = Time)
3.	$V = at$	(a = Acceleration)

From Sweller et al., 1983.

novice stage by using feedback to create a schematic representation of the landscape of possible moves.

Although Sweller et al. found that schematisation enabled solvers to look ahead during problem solving, not all of its effects were entirely benign. Schematisation was also accompanied by a mental set which deterred the solver from considering alternative solution paths to those that had been practised. As this outcome had been anticipated, the experimental design included two test problems inserted into the series, one at the beginning and one at the end, which, although soluble using equations 1 and 2, could be solved more directly using equation 3. On these problems, mental set effects were found to be most prevalent for solvers who had adopted the forward chaining method. (We will consider some of the pedagogic implications arising from this finding in Chapter 12.)

Analogical problem solving

Another heuristic device available to the problem solver is to look around for a similar problem to the target problem that has been successfully solved in the past. If such a source problem can be found it may then be possible to adapt its solution to the current situation. In fact, the status of analogy as a powerful problem-solving device has long been recognised. Generations of children have been familiarised with fractions by drawing an analogy with parcelling out sweets, and modern students have been introduced to computing procedures by drawing analogies with office filing procedures. Analogical problem solving also commands a significant role at the highest levels of scientific and artistic endeavour (see Weisberg, 1992). Not surprisingly, therefore, considerable effort has been devoted towards trying to understand when analogical transfer is likely to occur and how the cross mapping from source to target is managed.

Detecting a source

Recommending resort to analogical methods presupposes that solvers can undertake memory search with a reasonable hope of locating a source problem. It matters little that a valid analogy exists if the solver cannot reactivate it when it is needed. Yet we have already seen from the work of Gick and Holyoak (1983) that detecting an analogy can be far from straightforward. Despite their strenuous efforts at highlighting the analogical links between the actions of the general in the military story and the actions of the surgeon in the medical problem, most subjects stubbornly refused to see what was in front of them.

Of course, the general and the surgeon problems did differ in their surface details but, once we compare their joint solutions, we find there are many correspondences. If the fortress is seen as structurally similar to the tumour, a number of other correspondences fall into place; the mined roads are equivalent to the surrounding tissue, the groups of soldiers correspond to the rays and, so far as the solution is concerned, convergence provides a satisfactory resolution in both cases. After comparing the efficacy of different types of hints for activating the source record, Gick and Holyoak concluded that a key part of the detection process resides in the semantic similarity between the source and target situations. The more semantic features shared in common between source and target, the more likely it is that the analogy will be activated and used.

Mapping and adapting source to target

Once an analogy has been found, the solver next has to decide how features in the source map onto features in the target. As the most satisfying analogies tend to be those that appear to have little in common with the target, specifying how the mapping operations should proceed presents us with an apparent paradox. Successful mapping seems to demand substantial levels of understanding in both domains because, if this is lacking, the whole exercise can go badly wrong. Treating the heart as analogous to a mechanical pump works well provided it is the circulatory function that is being highlighted. It will break down if the emphasis is on their constituent materials. Successful mapping, therefore, entails (1) knowing what features of the source to ignore, (2) what features to carry over, and (3) how the feature correspondences between source and target should be set up. None of this seems to be possible if we lack a good understanding of both sides of the analogical relationship but it was the lack of comprehension of the target situation that prompted the need for analogical help in the first place. One way out of this predicament is to map the source onto the target as best we can, leaving any fine tuning until later. Although this may seem an unsatisfactory, hit or miss affair, things are not as bad as they appear. In many cases there are general constraints operating that can keep the mapping on the rails.

Gentner and Toupin (1986) report that the ease with which a source problem can be mapped onto a target depends on two distinct factors; their similarity or "transparency", and the degree of coherence or interdependence shared by the features in the source domain—which they term "systematicity". Successful mapping can be expected when both of these factors are present.

They tested the role of these two factors in analogical mapping by getting two groups of children, (4–6 years and 8–10 years), to listen to a story in which various animals played different characters. After listening to the story the children then had to act out an analogical version of the actions described using new animal characters. Different levels of transparency between source and target versions were introduced by manipulating the similarity between the types of animal chosen to play equivalent roles in the two story forms. Under high transparency (SS), the same roles were played by similar animals. Under an intermediate condition (D), particular roles in the first story were assigned to different types of animals in the second, acted version. Low transparency (SD), entailed the same animals taking on different roles in the first story and the acted version. Systematicity was manipulated either by tagging a moral onto the first story which was intended to tie the content together (high systematicity), or by leaving it out (low systematicity).

Analyses of the degree of transfer to the acted version revealed that high transparency (SS), facilitated performance at all ages. High systematicity, on the other hand, only benefited the older subjects, and then only in the low transparency (SD) condition. In other words, for the younger, less experienced subjects, ease of analogical mapping depended on the similarity of the surface features associated with the source and target domain. For older and more experienced subjects, underlying structural principles were starting to play their part as well.

Transparency effects in analogical transfer are not necessarily restricted to young problem solvers. It is not age so much as experience within the domain that permits the solver to delve beneath the surface and to register any systematic correspondences. At first, when we learn new techniques, the superficial context of learning can set severe constraints on how the learning is generalised. Thus, Ross (1987), having taught (naive) adult subjects the principles of probability using training problems drawn from medicine, found that transfer to new problems only occurred if they remained within the medical setting. Subjects soon experienced difficulties if the setting shifted from a medical to an educational setting. Indeed, surface similarity remained an important determinant of transfer even when the subjects had the necessary equations set out in front of them. This restriction can be expected to relax as the solver's experience increases and eventually systematicity should take over from transparency in determining whether or not a mapping from source to target problem will occur.

Estimates of the relative contributions of surface and structural similarities to the mapping between source and target problems have been provided by Holyoak and Koh (1987). This investigation employed a new set of analogies for their tumour problem constructed around the repair of an expensive lightbulb which could proceed in any of four ways.

One version ("Fragile glass/Laser") describes the bulb being repaired by fusing the filament using converging laser beams. This arrangement was justified by a cover story referring to the risks of breaking the surrounding glass and, in this form, it presents both a high surface similarity and a high structural similarity to the tumour problem. In the second version, ("Low intensity/Laser beam"), there was no mention of the danger to the surrounding glass but, as only low intensity lasers were available in the laboratory, there was still the need to summate the beams to the particular intensity required for fusion. This version, therefore, bears a high surface similarity to the tumour problem while being low on structural similarity.

The two remaining versions referred to repairing the filament using ultrasound instead of laser beams—a switch in procedure that serves to reduce the surface similarity to the medical problem. The combination of low surface similarity combined with high structural similarity was achieved by means of a storyline that referred to a strong sound source as likely to break the glass ("Fragile glass/Ultrasound"). Consequently, sound beams from weaker sources had to summate at the filament in order to complete the repair. The final combination of low surface similarity and low structural similarity ("Low intensity/Ultrasound") occurred when there were only low-intensity sound generators to hand. Here too, it was necessary to set up a number of generators and sum their products to arrive at the intensity required to fuse the filament.

Subjects who read the lightbulb story in the Fragile glass/Laser version were most likely to propose a convergence solution for the tumour problem. In contrast, subjects reading the Low intensity/ Ultrasound version were least likely to come up with this analogical solution on their own. Giving subjects the hint that the lightbulb story could be used to solve the tumour problem and then asking them to list all possible solutions revealed that analogical transfer was best when the source version was structurally similar to the medical problem. Thus, although both surface and structural similarities are involved in recognising an analogical source, it seems to be the structural detail that participates in the actual mapping.

Analogical mapping and constraint satisfaction

We can represent the features of the medical and military problems originally employed by Gick and Holyoak as elements in an associative network. For example, in Fig. 10.1 the constituent elements from these problems are represented as individual nodes in a single network which also specifies some of the possible cross mappings that could apply and their associated constraints.

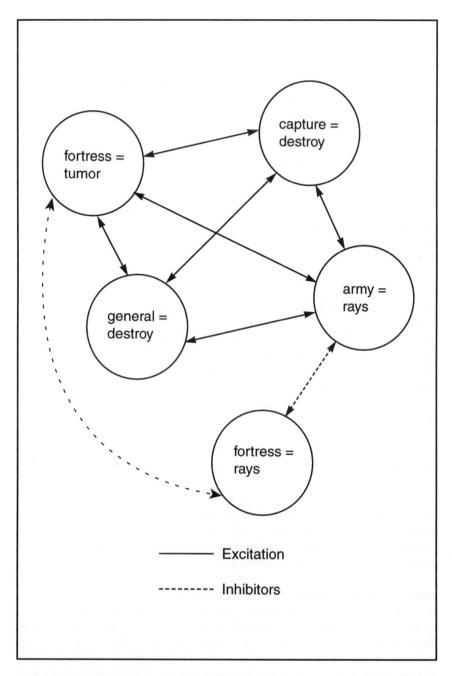

FIG. 10.1. Constraint satisfaction network for mapping fortress onto tumour problem. (From Holyoak, 1990.)

As indicated, if "capturing" is paired with "destroying" then a series of additional consequences immediately follow; "army" maps onto "rays" (the agent of destruction in both cases), "general" maps onto "doctor" (the planning agency), and "fortress" maps onto "tumour" (the object of attack). Together these cross mappings form a mutually consistent set whose component elements act to reinforce each other. A further constraint arises from the fact that mapping needs to be one-to-one; once an element from the source has been paired with an element in the target it is then inhibited from pairing with some other element. If "fortress" maps onto "tumour" it obviously cannot be a candidate for mapping onto "doctor" at the same time and the arrows in the diagram indicate these positive or negative relations between the possible decisions. In other words, as the process of mapping the properties of a source onto a target problem calls for the simultaneous satisfaction of a series of interdependent constraints, we have another instance of a task that can be effectively modelled using constraint-satisfaction networks.

One such model, ACME, has been proposed by Holyoak and Thagard (1989) and it simulates analogical problem solving by employing a network whose units represent the set of possible hypotheses to be mapped and whose weights reflect their inferential dependencies. Within the network, the activation level of a unit indicates the plausibility of its corresponding hypothesis (e.g. general maps to surgeon) while the positive and negative links between the network's units indicate which hypotheses are mutually consistent and which are mutually inconsistent.

From this standpoint, the factor of "systematicity" now resides in the network's connection strengths, whereas the factor of "transparency" is handled by means of a specially designated processing node within the network. This particular unit becomes increasingly active as the degree of semantic similarity increases between features in the source and target examples. ACME also contains another dedicated unit which is responsive to the pragmatic utility of certain correspondences during mapping. This allows for certain potentially irrelevant correspondences to be ruled out in advance based on the solver's general knowledge concerning the purpose of the analogy.

In this form, ACME has been used to simulate the Fortress to Tumour mapping by setting the activation values of the semantic and pragmatic units to 1 and by setting the activation of the other units to some minimal value. The final relaxation state of the network is then taken as representing the best fit to the overall constraints on the system. The units that end up with the highest activation values define the optimal mapping arrangements for the analogy in question. As well as the

Fortress/Tumour example, ACME has also been applied to the Lightbulb/Tumour variants (Holyoak & Koh 1987) and the data from Gentner and Toupin's (1986) work with children using the animal stories. As in all of these cases we have typical performance data from human subjects indicating the relative difficulty of the different problem situations, we can compare this data against ACME's performance under the same circumstances.

Taking the number of cycles to solution as a measure of the relative difficulty of a particular mapping, there was a reasonable degree of correspondence between the simulated and observed data. Thus, the number of cycles that ACME required to reach a stable state increased from 3 to 38 for Genter and Toupin's SS and SD stories in their systematic versions and from 3 to "no success" in their non-systematic versions. Similarly, for the various versions of the lightbulb stories employed by Holyoak and Koh, ACME experienced the same order of difficulty with these particular mappings as did humans.

Schema induction

Following successful analogical transfer, the solver has the opportunity to form a more abstract schema for the class of problems represented by the source and target examples (Novick & Holyoak, 1991). This schematic representation can then be recruited as a potential source for subsequent problem solving. However, although analogical reasoning is typically seen as involving memory search for a suitable source problem, other and more creative processes can also be implicated. Analogies may be created on the spot rather than recycled from memory. This is an aspect of analogical problem solving that is easily overlooked so long as experimental studies restrict themselves to simple problems or to inexperienced subject populations. Both of these restrictions were avoided in a study reported by Clement (1988) in which physics professors were asked to think aloud while deciding whether a coiled spring would stretch further if the diameter of the coils was increased. Of the 31 significant analogies generated by the sample of 10 subjects, the majority (18) arose through the solver modifying some feature in the target problem (e.g. uncoiling the spring); memory search to detect possible source problems generated only eight examples.

Generating analogies may be an extremely effective technique but it is one of a number of heuristic devices we have at our disposal. Yet other heuristics are employed when we are called upon to calculate the probabilities associated with the possible outcomes of a given situation and we have to decide which of these outcomes best meets our needs.

DECISION MAKING

Shall I buy a car now or wait until later? Shall I go on holiday this year or save the money? Will this candidate fill the vacant post or not? We are continually making decisions of this kind throughout our daily life yet, despite all this practice, we do not appear to be particularly good at doing all that is required. At least, this seems to be the conclusion if our efforts are judged against standards derived from formal logic or probability theory. Time and again we can be observed to fall short of these ideal standards—largely because we are prone to convert complex situations into simpler forms. Instead of entertaining the full set of possibilities inherent in a given situation, we turn for support to special heuristics whose function is to simplify what is at stake.

Tversky and Kahneman (1974) have identified three types of heuristic that subjects are likely to use when arriving at a judgement in situations where a number of potentially relevant variables are implicated. These are:

1. *Representativeness*, which stipulates that we select from the available information whatever subset is most representative of the problem as given.
2. *Availability*, which states that information that is easily accessed in memory plays a prominent role in shaping our conclusions.
3. *Anchoring plus adjustment*, which holds that we arrive at a judgement on a continuous dimension (e.g. when estimating size or frequency values) by focusing first upon some initial value and then by fine-tuning it to the current circumstances.

Each heuristic offers us the chance to cut through a great deal of extraneous detail while introducing the risk that we will be lured towards plausible but false conclusions.

Typical tasks that are likely to elicit one or other of these strategies have been reproduced in Table 10.2. The entries in brackets are the percentages choosing the alternative options based on a sample of student respondents (N = 250). In every case, the majority choice does not coincide with the correct or the most rational response to the question as posed.

The sketch involving Linda offers the choice between Linda graduating to become a bank clerk or graduating to become a bank clerk who is also a member of the feminist movement. Elementary probability theory states that the probability of both X and Y occurring cannot be greater than the probability of X occurring alone. However, most people

TABLE 10.2
Judgemental heuristics

Representativeness

1.   Linda is 31 years old, single, outspoken, and very bright. She graduated in philosophy and as a student she was deeply concerned with issues of social discrimination and social justice. She also participated in anti-nuclear demonstrations.

Which is now probable?

(a) Linda is now a bank clerk (17%)

(b) Linda is now a bank clerk who is active in the feminist movement. (83%)

Availability

2.   If we took words at random from a dictionary, which would occur more frequently?

(a) Words with initial letter K (75%)

(b) Words with third letter K (25%)

Anchoring plus adjustment

3.   Was the number of students at universities in the UK, in 1985:

(a) Greater or less than 10,000

(b) Estimate the number. (Median sample estimate, 100,000)

Based on Tversky and Kahneman, 1974.

faced with the choice in this form disagree with this apparently obvious conclusion. Of the sample of 250 first-year university students, 83% decided that the combination of bank clerk and feminist was more probable. In choosing this option the subjects have gone for the outcome that is most representative of the information as given. After all, why bother to tell us about Linda's social conscience if it isn't relevant? It seems we can work to different rules than those based on multiplying probabilities.

The second problem deals with the frequency of particular words in the language and here the majority choice picks out "words with k as the first letter" as the larger set. According to Tversky and Kahneman, this comes about because we assess the size of the two sets of words (initial letter k or third letter k) through the ease with which we can bring actual instances to mind. Other things being equal, this is a sensible strategy as larger sets will have more instances available. But other things are not equal when it comes to searching memory. As any crossword enthusiast can confirm, the initial letter of a missing word is a better retrieval cue than letters from other serial positions. As it is easier to generate instances of words beginning with k than it is to find words where k is the third letter, this creates a strong bias towards the conclusion that the former define the larger set.

The third problem calls for a numerical estimate of the numbers attending UK universities in 1985 and a spuriously low value (10,000) has been offered as an anchor point. The median estimate from the student sample came out at 100,000, which is less than half the real value obtaining at the time. Typically, the adjustments upwards from the anchor were insufficient to compensate for its inadequacies. The result is a significant underestimation of the true value.

Untutored human judges, it seems, prefer to work with a subjective logic that eschews formal rules in favour of heuristics attuned to the details of specific situations. Such context-sensitivity can be interpreted as an unfortunate flaw in our decision making but this not the only way of interpreting what is happening. All of the heuristics illustrated here, work by exploiting the information actually to hand at the time the judgement is required. What they do not involve is dredging up each and every item of information that might conceivably be relevant. Suppose, however, that we did stop to think deeply about each and every situation. Would this necessarily make us better judges? If our prime concern is to arrive at the answer that is most likely to be correct in the circumstances, then the answer surely has to be yes. But if the time taken to decide is also relevant (as it surely is) the assessment is not so straightforward. Everyday transactions with the world involve a trade-off between the time taken to reach a decision and the depth to which the situation is analysed. External events can sometimes move faster than we can assemble our thoughts and the animal that hangs around pondering the frequency of tigers in this part of the jungle is much more likely to end up dead than one that treats stripes as "oncoming tiger" and flees accordingly. As world events run on time-scales that are not of our making, the evidence pointing to the precipitateness of human judgement—far from defining fatal flaws—reveals, on the contrary, a very effective system for exploiting what we know at the time when it can be of most use. We can live with the resulting false positives just as we can live with our failures to be dead certain.

Although formal models of decision making have been proposed, they tend to be too inflexible to deal with the variations found in many real-life situations. For example, von Neumann and Morgenstern (1947) proposed that the choice of one option over another can be determined by listing the utilities associated with each option and comparing their combined values. Decision making is then simply a question of maximising the expected utility. However, as Shafir, Simonson, and Tversky (1993) observe, such formal models are not easily applied to "complex real world decisions" and they tend to override significant nuances in how subjects choose to respond. They cite as a case in point, the situation where a judge either has to select one of two options (A and B) or reject one of them. On a formal analysis this difference in the judgement task shouldn't matter; if A is preferred then B should be rejected. But the way the task is presented does make a difference, as instanced by the problem set out in Table 10.3. Here, subjects instructed either to state which holiday they would select or reject, tended to weight the information differently as their task changed.

The two locations differ in that resort A is middle of the road whereas resort B has both outstandingly good and bad aspects. It is these features that come in and out of focus as the task changes from selection to rejection. The outstandingly good points for B make it a likely preference while its outstandingly bad points also single it out for rejection. The result is that spot B's share of the total preferences and rejections exceeds that of spot A. In other words, formal, value-based models of decision making have difficulty in coping with the vagaries in performance that are created by contextual changes. Alterations in context that (in terms of the model) have no significant bearing on a

TABLE 10.3
Asymmetry of preferences and rejections

(PREFER) Imagine that you are planning a week's vacation in a warm spot over the spring break. You currently have two options that are reasonably priced. The travel brochure gives only a limited amount of information about the two options. Given the information available, which vacation spot would you prefer?

(CANCEL) Imagine that you are planning a week's vacation in a warm spot over the spring break. You currently have two options that are reasonably priced, but you can no longer retain your reservation in both. The travel brochure gives only a limited amount of information about the two options. Given the information available, which reservation do you decide to cancel?

	Prefer	Cancel
SPOT A: Average weather Average beaches Medium-quality hotel Medium-temperature water Average nightlife	33%	52%
SPOT B: Lots of sunshine Gorgeous beaches and coral reefs Ultra-modern hotel Very cold water Very strong winds No nightlife	67%	48%

From Shafir et al., 1993.

decision nonetheless can exert a significant influence on the outcome. And much the same can be said about the vagaries that arise when we attempt to engage in formal reasoning in different contexts.

FORMAL AND INFORMAL REASONING

Reasoning may proceed formally, as when we pursue a train of thought to a logically justified conclusion, or it may occur informally, as when we defend our views against attack during a public argument. Formal reasoning typically applies when we solve problems whose givens are specified in advance, as found with logical syllogisms where all of the relevant information is contained within the problem as set. Informal reasoning is a more open-ended procedure and far more typical of everyday reasoning. It occurs whenever we engage in planning or evaluative argument. In these cases, deciding exactly which information to use is itself a critical part of the reasoning process. We will look (briefly) at each of these areas in turn and then consider how they might be related.

Deductive reasoning and content-free rules

To the extent that we can reason successfully in unfamiliar and novel domains this can be taken to imply that we have access to content-free rules for generating valid conclusions. Thus, traditionally it has been asssumed that deductive reasoning draws upon formal rules that apply to the syntactic form of an expression, not its semantic content. An argument that proceeds:

If the time is twelve p.m. then John is in bed
It is twelve p.m.
Therefore, John is in bed

would rest upon the use of the formal rule:

If p then q
p
Therefore, q.

Changing the content of p and q to, say, the presence of circles and triangles, in no way alters the way in which the rule operates. People frequently use this *modus ponens* rule to deduce a conclusion, and its successful application does not require any prior familiarity with the content of the arguments. However, people are noticeably less confident when it comes to the *modus tollens* deduction. Here, given the conditional:

If there is a circle then there is a triangle.
(and told) There is not a triangle.
(we may not deduce) Therefore, there is not a circle.

The fact that people tend to go astray when making this type of deduction presents difficulties for the argument that we rely upon formal rules. Of course, an accommodation can be reached. We could propose that while there is an explicit rule for modus ponens, there is no equivalent rule for modus tollens and the performance variations point to the presence of some logical rules but not others.

A strong version of a rule-based approach to human reasoning can be found in Piaget's description of Formal Operational thought—the final stage in thinking associated with mid-adolescence. According to the developmental model, this stage is reached when the rules of the propositional calculus can be put to use in the service of deductive thought. When the formal operational thinker evaluates an hypothesis, hypothetico-deductive reasoning is said to be deployed in a search both for instances that confirm the tentative hypothesis and for instances of possible counter-examples. Yet actual examples of such dispassionate and controlled evaluation are relatively rare phenomena. Mature subjects faced with abstract arguments often end up reaching illogical conclusions that they would be quick to reject if the same logical problem had been presented to them in a more familiar form. Once again, we can accommodate such data by revising the proposed rule systems with the aim of explaining deductive error as well as deductive success. Reasoning errors could arise, not because people lack the appropriate formal rules, but because they represent the premises incorrectly or they make unnecessary assumptions along the way (Braine & O'Brien, 1991). Alternatively, we could give up trying to ground formal reasoning in the application of content-free rules and postulate context-dependent rules instead.

Pragmatic rules

The existence of content-dependent reasoning has been graphically illustrated through a deductive reasoning problem first reported by Wason in 1966. In its original version the task took the form of four cards spread out in front of the subject so that each face showed a single symbol, say, A, B, 2, and 3. Subjects were told at the outset that each card had a letter on one side and a number on the other and their task was to establish the truth of the following rule:

"If a card has an A on one side then it has a 2 on the other side".

They were to select just those cards that needed to be turned over in order to determine whether the conditional rule was true or false. Far from proceeding logically in this situation, Wason found that his (student) subjects made characteristic errors when they selected their cards. Around 90% of the subjects tested failed to turn over the correct cards. The majority of choices focused upon just one card (the A card) or, if two cards were selected, these tended to be the A and the 2 card.

The failure of subjects to select the card bearing the 3 is significant because, if it has an A on the reverse, the rule has not been followed and is thereby disconfirmed. It may not be possible to prove beyond doubt that a rule is true but it is certainly possible to prove that it is false. Ideally, therefore, subjects should turn over the card with the A in order to establish that there is a 2 on the reverse (the rule has been followed) and the card with the 3 in order to establish that there is not an A on the other side (the rule has not been violated). None of the other possible card selections is logically implicated in establishing the truth of the rule. The B card has no bearing on the rule as stated and the letter on the reverse of the 2 card is irrelevant because the rule only refers to legitimate pairings for all As.

In the time since the four card task was first reported, no card has been left unturned in a determined search to find out just what is going on. Why are intelligent subjects being misled in this test situation and are there other situations where they might do better?

There are certainly situations where exactly the same logical problem is much easier to handle. These apply when the conditional rule is given an appropriate background context. For example, presenting the selection problem in the form shown in Table 10.4 leads to a dramatic improvement in the observed levels of performance.

TABLE 10.4
Adding familiar context to the Wason rule

"As part of your job as a Sales Assistant you have to check sales receipts to make sure that any sale over $30 has been approved by the head clerk. The amount of the sale is written on the front of the bill. Given these four bills, which of the four would you have to turn over to make sure that the assistants had acted properly?"

Rule: "If a purchase exceeds $30, then a receipt must be signed by the store manager"

Bills	$15	$45	Signed	Not signed

From Rumelhart, 1980.

Under these circumstances, a majority of subjects (correctly) chose to turn over the $45 bill to see if the rule had been observed and the "not signed" bill to see if the rule had been broken. Similar results have been reported by Johnson-Laird, Legrenzi, and Legrenzi (1972), when they presented the task as a conditional decision associated with sorting letters at the Post Office as compared with an abstract version that simply stated the rule without providing contextual support. Of the 24 subjects tested, only 2 failed to make the correct choices in the concrete version whereas 22 failed to do so when faced with the abstract version.

If solvers are not using the rules of formal logic to guide their actions, they may well be using schematic rules, i.e. context-sensitive, production rules that can be implemented under the right external conditions. Such rules may not be triggered if the selection problem is presented in an abstract form but they are likely to be matched when the test situation mimics the situations occurring in everyday social life. For example, in the course of social interaction, we frequently come up against "permission" rules of the kind:

"If one is to take action A, then one must first satisfy precondition B".

The rule applies to many of the rights a society conveys on its citizens (If you are over 18 then you can vote) and it also applies to most commercial transactions (If you pay the entry fee then you can participate). By virtue of being exposed to structurally similar situations of this kind, we could be led through induction to construct a "permission schema" built around production rules relating to the antecedents and consequents associated with granting permission. Cheng and Holyoak (1985) have proposed that such a schema could be constructed around four rules:

1.   If the action is to be taken then the precondition must be satisfied.
2.   If the action is not to be taken then the precondition need not be satisfied.
3.   If the precondition is satisfied then the action may be taken.
4.   If the precondition is not satisfied then the action may not be taken.

As a permission schema would be invoked by certain presentation formats but not others, this would explain why performance on the selection task waxes and wanes in the manner reported.

A pertinent example is provided by Girotto, Light, and Colbourn (1988) who presented children with a rule relating to honey bees and their habits while varying the contextual background in such a way as to elicit either a permission schema or some other knowledge schema. The children were first shown a display in which some bees were in the hive while others were outside. They were then given a probe which, when applied to individual bees, indicated audibly whether or not they should be in that location.

In order to evoke a permission schema, the (10-year-old) subjects were told:

"All buzzing bees must stay inside the hive in the evenings following instructions from the Queen Bee".

The children were then asked to test whether any bees were breaking the rule (i.e. by testing those that were outside the hive). In a second condition (Formal), the same situation was described in terms of the formal rule:

"All buzzing bees are now inside the hive".

Here, the children were required to test the rule in the absence of any contextual support. Under the third condition (Diagnostic), the situation was backed up by additional description which, while not eliciting a permission schema, did activate a degree of relevant background knowledge. Now the hive was described as being underground and occupied by two types of bees; those living underground and those above ground. Each subject was to test whether:

"All the buzzing bees live underground".

The children's performance varied considerably over the three conditions. Under the Permission format, the success rate averaged at 78%, this dropped to 56% for the Diagnostic condition, and then dropped again to a low of 28% under the Formal condition.

These performance variations can be interpreted as dependent on the likelihood that a given contextual background elicits an appropriate production rule within the pragmatic schema but it still leaves certain problems unresolved. As we move away from the original version of the Wason conditional rule, it is possible that the subject's perception of the task may change. In treating a conditional rule as a statement of obligation or permission, subjects are no longer concerned with deciding whether the rule is true or false in the given circumstances so much as deciding what one should do under these circumstances (Over & Manktelow, 1993). Furthermore, as both these authors and Johnson-Laird and Byrne (1991) have argued, pragmatic schemas cannot on their own provide an adequate account of such "deontic reasoning" so long as the deontic terms "must" and "may" remain unanalysed.

Manipulating mental models

All of the reasoning tasks just discussed have required subjects to comprehend a relatively complex body of discourse, whether dealing with retailing procedures, postal practices, or the habits of bees. Subjects must first comprehend these cover stories before they can make further progress. Consequently, we can expect the text base and mental model that accompany text comprehension to bear directly upon the quality of reasoning that then follows. In fact, according to Johnson-Laird and Byrne (1991), it is the mental model dealing with what the discourse is about that gets to the crux of the reasoning process. It is the properties of mental models (not formal rules or pragmatic schemas) that determine the course reasoning is likely to take, as they control the hypotheses we are likely to entertain and hence whatever tests we then think necessary for deciding their validity.

As we saw in Chapter 9, in principle, the reader can draw upon whatever general knowledge may be deemed relevant when constructing a mental model for a situation as described. Consequently, this perspective provides a broader framework for explaining reasoning variations than either of the frameworks based on formal rules or pragmatic schemas. Formal rules may account for successful reasoning in novel situations but they do not readily explain the vagaries of content-dependent reasoning. Content-specific rules may account for content-dependency during reasoning but they do not readily explain how we reason in novel situations. Explanations based on mental models can be extended to cope with both types of demand.

Grounding reasoning in the formation and comparison of mental models implies that at least three processing stages need to be distinguished. As we attempt to deduce a conclusion from a given set of premises, there will be a preliminary stage where the stated premises are used as a springboard for creating a mental model of the situation being described. It may be that one model will suffice for this purpose but, typically, more than one will be needed. With these models in mind, the reasoner then enters into a second stage where an attempt is made at deriving information consistent with the properties of the models but which has not been supplied by the premises themselves. This derived information is then evaluated in the third and final stage where it is checked by reference to any alternative models that might exist which are consistent with the premises as stated but are incompatible with the putative conclusions.

The first two stages are part of normal discourse comprehension. It is only in the third and final stage that specific, deductive processes are brought into play and it is during this stage that errors in reasoning are likely to arise should subjects fail to consider the full range of models compatible with the premises as stated. Where we arrive at a deduction that we find easy, this is because the associated model building has been straightforward and undemanding. Where we find a deduction to be difficult and prone to error, this is because the mental models being entertained are not fully representative of the situation that is being described.

To take a concrete example: on this argument the difference in the difficulty of the modus ponens and modus tollens deductions resides in the way in which the two sets of premises come to be represented in their respective mental models. Following Johnson-Laird and Byrne, we will assume that when reasoners are setting up tokens for the entities involved, they try to keep as much information as they can in an implicit form. Hence, given:

If there is a circle then there is a triangle

this premise is taken to support an explicit model containing a token for a circle and a token for a triangle. Another model that is compatible with this assertion, (e.g. the state of affairs where there is not a circle) is unlikely to be represented explicitly, and it can be left implicit in the form of a dummy model (indicated by ...) which can be fleshed out later if required. This gives rise to a mental representation such as:

Circle   Triangle
...

where the categorical premise for modus ponens (There is a circle) is accommodated by the first, explicit model. In this form it supports the valid conclusion—there is a triangle—as no other model can be derived from the premises that falsifies it.

If we now apply the same analysis to modus tollens, the categorical premise (There is not a triangle) calls for the elimination of the first model which contains the triangle. This means that the implicit model now has to be fleshed out to accommodate the information from the categorical premise that there is not a triangle:

¬ Triangle

In this form the model represents only the categorical premise and it appears to suggest that no valid conclusion can be drawn—the error people typically make in these circumstances.

Proceeding to a correct conclusion requires a further step in model building where the information that has been left implicit is now made explicit. This requires three models in all:

Circle   Triangle

¬ Circle   Triangle

¬ Circle   ¬ Triangle

Reference to these models ensures that, given the categorical premise "there is not a triangle" (tokened here as ¬triangle), the first two models can be eliminated. This leaves only the third model which supports the valid deduction that there is not a circle. Hence, modus tollens is the more difficult deduction because it calls for a more extensive set of models than modus ponens. Furthermore, a similar analysis can be applied to other forms of deduction (see Johnson-Laird, Byrne, & Schaeken, 1992).

If we subject the Wason task and its conditional rule to the same scrutiny, once again we find that the quality of a subject's performance will depend on whether or not models have been created that include explicit tokens for negative instances. In the original version, the neutral conditional:

If there is an A then there is a 2

yields two models; an explicit model which satisfies the antecedent and the consequent, and an implicit model which allows for the case where the antecedent is not satisfied:

[A] 2

...

(Here the symbol [A] is taken to mean that there is an exhaustive representation of the possible occurrences of A—it cannot occur in any other models.)

As with the previous example, in the second model (...) the detail has been left implicit. There are alternative representations but there has been no attempt to specify what they might be. Subjects approaching the Wason task with just these models in mind will select only those cards that are explicitly represented and this means selecting the card depicting A and that depicting 2, which is the typical (and erroneous) response.

Representing the full set of possibilities means entertaining three mental models:

$$
\begin{array}{ll}
[A] & 2 \\
\neg A & 2 \\
\neg A & \neg 2
\end{array}
$$

As ¬A can occur with either 2 or ¬2, it cannot reveal whether the rule is true or false and hence subjects will be unlikely to choose this card. On the other hand, subjects who are entertaining this combination of models will be drawn into considering the ¬A and the ¬2 cards. As indicated, the ¬2 card would falsify the rule if it occurred with the A card, and it should, therefore, be turned over.

Evidentally, any manipulation that encourages subjects to work with more detailed models of the situation and its possibilities should boost the quality of their performance. Thus the contextual biases asssociated with the Wason task can easily be accounted for both as they bear upon the explicit tokening of the critical cards and the extent to which a search for counter-instances is conducted. Furthermore, the mental model approach can be extended to account for other forms of reasoning besides deduction. As Legrenzi, Girotto, and Johnson-Laird (1993) point out, the attentional focusing effects contingent on the mental models subjects happen to entertain can also be used to explain performance variations during decision making. For example, the assymetries associated with the selection or rejection of holiday resorts described earlier could readily be related to the content of the different mental models likely to accompany each type of decision.

Informal reasoning

There are many occasions when we reason our way through to a conclusion that seems to be the best bet in the circumstances without any certainty that we are right. Should we take on private health insurance given that the state health service appears to be breaking down? Will the quality of higher education be reduced by extending the teaching year and cutting down on the length of the degree? Compared against testing the truth of a conditional statement or the products of syllogistic reasoning, such problems are far more unstructured and open-ended. They are also more typical of the day-to-day demands made upon our reasoning abilities.

Table 10.5 reproduces some of the differences that distinguish formal from informal reasoning (see Galotti, 1989).

The predilection for studying formal reasoning over informal reasoning tends to be justified in terms of the potential links between

TABLE 10.5
Differences between formal and everyday reasoning tasks

Formal	*Informal*
All premises are supplied	Some premises are implicit and some are not supplied at all
Problems are self-contained	Problems are not self-contained
There is typically one correct answer	There are typically several possible answers that vary in quality
Established methods of inference that apply to the problem often exist	There rarely exist established procedures for solving the problem
It is typically unambiguous when the problem is solved	It is often unclear whether the current "best" solution is good enough
The content of the problem is often of limited academic interest	The content of the problem typically has potential personal relevance
Problems are solved for their own sake	Problems are often solved as a means of achieving other goals

From Galotti, 1989.

the two although, as Galotti has noted, these links are more often assumed than demonstrated. In this respect, explanations of formal reasoning based on mental models have the edge over competing explanations because they ground both forms of reasoning in the processes serving discourse comprehension in general.

That said, the mental models account is relatively silent when it comes to the principles determining the transition from the text base encoding the problem as set and the formation of the situation model encoding its referential meaning. This may not be so critical for problems that are self-contained but it becomes more of an issue for the complex situations associated with informal reasoning. How should we parse a complex situation into its salient and peripheral components? How should salient details be linked together in the right order? The answers to these questions will have a critical bearing on the format of the mental models we bring to mind and *pari passu* on the tests and conclusions we are led to entertain.

Narrative representation and informal reasoning
Looking back over the topics of problem solving, decision making, and reasoning it seems that our endeavours in these areas are neither purely logical nor entirely dependent on a collection of *ad hoc* heuristic devices. Rather, as Lloyd (1988) has indicated, our endeavours typically occupy the middle ground between these extremes. Mental models are part of this middle ground but it is also occupied by other discourse processing skills including those that inform narrative comprehension. Indeed, we

can suppose that it was narrative comprehension, not syllogistic reasoning or hypothesis testing, that situation models evolved to service in the first place.

All of which suggests that we can use narrative schemas to determine what should be included or excluded from an associated mental model and hence we can expect to find our attempts at reasoning to be the more successful the more the problem situation can be accommodated within the narrative format. For Lloyd, this is taken to mean that there is a primary mode of reasoning which relies heavily upon the processes involved in narrative comprehension. The other styles of reasoning which rely on specialised rules for cross checking and evaluating our putative conclusions have arisen subsequently as a secondary development from this primary source.

The primary reasoning mode would be grounded in the stories we spin as we try to give coherence to the flow of everyday events. These storylines are then used to shape the hypotheses we choose to test concerning the properties of the situation in question. Provided this exercise can proceed without too much shoving and straining, we come to accept the cover story as a true account of what happened. If no such accommodation is possible—say, critical events are left floating, unanchored to any plausible antecedent causes—we can then conclude that we are being presented with only half the story. Either way, it would be the casting of the flow of events into a narrative frame that informs our attempts to decide what is to be accepted as true or false.

Lloyd points out that a default mode of reasoning based on narrative understanding makes sense of the division between those situations in which we find it easy to reason our way to a conclusion and those in which we find it difficult. The division falls between those problem situations that can be readily assimilated to a narrative framework and those that cannot. We seem to be more at ease when reasoning about specific people doing specific things at specific times. We are less at ease when reasoning needs to call upon universal statements, the negation of prior information, and atemporal settings. The former circumstances are those in which we can spin stories to ourselves, the latter circumstances are those in which this is difficult or not possible. For Lloyd, therefore, narrative representation emerges as the primary, default mode for interpreting events and as the preferred route to the construction of a mental model. We may then add to this resource by using the tools of logic to extend and refine the model and to test any conclusions it may support, but this secondary reasoning mode may well be left dormant if the original storyline seems strong enough on its own.

Ultimately, Lloyd's theoretical position is not that far removed from Johnson-Laird's in that both of these theorists attempt to relate reasoning strategies to more general modes of human understanding. However, their emphases are rather different. Lloyd has little to say about Johnson-Laird's third, deductive stage and concentrates instead on the earlier stages. He also differs in taking the primary purpose of narrative-based reasoning to be that of injecting coherence into the flux of experience, not that of creating true and justified beliefs. As he remarks, "in arriving at the plot, we may also come to believe that we have hit upon the proof".

NARRATIVE REASONING

So far, the claims in favour of a narrative mode of reasoning have been based on a selective trawl through the experimental evidence rather than on a detailed analysis of narrative reasoning at work. We have a plausible story but no real proof. This deficiency can easily be rectified, as it is possible to identify certain situations where it seems the narrative mode is predominantly being used to structure and evaluate a complex body of evidence. In courts of law up and down the country, juries are required to reason about the guilt or innocence of people brought to trial. In order to reach their decision, jurors must listen to a series of accounts, which are often contradictory in themselves, but are certainly contradictory when viewed through the eyes of the defence and the prosecution. In such cases, it seems that jurors cope with the conflicting evidence by searching for plausible stories that can tie the various strands of evidence together. They then reach their verdict by selecting whichever narrative version they think best represents the case as charged. Just how successful these efforts are likely to be will depend on (1) the actual information presented during the trial, (2) the juror's general knowledge of similar situations, and (3) the juror's tacit use of story macrostructures to sift critical episodes from incidental detail, (see Pennington & Hastie, 1986, 1988).

The evidence as presented to the court will determine the main constituents of the story that is being created but not necessarily how and where they will feature in the developing narrative representation. This aspect may be determined by jurors finding analogous stories from the past or by making one up on the spot. Either way, as a particular narrative is pieced together, the emergent macrostructure helps to define when vital information is lacking. If stated antecedents are not balanced by their consequences the presence of such an imbalance in the burgeoning storyline indicates the account being offered is suspect.

Should jurors find that they are able to construct more than one story to fit the evidence, it is still likely that one of these versions will stand out as optimal. This will be the version that provides the best coverage for the facts as stated, that has the greatest degree of internal coherence and which offers the best fit to the juror's knowledge of similar cases. Once the best story version has been selected it can then be matched against the verdicts available to the court in order to bring the proceedings to a conclusion.

Empirical evidence for equating juror decision-making with narrative cognition has been derived by Pennington and Hastie (1986, 1988) based on jury simulations. This work has shown that subjects (*qua* jurors):

1. Spontaneously used narratives to summarise the evidence put before them.
2. Arrived at different verdicts if they had created different stories for the same evidence.
3. Could be swayed to one or another verdict if the trial evidence was presented in a form that favoured one narrative version over another.

The same experimenters have also found that subject jurors find it easier to weigh the evidence before them when they are allowed to assimilate it in story form (Pennington & Hastie, 1992).

In this experiment, the same trial evidence was presented, either as the event details had arisen over time (thus favouring story construction) or by grouping the details according to the legal points involved (making it more difficult for the subjects to recast the details into story form). Critical evidence relating to the credibility of a witness's testimony was found to have more effect on the final verdict when it occurred against a story background than when it did not—as though assimilating the caveat into a story framework invested it with a global significance which was lost or overlooked when the presentation took on a non-story format.

Admittedly, this finding could simply mean that the "legal" version was perceived as being a more haphazard presentation of the facts than the story version and it was this factor, not the story framework, that determined the subsequent weightings. But, as it has been found that jurors who assigned different stories to the same evidence were drawn towards different verdicts, this outcome is compatible with the storyline being important in its own right (see also Pennington & Hastie, 1993).

For some observers, the fact that we are so good at spinning stories is taken to mean that all forms of reasoning can be understood as an exercise in storytelling, including scientific reasoning (Rouse, 1990). However, just because it may be possible to substitute one mode of reasoning for another does not license the conclusion that one mode, the default mode, must always hold sway. Logic, mathematics, and scientific method all testify that other modes of reasoning than narrative cognition exist. Equally, by the same argument, because they exist, we cannot then conclude that they necessarily provide the only vehicles though which reasoning can occur even if they happen to offer the best means for getting at the truth.

ESTABLISHING TRUE AND FALSE BELIEFS

Where there are conflicting versions relating to the same event, this places an obligation on the would-be judge to suspend belief in order to treat all the evidence impartially. An impartial judge should not simply accept all that is said as being true, rather, he or she should adopt a neutral, non-committal stance towards the competing claims until all the evidence is in. Unfortunately, although steadfast neutrality under these circumstances may be logically desirable, it may not be humanly feasible. In coming to understand we may also come to accept by default that which we have understood.

In a preliminary study addressing this issue, (Gilbert, Krull, & Malone, 1990), subjects were told that they were participating in a language-learning exercise which was intended to match the tenor of everyday learning conditions. Accordingly, they were provided with a translation of "Hopi Indian" terms and, for some of these terms, they were told shortly afterwards whether they had been given a true or false translation. This procedure was said to be typical of everyday life where "we often hear new words and guess their meaning from context (but) later we may find we were right or wrong or get no feedback" (p.603).

During this first learning phase, subjects were also informed that because their "speed of response is related to the ability to learn languages", on certain trials only, they would be interrupted in order that their response speed could be tested. This was done by presenting tones to which they were to respond by pressing a button as quickly as possible. The real purpose behind this interruption was to truncate the subject's assessment of the feedback about a definition's truth status.

Altogether, a subject saw 28 word-translations (e.g. "A Twyrin is a Doctor"), 12 of which were signalled as true or false. Within this set of twelve, four translations were interrupted by a tone coming 750msec after the true or false signal. This happened on two occasions following "true" feedback and two occasions following "false" feedback. In the second phase of the study, subjects were then shown 21 questions testing what they had learned (e.g. "Is a twyrin a doctor?") or posing new, unseen definitions. Subjects were to respond to these questions by indicating whether they were true or false, thus providing a measure of what had been learned in the first phase as well as indicating how the interruptions had affected this learning.

It transpired that although interruption had no effect on the correct identification of true translations, (55% correct when uninterrupted versus 58% correct when interrupted), interruption did reduce the incidence of correct identifications of false translations. Uninterrupted, 55% of these translation were correctly identified but following interruption this measure fell to 35%. In other words, the interruption had an asymmetrical effect; it increased the percentage of false statements misidentified as true but did not affect the percentage of true statements misidentified as false. Under resource depletion, it seems that false statements are particularly prone to less accurate processing than true statements.

In a second study, subjects were informed that they were participating in a "lie detection task" and they were to watch a series of smiling faces which represented either genuine or feigned happiness. Information about which face was which could come before or after a face had been displayed. As in the previous experiment, subjects were interrupted at various points in order to truncate their processing of the true/false labels. Once again it was found that the interruptions exerted an assymetrical effect. Whereas an interruption caused subjects to mistake false faces for true ones, the reverse pattern did not occur.

The results from these two experiments could be explained if subjects in the course of comprehending a statement also go on to treat it as true by default. That is, when comprehending, we start off by accepting a statement as true, and only afterwards is this belief ascription altered should it be shown to be necessary. Feedback that a statement is false, therefore, would require an extra processing stage compared with feedback that it is true. Should a subject's attentional resources be depleted during the belief adjustment phase, this will necessarily have different implications depending on whether the feedback states that something is false or that it is true. In the latter case, truth status will coincide with its default status so the interruption is of little consequence. In the former case, the readjustment from true to false may be blocked by the interruption. Hence, by linking comprehension and acceptance we can account for the asymmetric effect of the interruptions.

Further experiments have indicated that subjects in a "holding" situation (where the truth status of a statement had still to be resolved) not only remembered that information as being true, they also acted upon this information as if this was the case (Gilbert, Taforodi, &

Malone, 1993). None of which marks out the human agent as engaging in dispassionate reasoning prior to arriving at a measured and rational conclusion.

HUMAN RATIONALITY

We have found little in this review to bolster our faith in the rationality of individual human thought. On the contrary, we have found that plot may be taken as proof, pseudo-evidence may be favoured over genuine evidence and, in coming to comprehend, we are inclined to accept uncritically what we have read or heard. All told, a picture that is not that removed from the state of "punctate cognition" held up to ridicule by Fodor and Pylyshyn (1988).

It is also a picture that is at odds with the concept of the "rational mind" which has played an important role in the history of Western thought since the time of the Enlightenment. It was at that historical juncture that, according to Flanagan (1984, pp.208–209), faith in God as the primary route to true knowledge was replaced by the powers of human reason:

> ... and the human project was reconceived as the project of coming to possess justified true beliefs, as opposed to beliefs that were edifying and comforting, but nevertheless unsupportable and superstitious. Rationality was to be the road to these justified true beliefs ... [where] ... you are rational just in case you systematically instantiate the rules and principles of inductive logic, statistics, and probability theory on the one hand, and deductive logic and all the mathematical sciences, on the other.

As it would be a singularly jaundiced view that claimed there has been no progress in the sum total of human knowledge since the Enlightenment, either the reported defects in individual rationality are not as dire as has been painted or there is another dimension to rationality that has not yet been addressed. Both reservations are justified.

Gigerenzer (1993) has mounted a compelling argument to the effect that studies such as those by Tversky and Kahneman dealing with defects in handling probabilistic information have missed their target. Consider again the problem of predicting Linda's current occupation. In its original format, the problem referred to a single case (Linda) and it was found that subjects opted for the illogical choice. When Gigerenzer reworded the problem so that the experimental subjects had to make frequency judgements rather than a probability estimate, they now fared much better. Under this revision, subjects were provided with the description of Linda and were then asked:

Out of 100 people who fit this description, how many are bank tellers? / Banktellers who are active in the feminist movement?

Under these circumstances the majority of subjects were not lured into making the mistake of choosing the less probable alternative. In accounting for this reversal, Gigerenzer adopts an evolutionary perspective, arguing that whereas selection is likely to have favoured cognitive algorithms for dealing with the frequencies of events, this would not be the case for calculating percentages or probability estimates. In other words, the cognitive algorithm(s) employed to reach an appropriate decision will be engaged by certain experimental tasks but not others. We may not be consistently rational but, there again, we are not consistently irrational either.

Such a state of "bounded rationality" is entirely compatible with the resource limitations that necessarily attend the exercise of individual cognition. It was limitations in attentional resources and processing capacity that determined the piecemeal and partial updating accompanying the assimilation of new information into a knowledge base, as discussed in Chapter 6. So we should not be surprised that these same limitations have now resurfaced in the context of rational thought. Human rationality may have definite limits—there are boundary constraints that derive from our limited computational resources—but this is not the same as saying that the human mind is intrinsically irrational. Bounded rationality is still a form of rational thinking. Pursuing this line of reasoning has led Oaksford and Chater (1993) to decry the fact that the implications deriving from the Frame Problem have not penetrated into the mainstream, psychological analyses of rational thought. Rectifying this deficiency, they suggest, calls for "more ecologically valid" investigations to be conducted which concentrate on how people cope with updating their beliefs in real-life situations. And they cite jury studies as an example of how to proceed.

Obviously, their proposal is entirely congruent with the tenor of the arguments we have been piecing together both here and in earlier sections. However, for Oaksford and Chater, the significance of the court room is that it would allow us to investigate *the individual* as he or she grapples with shifting bodies of evidence under real-life conditions. While endorsing that view, there is another branch to this ecological argument which grows out of the fact that "jury" is a collective noun. It is no coincidence that standard court-room procedure explicitly avoids relying on the deliberations of a single juror for delivering a verdict. The lessons of legal experience have taught that a more balanced outcome is likely when individuals are required to work *collectively* towards reaching an agreed verdict. Expressed somewhat differently, individual rationality may indeed be bounded, but the belief systems produced by individuals working collectively on a common problem may be significantly less constrained.

There are two principles operating at the collective level to suggest why this should be so. First, different individuals are unlikely to formulate identical beliefs from their experiences. This means the potential is always there for a clash of opinion as one viewpoint is set against another. Where such disagreement draws us into public debate, we may then find our ideas being exposed to a flurry of criticisms which serve to expose inconsistencies in the line of argument we have adopted. Inconsistencies that we had signally failed to detect through the exercise of our own reasoning skills.

Second, locating individual cognitive processes within a collective or social context enables us to recognise the full extent to which our limited individual resources can be supplemented by the much wider resources of a host culture. The most obvious example here is the way in which scientific procedures have been developed which provide an iterative series of checks and balances on the products of individual minds. This has resulted in a cumulative refinement in belief systems which is far in excess of anything that could be achieved in the lifetime of the individual thinker—whether acting alone or in concert with others. In other words, our transactions within the wider social community are also germane to the issue of individual rationality.

Recognising that people conduct their reasoning in the company of others and against a cumulative, historical setting may seem obvious and unexceptional. It is indeed commonplace. Nonetheless, once we start to address the collective aspects of cognition we soon come up against qualitatively new principles at work which bring into question the adequacy of the cognitive models that have been assembled from study of the individual case. We will explore some of these issues in the final section. It begins by asking whether the phenomena studied under the banner of social cognition can be fully assimilated within the cognitive frameworks predicated on the study of the individual mind.

SECTION FOUR

Knowledge in minds

CHAPTER ELEVEN

Social cognition

Social cognition deals with the manner in which we construe the thoughts and actions of other people against the backdrop of our own plans and goals. We have already considered the analogue case with fictional characters and we can expect the same basic processes that were involved there to be equally central in social cognition. However, they are labelled differently. Categorisation comes under the heading of social stereotyping; reasoning comes in the form of social attribution; and knowledge updating appears in various guises including impression formation, attitude change, and persuasion. The research parallels are real and substantial and they reflect large-scale borrowings by social psychologists from methods and explanations that were first developed in the cognitive laboratory.

The extent of this borrowing would seem to corroborate the widely held view that individually derived cognitive models can be adapted (with some local changes) to cover the full range of social cognitive phenomena. Perhaps so, but there are other, more radical opinions that have set out to unsettle or, indeed, sever this dependent relationship. Moscovici (1988) has argued that the classical stance of treating knowledge as in the private possession of the individual needs to be supplemented by reference to the collective representations shared by members of particular social groups. Proponents of "social constructionism" such as Gergen and Gergen, (1991) have gone much further down this road in holding that all forms of knowledge are to be understood as social constructions arising out of the dynamics of social exchange. By this point, the boundary between internalised representations and their external referents has effectively been dismantled—along with the need for cognitive mechanisms designed to straddle this division.

We will look at the most conservative position first of all. This holds that it is quite possible to incorporate the phenomena of social cognition within the information processing framework as individually understood. Accordingly, we will see what this means for the processes of social categorisation and social attribution.

SOCIAL CATEGORISATION AS
INFORMATION PROCESSING

Social categorisation occurs when we assign individuals to some particular social group, as, say, when new acquaintances are categorised in terms of their ethnic status. The basic knowledge that is being called upon here can be modelled through an associative network, much as for other forms of declarative knowledge. However, unlike instances from inanimate categories, people are inclined to object when they find the properties of a general category are being used to override their individual identity—especially if the resulting stereotype works to their marked disadvantage, as is often the case.

Stereotypes incorporate our default beliefs about the characteristics of target social groups. Initially, investigators attempted to elicit the content of these beliefs by getting respondents to list the characteristics they associated with particular ethnic labels. Thus, Katz and Braly (1933) found considerable agreement among their respondents on the supposed characteristics of different national groups although for many such groups this meant being saddled with some extremely negative traits. A replication conducted two decades later suggested that, although the more extreme judgements had been modified in the intervening years, there was still a significant degree of inter-subject agreement (Gilbert, 1951). These later respondents were far less inclined towards the blatant stereotypes reported by Katz and Braly although this is not to say that they avoided the less obvious distortions associated with stereotyping (Pettigrew & Meertens, 1995).

Stereotyped judgements come enshrined in statements such as "the English are reserved" or "the Italians are passionate". In each case, we find a target group is being tacitly compared to some other group (or groups) which, by implication, are less reserved or less passionate. Hence, one of the direct consequences of stereotyping is to highlight presumed inter-group differences. As "inter-group accentuation" also occurs when inanimate objects are labelled as belonging to different groups, this suggests that the phenomenon is not specific to social cognition but rather draws upon some very general cognitive mechanisms.

Consider the case of skin colour. Whereas different individuals can be expected to occupy different positions along this continuous dimension, labelling one half of the series "black" and the other half "white" serves to impose a strict dichotomy on the population members. Skin colour will continue to vary continuously but the presence of the labels introduces an abrupt rather than a graded transition between the two classes. Should subjects make judgements of skin colour under these circumstances, they are likely to respond by exaggerating the differences between two instances which, while being close together on the physical continuum, carry different labels.

The simplest account of why this should happen is that inter-class accentuation arises when joint sources of information (skin colour and label) are combined to form a single judgement. This explanation was first put forward by Tajfel in 1957 and, a few years later it was tested under very basic psychophysical conditions (Tajfel & Wilkes, 1963).

The experimental procedure called for absolute judgements of the length of each of eight lines under three presentation conditions. In the classified condition, the (four) smaller lines were all labelled A and the (four) larger lines were all labelled B. In two control conditions, the lengths were either unlabelled or were assigned labels at random. As Tajfel had predicted, the presence of the consistent classification did serve to increase the judged difference between physically proximate stimuli occupying different classes, both when compared against the actual scale differences and the judgements obtained under the control conditions. The consistent labelling, it seems, encouraged the judges to "stereotype" the component lengths in terms of their assigned categories. Subsequent studies have shown that similar accentuation effects can be demonstrated in other, more obviously social judgement conditions—see Eiser and Stroebe (1972) for a comprehensive review. Thus, at least some of the judgement biases associated with social stereotyping appear to be intrinsically related to the way in which we as individuals are disposed to process compound sources of information.

More generally, stereotypes can be conceived as schematic knowledge structures which act to structure (and sustain) our expectations about the behaviour of members of target groups. If we believe that the English are reserved and the Italians are passionate, this outlook leads us to behave in different ways when we form new encounters. With members of the first group we may be wary of being rebuffed if we attempt to strike up a conversation; with members of the second group we may welcome the distraction. Given such predispositions in how we approach target groups, the expectations involved can then become self-perpetuating as the feedback from each transaction is selectively distorted in the direction of the active stereotype (Hamilton, Sherman, & Ruvolo, 1990). There will be occasions, however, when target individuals act out of line with the stereotypical content and we are forced to face up to the conceptual conflict that then ensues. People who expect the English to be reserved may be taken by surprise when they encounter the supporters of her national football team.

In Chapter 6, it was argued that schema inconsistencies of this kind are likely to be especially noticed and recalled, provided they are germane to the schema content. The equivalent findings for stereotypic inconsistencies present a somewhat more varied picture although, on balance, they do tend to fall into line with this conclusion. Following a meta-analytic survey of some 60 such studies, Rojahn and Pettigrew (1992, p.81) concluded that there is "a slight overall memory advantage for schema inconsistent information". They report that the studies that supported this conclusion tended to be the ones where:

1.   The proportion of schema-inconsistent detail was not too great so that the person could still be seen as falling into a particular category.
2.   The relevant schema had been active at the time of encoding.
3.   The inconsistency involved was relevant to the schematic content.

In a number of significant respects, therefore, social stereotyping turns out to be quite consistent with other, non-social accounts of categorisation and schematic processes at work.

CAUSAL INFERENCING AND CATEGORY MEMBERSHIP

As people characteristically belong to not one but a number of social groups, there will be many occasions when we try to justify to ourselves how it is that the same person could belong to two or more apparently disparate groups. Kunda, Miller, and Claire (1990) have reported on the results of a series of studies where their subjects attempted to predict a person's attributes under various combinations of class membership. They found that when the combinations were surprising or unusual, the subjects typically turned to causal reasoning to justify the combination. Given an unusual example of dual class membership (such as a

"Harvard-educated carpenter"), subjects proceeded to ask themselves "How could a person belonging to category A come to acquire membership of category B?" This then led them to invent narrative vignettes which explained the link by invoking "emergent attributes" that were not part of the constituent categories. Thus, for the Harvard-educated carpenter, certain subjects introduced "non-materialistic" into the picture and then used this trait as the causal antecedent that prompted the transition from cloisters to carpentry. Once they had constructed a plausible storyline that could accommodate the two roles, they were satisfied.

In fact, a goodly part of everyday reasoning is taken up with searching around for causal explanations that will explain the behaviour of those around us. "Why did a colleague support that political line?" (was it conviction or expediency). "Why have the neighbours constructed that large fence and installed a guard dog?" (do they like privacy or are they frightened by my friends). As these examples indicate, when attributing a cause to an action we can choose to locate the cause either within the actor or within the eliciting situation. Which type of cause we select, internal or external, will then determine how we construe the behaviour in question. If we believe that criminal behaviour is due to some intrinsic failing in the individual criminal then our prescriptions for dealing with crime will differ from those who believe that criminals are the victims of oppressive social controls. All of which prompts the question—if both options are available, what leads us to choose one locus over the other?

Part of the answer to this question lies in the way in which we can use different combinations of events as pointers to internal or external causation. When we learn that John fails to be selected for a job, a probable cause for this failure may exist within John or it may lie with the employing agency. In the former case, John fails because of a dispositional cause—he may be a poor interviewee. In the latter case, he fails because of an external cause—he was unfortunate in applying to a company with stringent selection criteria. The internal attribution implies that John is unlikely to fare any better with other job applications. The external attribution suggests there is every reason for him to keep on trying. If we know that many other applicants, not just John, have been turned down by the company (consensus information) this strengthens the case for an external cause. Conversely, if we know that John has been turned down by a number of other employers (distinctiveness information), then this swings us in the other direction towards an internal locus (see Brown, 1986).

The direction of causal attributions will also be influenced by the extent to which we attend to the range of information on offer. This point has been well understood by generations of conjurers whose magical illusions frequently depend on the way in which attributional decisions are open to attentional manipulation. A telling example occurred in 1856 when Robert-Houdin (conjuror, illusionist, and inventor) was brought out of retirement by the French government to help settle an uprising in Algeria. The idea was to use his magical skills to demonstrate that France could call upon powers that were dramatically greater than those available to the religious rebels. To this end, Robert-Houdin put on a public performance in Algiers where one of the items in his repertoire was the Light and Heavy Chest. According to Dawes (1979, pp.125–127) when this trick had been performed in Europe it was presented as:

> ... a small, light, wooden box with a brass handle that becomes so heavy it can't be lifted. ... For political reasons however, the Arab audience received a presentation that was entirely different. [This time it demonstrated how] ... the most powerful man would be deprived of his strength.

People participating in an event are also likely to make different attributions to those made by observers who are on the fringes of the action. Observers tend to underplay the significance of situational factors, whereas actors are more likely to favour situational forces as the cause of their behaviour—a phenomenon that has been termed the "fundamental attribution error" by Jones and Nisbett (1971). An illustration can be found in a study by Ross, Amabile, and Steinmetz (1977) who staged a public quiz in which half of their experimental subjects acted as quizmasters, (asking questions on topics of their own choice), and the other half served as the contestants providing the answers. At the end of the quiz, both members of the pair, questioner and respondent, were called upon to rate their own and the other's level of general ability. Questioners' ratings indicated no difference between themselves and their yoked partners but the respondents saw things differently. Their ratings placed questioners above the average level of ability and located respondents (themselves) below this criterion. Whereas the questioners were well aware of the advantages accruing from picking their own questions, the respondents either overlooked or underestimated this relevant factor.

Explanations of these vagaries in attributional reasoning have been sought by postulating an internal "natural logic" (Jaspers, Hewstone, & Fincham, 1983) but this approach has met with the same types of criticism as were levelled at logical, rule-based explanations of formal reasoning. As with formal reasoning, the subsequent search for alternative explanations has tended to focus upon the pragmatic, contextual factors that accompany the attributional judgement. According to Hilton and Slugoski (1986) social attributions are made once the judge has determined how the target situation has deviated from the normal pattern. Once the source of the deviation has been identified this information is used to determine the direction the attribution should take.

It seems, therefore, that the adoption of a conservative stance towards the phenomena of social cognition has much to commend it. If such quintessential social phenomena as stereotyping and social attribution can be accommodated within the information processing framework without too much strain there seems every reason to suppose that other aspects of social cognition can be brought within the scope of cognitive mechanisms as individually defined. In which case, social psychology may have borrowed extensively from the bank of ideas in cognitive psychology but it can also point to a good return on the investment. On the other hand, if we ask why different people come to share commonly held assumptions about social groups, this generalisation begins to look somewhat less secure.

Consider again the phenomenon of stereotyping, this time in the light of why it is that certain social categories come to be shared by a significant proportion of the population. For stereotypes to be distributed in this way a process of diffusion must have occurred—a process that has not been addressed in the account just given. According to Tajfel (1981, p.145), there are two central issues associated with social stereotyping which need to be tackled in tandem:

> The first concerns an analysis of the functions that stereotypes serve for a social group within which they are widely diffused. The second question concerns the nature of the links between these social or group functions of stereotypes and their common adoption by large numbers of people who share a social affiliation. It is the asking of these two questions which defines the difference between the study of stereotypes *tout court* and the study of social stereotypes.

Although this pronouncement could be read as calling for more effort to be devoted to the study of the social institutions within which individuals exercise their intrinsic cognitive skills, this would be to misjudge the scale of the reassessment that is being proposed. Situating cognitive skills within the larger social framework not only means focusing on the collective context in which the operations of memory and thinking unfold, it can also mean treating this social milieu as integral to *how* they are exercised. Conceivably, there are social parameters to cognitive operations which are as much part of their *modus operandi* as the capacity of working memory or any of the other individually derived parameters of the cognitive architecture. Needless to say, this is a contentious claim but we will try to see why and how it has been made.

SOCIAL MEMORY

So far we have assumed that the memory stores and retrieval mechanisms that comprise the human memory system have been firmly located within individual heads, but there are other ways of proceeding. Collective or social models of memory, (e.g. Ostrom, 1989), largely reject this circumscribed view in favour of an alternative version in which memory operations are conceived as being distributed across different individuals. Ostrom cites the case of a couple travelling abroad, one driving and the other navigating, where each can be expected to encode different aspects of the same event. In effect, the "memory representation" for the journey is shared between them. Such situations are hardly uncommon; similar shared memories will arise whenever there is more than one witness to an event. And, as each participant is likely to be aware of this shared aspect of memory, subsequent recall can capitalise on this fact. It will be recalled from Chapter 4, that when Wagenaar found there were autobiographical events that he could not reconstruct on his own, he turned to others who were also present at the time for their help in bringing the events back to mind. Everyday recall, it seems, is not just a matter of individual memory stores and internal retrieval mechanisms, it can also "reduplicate" these aspects at the interpersonal level.

A similar line of argument has been proposed by Wegner, Erber, and Raymond (1991). They refer to "transactive" memory as a "shared system for encoding, storing and retrieving information" which applies when people sharing in a close relationship take on different responsibilities in the conduct of a joint task. Under these conditions they come to develop a transactive memory whose properties are presumed to be greater than either memory system when taken alone. As a result (Wegner et al., 1991, p.923):

> ... individual memory systems can become involved in larger, organised social memory systems that have emergent group mind properties not traceable to individuals.

If a transactive memory is to work effectively, each participant needs to know which component knowledge is currently being held by others, and this means that directories for indexing this information will need to be created and constantly updated. This requirement, however, can be mitigated if participants agree to take on differing spheres of responsibility and each can rely on the others' specialised abilities.

Wegner et al. provide partial support for this analysis when they demonstrated that subjects accustomed to a co-operative relationship on a shared memory task were thrown off balance when a distributed memory structure was imposed upon them from outside. But this hardly constitutes strong evidence for their additional claim that emergent properties can arise within transactive memory systems.

Upholding this claim, as Meudell, Hitch, and Kirby (1992) have recognised, requires rather more than just showing that two people together can remember more than either can recall alone. This outcome could arise for potentially trivial reasons. It could occur because, (1) they attended to different things at the time of encoding, or (2) because each happened to retrieve different things at recall. Neither of these features could be said to have "emerged" from their joint collaboration. Somewhat more significant would be the situation where, (3) the features that are recalled in the joint situation are features that neither participant could remember at all when recalling alone. Despite using a variety of memory tasks, Meudell et al. could find no evidence of features emerging in this way during social recall. In other words, the strong claims for the emergent properties of collective memory systems are either misplaced or at least premature. Still, it may be wrong to dismiss the first two points entirely out of hand. There are circumstances where the fact that participants in an event attend to and remember different things can exert an important influence on the content of individual thinking.

Assigning a collective dimension to memory, even if it is no more than different people remembering different things about the same situation, invests others with the power to influence what we are likely to remember or forget. In introducing this apparently innocuous point, we find that some far from innocuous implications for memory phemomena follow in its wake; implications that make little sense so long as we remain wedded to the individual perspective. Once we start to enquire "Who controls what will be selectively rehearsed and remembered?", and "What interests are shaping this choice?", we find ourselves being drawn into distinctly new territory.

Social institutions, such as governments and other interest groups, are far from indifferent to the ways in which past events are interpreted by the community at large. Indeed, they are often responsible for the historical record being rewritten to bring it into line with their preferred version. Favoured lives and events are chosen for celebration while other lives and events are passed over in silence. The process of deciding what is in or out—what should be commemorated or neglected—can set different vested interests against each other as each side tries to have the controlling say. Whichever side wins this struggle gains the power to legitimate their version of the historical record at the expense of rival accounts (see Middleton & Edwards, 1990).

Thus, in allowing for a degree of social control over what is collectively rehearsed, we find that an apparently clear boundary between the individual and society has begun to dissolve. It is no longer quite so obvious which of the processes contributing to knowledge construction are located within the individual and which are located within society at large.

SOCIAL REPRESENTATIONS

According to Moscovici (1988), there are certain types of cognitive structures that, although internalised by the individual members of specific social groups, nonetheless are best understood at the collective level. These "social representations" serve to structure reality in specific ways and, given that they are shared, they act as a common code for expressing and developing a particular point of view. Moscovici (Farr & Moscovici, 1984, p.133) conceives of social representations as having:

> ... a logic and language of their own [and they serve] a two fold function; first to establish an order which will enable individuals to orientate themselves in their material and social world and to master it; secondly to enable communication to take place among members of a community by providing them with a code for social exchange and a code for naming and classifying unambiguously the various aspects of their world and their individual and group history

Thus, in addition to the schemas, scripts, and belief systems that constitute the store of individual knowledge, Moscovici posits a further layer of knowledge structures that he locates within the larger social group. Social representations provide selected individuals with the means of accommodating unfamiliar events within an accepted frame of reference. They also allow for a degree of social consensus to be created where none may have existed before. The end result is that our experiences come to be invested with a layer of meaning that will be missed just so long as we insist on adopting a purely individual perspective. Although social representations appear to possess many features in common with individual knowledge schemas, unlike schemas they serve to highlight those components of general knowledge we happen to share with others whose views we respect.

These ideas were originally developed in the course of an investigation into the manner in which psychoanalytic theory progressed from being an esoteric outlook adopted by a small professional group to its being absorbed into the common language of French culture (Moscovici, 1961). Since then the role of social representations in making the "unfamiliar part of the familiar" has been investigated in a number of other contexts including the rituals of laboratory experimentation and the social diffusion of concepts relating to childhood and mental illness (Farr & Moscovici, 1984). The thrust behind all of these studies has been towards explaining how knowledge originally formulated in one (restrictive) context becomes translated into some more accessible version. Which is to reactivate a theme we have met before.

Moscovici's account of the role of social representations in the diffusion of specialised knowledge can also be understood as defining a further stage in the knowledge redescription process identified by Karmiloff-Smith (1992). It implicates processes occurring beyond the individual knowledge level that can be set in train once the individual memory code can support conscious access and verbal report. That is, diffusion based on social representations appears to serve a similar function on the collective level to that served by metareflective activity on the individual level. In each case, specialised, context-specific knowledge becomes converted into some more accessible version. Whereas individual metareflective processes culminate in knowledge representations supporting verbal report and conscious awareness for the individual concerned, social representations appear to play a similar role in extending their accessibility yet further into the community at large. Novel ideas that were once restricted to just one or a few originators now begin to transfer to selected others within the larger community. At which point, the future development of that body of knowledge becomes intimately tied up with the nature of the social transactions occurring within the social subgroups that happen to have got involved. But adopting this line of argument not only serves to blur the traditional conception of human knowledge as the product of individually defined computational processes, it can also be used to undermine the very foundations of the classical computational framework itself.

SOCIAL CONSTRUCTIONISM

The classical view refers to the human mind acting as "a mirror of reality" where symbols representing features in the external world are continually being "polished" so as to reflect the properties of the world more and more accurately. It has culminated in the physical symbol system and the cognitive architectures described in Section 1 and it is this framework that proponents of "social constructionism" have rejected wholesale. They hold that human knowledge is a purely social construction deriving from the dynamics of publicly shared discourse. Whatever knowledge of the world we may happen to possess will have been derived from the interplay of interpersonal forces where contingent factors such as negotiation, power, and collusion have steered our beliefs in particular directions.

For example, Gergen and Gergen (1991) cite the work of T.S. Kuhn as demonstrating that revolutions in scientific thinking depend not only on hypothesis testing but also on a wider set of social variables including the exercise of rhetoric and persuasion. For Gergen and Gergen, it is these social variables above all else that license what is to be treated as true or false. Beliefs about the world are not so much inductions from observation, as historically contingent conventions whose truth or falsity are matters of social determination. In this system, experimental observations play no privileged role because observer bias and the social properties of the language used to express the experimental results all militate against the separation of "knower" from "known". There is no such thing as an "independent observer" seeking the meaning behind events, rather meanings are constructed as people (Gergen & Gergen, 1991, p.78):

> ... collectively generate descriptions and explanations in language. ... In this sense what we take to be knowledge is not placed within individual minds, nor is it contained within abstract descriptions and explanations. Rather, from the constructionist standpoint, knowledge (as it is represented in language) is part of the coordinated activities of individuals which are used to accomplish locally agreed upon purposes concerning the real and the good.

Such theorising runs squarely and deliberately against the whole empirical, experimental tradition which is now relegated to the status of being just one of many ways for bringing about the consensus that legitimates one set of beliefs over another.

This is a minority view and likely to remain so (the irony is intended) but, in rejecting the radical and uncontrolled methodologies espoused by social constructionism, it does not follow that collective principles acting to supplement the individual's own efforts at knowledge revaluation are thereby ruled out of court. For example, there are aspects of interpersonal persuasion that can be seen to work with the grain of the cognitive architecture as traditionally understood, but there are yet other aspects that are effective precisely because they exploit principles that are best understood on the social plane.

PERSUASIVE TECHNIQUES

Before advertising standards were drawn up and policed, advertisers could make the most outrageous claims for their product. Then, once it became a legal requirement that all the claims stated in an advertisement should be truthful, the device of direct lying as a means of selling a product was effectively closed. The net effect was to reorient advertisers towards new presentational techniques that would have the same outcome. It may be untrue (and therefore illegal) to state that your product is the best on the market, but it may still be possible to get the same message across by prompting the reader to infer this illicit item of information. As we saw from the earlier discussion of text comprehension, inferences made during reading are added to the text base in the same way as actually stated content. Consequently, it can be as good as stating a fact, if the reader can be made to infer that same information.

Suppose we want to say that Brand X powder washes whiter than all other brands on the market. It may not be true but, as Harris and Monaco (1978) have demonstrated, there are various ways of phrasing the message so as to elicit this claim as an inference. For someone reading the slogan "Brand X gives you a whiter wash" the presence of the comparative adjective (whiter) is likely to prompt inferences about the inferiority of the competition and the superiority of Brand X. Similarly, for someone reading the slogan "Get your wash really white. Get Brand X" the presence of the juxtaposed imperatives can prompt an inference about the causal link between the two actions as the reader re-establishes local coherence through the introduction of a bridging link.

More subtly, perfectly true statements may be stacked together so that, while each taken alone is individually true, the composed product is not true. Someone who reads a "piecemeal survey" to the effect that:

Brand X is cheaper than Brand A
Brand X is faster-acting than Brand B
Brand X is longer-lasting than Brand C

is likely to form a representation in memory to the effect that Brand X is cheaper/faster/longer-lasting than each and every one of its competitors.

Searleman and Carter (1988) investigated the effectiveness of these stylistic devices by comparing the recall of experimental subjects for the *literal* content of messages that either stated a claim directly or implied that claim indirectly. Subjects read each message and then, either immediately or after a short delay, judged which of a series of test statements were true as stated in the original message. The percentage of subjects misled into thinking a claim had been stated, as opposed to being prompted by one of these linguistic devices, increased significantly over a five-minute delay. Using comparative adjectives, 22.5% of subjects indicated the literal presence of an implied claim on immediate recall but this rose to 55% after the delay. Similarly, using juxtaposed imperatives the equivalent measures were 62.5% and 87.5% and, for a piecemeal survey, 55.0 and 80.0%, respectively. Given time, the methods clearly do work. Professional persuaders, it seems, have learned to work with the grain of the cognitive system in turning its activities and products to their own ends. These examples of persuasive techniques fit comfortably within an information processing framework as individually understood. Yet other techniques appear to work their effects by exploiting collective principles governing the conduct of social exchange.

The classic advice concerning salesmen is not to let them get their "foot in the door" or you will regret it. It is good advice. A subject who has complied with a small request is more likely to go on to agree to a larger request than some other subject who has missed out on the softening-up stage. In a study reported by Freedman and Fraser (1966) a random sample of housewives were asked if they would open up their home to allow a group of men to go through "cupboards and storage places" in order to list the household products that had been purchased. Not unexpectedly, a majority (78%) of the subjects directly confronted with this request refused outright. Other subjects, however, were first asked if they would agree to answer some questions concerning their shopping habits. Only after this small request had been made and accepted were they then confronted with the extreme request about opening up access to their home. Under these conditions a majority (63%) agreed to do precisely that. Freedman and Frazer attribute the efficacy of the technique to the subject's need to maintain a consistent public face. Having adopted one position in public, the subject feels some obligation to continue to live up to this position the next time around.

A variant on this double-edged approach is to reverse the order of magnitude of the two requests. Subjects are first confronted with an extreme request (which they are expected to refuse) and then encounter a second request that is less demanding than the first—although it may well have seemed unreasonable if presented on its own. This technique was used by Cialdini et al. (1975) when their primary aim was to get student subjects to agree to "act as chaperone to a group of juvenile delinquents on a 26-hour trip to the zoo". Only 17% of a student sample agreed to take part when asked outright. Subjects who had been faced with a more extreme request beforehand were much more compliant. They had first been asked if they would volunteer to work for two hours every week, over a period of five years, as an unpaid counsellor to a group of juvenile offenders. Having received the expected refusal, the experimenters then came out with their intended request—that subjects act as a chaperone. At this point the agreement rate shifted from 17% to 50%.

There are various ways of interpreting why this technique works. It could be interpreted as a judgemental anchoring effect where the first request makes the real request appear less extreme. However, as the persuasive effect disappears when a different person is brought in to spring the second request, an alternative explanation based on the principle of "reciprocal concession" has been suggested. A subject who refuses to comply with the first request forces the person making the request to concede ground. Consequently, at the time the second request is made, there is pressure on the target to make a reciprocal gesture by acceding this time around. This clearly yokes the efficacy of the technique to the principles governing social exchange rather than to the principles governing individual decision making. Nonetheless, anchoring effects cannot be entirely ruled out. Even a psychophysical task such as judging of a series of weights need not show anchoring effects provided the anchor stimulus is not construed as being part of the judgement task itself (Brown, 1953). Thus, the device of introducing another person to make the second request may have simply "gated out" any anchoring effects arising from the extreme request. Of course, these explanations are not necessarily mutually incompatible. Both factors could work in consort to bring about the observed effects.

RHETORIC AND ARGUMENTATION

It is not essential for would-be persuaders to resort to devious means to achieve their ends—the exercise of skilful argument can also fulfil this purpose. The use of rhetorical argument as a tool of persuasion has a long and distinguished pedigree although evidence of its use may be less obvious today than in the past (Pratkanis & Aronson, 1991).

Argument and debate occur when people who hold different attitudes on the same topic express their views publicly. As each of us is likely to hold a number of attitudes about a complex topic such as politics, it is implausible that there will be a single attitudinal statement that sums up our position. Consequently, although our attitudes and beliefs will determine when and how we engage in public debate, we are unlikely to take exactly the same stance each time we are drawn into political argument. Indeed there are times when we may find ourselves arguing in favour of a position we would normally reject if the corresponding counterarguments are sufficiently extreme. Under these circumstances, socialist voters may find themselves justifying free market forces in the face of hardline Marxist argument, while conservative voters may find themselves arguing for some social controls when confronted by arguments for reintroducing climbing boys for sweeping chimneys.

Given this potential variability in how we may choose to defend our corner, it is not at all unlikely that we find ourselves in the position where we start to contradict ourselves. At this point, inconsistencies in our reasoning that may not have disturbed us previously, by virtue of being made public before a critical audience, now call for a degree of self-justification and repair.

These arguments are derived from Billig (1987) who states (p.162) that:

> It is not inconsistency per se which is disruptive but the criticisms of inconsistency and it is the criticisms that raise the need for defensive justification. It does not matter whether such criticisms are made by others or whether they originate from our own internal voices of criticism. They still possess the capability to disturb and to provoke the intention of justification. Thus any workings of our minds are not governed by the threat of inconsistency in any absolute sense but only by those inconsistencies which form the basis of criticisms.

This is to mark out public (and internal) debate as an important factor in knowledge updating because it can expose inconsistencies in our knowledge which left to our own devices we may not have registered or, if registered, whose implications have not been tracked down. In other words, the partially resolved updating situations that we encountered in Chapter 6 can be repaired as public argument sets in train a greater awareness of the limitations of our own beliefs.

The process of argumentation

Arguments are conducted by setting out justifications for what we believe and by rebutting through counter-argument the contrary views put forward by our opponents. For Billig, computational models of thinking are misleading precisely because they emphasise logical, rule-governed principles at the expense of the rhetorical strategies that inform public debate. He caricatures information-processing models as akin to bureaucratic routines in which thought is presented as little more than searching for an appropriate pigeonhole for the information concerned. Once a suitable slot has been found, thought can proceed on its way as set rules and preformed schemas take over; the whole exercise being conducted with the maximum of efficiency and the minimum of fuss. Mental models, with their emphasis on the importance of counterexamples in formal reasoning, are criticised as falling short of providing an adequate account of the argumentational process because (Billig, 1987, p.99):

> Within rhetoric the counterexample does not occupy a particularly privileged position; a telling counter example might be used to criticise an opponent's argument but an apposite example will be just as useful for one's own argument.

Similarly, although the course of argumentation could be interpreted through the execution of the relevant scripts, this too falls short of being the whole story. It is in the very nature of argument to call into question the status of any script and any or all of its rules. And, as we switch from criticism to justification and back again, we create the very conditions that favour a revision of the script itself. In this respect engaging in argument entails a process of self-discovery; we may be unsettled by what we are driven to defend and we may be changed in the process. Through social argumentation we can hold a mirror to our beliefs and the refractions created by other perspectives can serve as a potent factor for initiating the inner reflection that enables us to track down unexpected ramifications stemming from the beliefs in question. At the conclusion of the argument we may not have persuaded the opposition of the justice of our case but we may well have persuaded ourselves.

Unfortunately, Billig supplies little in the way of quantitative evidence that individuals really do employ their argumentative skills in the ways he describes. However, he is not alone in this respect. Exactly how people set about arguing their corner—the strategies they use when justifying their beliefs and when challenging the beliefs held by others—has received remarkably little attention. An exception can be found in a study by Kuhn (1991) which was specifically designed to tease out the styles of argument people could employ when defending their own views on a topic and when rebutting alternative interpretations.

In the course of the investigation, adult subjects were asked to state their views on a series of contentious topics such as "crime", "school failure", and "unemployment"—topics on which all of the respondents were likely to hold definite views and which they could be expected to defend aloud. The subjects varied in age (from teenage to 60s), gender, and educational level (college and non-college) and their rhetorical skills were assessed through a variety of subtasks intended to elicit different styles of argument. For example, subjects were asked to state their views on the causes of crime and then, in order to see how they justified these views, they were asked to generate an opposing position and explain how they would rebut this alternative interpretation. They were also required to supply a remedy for crime (to see if this was consistent with their earlier view) and a series of "epistemological questions" dealt with their awareness of their own beliefs.

In a second session, the same subjects were next asked to evaluate new evidence supplied by the experimenters which was either underdetermined or overdetermined. In the former case this meant offering anecdote rather than real evidence. In the latter case it meant offering up to three different reasons for crime, each supported by an authoritative source. The resulting subject protocols were then analysed for, (1) the quality of the causal theories put forward, (2) the evidence provided in support, (3) awareness of alternative theories, (4) responses to counterargument, (5) reflective awareness, and (6) reactions to different kinds of evidence and expert opinion.

Most of Kuhn's subjects could come up with relatively developed "theories" for the topic in question. Thus, 19 possible causal chains relating to crime and 30 causal chains relating to school failure were proposed overall. The most common causal chain for persistent criminal behaviour took the form:

[Lack of education→lack of skills→lack of employment→lack of income→monetary needs→return to crime].

For school failure, the preferred causal chain was somewhat less complex:

[Physical problems (hearing, eyesight, nutrition)→School failure].

Once they had selected a particular causal sequence, subjects were then probed for the type of evidence they could produce in its support. This evidence was classified under three headings; genuine evidence, pseudo-evidence, and non-evidence.

Genuine evidence was identified by being distinguishable from the causal sequence being defended and as having a bearing on its correctness. This might entail pointing to a link between an antecedent and an outcome and, at its weakest, this could mean little more than pointing out their correspondence. A stronger justification would be one that drew upon correlated change, where change in the antecedent is related to change in the outcome. Other types of genuine justification arose when subjects went beyond the supposed causal link in order to search for additional external factors. Examples here would include the use of counterfactual argument (what would happen if the causal antecedent were absent); introducing analogies; making general assumptions (e.g. original sin), or discounting some alternative explanation. Pseudo-evidence arose when subjects justified their case by providing a narrative or scenario that merely offered a depiction of how the phenomenon might occur. Instances of "no evidence" arose when subjects argued there was no need for proof—it was obvious—or they argued a case that was unrelated to the theory in question.

Applying these classifications to the arguments obtained from the whole sample, less than half of the subjects were able to provide genuine evidence for their professed beliefs on any of the topics tested. In fact, for many subjects, providing a good storyline (pseudo-evidence) was perceived to be as good a justification for a theory as providing genuine evidence in its defence.

When generating counter-theories to their own, subjects were judged as having met this request if, (a) there was a genuine contrast between the old and new theory, and (b) the subject regarded the counter-theory as something that could be argued against. Half of those who managed to produce a counter-theory had previously produced genuine evidence for their own position. Of the subjects who failed to come up with a counter-theory, only 30% had generated genuine evidence previously. Reliance on pseudo-evidence, it seems, diminished awareness of the possibility of alternative theories.

Subjects who complied with the request to suggest a rival theory of crime that might be held by another person were also asked "what evidence might this person give to try to show that you were wrong?" and then "What could you say to show that this other person was wrong?". Where subjects did come up with counter-arguments, their quality was not very strong. Yet other respondents took the view that counter-arguing was not possible because if the antecedent was present then that was the end of the matter. These subjects held that (Kuhn, 1991, p.144):

> If it is known that family problems are prevalent ... then it is impossible to contest the claim that these family problems are the cause of school failure. Because the antecedent occurs in the presence of the outcome it must have the status of a cause.

This observation is particularly noteworthy for the strong confirmation bias it reveals and it was found to be present for all of the topics under test. As a result, up to half of the subjects in the sample failed to appreciate the relevance of counter-instances in the conduct of argument.

Rebuttals were elicited by getting subjects to generate counter-arguments to the evidence they thought would support a competing theory to their own. In principle, rebuttal could proceed by showing that the counter-theory and its supporting arguments were wrong, by showing that the original theory and its arguments were stronger, or simply by taking the counter-arguments in isolation and criticising them in succession. About the same proportion of subjects generated successful rebuttals as generated successful counter-arguments (between 40–50% across topics). This measure, however, dropped to around 30% when it came to rebuttals that attempted to address the counter-arguments while, at the same time, demonstrating that the respondent held the stronger theory. The majority of subjects failed to make this dual comparison, as though they were disinclined to question the extent to which their own preferred theories were likely to be correct.

Overall, Kuhn's findings do not do much to bolster the case for group debate serving to iron out inconsistencies in the positions people choose to adopt. The general run of arguments were too transitory and too unfocused to sustain any significant advances on this front. Nonetheless, Kuhn's subjects were debating with an imagined opposition. Had an actual opposition been present in the flesh, possibly they would have been drawn either into mounting a more convincing set of arguments or experiencing greater pressure to change their position. We will look at the latter possibility in more detail. First, from the perspective of simulation studies of group discussion and then in the light of some genuine case histories.

Simulating group argument

Running simulations of group debate enables us to explore the range and dynamics of the kinds of exchange that can occur in a group setting. For example, an individual's predilection towards a confirmation bias (searching for evidence to support a prior hypothesis and ignoring counter-evidence) could be attenuated in actual group discussion if the other members of the group expressed different positions. Whereas confirmation bias inhibits the individual from searching for alternative ways of explaining a given body of evidence, the presence of other people labouring under the same bias but espousing different explanations could work to diminish its effects. Where other people happen to have come to different conclusions, the resulting group debate could go some way towards opening up the "interpretation space". Alternatively, if during this debate certain viewpoints happen to be expressed very forcefully, the debate could go in the opposite direction of closing down the interpretation space. In these respects, the group could come to demonstrate different cognitive properties to those displayed by individuals on their own. How different, will depend on the communication patterns adopted by the group members—who talks to whom and how persuasive they are.

In group discussion, therefore, where information is distributed across the group members, constraints on individual hypothesis-formation will derive both from the external evidence and from the views of the group members themselves. These same constraints will also jointly determine whatever conclusion emerges as being mutually acceptable for the group as a whole. In other words, groups trying to arrive at a consensus position furnish another example where constraint-satisfaction networks can be used as tools for modelling the dynamics involved. By treating the social group as a community of constraint-satisfaction mechanisms, where each network is attempting to settle into an appropriate relaxation state, it should be possible to model the progress of a debate and any emergent properties that arise from the group functioning as a whole, not just as a collection of individuals.

Hutchins (1991), has proposed that each group member be represented by an individual constraint network. The group as a whole can then be represented by the total system created when the individual networks are linked together. At the individual level, a preferred schematic interpretation for a body of external evidence will reside in the pattern of interconnectivity between the units that make up the network. Actual individual preconceptions can then be represented by setting up some prior pattern of activation over each of the units in the network. External inputs to the network can be used to represent whatever evidence exists for or against the hypothesis that is being favoured.

Now, suppose we couple two or more such networks together in order to simulate some larger community which is also trying to arrive at an interpretation of the available evidence. This will have the effect of introducing a new set of parameters bearing on the final settlement states. These parameters derive from (1) the variations that exist between the individual networks that comprise the community (i.e. the different schemas and preconceptions being attributed to the different community members) and (2) from the manner in which the nets themselves are interconnected (i.e. how the group members communicate with each other). Table 11.1 lists the principal parameters that can be derived from these two sources and their corresponding interpretations when applied to real communities.

Communication between nets can vary according to (a) which nets are allowed to intercommunicate, (b) which individual units are involved in these communications, (c) the degree of activation that is passed from a communicating unit to a receiving unit, and (d) the time course over which information exchange can occur. By manipulating these communication parameters, different forms of group debate can be simulated. If the amount of activity that is transmitted from a unit in one network to a corresponding unit in another network is increased

TABLE 11.1
Principal parameters of simulation models and features of individual and group processing they represent

In the model	In a human system
Distributed propeties	
Pattern of interconnectivity among units in the net	Schemata for data
External inputs to particular units	Access to outside evidence
Initial activation across units in net	Predispositions, current beliefs
Communication parameters	
Patterns of interconnections among the nets in the community	Who talks to whom
Patterns of interconnectivity among the units of communicating nets	What they talk about
Strengths of connections between nets that commmunicate	How persuasive they are
Time course of communication	When they communicate

Adapted from Hutchins, 1991.

or lowered, this is tantamount to varying the degree of persuasion that is being applied by the group to each of its members.

Suppose we have a community of such networks where each net has the same underlying constraint structure, the same access to experimental evidence, and slightly different prior activation patterns. If the networks are arranged to be in open communication with each other (all networks intercommunicate, all units are interconnected with all other units, and information exchange is continuous), setting persuasiveness at zero (communication strength is set at zero) will mean that each network settles into a relaxation state that is determined solely by its own resources and predispositions.

Next, suppose the level of persuasiveness is allowed to increase. Minority interpretations of the data will now be increasingly overridden as the group moves towards a consensus on the "correct" interpretation. Indeed, persuasiveness can be increased to a point where no amount of external evidence to the contrary may shift the group from its chosen interpretation. Hence, through this simulation exercise, Hutchins has managed to show that there are circumstances that result in the group displaying an even more extreme form of confirmation bias than is found for its individual members. According to Hutchins (1991, p.299) these circumstances arise when the communication level is set so high that the individual nets are converted into one large net:

> Wherever the nets go in interpretation space, they go hand in hand and stay close together. Because they are in continual communication, there is no opportunity for any of them to form an interpretation that differs much from that of the other. Once in consensus they stay in consensus even if they have had to change their minds to reach consensus. [Ultimately] When the strengths of the connections between networks is increased to a point where it far outweighs the strength of the connections within networks, the nets all move to a shared interpretation, that is incoherent. In this condition, the importance of sharing an interpretation with others outweighs the importance of reaching a coherent interpretation.

Other patterns of communication that assign more or less voting power to particular nets can lead to situations where additional and different hypotheses come to be entertained (at the expense of a degree of indecisiveness) or to less diversity of interpretation (at the expense of disregarding some of the evidence). In short, despite holding the cognitive properties of the group members constant, different patterns of group communication can result in emergent properties at the collective level.

Of course, the situations that Hutchins is describing are laboratory simulations. Nonetheless, they provide telling illustrations of how, under extreme conditions, social groups could arrive at consensus views that take little or no account of the external evidence for those beliefs. The critical question is whether such extreme levels of irrationality do occur within social communities. Can actual cases be observed where group persuasion is set at a such a high level that "the importance of sharing an interpretation with others outweighs the importance of reaching a coherent interpretation"? Although group situations of this kind are rare, there are certain practices that do seem to reproduce what is required.

THOUGHT-REFORM PROGRAMMES

When the persuasiveness of the exchanges between group members was maximised, the connectionist simulation just described indicated that it became more important that the participants agreed amongst themselves than that they respected the constraints imposed by evidence from the external world. As a result, the group ideology came to prevail over whatever evidence existed to the contrary. Outside the laboratory such conditions are fortunately not commonplace, but they do exist. And if milder forms of persuasion appear to work with the grain of cognitive processes, the more oppressive methods of "thought reform" grind away at their very foundations. In the process, however, we are provided with an opportunity to observe how the characteristics of the individual cognitive architecture and socially distributed cognition can be jointly exploited to produce an extremely radical form of knowledge updating.

That it is possible to achieve the seismic shifts in individual belief systems that have been described by observers of thought-reform techniques seems at first both surprising and disturbing. Nonetheless, the means for achieving these ends are not drawn from some remote and arcane domain, they are already familiar. "All" that is needed is a ruthless exploitation of the individual and collective cognitive principles we have already encountered. To justify this claim, we will first consider in some detail a case history dealing with the application of a particular thought-reform programme, After that, we will take stock by reflecting on why these practices appeared to work as intended.

In 1954, Lifton (1961) took the opportunity, provided by a visit to Hong Kong, to reopen his investigations into thought-reform procedures which had started when he was involved in the psychiatric evaluation of American POWs returning from the Korean war. This time around, over the course of the next 17 months, he recorded the methods employed by the Chinese authorities as part of their reform programmes for both their own Nationals as well as Westerners who were being held as political prisoners. Altogether, Lifton interviewed 25 Westerners who had experienced these pressures prior to being released and 15 Chinese Nationals who had undergone similar experiences before escaping from mainland China to Hong Kong. In his account, Lifton treats these two groups separately, but there were sufficient similarities to warrant looking at the sample as a whole—at least so far as the basic techniques were concerned.

At the outset, Lifton identifies a distinct pattern of demands associated with thought-reform programmes which serve to distinguish them from educational, religious, or therapeutic programmes. In these other cases, although the boundaries can easily become blurred, a creative tension exists between the teacher, the taught, and the focal ideas. This tension is not present in the case of thought reform where everything has to be subordinated to the ideological issues.

Such ideological control can be achieved in a variety of ways. "Milieu control" ensures that all forms of communication other than the "correct" versions are kept from the victim. "Mystical manipulation" aims to yoke the correct mode of thinking to some higher law of nature. A third stratagem entails the purging of wrong beliefs and attitudes by demanding "purity" of thought and confessions of past wrongdoings. A fourth procedure is the use of a specially loaded language such as "imperialist thinking" or the "way of the people" which function as truth-terminating clichés. These slogans serve to separate beliefs into those that are desirable (they relate to ultimate truths) and those that are immoral (they act as obstacles to ideological progress). Thought reform can get underway when all of these stratagems are brought together within an institutional context which has no intention of allowing individual rights to get in the way of progress towards the establishment of a collective doctrine.

Such programmes have been found to bring about radical and long-lasting changes in the ideological outlook of their participants although we can expect to find variations in the degree to which actual individuals conform and submit. Thus, Lifton found that although a few subjects held to their new point of view after their release (some for years after), most came eventually (in a different political climate) to adopt stronger antagonisms towards Chinese communism than they had held before imprisonment. However, none of those involved was unaffected by their experience, which is hardly surprising given the harshness of the regime. The changes wrought by the reform programmes may not have resisted the shift to a new political scene but they did suffice, at the time, to bring people to the point of confessing to things they had not done and to repudiating beliefs and values they had previously held to be important. By combining accounts from different case histories we can assemble something approximating to the typical course of events once the individual had been caught up in the system.

A paradigm case

On arrest, the victim was placed in a cell with others who were also undergoing the reform programme but were at more advanced stages of reform. These cellmates were under pressure not only to reform themselves but also to reform their companions, as success on this front would increase their own chances of release. Consequently, from the first moments of incarceration a victim was exposed to group pressures focused on his or her ideological wrongdoings. Each companion in the cell was motivated to denounce the prisoner as an "imperialist spy" and to urge a confession. The fact that at this stage the victims believed in their innocence and had nothing to confess was irrelevant. A prisoner who made this protest would be met with the counter-argument that "The government doesn't arrest the innocent".

Lifton refers to the ensuing within-cell encounters between the new arrival and the cellmates as "struggle" and during these encounters there would be extensive probing into the victim's background in order to find what was wrong. Eventually this information will form the basis of the confession that is the ultimate aim of the programme. The struggle may continue for several hours prior to the victim being summoned to the first round of official interrogation.

At the first interrogation, the prisoner is questioned about his or her past actions and work patterns going back several years. When (inevitably) the answers provided are insufficient to satisfy the presiding judge, a combination of hints, threats, and promises starts to emerge (Lifton, 1961, p.21):

> The government knows all about your crime. That is why we arrested you. It is now up to you to confess everything to us and in this way your case can be quickly solved and you will soon be released.

Interrogation can continue for many hours and, if the prisoner insists on asserting innocence, the judge is likely to call for the prisoner to be handcuffed. After a short break the interrogation then continues. Further protestations of innocence lead to leg chains being applied prior to the prisoner's return to the cell.

A prisoner who rejoins the cell in a shackled state is clearly marked as unreformed and this provokes a further, more intense period of struggle. And so the process continues, alternating between struggle and interrogation with no opportunities for the victim to escape into sleep. Under these mounting pressures, a prisoner may eventually respond by inventing a "wild confession" by citing things known to be untrue in the hope of gaining some respite. Thus, a victim might claim to have been the leader of an espionage group reporting to a local foreign embassy. If so, this confession is duly probed during subsequent interrogations and, when found to be inconsistent and contradictory, it is rejected.

With one confession made and rejected, the interrogation now focuses upon the details of the prisoner's work and acquaintances, probably delving back over many years. Now, when the victim returns to the cell it is under instructions to dictate a report to another prisoner containing all that had been said previously. After say eight days and nights of alternating struggle and interrogation and little or no sleep, a confession begins to emerge that, while still "wild", is becoming more closely tied to real events.

Over the next few weeks, the prisoner is required to talk about earlier acquaintances, giving their addresses and their affiliations, and in this manner the victim's autobiographical memories become part of the chimera that is being assembled. If at this stage the prisoner shows signs of being ready to admit to a catalogue of crimes (i.e. not just to agree to accusations but to freely elaborate upon them) a new leniency is introduced into the regime. The shackles are removed, more rest is allowed, and the level of overt pressure is generally reduced. These signs of progress are also evident to the other cell members who are on hand to offer the prisoner friendly guidance in writing a revised confession. Any show of resistance brings back the handcuffs and leg chains.

Shortly after the new leniency has been introduced, the prisoner may be judged as sufficiently advanced to participate in the daily struggle and to help with the re-education of other cell inmates. This phase entails not just reading the official goverment literature but publicly expressing a personal opinion on the contents and using it to criticise the ideological stance adopted by others. Everyone is required to participate and each has to express the correct opinion as determined by the cell chief. Furthermore, these discussions are not just confined to intellectual issues—emotional and personal reactions to the materials are also monitored.

By this stage, the victims may have progressed from paying lip service to the correct point of view, and moved towards accepting these standards inwardly and applying them to themselves. They have now become used to expressing spontaneously all of their reactions and to identifying their wrong thoughts. In short, they have become "more and more enmeshed in the special problem solving techniques of this ideological world".

After perhaps a year of such experiences, the prisoner will be participating in interrogation sessions that are more linked to real events. This is likely to produce a series of confessions which are then continually refined to make them more concise, logical, and, ultimately, more convincing. At this point the prisoner is moved to a new wing in the prison with better living conditions. This marks that the time has come for a public ceremony where the final version of the confession is personally endorsed and signed.

Stratagems and mechanisms at the individual level

Lifton's analysis of these case records was aimed at determining why different people responded as they did; why some succumbed and why others resisted or became confused. Our concern is rather different. To the extent that the manipulative techniques appear to lead to major reorientations in belief, how might they be accommodated within the analytical framework we have been gradually piecing together? The following analysis is meant to be suggestive and no more. It is certainly not an exhaustive review of the principles involved. Even so, we find that if we are to begin to grasp the full magnitude of what is going on, we need to appeal to a set of principles drawn from both the individual and social levels. Neither level alone quite captures the full range of powers that is being exercised.

In previous chapters we have referred to some of the basic cognitive processes whereby knowledge is acquired, organised, and partially updated. Thought reform may be an extreme exercise but ultimately it must work through these same mechanisms. Consequently, it should be possible to isolate the mechanisms through which the pressures for belief revision can be most effectively channelled. First of all, we will see what would be predicted from the properties of the individual cognitive architecture.

Reality testing.   Sleep deprivation and the continual exhortation to think about possible crimes obviously plays havoc with reality-testing mechanisms relying, as they do, on different internal signatures for imagined and real events. Bringing victims to the point where they start to confuse imagined and real events constitutes a major step along the reformist route.

Belief acceptance. Making false confessions to others and writing them down, however wild they may be, enjoins victims to entertain ideas about things they have not actually done. If simply being asked to comprehend statements leads to acceptance by default (see Chapter 10) this is to exploit another route through which thought reform can be pursued. The last thing victims are allowed is the time or space to assert the subsequent falsity of these beliefs, rather the whole time is to be spent adding to their number.

Mood state dependent memory. People exposed to these practices will experience a great deal of emotional turmoil as they realise how friends and colleagues are being betrayed. Guilt, shame, and fear will be repeatedly elicited in the course of the daily struggles which will then become closely associated with the intellectual content of the reform process. This is mood state dependent memory with a vengeance and it can be made to work in concert with the aims of the reform programme by keeping the critical beliefs in focal awareness.

Thought suppression. If the victim tries to keep certain areas of the self private, and tries to hold back certain secrets from the "helpers", it will be necessary to suppress these thoughts at the times when they threaten to break out into the open. Suppression attempts of this kind are likely to link the illicit thoughts to the central topics under discussion, so that, far from doing the job intended, this will make it that much more difficult to keep the illegitimate thoughts suppressed and free from outside criticism.

Self-criticism, conflict and cognitive change. The most dominant feature associated with thought-reform techniques is the use of conflict to bring about cognitive reorganisation. From Lifton's records it is immediately evident that great emphasis is placed on self-criticism being exercised by victims which may continue for years as the minutiae of their lives are gradually reassessed against the new ideological standards. We have argued elsewhere that purging errors from a knowledge base is a slow and gradual process. It is slow and gradual because there is no automatic route to be followed; before each and every item of knowledge can be revised it needs to be activated in the context of the new standard if any change is to be effected. Whatever does not participate in this process remains unreformed. It seems that the authors of this reform programme not only understood this point very well, they did not flinch from the implications that massive amounts of continuous and extensive monitoring would be called for.

To take stock so far, if we had been called upon to design a thought-reform programme using current individualistic models of cognitive processing as our guide, we would arrive at something not unlike the regime Lifton describes in such detail. Nonetheless, had our efforts stopped at this point they would fall short of the full powers of the Chinese system which typically eschews placing the victim in solitary isolation. Given the rigours of other parts of the programme, this is unlikely to be a humanitarian gesture but an acknowledgement that more can be achieved by the group than by the individual acting alone.

Stratagems and mechanisms at the social level
The incorporation of the prisoner into a social group where all are working on the same problem (their release) potentially introduces a number of new aspects into the account, although only three will be mentioned here; the distribution of critical knowledge among members of the group, the distribution of critical monitoring, and the requirement on the group members to co-ordinate their different ways of construing the same information.

Socially distributed memory. To the extent that all prisoners will come to share a great deal of information about each other, they are likely to register when a critical piece of information has been held back in a new context of debate. Whether the victim genuinely fails to bring the item to mind or deliberately suppresses it doesn't really matter. There will be a greater likelihood that the failure will be recognised by someone else in the group situation than if the subject were acting alone. Thus the cell members, by serving as a distributed memory, can only intensify the level of self-criticism that is made possible.

Socially distributed monitoring. Enlisting not one but many judges of the quality of a victim's adjustment to the received point of view brings about another turn of the ratchet in the desired direction. Critical evaluations that the individual could not achieve alone can be generated within the group on a number of different fronts. These may not be subtle but they do not need to be. Distributing the responsibility for criticism among the group members means that it can be kept going relentlessly; where one flags, another may take up the chase, to be replaced in turn as this becomes necessary. Superficial answering or the use of humour to abort critical lines of thought are also effectively annulled by this arrangement. No one is allowed to detach themselves from the group by retreating behind cursory answers and no one is allowed to take refuge in flippant answers for the same reasons. In these respects, the limits on what individuals could achieve on their own can be very effectively transcended in this specialised group setting.

Co-ordinating different perspectives.   Not all members of the group will interpret events in the same way. Those who are more advanced along the reformist route will be able to raise issues that others are likely to miss. In coming to understand and co-ordinate these other views, less advanced members then "benefit" from these insights. Especially so, as the nature of the situation gives them no choice but to attend to the implications of the new information. As we will see in the next chapter, although individuals can and do monitor their own levels of understanding, the metacognitive skills involved are not particularly sensitive. Combining novice with more advanced practioners provides an effective remedy for this defect.

Finally, we might note that the group dynamics associated with thought reform are precisely those that simulation studies predict will be most effective in moving its members towards adopting a collective ideology in the face of external evidence to the contrary.

Although this paradigm case has been matched, point by point, with an itemisation of the specific principles that appear to be in play, it still remains a one-off study. Even so, despite major differences in ideological content and environmental control, it seems that much the same principles inform the practices of religious cults. Under the heading "How to become a cult leader", Pratkanis and Aronson (1991) proceed to list "seven mundane but proven effective tactics for creating and maintaining a cult." These tactics correspond closely to the gist of the preceding account. Despite the procedural differences attendant on subjects who have been physically imprisoned and subjects who have volunteered to become cult members, and despite major discrepancies of time and place, the significant features of Lifton's account do appear to generalise beyond the confines of Chinese political prisons.

The primary purpose behind this excursion into the pathology of social groups was to illustrate how the principles contributing to individual knowledge formation are jointly located on both the individual and the collective levels. Although thought reform is an unusual case, there remain other, more prosaic situations where a similar conjunction of cognitive principles works collaboratively towards more laudable ends.

None of us, left entirely to our own devices, can hope to discover anything like the full range of ideas, theories, and artefacts that our culture has found to be useful. But we can be taught a significant proportion of this inheritance. Formal education provides another context, therefore, where individual and collective processes are interweaved for the purpose of turning out better-informed members of society. Equally, these same principles contribute to the production of a more informed society. Together, these two issues constitute the two sides of one dialectical equation and they constitute the topics of the next two chapters.

CHAPTER TWELVE

Cultural transmission of knowledge: Formal education

No society leaves entirely to chance how its members come to acquire their cultural heritage. The tuition on offer may amount to little more than putting the novice to work alongside those with more experience, but as a society grows dependent on the technological skills of its citizens, more formal programmes of teaching become unavoidable. In which case, the novitiate may be faced with a schedule of specialised instruction for anything up to 10 or 15 years before being accepted as a fully qualified member of society. Our immediate concern is to see how the principles of knowledge representation and updating pieced together from individual and collective levels of analysis can inform our understanding of formal modes of instruction and study.

Instructional or expository texts are designed to convey new factual information to their readers although it can be a hit or miss affair. Their expository function can be enhanced by restructuring texts according to principles derived from individually based models of information processing. Even so, novice study practices can fall well short of what is intended. Left to their own devices, learners tend to be drawn into a shallow processing of instructional materials while at the same time developing an overconfidence in what they have actually acquired through these efforts. However, these individual deficits can also be mitigated by recruiting other people into the learning situation.

EXPOSITORY TEXTS

Expositions refer to forms of discourse designed for the express purpose of conveying new factual information to an audience. Typical examples would include textbooks, technical manuals, scientific reports, and any amount of official leaflets. All of these materials will have been written on the assumption that they can play a primary role in the diffusion of new knowledge, although the extent to which particular specimens actually measure up to this responsibility can be a moot point.

Expositions differ from narratives both in their style and their content. Whereas narratives deal with the details of human intentionality in an episodic format which can make use of an informal expressive style, expositions require their readers to assess the truth status of formal statements linked together via logic rather than the vagaries of human intentionality (Graesser & Goodman, 1985). In other words, expository texts bring together a constellation of properties which, when set against the previous discussion of the qualities of abstract reasoning, do not bode well for the levels of comprehension they are likely to elicit in their readers.

According to Graesser and Goodman, expository texts are read more slowly than narratives and they tend to elicit much lower levels of inferencing—mainly because a large part of the reader's resources are tied up with establishing local coherence. Readers may well slow down when reading expository text but they can also miss glaring errors—even if the topic is familiar to them.

In a study reported by Baker and Wagner (1987), college-level subjects were required to read a set of passages describing contemporary political figures and to underline any content they found hard to understand or that they knew to be incorrect. One of the passages referred to Ronald Reagan as "Governor of Montana" and a mere 24% of the student sample identified this statement as incorrect. Supplying an advance warning, "to expect inconsistencies", improved their performance but not by much. Despite being alerted in advance, 49% of the sample still remained unaware of the mistake. It was not that the students did not know that Reagan was Governor of California, they knew this perfectly well. Even so, it was evidently not activated at the time the error was encountered.

Glover and Krug (1988) have reported similar findings. In their study, subjects read a 2500-word essay on "European Events, 1946–51" in which no fewer than 15 sentences had been altered in order to make them blatantly false. For instance, the correct sentence "The Soviet army continued to occupy Poland at the outset of the 1950s" was altered to read "The British army continued to occupy Poland at the outset of

1950s"—a transformation that, were it true, would mean rewriting the entire course of post-war politics. Subjects were asked to read the passage carefully and to underline any part that seemed hard to understand, that contained inconsistencies, or was incorrect. On average, they managed to detect only four out of the fifteen errors despite being primed to look for inconsistencies. The experimenters did manage to improve these error-detection rates by providing the readers with "advance organisers" for the passages (see later) but the fact remains that under normal reading their subjects fell far short of the standards we might expect to take for granted. So, what can be done to ease the reader's burden and to raise levels of understanding?

Readability of text

Intuitively, we are well aware that some ways of expressing information are clearer than others. The same information can be expressed with crystalline clarity or so opaquely that even after many re-readings we are still unclear about the author's intentions. Stylistic differences of this kind tend to be lumped together under the general heading of text "readability" and there have been various attempts at producing formal measures that, if not identifying the principles of good stylistic practice, at least serve to differentiate the good from the bad.

One of the first such measures (Flesch, 1948) differentiated between simple and complex texts by assigning each text a global score based on a weighted combination of its word and sentence length. Flesch scores of 50 or below indicated "difficult to very difficult texts" accessible to only around 25% of the population, and scores of 70 and above indicated "easy to very easy" passages accessible to the majority of citizens (see Ley, 1977).

Although simple to calculate, the Flesch formula is misleading in treating readability as an absolute property of a text. A text that appears difficult to one reader may appear easy to another and this failure to bring the reader into the picture also applies to the alternative, Cloze technique as described by Taylor, 1953. This method involves replacing, say, every fifth word in the text, with a blank, and getting the reader to guess the missing word. On average, a text with a high Cloze score should be more readable than one where the majority of readers can only fill in a few of the gaps. Neither of these measures, however, does much to address the range of comprehension strategies readers are known to employ. Rectifying this deficit calls for a theoretical analysis of text comprehension viewed as a whole, which brings us back to the studies conducted by Kintsch and his associates. At least within this cyclic model it is possible to conjecture on what is likely to happen when skilled and less skilled readers embark on the comprehension of given texts.

Readability and the formation of a text base

If different readers chunk different amounts on each reading cycle, this will directly affect their efforts at establishing local and global coherence. The more propositional content retained in working memory from cycle to cycle, the easier it will be to form the appropriate text base. A reader working with a buffer of less than average capacity is likely to find that the propositions required for local coherence are not directly available when they are needed. As a result, the flow of comprehension will be suspended while search and reinstatement operations take place. Consequently, a text can be expected to become less and less readable as these search and reinstatement demands increase. This may come about because the text is badly written, because the reader is hampered by a low reading span, or because both of these features apply. Whichever way, if we can estimate the reinstatement and inference demands associated with particular conjunctions of texts and readers we should be in a good position to predict any dependent variations in readability.

Miller and Kintsch (1980) tested this relationship by using the cyclic model to simulate the formation of a text base, both when different text structures were presented and when the model parameters (e.g. for buffer size) were allowed to vary. As a result they were able to estimate the number of bridging inferences and reinstatements associated with different samples of text and different levels of reading ability. The same passages were then given to a "homogeneous" sample of readers and their reading times and recall accuracy scores were recorded. The estimated inferencing and reinstatement demands were found to correlate with the observed reading times and, to some extent, they also predicted the content of the recall protocols. In comparison, Flesch scores for the same passages, while correlated with the reading times, did not predict recall accuracy to the same degree.

Using the same procedure, Vipond (1980) found that both micro- and macropropositional operations were linked to text readability although their exact role interacted with reading skill. For semi-skilled readers, estimates of the bridging inferences and reinstatements required for the formation of the propositional text base gave the best predictions for reading performance. For skilled readers, the best estimates were provided by the bridging inferences and reinstatements involved in the formation of the text macrostructure.

Some progress, therefore, has been made towards the goal of developing a sensitive and valid measure of text readability but there is clearly a long way to go before textbooks can be vetted against some agreed set of standards. Until that time, the quest for textual clarity will have to persevere with the coarse measures of readability currently to hand, supplemented by any intuitions we may have concerning good and bad practice.

Intuitions about how to write well are not exactly thin on the ground. A list of maxims for would-be authors of expository documents has been compiled by Mayer (1985) although it can be be condensed, more or less, into two methodological categories; (1) extrinsic methods—which are directly under the writer's control, and (2) intrinsic methods—which shift a greater burden of the responsibility onto the reader.

Extrinsic cues for boosting comprehension (e.g. adding headings and indentations to a text) incorporate explicit features as part of the written text which serve to signal the location of important content. Intrinsic devices, on the other hand, are aimed at initiating problem solving and self questioning in the reader at key points in the text. Both types of manipulation have received a degree of experimental support but once we embark on using these devices, it can be difficult to know where to stop.

Advance organisers

"Advance organisers", as the name suggests, are extrinsic cues supplied at the outset of reading intended as primes for the main topics dealt with in the text. This could mean just providing the passage title and no more, but, typically, advance organisers entail a set of topic labels or a brief outline of what is to come. Such advance cueing can produce some gains in memorability but in practice these gains are unlikely to be very great.

Royer (1977) presented a taped lecture to three different groups of college students either with or without advance cues. One group was given a set of topic headings beforehand, a second group was given the same headings afterwards, and the third group received no assistance of this kind at all. On a post-test, the percentage recall scores were highest for the subjects receiving advance cueing, who averaged 39% accuracy at recall. The group receiving no prior assistance averaged only 29% at recall and the group receiving the headings at the end fell between these scores, averaging around 35% recall accuracy. Similar gains for advance organisers have been reported by Glynn and DiVesta (1977) and it will be recalled that when Glover and Krug (1988) supplied advance outlines this significantly increased the detection rate for false statements. Thus, there are advantages to be gained from adopting this procedure but it is unclear where to draw the line; just how much additional advance information is reasonable?

Adjunct questions

Self questioning and comprehension are intimately linked and another route towards improving comprehension is to embed questions within the text itself which the reader has to answer. "Adjunct questions", as they have been termed, have been found to produce gains at recall similar to those reported for advance organisers but their specific effects depend on whether the questions precede or follow the critical text content. If they come after the relevant content, they act both to increase recall for the target content and the surrounding context. If they come beforehand, their effects are more localised in that they boost memory for target content at the expense of other material (Anderson & Biddle, 1975). As with advance organisers, there is no clear set of principles to constrain how adjunct questions should be used. It is left to the individual to decide in any particular case, how many questions are appropriate and what degree of specificity they should aim for.

Illustrations

Adding illustrations to a text is another device for boosting the reader's understanding of the topic in question. Many scientific and technical texts require the reader to understand how the states of a device or system change over time and authors frequently have recourse to diagrams as supplements to the written word. Again, however, there are difficulties arising from the many and varied forms illustrations can take. For example, if the aim is to explain the workings of a mechanical device such as a pump system, the author has the option of using different kinds of diagrams. An accompanying diagram could depict how the component parts fit together, how the states of the system undergo stepped changes, or both kinds of information.

In order to differentiate between these options, Mayer and Gallini (1990) compared four groups of subjects who read different accounts of mechanical pump systems while trying to represent the causal rules and associated state changes in the form of a mental model. Under the control condition, no illustrations were present. Under the experimental conditions, three different modes of illustration were used; diagrams depicting parts alone, depicting steps alone, or depicting both parts and steps together. Subjects with high or low levels of prior knowledge were included in each condition and they were tested both for their verbatim retention of the passage content dealing with the workings of the pump and for their creative understanding of the system as revealed through problem solving. It was found that, compared with the control group reading the unillustrated version, low-knowledge subjects who saw the parts plus steps illustrations did benefit significantly when recalling conceptual information and when solving problems in the area. No such gains were observed for high-knowledge subjects under these conditions, nor for low-knowledge subjects exposed to the other types of illustrations. Certain kinds of diagram, therefore, can facilitate comprehension by focusing the reader's attention on new conjunctions of information that would probably be missed in an unillustrated version. Provided the diagram enables salient propositional and perceptual information to be brought together in working memory, it can serve as an "inference generator" as discussed in Chapter 3. Nonetheless, photographs, outline diagrams, caricatures, graphs, and moving pictures, while they are all illustrations, constitute a very mixed set and there is no good reason why each type should complement discourse comprehension in the same way. When Gehring and Toglia (1988) compared a 15-minute taped lecture on selling pharmaceuticals with the same lecture supplemented by no fewer than 139 slides, they found no additional gains arising from the presence of the slides. On the other hand, a videotaped accompaniment did produce some gains over the unillustrated control condition.

Rhetorical structures of texts

The conventional format of a scientific article is different from that adopted by user manuals for technical apparatus, which is different again from the format of a mathematical paper. A reader who understands these canonical forms can anticipate where specific categories of information are likely to be found but, for beginners at least, should a specialised rhetorical form deviate from the conventions of normal practice, this may introduce unnecessary complications (Dee-Lucas & Larkin, 1990). Different macrostructures can facilitate comprehension by directing the reader to the likely location of important content but they can also work in the opposite direction if information is withheld when it is expected or needed.

Where a text is accompanied by worked examples as, say, with arithmetical primers, their presence is intended to provide the learner with the opportunity to practice procedural skills. However, worked examples need not always bring about the effects intended; readers may be so preoccupied with getting the right answers that they fail to reflect on what they are doing and the principles they are employing. In Chapter 10, the work of Sweller, Mawer, and Ward (1983) was described which dealt with changes in problem solving strategy as subjects practised away at a series of kinematic problems. Evidence for schematisation of the principles involved was associated with subjects shifting from the use of means–end strategy to using a forward strategy. It was observed at the time that not everybody demonstrated this shift.

Some subjects stubbornly persisted with their initial, means–end strategy throughout.

The failure of these subjects to follow the normal pattern led to the conjecture that they had not fully appreciated the dual nature of their learning task. As a result, they mismanaged the trade-off between the task components by focusing too much on the differences between current states of the practice problem and the goal state and too little on which operators were being selected and their outcomes.

This line of reasoning implies that if the worked examples were restructured to allow the solver to pay attention, not only to getting the right answer but also to how that answer was reached, it should have the effect of boosting the number of subjects who schematised their solution methods. In a subsequent study, Sweller (1988) presented solvers with similar practice problems to those used previously but this time the instructions were changed. Now, instead of trying to solve each kinematic problem for a given variable (e.g. for height or for speed), solvers were shown a problem and told, "given this set of values calculate as many different additional variables for the situation as you can". Sweller reports that this "unfocused" practice condition did lead to an increase in the number of subjects adopting forward reasoning strategies and to an increase in the number of subjects showing mental set effects—both of which were taken as signs that schematisation was taking place. It was also predicted that, compared with the focused method, these subjects would remember more about the computations they made during the practice sessions. This outcome too was confirmed. Subjects using the unfocused method recalled more of the problem givens and their solution paths than subjects who followed the traditional method.

Sweller's dual task hypothesis implies that training materials should avoid introducing any extraneous cognitive load that could detract from reflective learning. Yet most training materials tend to fall well short of this criterion. Indeed, according to Sweller, Chandler, Tierney, and Cooper (1990) the majority of texts they consulted did exactly the opposite of what was required by confronting their users with a series of arbitrary subtasks that gratuitously dissipated their attentional resources. They describe a typical training sequence as setting out to give (1) an explanation of the principles involved, (2) introducing one or more worked examples, and (3) providing similar problems for learners to solve on their own. At each of these stages they found suboptimal procedures were being employed. Nonetheless, in the light of the preceding arguments it was evident how they could be improved.

For example, dropping the third step altogether should significantly reduce the learner's extraneous load and it was shown subsequently that learners did benefit if this change was introduced. Applying the same principles to the second step (where worked examples were displayed) calls for examples that do not introduce gratuitous processing demands of their own. Bad practice would arise whenever the examples required the learner to integrate different sources of information—as when linking an item in the text with a feature in a separate diagram. Under these circumstances, the resulting division of attention would serve to inhibit rather than facilitate schema formation. The problem could be removed, however, if all relevant detail were contained within the diagram itself. When it was arranged for subjects to practise with worked examples that had been restructured in this manner, not only was the time needed to work through the practice set reduced, it was also accompanied by faster and better performance when the subjects worked on transfer problems.

At this point, Sweller et al. had restructured the standard training procedure by getting rid of step 3 (where students work out problems for themselves) and by rearranging step 2 (to employ integrated worked examples). This just left step 1 (the explanation of the solution principles involved) to be assessed in the same terms. When they improved the readability of the explanatory introductions by reducing instances where the relevant information was fragmented, this too resulted in a further facilitation in problem solving. Taken overall, the combination of integrated explanatory texts and integrated worked examples gave rise to major learning gains compared with conventional materials. Furthermore, it was shown that the same restructuring principles generalised across problem domains. The introduction of these instructional changes was shown to facilitate not only the teaching of co-ordinate geometry but also the teaching of engineering skills.

METACOGNITIVE SKILLS AND LEARNING

The moral that emerges from the studies just described is that, without a great deal of external guidance, most learners are not especially adept at focusing their cognitive resources as required. This shortcoming can be further exacerbated by the tendency of learners to nurture an undue optimism about the quality of their own learning. Consider the simple make/break buzzer depicted in Fig. 12.1, which is taken from de Kleer and Brown (1981).

The functioning of this device can be easily explained by a small set of rules (De Kleer & Brown, 1981, p.289):

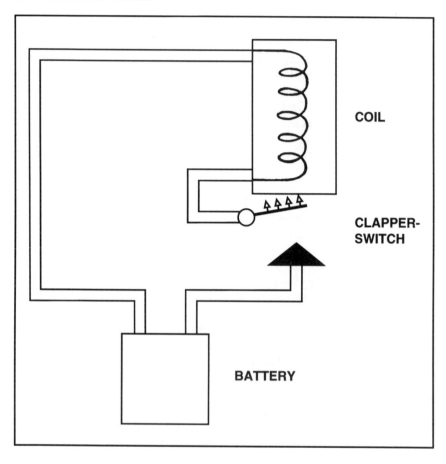

FIG. 12.1. Make-break buzzer. (From de Kleer & Brown, 1981.)

The clapper switch of the buzzer closes, which causes the coil to conduct a current, thereby generating an electro magnetic field, which in turn pulls the clapper arm away from the switch contact, thereby opening the switch, which shuts off the magnetic field allowing the clapper arm to return to its closed position, which then starts the whole process over again.

Having read these rules, it seems we are in a good position to envision how the device functions and we may feel quite confident about this—even though our confidence is misplaced.

Concealed deficiencies in understanding can be brought to the surface if we are asked about the functioning of the device when relatively minor changes are introduced. For example, what happens to the output if we reverse the leads of the battery, or, if the switch arm is made lighter or heavier? As we grapple with these questions it soon becomes clear that our original sense of understanding can appear highly optimistic, if not downright misleading. Understanding how the make/break buzzer functions entails constructing a mental model in which we can envision how state changes are caused by the components working as a whole. A typical mental model for this device incorporated content relating to the rule that closing the switch causes the coil to conduct current, but left implicit how the circuit components should be set up to enable this to happen. It seems, therefore, that strong feelings of knowing can conceal weak levels of understanding and our metacognitive promptings are, at best, an unreliable guide to the quality of our actual learning. Yet, if this is the case, how else are we supposed to monitor our state of understanding?

Monitoring comprehension

In the course of learning new information it will frequently happen that we reach a point where we do not understand part of what is being said. If we are reading, this sense of bafflement may prompt us to backtrack and reread the relevant section in order to remove the difficulty. It is a reasonable reaction because rereading can provide a way out of the difficulty by bringing new content into conceptual focus. Hence, self-monitoring of the quality of comprehension would appear to be an indispensable factor in this reorientation process as, deprived of its promptings, we would find ourselves unable to proceed except in the most superficial of ways. Nonetheless, many investigations into comprehension monitoring have cast doubt on its reliability and therefore on its utility in providing informative feedback to the learner. Glenberg and Epstein (1985, 1987), have consistently found that learners' ratings of self-confidence in their level of comprehension of a text did not predict their actual performance when they answered inference questions later. High levels of expressed confidence were not necessarily associated with good test performance.

The Feelings Of Knowledge (FOK) on which the confidence ratings were based arose, not so much from careful checking of the text content against prior knowledge, as from a more amorphous assessment based on how familiar the text content appeared to be. When Glenberg and Epstein (1987) asked physics and music students to rate their FOK for texts in their own or the other subject they found a relation between FOK and performance for the unfamiliar domain but not for the familiar domain. Physics students reading articles on physics and music students reading passages about music could not rely upon their feelings of knowing to predict which inference questions in their own subject area they would get right or wrong.

More recent work suggests that the relationship between rated level of confidence and the quality of subsequent levels of inferencing may not be quite so tenuous as these data suggest. In particular, Weaver (1990) has criticised the scope of Glenberg and Epstein's measure of comprehension, noting that it could be based on no more than a single inference question for each paragraph of text. When Weaver increased the number of inference questions he found that this change was sufficient to produce a significant, positive correlation between rated confidence and performance. Even then, the measured relationship was still quite low, (r = +.40), implying that the subjects continued to be overconfident when assessing the amount they had learned.

Maki, Foley, Kajer, Thompson, and Willert (1990) have also questioned the inability of subjects to calibrate their own comprehension. They found that when learners were encouraged to increase their level of processing this manipulation served to increase the predictive value of their comprehension ratings. Similarly, with regard to paired-associate learning, Nelson and Dunlosky (1991) report that introducing a slight delay between the learning task and ratings of FOK brought about a significant improvement in the utility of the ratings for predicting subsequent recall.

In general, although learners can and do use metacognitive monitoring to predict the quality of their learning, its promptings appear to be less well calibrated than we might think. For authors of instructional texts this means that they just have to take the gamble that their intuitions on where and how to prompt the reader into adopting a deeper level of processing will work as intended. For teachers engaged in face to face contact with their audience there are more direct ways of detecting when their message is failing to get across.

ORAL MODES OF INSTRUCTION

Reading is primarily a solitary activity where the author is distanced from the eventual audience. In contrast, when lecturing to an audience that is physically present, lecturers can use feedback from their audience to determine when communication seems to be breaking down and proceed to repair on-line a message that is failing to get across. Exactly what constitutes good lecturing practice in this regard is difficult to define *a priori*, but it is always possible to observe different lecturers in action and then to partition out what the "stars" on the lecturing circuit are actually doing that marks them out from their lesser colleagues.

A study along these lines, has been reported by Murray (1985) based on observations of 48 lecturers from the Faculty of Social Science in the University of Western Ontario. During the last two weeks of their course, student ratings of the teaching effectiveness of their lecturers were obtained which were averaged to give a single score for each lecturer. These effectiveness scores were then correlated with independent measures of how the lecturers performed when lecturing. Thus, the study is not concerned with how teaching strategies affected student performance but with how these practices were received by the student audience at the time.

Independent observers had visited each lecturer's class at least three times in order to make unobtrusive recordings of their styles of behaviour and these ratings were averaged to give summary scores on a number of behaviours. For example, teachers were judged on the extent to which they gesticulated while lecturing or on the extent to which they provided advance warning of what was to come. As a result, by the end of the study around 100 aspects of behaviour had been rated for each lecturer. These data were then collapsed under the six headings of Enthusiasm; Clarity; Interaction; Task Orientation; Rapport; and Organisation. The correlations that obtained between certain of these categories and the student ratings of teaching effectiveness are given in Table 12.1.

Evidently, the behaviours grouped under "enthusiasm" all had a significant bearing on student opinion. Equally evident was that most of the activities grouped under "organisation" had met with a pretty dismal, if not frosty, reception.

The pervasive role of instructor enthusiasm warrants further comment. Not surprisingly, it does not feature in comprehension models based purely on textual materials, as the printed page distances the author from the reader, obscuring, if not removing this factor altogether. As we move towards face-to-face contact, however, enthusiasm and its concomitant behaviours become increasingly prominent and appreciated. One possible explanation for this link lies in the way in which instructor enthusiasm bears on the incidence of self-questioning in the learner.

In coming to understand a new topic we need to do more than just register the basic details, rather we also need to question the significance of what is said. Why do the facts take the form they do? What would it mean if they were different? Where have I come across this pattern before? Each interrogatory probe serves to bring the new information into conjunction with different aspects of our previous

TABLE 12.1
Correlations between lecturer behaviour and students' ratings

	Correlation with efficiency
[ENTHUSIASM]	
Speaks expressively or emphatically	.63*
Shows facial expression	.47*
Uses humour	.49*
Reads lecture verbatim	−.33*
[CLARITY]	
Gives multiple examples	.30*
Stresses important points	.47*
[INTERACTION]	
Addresses students by name	.32*
Encourages questions and comments	.42*
Praises students for good ideas	.37*
[RAPPORT]	
Friendly, easy to talk to	.35*
Shows concern for student's progress	.45*
[ORGANISATION]	
Puts outline of lecture on board	−.08
Gives preliminary overview of lecture	.24
Signals transition to new topic	.31*

* significant correlation. Abstracted from Murray, 1985.

knowledge and our understanding stands to be consolidated in the process. But, before the advantages of self-questioning can be realised, two difficulties need to be overcome. The first relates to the apparent circularity that is involved—asking the right questions in a new domain presupposes knowledge that has yet to be acquired. Second, promiscuous questioning of each and every new detail would be counter-productive—somehow we must know when it is worth the time and effort. On the first front, it is evident from Table 12.1 that students appreciate when questions are set for them. On the second front (knowing when to question) an enthusiastic delivery provides students with a metacommentary on a topic which indicates where the "interesting" points in a topic are to be found and hence where self-questioning can be most useful in advancing understanding. Identifying these key areas is a skill that has to be learned anew for each content domain. In the meantime, learners can benefit by proxy through the instructor's own reactions to the topic as it unfolds.

SELF-QUESTIONING AND LEARNING

A preliminary account of the role of self-questioning in promoting understanding was given in Chapter 6 where the failure of early simulations of dynamic memory was linked to their inability to question inputs properly. Although CYRUS was designed to update itself as new information was acquired about the movements of the American Secretary of State, in practice, it did not do very well. CYRUS was designed to answer a question for which it had no direct information by transforming it into a version for which information did exist. But it failed to ask enough questions. When fed strange and out of the way facts, it remained insufficiently aroused to come up with a flurry of relevant questions.

Human learners do rather better than this although things can easily go wrong at a number of key points in the questioning process. In particular, problems can arise (1) when deciding where questioning will be beneficial; (2) when attempting to frame the question appropriately; and (3) when searching for information that will answer the question adequately. Failure at any one or more of these stages can easily jeopardise the quality of the learning outcome.

On the first point, it is evident that promiscuous questioning during learning will be of little value whereas restricting questioning to interesting cases of expectation failure could turn out to be extremely beneficial. Once our interest has been aroused, possibly because an explicit prediction has been directly contradicted, further questioning may home in on long-standing confusions that have previously gone undetected. But this then runs up against the second point. Conceptual advance will only happen if the question has been phrased at the right level. Questions dealing with local details will do little to further the learner's understanding whereas questions that deal with the ramifications of what has been learned for more remote areas of the learner's knowledge base can be highly beneficial. In short, we can conceive of a hierarchy of question forms where higher versions carry greater significance for the quality of learning that is likely to be achieved (Schank, 1987).

At the most basic level are those questions that deal with the specifics of what happened. One level up are questions aimed at clarifying whatever causal chains may be involved and a further step is taken when questioning attempts to relate the new experience to relevant, prior knowledge. At the top of the scale are those questions that serve to conjoin features of the current input with hitherto remote areas in the learner's knowledge base. It is at this level that, every once in a while, self-questioning delivers novel and powerful generalisations.

Nonetheless, formulating questions that are sufficiently searching in this respect is far from easy. In fact, framing well-formed questions even at the basic level, is not easy and, if it is carelessly done, the resulting answers may hinder learning rather than help.

Such an outcome applied in a study reported by Van der Meij (1990) in which the questions raised by fifth-grade students were recorded as they participated in a word definition task. The subjects were presented with a word and they then had to choose between five alternative definitions. In making their choice, they were told to make a putative decision first of all and then, before committing themselves, they were allowed to ask some questions about their choice. The questions were supplied by the experimenter and they fell into two types; specific questions which reduced the choices on offer and, global questions which were too general to be helpful in this respect. Under these conditions, a number of the students proceeded to ask questions that were both unnecessary and harmful. A question was deemed unnecessary if the putative choice was already correct. It was judged as harmful if the putative choice was correct but was then changed as a result of the question selected.

In a second study, the students were encouraged to follow their provisional answer by a question of their own making. Placing more of the responsibility on the subjects themselves only served to reduce the overall incidence of questioning and, for the low-ability subjects, it also tended to elicit global questions that were not particularly helpful to them.

We cannot assume, therefore, that even if an appropriate context for raising questions has been detected, the right questions will come unbidden. Equally, even if appropriately phrased questions are forthcoming, we cannot assume that they will then be answered adequately. There are many occasions when our response to questioning is, at best, cursory and, at worst, downright misleading. Self-questioning may be the royal route to knowledge consolidation but we may be tempted to spend more time handwaving than travelling.

We have seen both here and elsewhere that question answering can sometimes be a perfunctory process where we respond to a question by making a plausibility check rather than by analysing what the question means. When Erikson and Mattson (1981) asked their subjects "How many animals of each kind did Moses take into the ark?" they were frequently given the confident answer "Two", although their respondents knew perfectly well that it was Noah who was in charge of the passenger list. In arriving at their answer these subjects were clearly not delaying their reply until they had found an exact match between what they knew and the question as posed. Reder (1982, 1987) has explained such "mindlessness" by proposing that subjects can rely on two different strategies when answering questions. One strategy is based on direct search for the factual information encoded in memory. The other strategy rests on a more inferential approach to the question where a plausible answer is preferred over a factual reply. Which strategy will be employed depends on the subject's FOK responses as the question is comprehended. Direct search is employed when FOK indicates that search will be easy. Otherwise, a plausibility match is the preferred strategy.

To take stock so far, it seems that self-questioning aimed at consolidating understanding will only be useful if:

1. The learner realises when questioning is necessary and likely to be useful. Certain heuristics such as "interesting failed expectations" appear to influence this decision.
2. An adequate question can be formulated. Although this may appear to call upon the very knowledge that is being sought, a range of basic question frames is generally available which may lead on to higher-order levels of questioning.
3. The answer is based on a direct search of the relevant knowledge base and is not usurped by a plausibility match.

Thus, although the importance of self-questioning for consolidating understanding seems undeniable, in practice it can be beset by many attendant problems. It comes as no great revelation, therefore, that students left to study under their own devices often experience difficulties in doing the right things.

SPONTANEOUS STUDY METHODS

Anderson (1980) surveyed the preferred study practices of 400 students and recorded the frequency of the different learning strategies they spontaneously chose to employ. The most popular practices were: (1) Read and reread the text; (2) Underline in the text; (3) Review the material; and (4) Take notes. Somewhat less common were those practices that called for a more proactive reponse to the text content, e.g. (5) Write outlines of the text content; (6) Reflect on the material; and (7) Skim through the text beforehand. Distinctly unpopular were those practices that had the best chance of revealing potential gaps in understanding, e.g. (8) Self-testing on the content; (9) Writing summaries; and (10) Working through practice problems. This survey is instructive in contrasting differences in the depth of preferred study practices but it made no allowance for individual differences in student ability. Subsequent investigations have shown that student ability can be an important factor in determining preferences for shallow and deep modes of study.

Fergusson-Hessler and de Jong (1990) asked two groups of physics students, divided into good and poor learners on the basis of their previous examination performance, to read an article on the mass-spectrometer as if they were studying for an exam. Unlike normal study, this text contained signals at various points which indicated that they were to stop reading in order to report exactly what they had been doing just beforehand. Using this method, around 32 different study practices were identified which were further reduced by assigning them to one of four categories: (1) superficial processing; (2) integration; (3) making connections; and (4) a residual category for "other" types of response.

Superficial processing included such activities as comparing symbols in text to symbols in figures, taking something for granted, and the use of rote memorising. These activities do little more than establish the local coherence of the text. *Integration* referred to any attempts by the learner to link together on a global level what was being read. This could entail trying to separate essentials from side issues, drawing conclusions from the text, or searching for the presence of possible contradictions. *Making connections* referred to activities aimed at linking the text content with the reader's prior knowledge. It could mean explicitly recognising particular parts of an argument as having occurred in other contexts, thinking of new examples in addition to those provided, or reformulating the given argument in a different way. The remaining activities that could not be classified under these three headings, were assigned to a residual *other* category. Grouped under this heading were activities such as expressing a value judgement on the text content or simply making a note that certain points were not clear.

Although the two ability groups did not differ in how actively they processed the text, their study methods did differ qualitatively. Poor students preferred the more superficial methods and they were particularly inclined to report taking things for granted. Responses in the residual category were three times as common for the lower-ability group as for the good students and this group also paid most attention to the declarative passage content at the expense of procedural detail. Thus, the poorer students appeared to suffer from a distinct lack of insight into their own knowledge states which deflected them from questioning the value of what they are doing. Ironically, these were the students who were most inclined to report seeing "everything as clear"; good students were much more circumspect about the state of their own knowledge. Deep processing strategies, like confronting the text content with other ideas or making it more explicit, were largely confined to the higher-ability group.

COLLECTIVE LEARNING

One way of rectifying these individual processing deficiences is to convert the learning situation from an individual assignment to one in which other people are made part of the learning equation. Of course, to the extent that learners are already engaged in absorbing arguments put forward by others this has always been the case. Nonetheless, shifting the theoretical focus from individual learning strategies to a collective level serves to raise two new and substantial issues.

First, exposure to the received styles of reasoning adopted by different academic disciplines could well have implications for students' reasoning outside the lecture room. Individuals exposed to advanced training in areas such as logic or history, i.e. disciplines that possess specialised problem-solving techniques, have the opportunity to capitalise on this training when engaged in reasoning in general. We can expect trained logicians to utilise their logical skills when reasoning about their everyday world and we can expect trained historians to extract consistent storylines from apparently contradictory materials, whatever their source.

Second, where more than one person is engaged in a common learning task, this can improve the levels of comprehension for all concerned as they adjust to the perspective of other learners and as they co-ordinate this information with their own understanding. We will look at each of these issues in turn.

Formal education and general reasoning skills
The extent to which educational experience generalises outside the context of instruction is an issue that has long and chequered history (e.g. Perkins, 1986), and it would take us too far afield to attempt a review of the "formal training" literature. However, a narrower line of enquiry can be entertained by referring to the potential impact of highly specialised modes of training on students' general reasoning skills. Kuhn (1991) had found in her study into styles of argument, reported in the previous chapter, that a subgroup of philosophically trained subjects had argued their brief more effectively than their less educated colleagues. In similar vein, we can ask whether exposure to higher training in different, specialised disciplines can also instil distinct styles of reasoning in their students which can then transfer to new and different contexts.

Lehman, Lempert, and Nisbett, (1988) tested for transfer of this kind by comparing the performance of first- and third-year graduate students in chemistry, law, psychology, and medicine on a battery of different reasoning tests. Some of the tests had been designed to assess their everyday verbal reasoning, some to assess their statistical reasoning, and others to assess their logical reasoning. They found that increased exposure to certain disciplines did have measurable consequences for the tests in question. Although three years of postgraduate chemistry showed no differential effect on any of the reasoning measures, students in their third year of law were found to be better at logical reasoning than their first-year counterparts. Furthermore, students into their third year of medicine or psychology were better than their first-year equivalents on all three of the tests employed. Graduate training, it seems, can have general effects which are detectable outside the curriculum.

In a subsequent paper, Lehman and Nisbett (1990) reported on a longitudinal study that monitored the preferred reasoning strategies of students as they progressed through the four years of their undergraduate course in social science, natural science, or the humanities. This time it was found that an undergraduate training in psychology and social science exerted the most influence on how the students tackled problems in statistical and methodological reasoning whereas exposure to the natural sciences and the humanities had few significant effects on these measures. This situation was effectively reversed when conditional reasoning was assessed. On these questions, natural science and humanities students showed the most gains while social science students were less affected.

The investigators express some surprise at the gains in conditional reasoning displayed by humanities students, as though they expected this type of training to have little or no bearing on the students' reasoning skills. Yet, given the close alliance between narrative comprehension and informal reasoning described in Chapter 10, this outcome is not that remarkable. Students of history are explicitly called upon to evaluate different and often conflicting eyewitness reports and such training could well establish reasoning skills specifically tailored to the evaluation of complex and possibly inconsistent lines of argument.

Explicit evidence in support of this claim has been provided by Wineberg (1991). The study dealt with the content of protocols produced by a group of working historians and student historians as they thought aloud while reviewing "a series of written and pictorial documents about the battle of Lexington". Analysis of the data led Wineberg to identify three basic heuristics as used by professional historians. The first,

Corroboration, entailed identifying important descriptive details and then checking them against each other before accepting them as valid. The second, *Sourcing*, entailed evaluating the source of documentary evidence before trying to absorb the detailed content. The third, *Contextualisation*, was concerned with linking the documented detail with specific times and places.

The presence of these specialised skills reveals how everyday reasoning strategies can be further refined in the light of formal training to produce new versions capable of delivering a coherent argument through the elimination of misleading detail. Corroboration calls for a comparison of the consistency of one narrative form against another and it favours whichever version receives the most independent support. Sourcing depends on treating different protagonists in the action as unequal observers and alerts the reasoner to potential biases in witness statements that need to be detected and weighted accordingly. Contextualisation plays a similar role in weighting the quality of different reports by consulting the mental models likely to have been created by different obervers. It proceeds by drawing inferences from witnesses' testimony aimed at evaluating their perspective on the event in question; was the witness at the centre of things or way out on the periphery? For example, one experimental subject weighed the available testimony according to what was likely to have been seen "in the darkness of this New England morning".

Wineberg found that experienced historians employed these heuristics significantly more often than their students. Experts were three times as likely to look back to a previous document, three times as likely to evaluate the source of a document, and were significantly more sensitive to aspects of time and place. It was the judicious combination of these heuristics that enabled expert historians to detect patterns in the fragmented data at their disposal and to arrive at an overall sense of order that lay observers would almost certainly have missed.

More generally, we can expect to find a dialectical process at work as historians, and other scholars, are first inducted into their chosen discipline and as they then go on to contribute to this same methodology. Exposure to extant professional methodologies will impact on the reasoning styles of the novitiates, some of whom will then go on to make their own contribution to the pool of specialised techniques used for training new entrants. We will return to this point at the end of this discussion and in the following chapter. For the present, it serves as a salutary reminder that formal education is nothing if not a highly developed form of socially situated cognition.

Individual learning as socially situated

Although styles of reasoning acquired during formal training may generalise to outside activities, there again, they may not. Instead of transfer we can also find compartmentalisation taking place. A case in point was reported in Chapter 7 where Strauss's study of the child's grasp of temperature revealed a dissociation between what had been learned at school and what had been learned from everyday experience. Perret (cited in Perret-Clermont, Perret, & Bell, 1991) has similarly described how mathematical operations taught in the classroom often fail to engage with equivalent tasks experienced on the outside. In this case (Perret-Clermont et al., 1991, p.57), it was as though the children concerned had failed to develop:

> ... the expected metareflection about underlying rules, concepts and structures or about the teacher's background thoughts and intentions. ... Their responses were contextualised, deriving their meaning from the restricted setting in which they were constructed and were embedded in current and past classroom experience.

This is to raise once again the issue of knowledge redescription, but this time as it applies on the collective level where the learner's metareflective activity is linked to the social context in which the learning takes place. Certain contexts of learning may fail to engage metareflective processes in the learner. Equally, there are other social contexts where individuals can come to exhibit levels of performance in consort with others which would have eluded them if they had been left to struggle through on their own.

Peer teaching and co-operative learning

Left to ourselves, we are easily misled into thinking we understand when we do not. Hence, any study strategy that forces us into taking a more critical view of the quality of our own learning can only be beneficial; becoming aware that one doesn't understand is a critical first step towards putting matters right. Students who find it difficult to take this extra step on their own are likely to find that the device of drawing others into the learning exercise makes a considerable difference. For example, converting the learning task from one of private study (where one learns purely for personal benefit) to one of communication (where the learner must be prepared to teach what has been learned to others) has been shown to make a significant difference to the outcome. Consider a study reported by Ross and DiVesta (1976). They compared the learning of a lengthy passage dealing with the lifestyle of a foreign tribe when the task took the form of private study and when it served as a preparation for delivering an oral summary to other students. On a recall test administered one week later, they found major differences between these two learning conditions. Subjects who expected and later gave an oral summary recalled 25% more content than students who learned for themselves. Similarly, Annis (1983) has reported that subjects engaged in learning for the purpose of teaching others recalled up to twice the amount achieved by control subjects engaged in private study. Introducing a potential audience into the learning process can expose the deficiencies associated with shallow modes of study that otherwise would have gone undetected. After all, it only takes one awkward question from a potential audience to be anticipated to move the learner from a state of complacency to one of alarmed concern.

The importance of attending to the other perspectives is further supported by studies involving another form of socially facilitated learning—"co-operative learning"—where, unlike peer tutoring, all the participants are expected to be equally involved in the common learning process. Doise and his colleagues (e.g. Doise & Mugny, 1984) have shown that when children worked collaboratively on a conservation task, they gained in insight as a result of being exposed to the arguments put forward by others. In particular, non-conserving children came to agree with conservation judgements expressed by their partners and they maintained these judgements after the group session had been concluded. Even arranging for two non-conservers to collaborate on a conservation task appeared to have beneficial effects. If they could be brought to agree on a joint reponse, both were likely to show an improvement in their own conservation responses.

These improvements did not simply depend on each learner conforming to what could be observed in the group situation. Detailed analysis of the peer-group discussions (Perret-Clermont et al., 1991, p.44) both at the time and at a subsequent post-test revealed that:

> Those subjects who progress to the stage of conservation manage, in the posttest, to defend their newly acquired cognition with "new" arguments (i.e., different from those heard from their partners during the experimental session).

Other studies have questioned this conclusion (e.g. Emler & Valiant, 1982), but we have already encountered good theoretical grounds for predicting this type of outcome. Where the group situation served to bring unrelated strategies into the same mental workspace (this time emanating from both participants) each individual was presented with the opportunity to form a new structural synthesis.

"Co-operative learning" is something of a misnomer for this exercise—conflict tended to arise once children occupying different cognitive levels were let loose on the common task—but even so, their subsequent progress was not solely due to the clash of different viewpoints exposing the children to the inadequacies of their own judgements. Rather, the opportunity for social interaction *per se* also contributed to this outcome (see Perret-Clermont et al., 1991). Participating in social discourse about a common task had required each child to co-ordinate his or her perspective with that of others and this exercise in "reading other minds" had a significant bearing on the quality of the learning outcome.

Vygotsy and social scaffolding
Much of the work on the social facilitation of learning harks back to arguments that were aired in the 1930s when Vygotsky (1934; English translation, 1962) roundly criticised Piaget's developmental theories for their undue emphasis on internalised mental activities. For Vygotsky, Piaget's emphasis on individual cognitive principles determining the developmental progression from lower to higher mental processes was simply wrong. Rather, Vygotsky argued that the mental development of the child has its origins in the details of social exchange and in the psychological tools (such as language) that follow in the wake of these socialisation experiences. A child who participates in different social settings is exposed to new modes of thought which then, and only then, undergo a process of internalisation. As a result, modes of thinking in the child that orginally depended on the scaffolding provided by other group members come to occur in the absence of this support. In contrast to the Piagetian stance, Vygotsky's "general genetic law of cultural development" (cited Wertsch, 1985, pp.60–61) holds that:

> Any function in the child's cultural development appears twice, or on two planes. First it appears on the social plane, and then on the psychological plane. First it appears between people as an interpsychological category, and then within the child as an intrapsychological category. This is equally true with regard to voluntary attention, logical memory, the formation of concepts, and the development of volition. We may consider this position as a law in the full sense of the word, but it goes without saying that internalization transforms the process itself and changes its structure and functions. Social relations or relations among people genetically underlie all higher functions and their relationships.

The immediate import of this line of argument for instructional practice can be seen most clearly in Vygotsky's writings concerning the zone of proximal development. This zone is demarcated at one extreme by the level of problem solving a child can achieve unaided and, at the other extreme, by the level that can be reached when working in collaboration with another (more capable) person. As Vygotsky (1962, p.103) expresses it:

> Having found that the mental age of two children was, let us say, eight, we gave each of them harder problems than he could manage on his own and provided some slight assistance: the first step in a solution, a leading question or in some other form of help. We discovered that one child could, in cooperation, solve problems for twelve year olds, while the other could not go beyond problems intended for nine year olds. The discrepancy between a child's actual mental age and the level he reaches in solving problems with assistance indicates the zone of his proximal development: in our example, this zone is four for the first child and one for the second.

Group modes of learning can act to promote the child's growth in understanding because the participants are likely to have overlapping (but not exactly equivalent) zones of proximal development. Bringing together different and possibly conflicting perspectives on a common learning task can result in novice participants entertaining ideas that they had been incapable of formulating by themselves.

Eliciting self-explanations

Learning for the purpose of teaching others and co-operative learning are both instances where a social scaffolding has been erected around the learning process. Each procedure is designed to elicit patterns of self-questioning which the participants can then put to use in generating their own explanations for the topics under review. Nonetheless, solitary study is still the norm and it would be especially advantageous if individual modes of study could be found that retained the benefits attributed to social facilitation.

A recent investigation by Chi, de Leeuw, Chiu, and LaVancher (1994) suggests that this outcome could be achieved by incorporating "talk aloud" procedures within the routines of individual learning. Although their recommended method does not completely dispense with an audience (their students talked about their self-generated explanations to the experimenters who tape-recorded what they had to say) the underlying assumption is that given sufficient practice and positive feedback, individual students could go on to adopt these tactics as a matter of course.

Chi et al. identify "self-explanation" as occurring when learners spontaneously provide their own explanations for content they encounter during the course of their studies. In a previous experiment, (Chi, Bassock, Lewis, Reimann, & Glaser, 1989), they had found that the students who benefited most from studying worked physics examples were the ones who spontaneously generated the most explanations for the actions involved. The present study was designed to see whether equivalent gains in comprehension could be externally induced by prompting students come up with self-explanations.

The design of the experiment called for two groups of subjects (eighth-grade students) to read and digest a fairly complex passage dealing with the human circulatory system. At the outset, both groups were tested for their prior knowledge of the topic. Then, each group was given the opportunity to read through the text. Control subjects read the passage through twice before answering a series of post-test questions about the content. Experimental subjects read the passage just once (Chi et al., 1994, p.477) under instructions to read:

> ... each sentence out loud and then explain what it means to you. That is, what new information does each line provide for you, how does it relate to what you have already read, does it give you a new insight into your understanding of how the circulatory system works, or does it raise a question in your mind?

The test questions aimed at assessing the subjects' prior and subsequent knowledge of the circulatory system ranged from questions that could be answered using explicit detail contained in the text to questions that could only be answered through the generation of new knowledge. All subjects answered half of the questions in each category before reading the text and then answered the full set in the course of the post-test.

Whereas both groups gained on post-test, the prompted group gained most of all (32% vs 22%), especially with regard to the more difficult questions (22.6% vs 12.5%). Analysis of the self-explanations provided by this group indicated that 30% were generated by linking the new information to general background knowledge; 41% derived from global integrations within the text, and 29% depended on a variety of other strategies such as drawing analogies and logical inferences. Within the talk-aloud group, subjects who generated the most self-explanations tended to experience the greatest gains in comprehension, especially on the harder questions. Significantly, the conceptual gains associated with the subjects in the prompted group were not dependent on their abilities as measured by a standard achievement test.

INDIVIDUAL LEARNING AS HISTORICALLY SITUATED

At the end of a long and protracted period of training, the individual learner will be well versed in the cultural heritage of the host society. In fact, more well versed than we might at first think. In acquiring the culture's cognitive tools, the student has also been immersed in the culture's intellectual history. According to Resnick, Levine, and Teasley (1991, p.7), each and every cultural artefact, from the algorithms of a culture's arithmetic and science to its books and maps, will have:

> ... theories built into them, and users accept these theories—albeit often unknowingly—when they use these tools. ... The tools that one uses not only enable thought and intellectual progress but also constrain and limit the range of what can be thought. In these invisible ways, the history of a culture—an inherently social history—is carried into each individual act of cognition ...

Formal education is the principal means through which the products of this intellectual history are transmitted from one generation to the next. However, in absorbing the content of contemporary disciplines, the modern novice is often called upon to revise some strongly held intuitions about the properties of the physical world, intuitions that may be similar to those that informed earlier models of the phenomena in question. It is possible, therefore, that in coming to understand the contemporary outlook, the modern learner may be drawn into recreating the conceptual steps associated with the original process of discovery. Novice physicists learning about Newton's laws of motion could find themselves having to revise the same misconceptions in their own thought that informed the thinking of Newton's precursors.

The present chapter has been concerned with the manner in which individuals absorb the lessons of formal education. In the next chapter we will turn the perspective the other way around by enquiring into potential parallels (and discontinuities) between the individual and the historical records. The overall aim is to try to throw some light on the dynamic principles underlying the accumulation of knowledge on the collective level.

CHAPTER THIRTEEN

Cultural transmission of knowledge: Historical change

Knowledge is not just handed down inviolate from one generation to the next, it is also transformed as new contexts are created through its application and use. Thus, the accumulation of knowledge can be addressed on two fronts; cross sectionally, as viewed from the individual case, and longitudinally, where the individual is seen as a transitory actor in an ongoing sequence. If our grasp of the dynamic principles at work on the individual level is tenuous, this is doubly so when it comes to the principles that shape the historical growth of ideas. Nonetheless, attempts have been made to redress this imbalance by bringing together studies of how belief systems change from one generation to the next (mainly scientific beliefs) and studies of the course traced by individuals as they gain expertise in the same domains.

For the novice who is attempting to understand the current position, say in physics or biology, this may mean retracing some of the steps that comprised the historical route. Consequently, we can ask whether the collective and the individual histories are likely to share features in common. In the course of coming to understand current scientific belief is it possible that the individual learner pursues a similar route to that by which scientific understanding itself advanced? At first glance, it must be admitted that the likelihood of finding useful parallels seems extremely remote. Quite possibly, there are no connections to be made between the collective and the individual case history. If so, the very knowledge that such a dissociation exists should encourage us to pay attention to the nature of the differences involved. On the other hand, as we come closer to understanding the mechanisms of thought in the individual thinker, we may find that this same information can be used to interpret the historical record and vice versa.

The aim of the present chapter is to provide a preliminary survey of some of these issues and to see how historically situated accounts of cognition might fit within the theoretical frameworks we have employed so far. The account commences by considering T.S. Kuhn's influential analysis of the causes leading to radical change in the content of scientific theory and the manner in which such change is managed within the scientific community. Although Kuhn's account tends to overstate the non-progressive aspects of scientific change it does provide a useful framework for foregrounding some of the factors involved. It is followed by a review of some of the misapprehensions harboured by individual learners as they set out to absorb particular aspects of scientific theorising. These two sets of accumulative records are then compared to see what, if anything, they can tell us about possible mechanisms for change. The discusssion concludes with reference to the way in which models of the individual cognitive architecture have been used to simulate critical stages in historical, scientific debate. The whole exercise will, of necessity, do less than justice to the nuances and subtleties of the historical issues but at this stage we are not attempting to do more than search for some interesting questions that could link these areas together.

SCIENTIFIC REVOLUTIONS

In his book *The structure of scientific revolutions*, Kuhn (1962) addresses the possible causes leading to the overthrow of established scientific beliefs and the channels through which these forces operate. Early on in his account, Kuhn (1962, p.viii) introduces the concept of the "paradigm" which he identifies with:

> ... universally recognised scientific achievements that for a time provide model problems and solutions to a community of practicioners.

"Normal science" is being practised when a paradigm is in place that is largely accepted as setting the research goals of a particular scientific community. The ensuing research is directed towards exploring the paradigm's implications and it is this activity that gives rise to the findings deemed fundamental to theory construction. These are the findings that take pride of place in the textbooks of the period and it is through exposure to this corpus of work that succeeding generations of practitioners qualify for entry into the scientific community. Newton's *Principia* and Lyell's *Principles* came to dominate the research agenda within physics and geology respectively because, following their publication, their arguments were seen as intellectually more rewarding than their competitors and they pointed to a range of problems waiting to be solved. Routine scientific activity, in other words, is not so much concerned with testing the validity of the paradigm itself as with exploiting its capacity for organising observations of natural phenomena.

The prevailing paradigm does rather more than define which problems are to be judged as relevant and soluble. It also acts as a source for the intellectual faith and commitment that are crucially needed if individual scientists are to investigate their subject in meticulous detail. Committing one's creative future to a particular area of research is not a step to be taken lightly and the shared paradigm can shoulder much of the burden associated with this choice. It is this same commitment to scrupulous and detailed experiment that, sooner or later, will bring anomalous observations to light which can then set in motion the forces leading to paradigmatic change. As Kuhn explains (1962, p.53):

> Discovery commences with the awareness of anomaly—the recognition that nature has somehow violated the paradigm induced expectations that govern normal science. It then continues with a more or less extended exploration of the areas of anomaly ... (which period) closes only when the paradigm theory has been adjusted so that the anomalous has become the expected.

Under these conditions, Kuhn suggests that new goals arise within the scientific community which lead to a meta-analysis of the theoretical assumptions under threat. The conceptual tools that created the anomaly are themselves now put under scrutiny in order to resolve the problem. Exceptionally, if the crisis cannot be resolved within the confines of the prevailing paradigm, it may lead to the adoption of an alternative version which promises to do a better job at coping with the critical experimental data.

Kuhn's choice of the politically loaded term "revolution" to describe the process of paradigmatic change is quite deliberate. The breeding ground for political revolution is a general sense of growing dissatisfaction with the way existing institutions act to prohibit alternative modes of thought, along with the belief that some alternative system exists that will manage things better. For Kuhn, these same creative tensions serve to fuel the exchanges within the scientific community when alternative paradigms are brought into conflict. Such tensions will be further exacerbated wherever the alternative paradigm demands not merely some adjustment and retuning of the older ways of thinking, but a qualitative shift in outlook, where the phenomena in question are assigned different interpretations according to which paradigm is being used. The ensuing crisis sees a struggle for mastery enacted as each side attempts to impose its own definition of normal science.

At such times the rival camps will tend to talk past each other. Each movement will attempt to justify its case by appealing to facts and interpretations whose significance derives from the frameworks that are in dispute. Inevitably, this leads to major difficulties of adjudication. Scientific autonomy rules out a resolution based on appeals to some external authority, instead the solution must come from within the scientific community directly involved. Paradigm change allows for the deadlock to be broken through a structural revolution that alters the world view of the practitioners in the dispute. At the same time, the incommensurability of the competing positions implies that revolutions in scientific thought need not solely be driven by logic and reasoned argument. In which case, scientific change is not so much a linear progression towards some greater, more embracing state of truth than a process of selection where rival systems compete for recognition as the "fittest way to practise future science."

Kuhn substantiates his analysis by pointing to particular events in the scientific records where normal science was thrown into crisis only to be accompanied by paradigmatic change. Specific examples can be found in the shift from Ptolemaic to Copernican astronomy; the collapse of phlogiston theory in chemistry; and the events in physics that led up to the acceptance of Einstein's Relativity theory.

Following their first appearance in print, Kuhn's ideas received widespread attention and equally widespread criticism, as the postscript to the second edition (1970) makes clear. Some critics have objected to the way in which he understated the degree of variation that actually exists between practitioners doing normal science—as though there is a generic activity termed "Science" rather than an assortment of sciences each subscribing to different interpretations of their practices and values. Other critics have taken Kuhn to task for allowing the key concept of the paradigm to fluctuate between different meanings at different times. Nonetheless, Kuhn's central argument is both forceful and clear. Knowledge accumulates in the scientific community during periods of normal science conducted within a generally accepted paradigm. As its sphere of application expands, certain paradigmatic predictions may be disconfirmed, giving rise to a body of critical data that cannot be accommodated within the received framework without a major reorganisation taking place. Such conflict-induced crises can prefigure revolutionary change but this will only occur provided an alternative paradigm is waiting in the wings and enough converts can be recruited to its cause.

It will be evident, even from this condensed account of the arguments, that there are parallels to be drawn between Kuhn's collective model and models of individual knowledge reorganisation as set out in Chapter 7. Once again, we find conflict induced by expectation failure being proposed as a factor contributing to conceptual change which works its effects through the processes of metareflection it brings in its wake. Furthermore, although conflict provides the opportunity for conceptual change it does not in itself provide the resolution. Paradigm change also presupposes there is some alternative framework in circulation that is capable of accommodating the anomalous data and of opening up new opportunities for the practice of normal science. But we are dealing with extremely broad generalisations—matters could change significantly once specific content domains are considered in more detail.

NOVICE BELIEFS AND EARLY SCIENTIFIC THEORY

If we compare modern novices' explanations of physical phenomena with the content of the historical explanations that have led up to the current position we can proceed to enquire into possible correspondences between these two descriptive records. Although the notion of any literal recapitulation is certainly too strong (the mediaeval and modern lifestyles are too disparate to expect a simple reduplication of earlier ideas) there may still be similarities to be detected beneath the surface. Wiser (1988) has conducted exactly this type of comparison in the area of thermal physics. Her conclusion is that genuine parallels do exist: the early modes of understanding the concepts of heat and temperature show significant similarities with the representations employed by modern novices as they try to come to terms with these fundamental ideas.

Concept differentiation: Heat and temperature

The historical record reveals that it took some time before the concepts of temperature and heat were differentiated from each other. According to Wiser (1988, p.33), in modern thermal theory, heat and temperature are to be distinguished in that:

Temperature is the average kinetic energy of translation per molecule. It is therefore an intensive property. ... Heat is extensive ... If it takes a certain amount of heat to bring the temperature of a certain mass of substance from t1 to t2, it takes twice that amount of heat to bring twice the mass of the same substance from t1 to t2.

Although this is hardly the whole story, there is already quite sufficient here for novices to get very confused as they grapple with these concepts. Strauss (1987) reports that young children (and the not so young) were unlikely to understand that mixing two cups of water at 20°C with two cups of water at 80°C will give a mix of the same temperature as one cup of water at 20°C and one cup at 80°C. Thermal theory holds that in the case of the double amounts, although the resulting mix is at the same temperature as the mix with the single cups, twice as much heat will have been exchanged. Novices, who fail to differentiate between heat and temperature, make characteristic errors as they reason their way through such examples. The point at issue is whether these errors match up to those made at an earlier phase of scientific understanding when a similar failure in differentiation applied.

Historically, Wiser focuses on the work of the Italian experimenters in Florence at the beginning of the seventeenth century whose explanations of thermal phenomena were also based on different concepts to those applied today. The Source–Recipient model of the time assumed heat to be made up of particles of fire and held that heat is emitted spontaneously by very hot sources which communicate their heat to substances in contact with them. The recipients in this exchange are passive receivers; they have no effect on the heating process and the sources are not themselves affected by their action on the recipients.

One consequence of this asymmetry between source and recipient is that it does not allow for the view that cold is the absence of heat. Rather, within the source–recipient model, cold is viewed as a separate entity in its own right. Furthermore the model assumes that heat is to be measured by its intensity, or strength, not by its amount. Thus, while the source–recipient model did utilise a concept of heat, it was an undifferentiated mixture of what we would now term heat and temperature, combining together their intensive and extensive properties.

Wiser maintains that contemporary novices use something very like the source–recipient model when accounting for the kinds of phenomena analysed by the earlier experimenters. The modern subjects talked about heat acting as a force and they treated cold as a separate agent in its own right, possessed of its own sources and its own force. For the least sophisticated subjects, Wiser suggests that their thermal model "is identical in structure and very similar in content to the source–recipient model" (p.45).

Overall, Wiser concluded that novice concepts in this domain should not be viewed as impoverished or inadequate concepts but as different from the expert's and as embedded in a different theoretical model of thermal phenomena. This theoretical model is strikingly similar to the early source–recipient model and it serves to capture strong intuitions derived from everyday experience that are not easily discarded. Although Wiser sees no reason to suppose that subsequent developments within thermal physics would reappear as part of the novice–expert shift, she leaves as an open question whether the process of knowledge restructuring in the individual might still share "deep similarities" with the historical case.

Other psycho-historical comparisons have gone further in likening the modern novice's understanding of natural phenomena to Kuhn's pre-paradigmatic stage in scientific theorising. They argue that any content overlap with the historical record arises because the approach to theory formation is much the same in both cases.

Impetus theory and classical mechanics

McCloskey and Kargon (1988) have focused their investigations on lay notions concerning the motion of inanimate objects and, much as Wiser had reported for thermal phenomena, their respondents also tended to share similar misconceptions to the early practitioners who paved the way for classical mechanics. The misconceptions in question rested on an intuitive theory of motion that bore a "striking resemblance" to the pre-Newtonian theory of impetus.

The primary evidence for this claim was produced when McCloskey and Kargon questioned highschool students and college students for their predictions about the motions of objects in critical situations. For example, they were asked to draw the path taken by a ball as it exits from a spiral tube. Newton's first law of motion states that the ball will travel in a straight line once it is released, but half of the subjects questioned preferred the view that the ball would follow a curved exit path. Presenting the same problem in another form (e.g. a ball breaking away from the string on which it was being whirled around) produced similar anomalies with one third of the subjects claiming it would follow a curved path. All told, a substantial minority of the subjects believed that when an object is forced to move in a curved path, it will continue in a curvilinear motion for some time after it is released.

This belief turned out to be quite robust. When subjects were asked to make predictions about actual moving objects, similar misconceptions emerged. Asked to roll a ball so that it followed a curved path, some subjects attempted to impose a curved path on the ball's motion. Equally, more than half of the subjects, when asked where a ball would hit the ground if it was dropped from shoulder height by a man walking along, failed to appreciate that it would traverse an arc, hitting the ground at a point that is somewhat forward of the point of release. Some subjects suggested that it would fall straight down hitting the ground directly below the release point and a few were prepared to believe that it would move backwards. When subjects were asked to justify their predictions, they made use of an intuitive theory which held that setting an object in motion imparted an external force to the object that kept the object in motion just so long as it remained present.

McCloskey and Kargon note that impetus theories of this kind have a long history—at least commencing with Aristotle and persisting into the late Middle Ages. Impetus theory assumes that the act of setting an object in motion imparts an internal force or impetus that continues to operate after the object is no longer in contact with the original mover. As the impetus gradually dissipates, the object slows down and eventually comes to a stop. Newtonian mechanics, in contrast, states that just as no force is required to keep an object at rest, so no force is required to keep an object in motion. In the absence of an applied force, an object at rest will remain stationary, and an object in motion will keep moving at a constant speed in a straight line. In the Newtonian model, therefore, motion in a straight line at a constant speed is viewed as a natural state and it requires no further explanation. According to the impetus model, motion must have a cause, and a qualitative distinction is drawn between a state of motion (characterised by the presence of impetus) and a state of rest (characterised by the absence of impetus). From this perspective, a moving object comes to a halt because it loses impetus, whereas classical Newtonian theory holds that a moving object is brought to a halt because it is operated upon by external forces such as friction.

Given the strong similarity between the assumptions derived from impetus theory and the assumptions employed by contemporary novices, McCloskey and Kargon proceeded to probe the intuitive model the novices had in mind by exposing them to the paradoxical cases that led medieval theorists to modify the Aristotelian position. Medieval impetus theory shared the Aristotelian view that a force is required to keep an object in motion but, at this stage, a start had been made on distinguishing between physically necessary and unnecessary conditions. Whereas the Aristotelian view held that an external force was needed to keep an object in motion, the modified theory asserted that motion is maintained by an internal force impressed in an object once it is set in motion. A circular motion, once imposed on an object, can be expected to continue.

The observed commonalities between these early conceptions and the theories held by modern novices arise, according to McCloskey and Kargon, because of the ways in which we organise our experiences with moving bodies. In this respect both medieval and modern observers were (or are) faced with the same task—namely, to arrive at a satisfactory interpretation of their experiences in which relevant detail has been sifted from irrelevant detail. This is a process that calls for repeated observation and it typically involves a staged sequence whose later stages support increasing degrees of insight. At its most basic, the sequence starts with "defining a problem situation". It is followed by a second stage where effort is focused on "sorting relevant conditions from irrelevant". This can then lead into a third stage which McCloskey and Kargon associate with "defining theoretical entities and relating them into a rough theory". Progress beyond this point to stage four calls for "refining, testing and reformulating the theory". Stage three translates into a pre-paradigmatic stage in the understanding of impetus and it also characterises the level at which the modern novice approaches the same problems. By stage four, however, the collective and individual records can be expected to diverge.

For McCloskey and Kargon, therefore, any parallels between the growth of knowledge in the individual novice and the historical record are likely to arise not so much via content, where the modern student necessarily reproduces the conceptual detail of what has gone before, as via the cognitive strategies used to assimilate immediate experience to extant knowledge schemas. Much the same conclusion has attended Piaget's extensive investigations into the vagaries of the child's growth in understanding natural phenomena. However, for Piaget, the stages involved in psychogenesis (the growth of knowledge in the child) and in scientific theory formation are seen as cyclical in nature; arriving at stage four allows a return to stage one using new conceptual tools. It is the application of this cyclical mechanism that accounts both for any correspondences across the individual and collective records and their subsequent divergencies.

GENETIC EPISTEMOLOGY

Despite the well-nigh universal depiction of Piaget as a student of child development, his studies of psychogenesis were primarily directed towards understanding how information gained from experience is transformed into knowledge structures that permit insight into necessary truths about the world. Genetic epistemology sets out to use the psychogenetic data as a tool for understanding how scientific knowledge itself has developed. According to Piaget and Garcia (1989, p.28) it holds that:

> The goal of comparing historical and individual development, is not to set up correspondences in terms of content, but to show that the mechanisms mediating from one historical period to the next are analogous to those mediating the transition from one psychogenetic stage to the next.

We noted in Chapter 7, that Piaget described the growth of knowledge within the individual child as a staged affair where progression from stage to stage was characterised by the emergence of knowledge structures possessed of increasing degrees of equilibrium. Each stage arose through a reorganisation of the acquisitions of the previous level and equilibration was singled out as the key mechanism for bringing about structural change. Refinement of knowledge emerged from the cumulative resolution of internal inconsistencies within the knowledge base, resulting in a succession of knowledge structures capable of functioning in more and more content domains while maintaining their resistance to disruption. In effect, we are being offered a recursive model of knowledge reorganisation where the child has no sooner established one knowledge structure adapted to a particular context than it is being pushed to its limits in new contexts of application. Genetic epistemology holds that this model not only applies to the individual case, it also applies to the historical course of scientific change.

Intra→trans mechanism and historical change

When a new domain of enquiry is being opened up and the preliminary observations of physical phenomena are being made, the resulting information is assimilated to whatever knowledge schemas are available at the time. This is so, not only for the pre-operational stage of understanding in the child, it also characterises the early, pre-paradigmatic stages of scientific enquiry. In each case, the attentional focus is on object properties taken in isolation. During this preliminary phase (the "*intra-object*" stage of scientific enquiry) new concepts are formed which allow for actions directed towards modifying the objects in question but which do not allow for these actions to be co-ordinated as a whole. For example, the intra-object stage in chemistry applied when the early chemists concentrated their efforts on the individual properties of chemical substances taken in isolation, properties such as their taste and appearance.

Reorganisation of the knowledge base created during this phase depends on two types of reflective process being called into play.

"Empirical abstraction" extracts information directly from observed objects and events; "reflective abstraction" extracts a further body of information by operating upon the products of empirical abstraction. Through their joint operation, information comes to be represented in a form that can be generalised beyond the original context of observation. As a result, new features come to be detected in the external world which cannot be assimilated within the prevailing knowledge schemas and the ensuing disequilibrium leads to the formation of new, more equilibrated schematic versions.

With these revised schemas in place, a change in attentional focus for the phenomena in question occurs and interest shifts from object properties taken in isolation to whatever relationships may exist between these properties. This sets the stage for the *"inter-object"* phase of scientific enquiry and it finds its equivalent in the concrete-operational stage in psychogenesis. It is during this historical stage that investigation is mainly directed towards exploring and defining the transformations that can be applied to the external events in question. Thus, staying with the history of chemistry, the efforts that led to the distinction between acids and alkalis would constitute operations drawn from the inter-object stage.

Finally, it is when object relations and their possible transformations themselves become the focus of scientific attention, that the conditions are in place for the *"trans-phase"* to emerge. In the context of chemical theory, this would be the stage where the mutual relationships between acids, alkalis, and salts were being worked out, i.e. transformations identified at the previous level are now being synthesised as a whole. This phase in scientific enquiry also has its counterpart in psychogenesis, namely, the formal operational stage where intellectual transformations come to be synthesised as a whole.

Thus, the dialectical progression (intra- inter- trans-) is said to apply both to theory construction in different scientific domains and to the route traced out by the developing child. In consequence, the "intra to trans mechanism" is identified as "the most general of all commonalities between history and psychogenesis". Applied to the development of impetus theory, both with regard to its historical sequencing and its use by the individual novice, one and the same mechanism can be used to account for the commonality of content. Of course, there will be some differences. Progress is likely to be much faster in the individual as compared with the historical case, but this is due to the support and direction provided by the culture that has already absorbed these intellectual advances. However, this does not materially alter what is said to be happening.

Piaget and Garcia backed up their theoretical claims by arguing that sequential phases of understanding within classical mechanics can be mapped onto equivalent stages in children's understanding of the physics of moving objects. However, this exercise, and those discussed earlier, all presuppose that there is general agreement on how the historical course should be described. In fact, historians of science are rarely in accord on such matters and other descriptions of the course of events could fit less comfortably with the account they piece together. Indeed, as Piaget and Garcia approach their interpretation of history using the psychogenic model it is perhaps not surprising that they then find parallels. A more critical test would hinge on the extent to which other, independent historians agree with their analysis of how a particular branch of science emerged. Better yet would be a prediction from their model of how a current, pre-paradigmatic science is likely to develop. Perhaps, the move from folk psychology to cognitive science could serve as a candidate here. The most telling criticism, however, is one that we have met before—the cognitive mechanisms held responsible for the process of scientific discovery and change take the form of general descriptions rather than specifications for explicit mechanisms. Even so, Piaget and Garcia's psychogenic model does indicate how this line of argument could be developed.

As genetic epistemology equates scientific discovery with the processes involved in individual problem solving, it should be possible to exploit the latter to illuminate the former. That is, the computational models used to simulate individual problem solving should also be capable of simulating the historical course of scientific discovery. Although production systems have not been designed around Piagetian principles, if the thrust of the preceding argument is correct, they should, nonetheless, turn out to have a direct bearing on the course of the historical record. In fact, the gist of these requirements have been met by Langley, Simon, Bradshaw, and Zytkow (1987) who have deployed a battery of production models both to "discover" some of the foundational laws of modern science and to restage some of its classical theoretical disputes.

DISCOVERY PROGRAMS;
BACON, GLAUBER, AND STAHL

Langley et al. describe four production systems (BACON; GLAUBER; STAHL; and DALTON) which all function as discovery procedures while differing in the types of information they are able to handle. The first program (BACON) is designed to uncover whatever quantitative laws may lie hidden in a body of numerical data. The remaining programs have been designed to handle different types of qualitative data. GLAUBER operates on purely symbolic data (the properties of chemical compounds) and attempts to find appropriate ways of classifying different chemical substances and the qualitative laws that link these categories together. STAHL also accepts qualitative facts as input but aims to go beyond the generation of qualitative descriptions of chemical substances to generating explanations for their structures using, say, the fact that two different chemical reactions have products in common. The fourth program, DALTON, can take outputs from STAHL and use them as input data in order to assign molecular models and atomic weights to the substances involved.

In putting these various discovery programs through their paces, Langley et al. make the strong claim that they can simulate the problem-solving activities employed by major scientists in the past and, by implication, in the present as well. We will look at three examples to get the feel of how they operate; (1) the use of BACON to induce Kepler's Third Law, (2) the use of GLAUBER to simulate the qualitative reasoning of eighteenth-century chemists, and (3) the use of STAHL to simulate the stages of a classical dispute in chemistry—the conflict between phlogiston theory and oxygen theory instanced by Kuhn as an example of crisis leading to paradigm change.

BACON and Kepler's third law of planetary motion

BACON comes in a variety of different forms which differ in the number of heuristic operators they can employ. Its "experimental data" consist of lists of attribute–value pairs representing observations that have occurred together such as the distance of a planet from the sun or its period of rotation. Although BACON.1 has only been equipped with a few, very general heuristics it has, nonetheless, managed to work out a number of quantitative laws including Kepler's third law of planetary motion (1618). This states that "the cube of a planet's distance from the sun is proportional to the square of its period" and it can be re-expressed as:

$$D^3 / P^2 = c$$

where D is distance; P is the period and c is a constant. Table 13.1 gives examples of the type of (idealised) data BACON.1 has operated upon.

The table contains three directly observable attributes; the planet observed, A, B, or C; each planet's distance from the sun, D, and the period of the planet's orbit, P. The remaining entries (Terms 1, 2, and 3) refer to attributes induced by the program from this primary data. The heuristics employed to generate these terms are given in Table 13.2.

TABLE 13.1
Idealised data for planetary motion

Planet	Distance	Period	Term 1	Term 2	Term 3
A	1.0	1.0	1.0	1.0	1.0
B	4.0	8.0	0.5	2.0	1.0
C	9.0	27.0	0.33	3.0	1.0

Term 1 = D/P; Term 2 = D^2/P; Term 3 = D^3/P^2

From Langley et al., 1987.

TABLE 13.2
Heuristics employed by BACON.1

1.	If the values of a term are constant, then infer that the term always has that value
2.	If the values of two numerical terms increase together, then consider their ratio
3.	If the values of one term increase as those of another decrease, then consider their product

From Langley et al., 1987.

In Table 13.1, as D increases so does P, hence the second heuristic can be applied which states consider the ratio of D and P. This ratio (D/P) defines Term 1. Because its values decrease as D increases, this relationship brings heuristic 3 into play, which exhorts considering their product. This introduces Term 2 as D^2/P.

At this point, we find that Term 1 decreases as Term 2 increases, so once again BACON considers their product. This defines Term 3 as:

$$\text{Term1(D/P)} . \text{Term2}(D^2 / P) = \text{Term3} (D^3 / P^2)$$

As Term 3 takes a constant value, 1, for all of the planets, the first heuristic can now be applied and, according to Langley et al. (1987, pp.66–67):

The statement that the term is constant across planets is equivalent to Kepler's third law of planetary motion and the above protocol can be treated as a plausible trace of how one might discover this law.

Although BACON.1 can discover numerical relations between two variables, it needs new productions if it is to handle functions involving many terms. Another version, BACON.3, allows for different levels of description to be applied to a set of observations by using regularities at one descriptive level to create new descriptive clusters at a higher level. In other words, unlike BACON.1 which distinguishes between "observed" data and summary descriptions, later versions can apply their discovery heuristics recursively using the summaries as though they were data.

Subsequent versions of the program, BACON.4–6, were devised to handle nominal data and to introduce some "expectation" into searching the problem space by allowing the system to invent intrinsic properties (e.g. voltages and conductances) and to treat these as data. Adding these routines led to the successful generation of Ohm's law of electrical circuits; Archimedes' law of displacement; Snell's law of refraction; Black's specific heat law; the law of conservation of momentum; and the law of gravitation. All told, an impressive portfolio of discoveries whose diversity testifies to the general applicability of BACON's methods.

GLAUBER

The GLAUBER discovery program handles schematic qualitative information, as when laboratory observations on the properties of chemical reactions and compounds are thematically grouped. It is primarily intended to model the investigations conducted in the seventeenth and eighteenth centuries into the properties of chemical substances which led to the categories of acids, alkalis, and salts being introduced into the chemist's working vocabulary.

Each laboratory observation is expressed propositionally as a predicate plus one or more labelled arguments, thus enabling different inputs and outputs to be compared and grouped. For example, the chemical reaction between ammonia and hydrochloric acid to produce ammonium chloride, ($NH_3 + HCl = NH_4Cl$), would be represented by the proposition:

reacts inputs {HCl, NH3} outputs {NH4Cl}

Here the predicate (reacts) takes as its arguments the inputs and outputs of the reaction and, as the same symbols can occur in the arguments of several propositions, this makes an important contribution to the ongoing analysis. Thus, given:

Proposition 1. (reacts inputs {HCl NH3} outputs {NH4Cl}
Proposition 2. (reacts inputs {HCl KOH} outputs {KCl}

the occurrence of HCl in both propositions means that this relationship can be entered into a further round in the discovery process. Similarly, the observation that HCl tastes sour could be represented:

has—quality object {HCl} tastes {sour}

which furnishes another piece of information about hydrochloric acid that can initiate additional steps in the analysis.

Running the program on data represented in this form resulted in a classification of the different substances into acids, salts, and alkalis, and a general inference about their interrelations:

Reacts inputs {acid, alkali} outputs {salt}

Thus, GLAUBER generates a taxonomic schema capable of grouping together objects sharing similar properties. This type of exercise in the past has led to some vitriolic disputes as different scientists have come up with competing descriptive schemas for the same substances. The demise of "phlogiston theory" provides a textbook case.

STAHL and phlogiston theory
The beginnings of the phlogiston debate reach back to the end of the seventeenth century when, according to Dampier-Whetham (1929, p.197):

> The chief difficulty of the early chemists was to understand the phenomena of flame and combustion. When bodies are burnt, it seems that something escapes. This something, for long identified with sulphur, was called phlogiston, the principle of fire, by G.E. Stahl (1660–1734). ... Chemical science learned to express its facts in terms of this hypothesis. Owing to its influence, as well as to that of older theories, isolated investigations which pointed to more modern views failed to impress the minds of chemists; the facts had to be rediscovered and then reinterpreted.

Combustion occurs when substances are burned and we know from simple observation that substances differ in their inflammability. These variations Stahl attributed to the presence or absence of phlogiston—an interpretation that came under increasing attack towards the end of the eighteenth century when it was eventually replaced by the version put forward by Lavoisier based upon oxygen and its properties. A detailed account of the issues in this debate is provided by Thagard (1992) and the following discussion is based on this source.

Within phlogiston theory, acids were treated as "simple substances", whereas what we now know to be their constituents were treated as compounds. For example, within the Stahlian system, sulphur was taken to be a compound of sulphuric acid (oil of vitriol) and phlogiston. An alternative account was provided by Lavoisier who dispensed with the concept of phlogiston altogether arguing (correctly) that acids should be treated as chemical compounds not as simple substances and (incorrectly) that all acids contained oxygen. The resulting debate between these positions eventuated in Lavoisier's oxygen theory replacing phlogiston theory as the preferred mode for explaining combustion and related phenomena.

In Fig. 13.1A we can see the part relations assumed by phlogiston theory as applied to metals. The alternative arrangement of these constituent parts, as proposed by Lavoisier, is given in Fig. 13.1B. Also in Fig. 13.1A the constituents of metals are taken to be calxes (now termed oxides) and phlogiston. This interpretation could support explanations of a fairly wide variety of physical phenomena (e.g. respiration as well as combustion), although it did present some difficulties. If phlogiston is given up during combustion, then in order to account for the fact that metals gained weight when burned this meant that phlogiston had to be assigned a negative weight. Lavoisier's experiments led him to the alternative conclusion that the gain in weight was due to something being added from the air. If so, this would suggest a rather different arrangement of part relations (Fig. 13.1B) where oxides are compounds whose constituents are metals and oxygen.

Given these two rival theories, there were real difficulties in translating between them, and STAHL's discovery procedures were aimed at restaging this controversy. The program accepts an ordered list of chemical reactions as input and generates as output a list of the chemical elements along with the compounds in which they occur. The analytic procedure is thus intended to simulate the laboratory work of the theoretical chemists at the time the controversy was at its height.

Essentially, when STAHL is given information about different chemical reactions it uses its inferential heuristics to suggest components for the substances involved. For example, the heuristic rule "infer components", can be applied to the components of synthesis and decomposition reactions. It is stated as:

Infer Components: If A and B react to form C, or if C decomposes into A and B then infer that C is composed of A and B.

STAHL has similar rules for transforming complex descriptions into simpler versions which can then be matched by the "infer components" rule. Thus, the rule "reduce" is responsible for cancelling out substances occurring on both sides of a reaction:

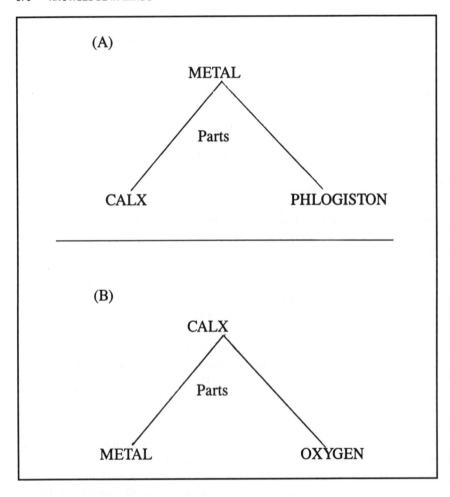

FIG. 13.1. A. Constituent parts according to phlogiston theory. B. Constituent parts according to oxygen theory. (From Thagard, 1992.)

Reduce: If A occurs on both sides of a reaction, then remove A from the reaction.

Although STAHL utilises the same heuristics during problem solving, variations in presentational factors can mean that it comes up with different descriptions at different times. Hence, its structural descriptions will depend critically both on the data it receives and the order in which they are presented. When supplied with the historical data in the phlogiston debate, STAHL reproduced the same kinds of contrasting acounts as those that fuelled the original dispute.

Furthermore its discovery process encountered similar problems to those reported at the time, implying that the whole debate arose, not because the disputants reasoned in different ways, but because they differed in their initial assumptions.

Evaluation

Computational discovery programs, therefore, have extended the scope of our previous discussion by implying three important claims about the process of scientific discovery, (1) it is reducible to the principles of ordinary problem solving, (2) these principles can be modelled using explicit heuristics and production rules, and (3) it is possible to use these principles to recreate the actual stages of historical discovery. There can be no doubt of the potential significance of this work but there is room for scepticism concerning all of these claims.

As Langley et al. run through their examples, one is immediately struck by the truncated nature of the discovery procedures being proposed. Although it could be argued that this truncation is precisely the measure of their success, an alternative interpretation is that their analyses seriously oversimplify what is at stake. It is the experimenters, not the programs, who determine what will qualify as data, and each simulation necessarily incorporates presuppositions about which observations should be retained and which observations should be ignored. In other words, by staking out the problem space in advance, a variety of difficult decisions have been avoided. After all, at the time Kepler was applying mathematics to celestial motion, the chemists of the period (alchemists) were searching for the philosopher's stone that would convert base metals into gold. It comes as no surprise that there is no discovery program (PARACELSUS, perhaps) specifically designed to be unleashed on this problem. Of course, it would put an end to this cavilling if the alchemists had gone on to discover the philosopher's stone, but one suspects that the attempt will not now be made. (In case this example seems too remote, it should be borne in mind that even Newton thought it worthwhile to spend a considerable amount of his time reflecting on the alchemical mysteries—see Debus, 1977.)

With regard to the historical claims that are being made, the picture is even less convincing. The research effort put into the design of the discovery programs is nowhere matched by an equal degree of concern for the details of the historical record. There are no detailed references to the actual workbooks and laboratory notes at the time, and this neglect of historical detail only serves to undermine the strength of their case. However, to be fair, the force of this criticism has been met head on elsewhere.

Kulkarni and Simon (1988) undertook to match the output of another heuristic discovery program (KEKADA) to the historical details of Krebs' work in the 1930s into the synthesis of urea in the body; work that eventually led to an account of the urea cycle. Kulkarni and Simon designed KEKADA to "model the heuristics Hans Krebs used in this discovery" and they made extensive use of data from a number of historical sources including the published papers, laboratory notes, and autobiographical details. This comparative exercise led them to conclude that, although there were minor disparities (which could be explained by small differences in initial knowledge and attentional variations) there were striking similarities between the simulation and the real thing. Setting minor differences to one side, Kulkarni and Simon (1988, p.171) state:

> ... KEKADA follows the same strategy of experimentation as Krebs and its motivations for carrying out various experiments are the same as the motivations of Krebs, whenever these are indicated by evidence in the diaries and retrospective interviews.

Kulkarni and Simon also concluded that as a large proportion of the heuristics used by Krebs were applicable, not only outside the urea synthesis problem but outside chemistry altogether, KEKADA could be treated as a general model for scientific experimentation.

Evidence testifying to the psychological validity of the heuristics themselves has been provided by Qin and Simon (1990). They asked student subjects (some sophisticated in science and mathematics, others not) to look at two groups of data and to try to find a relationship between them. The data are given in Table 13.3, which also defines the terms "s" and "q" as the distances of planets from the sun and their periods of revolution. In other words, the students were confronted with the same task as that assigned to BACON.1 when it derived Kepler's third law of planetary motion. However, this contextual information was withheld from the experimental subjects who were simply required to relate data group "s" with data group "q".

Subjects were encouraged to think aloud as they worked and the resulting protocols were analysed for the heuristics that were brought into play. Of the 14 subjects tested in this way, two found the law, one came near, and the others failed to find it. In the course of the study, "all the subjects used heuristics like BACON.1's" although not all subjects used all types and there were considerable individual differences in the heuristics actually selected and how long subjects persisted in using them. (We will return to some implications of these individual variations shortly.)

TABLE 13.3
Paired data used by Qin and Simon

	s [distance]	q [period]
[Mercury]	36.	88
[Venus]	67.25	224.7
[Earth]	93	365.3
[Mars]	141.75	687
[Jupiter]	483.8	4332.1
	(s = distance; q = period of revolution)	

From Qin and Simon, 1990.

We are now in a position to look again at Piaget and Garcia's claims about the cognitive mechanisms involved in knowledge reorganisation in the light of the operations of the discovery programs described earlier. In this respect, we find the limitations associated with BACON.1 to be similar to Piaget and Garcia's account of the preliminary phases of scientific enquiry. BACON.1 can draw upon the products of direct observation but it has no means of engaging in a further round of reflective abstraction aimed at exploiting these discoveries. However, later versions, in allowing for the recursive application of BACON's heuristics, do appear to implement the processes of reflective abstraction as described in the genetic epistemological model. When BACON.3 blurs the distinction between data and laws by operating on the results of its own processing, it deploys the same type of recursive operations that Piaget and Garcia identified as being crucial to the dynamics of historical change.

Additionally, Piaget and Garcia's arguments concerning the dialectical nature of the scientific process also receive a degree of independent support from this quarter. In the course of the phlogiston debate, the investigators returned to the natural phenomena in question using newly constructed intellectual tools to generate new observations and facts. In effect, we find a dialectical cycle in operation where each turn led on to further discoveries and new investigatory tools.

Apart from STAHL, the discovery programs described earlier are more applicable to the practice of normal science than to the management of scientific crisis. This particular aspect has been addressed by Thagard (1992) who has also used the techniques of computational modelling to simulate the process whereby one theoretical model may be displaced by a rival theory. According to this analysis, scientific revolutions hinge on the extent to which the theories under dispute exhibit different levels of "explanatory coherence". Other things being equal, faced with two rival theoretical systems, the one that offers the greater degree of explanatory coherence should be preferred.

THEORETICAL STRUCTURES AND EXPLANATORY COHERENCE

Consider the case where the same body of evidence can be explained by two different and competing systems of hypotheses. The observations may be unequivocal but their theoretical interpretations can go one way or the other. In coming to choose between these competing theories, we should pay attention not only to the manner in which they account for the attendant data but also to how each of the rival systems coheres as a whole. That is, we should assign greater weight to the theoretical system that, (1) explains most or all of the data, (2) does so parsimoniously, (3) provides explanations that are analogous to previously accepted modes of explanation, (4) consists of propositions that are themselves capable of further explanation as to why they should be true, and (5) avoids internal contradictions. If we register and weight rival systems on these properties taken together we will then be in a better position to decide which version is to be preferred.

By definition, arriving at such a global assessment entails taking all of these constraints into account simultaneously. Hence, as with schema instantiation and analogical problem solving, the assessment of explanatory coherence can be assigned to the computations of a constraint-satisfaction network. The choice between the rival theories is made once the network has relaxed into the best fit to the range of explanatory constraints that happen to be present.

ECHO

The computational model designed for this purpose, ECHO, consists of a local connectionist network whose units serve both to encode the observational data in question and the different propositions that have been put forward to explain these data. Where two propositions are mutually consistent (cohere) they are given an excitatory link. Where two propositions are inconsistent (incohere) the link is made inhibitory.

A principle of Data Priority ensures that propositions that describe experimental results are given "a degree of acceptability on their own" and this is handled by a special evidence unit in the network with links to each data unit. This special unit is clamped at a value of 1. When running the network, activation spreads from this unit to the other units in turn.

To see how such a network operates, consider a simple hypothetical situation where the data set (E1; E2) can be assigned rival explanations (H1) and (H2). Because these explanations incohere there will be an inhibitory link between these units. Where H1 is capable of explaining both E1 and E2 but H2 can only explain E2, running the network will result in a greater amount of activation being propagated to the unit for H1. And, other things being equal, it will settle into a state where the unit for H2 is deactivated and only the unit for H1 has an activation value above 0. In principle, the same decision procedure can be scaled up to tackle cases where the rival hypotheses differ not only in terms of explanatory breadth but also in terms of their parsimony and degree of internal consistency.

In this form, ECHO has been applied to a variety of decision situations ranging from plotting the course of scientific historical debate to the simulation of jury decisions in murder trials (see Thagard, 1989). It has also been used to adjudicate on the phlogiston debate described earlier. In contrast to Kuhn's account where the incommensurability of the competing paradigms had been emphasised, Thagard's analysis indicated "considerable cumulation of evidence from the phlogiston to the oxygen theories" (p.107). Thus, in allowing for a greater degree of exchange between rival positions, Thagard is effectively calling into question Kuhn's emphasis on the non-progressive aspects of scientific advance.

SCIENTIFIC CREATIVITY AND SCIENTIFIC COMMUNITIES

The beliefs that most of us come to hold about the world, where they are our own, are likely to be mundane and where they are not, they are likely to be second hand. Even so, at some time or other certain individuals have been able to make a significant contribution to the store of human knowledge. Although practically nothing is known about the algorithms that sustain genuinely creative thought, (assuming they exist; Johnson-Laird, 1993; Penrose, 1989), this has not prevented the topic from being addressed within the computational framework.

It was noted earlier that Qin and Simon reported significant individual variations in the problem-solving strategies employed by their experimental subjects which had a direct bearing on the extent to which their subjects came near to detecting the underlying mathematical law. More generally, such variations could also bear upon creative thinking at large. That is, one dimension of creative thinking could well hinge on the manner in which individual investigators sample the pool of problem-solving algorithms available to them. Investigators who use atypical algorithms or who employ standard algorithms in an unusual order would be more likely to come up with novel solutions than if they had conformed with normal practice (Goldman, 1986). Alternatively, as Boden (1994) has suggested, the origins of creative activity could depend on the extent to which solvers are capable of analysing the properties of their own data representations and the problem spaces in which they are embedded.

However, both of these approaches to the dynamics of creative thought insist on adopting the perspective of the individual thinker. As a result, to return to an earlier concern, we can be drawn into overstating the parallels to be found between the musings of the individual novice and the historical record. Professional scientists are primarily concerned with formalising their observations and with co-ordinating their views with those of others active in the field. Novices, on the other hand, are not working under these pressures and are unlikely to arrive at the same degree of conceptual differentiation for the phenomena concerned. With regard to the phlogiston debate, novices are unlikely to be confronted with the conceptual reorganisations that faced the participants in this dispute. As Thagard points out, the rearrangement of kind/part relations that accompanied the shift from Stahl's position to that adopted by Lavoisier constitutes a level of complexity that falls well outside the novice's purview.

Conceding this point implies that scientific problem solving cannot simply be seen as individual problem solving writ large. Once a scientific domain has passed beyond the pre-paradigmatic stage, its subject matter not only calls for resources that are not available to the untrained thinker, but for resources that exceed those available to the individual scientist working alone. There is a distributed aspect to the scientific enterprise which draws upon the collective resources of whole scientific communities.

In a study that, unusually, focused on scientific reasoning in real laboratories, Dunbar (1994) noted how the incidence of creative problem solving rested not so much on the abilities of individual scientists as on the mix of abilities to be found within a laboratory team. On those occasions when inconsistent data were obtained that called for a new type of explanatory hypothesis, he observed how individual scientists working alone were inclined to minimise what had happened. They tended to attribute the inconsistency to "... error of some sort and [they] hoped that the finding would go away." Matters changed significantly when the same findings were presented to a group of fellow scientists. Under these conditions, Dunbar notes (1996, p.385):

... the other scientists tended to focus on the inconsistency to dissect it, and either (a) suggested alternate hypotheses or (b) forced the scientists to think of a new hypothesis. This happened at numerous lab meetings and was one of the main mechanisms for inducing conceptual change in scientists when inconsistent evidence occurs.

Furthermore, Dunbar found that the extent to which a particular laboratory made use of analogical reasoning to resolve anomalous data critically depended on the extent to which its members were drawn from different scientific backgrounds. Where all of the laboratory members shared a similar theoretical background and had the same knowledge at their disposal, the group was no better at throwing up analogical suggestions than the single individual. It was when the members of the scientific team could draw upon different bodies of knowledge that the most fruitful analogies were most likely to emerge. That is, the "social structure of the laboratory has an effect on types of reasoning and conceptual change".

Once again, therefore, we are faced with the need to supplement individually based accounts of cognitive activity by reference to the collective context in which they come to be executed. Indeed, this is especially true in the case of scientific research where highly specialised communities have evolved for the express purpose of advancing knowledge. How well different scientific communities live up to this aim in practice and why some appear to be more successful than others are issues that have barely been addressed, although Kitcher (1993) provides a more detailed commentary on these matters.

We embarked upon this chapter with the aim of bringing the individual and the collective historical records together in the hope of getting a better fix on the mechanisms and principles governing the accumulation of knowledge. As it has turned out, the exercise has been relatively encouraging because the commonalities and disparities that have emerged can be readily assimilated to the account that has been pieced together in earlier sections. Commonalities have arisen where problem-solving mechanisms, as individually defined, have been applied to the practices of pre-paradigmatic science; see the discussion of Wiser (1988); McCloskey and Kargon (1988) and Piaget and Garcia (1989) set out earlier. With the advent of "normal science", significant disparities start to emerge. Although the work of Langley et al. (1987) and Kulkarni and Simon (1988) would appear to suggest that normal science can be subsumed under problem-solving mechanisms as individually understood, other studies suggest that they are not providing anything like the whole story. In this respect, both the work of Thagard (1992) and Dunbar (1994) underscores the contribution of the professional, social environment in which scientific research is practised.

That said, it has to be acknowledged that the studies just referred to are hardly representative of the historical record dealing with the development of Western scientific thought, let alone representative of developments in other quarters. It would be extremely hazardous to try to draw hard and fast conclusions from this limited source material. Set against the selectional pressures that have shaped the mechanisms and functions of the modern mind, scientific thought, however widely drawn, constitutes a very small cross section of this broader historical record. Our final task, therefore, is to see how locating human cognition within a broader (evolutionary) context has enabled the constituents of our earlier discussions to be reassembled within a more coherent framework.

CHAPTER FOURTEEN

Evolutionary constraints and the modern mind

The resource limitations that accompany human information processing place significant constraints on the extent to which any particular knowledge base is likely to be modified as a consequence of new learning. Nonetheless, modifications that cannot be done on one pass may be achieved iteratively through our repeated transactions with the physical world. Or, there again, they may be achieved vicariously by adopting them wholesale from the cultural resources that surround us. The individual and the collective aspects of human cognition are intimately and symbiotically related. The aim of this chapter is to seek a deeper understanding of this inter-relationship by bringing evolutionary biology into the discussion.

EVOLUTIONARY EPISTEMOLOGY

Darwin's original arguments were primarily directed towards explaining "speciation" (how different species have come into existence) where the unit of selection was the individual organism. However, the thrust of the arguments can be readily generalised and the "modern synthesis" has been used to inform the search for innate cognitive mechanisms adapted to the salient features of the organism's physical and social environment. We will refer to work on both of these fronts and then see how an evolutionary story has been compiled which, in linking the modern mind to its ancestral forms, has also managed to link together a number of our previous concerns.

The core concepts of Darwin's theory of evolution are, (1) variation—individuals within a population vary in their physical and mental characteristics, (2) selection—environmental pressures serve to select some characteristics over others, and (3) inheritance—it is the fittest individuals who are most likely to survive and reproduce and thus are most likely to transmit their characteristics to their offspring. Subsequent attempts to apply these arguments to psychological phenomena initially rested on the concept of "recapitulation". This concept held that if an ability depends on an innate cognitive module formed by natural selection then we can expect to find parallels between phylogeny and ontogeny. Stages in the developmental history of the species should be mirrored in the stages comprising the developmental history of the individual organism. Such a recapitulation hypothesis had featured as part of Darwin's original arguments (where anatomical changes in the growth of the embryo were interpreted as mirroring different stages in the evolution of the species) and, if recapitulation could be observed for organic structures, it was surely worthwhile looking for similar parallels with regard to the mechanisms underlying cognition.

Langer (1988) has singled out Hobhouse (1901) as the first theorist to provide a systematic and comprehensive application of the comparative method to psychological phenomena. Within phylogenesis, Hobhouse discerned six discriminable and sequential stages in the organisation of cognitive activity which he thought were echoed in the mental development of human beings. Starting from blind reflex activity, organisms have progressed through trial and error; assimilation activity (where some modification of the critical behaviour became possible); practical judgement (where actions were differentiated but still based on direct experience); conceptual thought (actions were freed from perceptual constraints); and, ultimately, arrived at logical operations (where actions came to be based on logical analysis of the situation). As Langer comments (1988, pp.68–69):

> These six means of activity characterize the direction of mental development within both phylogenesis and human ontogenesis ... the two most advanced means, conceptual thought and logical analysis, (however) evolve in human ontogenesis only. Human cognition goes beyond the information given by perceptual experience.

Subsequently, Baldwin (1915) extended recapitulation theory to include "ethogenesis" by bringing historical and cultural processes within the same comparative framework and thus laid the foundations for the studies in genetic epistemology as practised by Piaget and his colleagues in Geneva.

Although the simple application of recapitulation theory seems to have run its course (e.g. Medicus, 1992) there remain other, more sophisticated ways of applying evolutionary principles to mental phenomena. Which is not to say that the conclusions that are then reached will necessarily be mutually compatible. Where Anderson (1993) has used evolutionary principles as a means of refining ACT* into ACT-R, (see Chapter 4), the same principles have also been employed as a weapon for attacking the computational approach as a whole (Edelman, 1992).

Edelman's criticisms rest on the significance he attributes to individual variations in neuro-anatomical organisation. Although individual variation is a fundamental biological concept, outside the biological sciences (and this includes cognitive science) it tends to be treated as a "sampling error"—something that has to be partialled out before proceeding further. This difference in theoretical stance is hardly cosmetic and Edelman places great emphasis on the fact that the neural organisation of individual brains does not rely on the point-to-point wiring typically found in computer architectures. Rather, human neuro-anatomy exhibits levels of individual variation which are simply too extensive to be dismissed as random noise. For Edelman, its presence is taken to imply that the transfer of information from the environment to the individual occurs, not by instruction, but by selection where the human brain functions as a "Darwinian machine".

"Evolutionary epistemology" aims to apply Neo-Darwinian principles both to the emergence of the cognitive mechanisms that comprise individual intelligence and to the emergence of the cultural representations that have accompanied their application. It is assumed that human intelligence and human culture can be interpreted as secondary and tertiary adaptations arising through the processes of natural selection. On both of these fronts, adaptations have occurred that work to compensate for the inevitable shortcomings that will be associated with primary biological adaptations. Of necessity, primary adaptations are hard-wired and fixed and, in this form, they can only provide a "best bet" for the organism's survival at any one time. According to Plotkin (1994, pp.137–138), left to her own resources, Nature consigns:

> ... organisms to a future about which there can be no certainty, with a set of instructions for the building of adaptations which may no longer be right for the job. This

danger of always being "out of date" in one's genetical knowledge of the world must somehow be countered.

A solution to this "uncertain futures" problem can be reached if the individual organism is allowed to respond to unpredictable changes in its world by matching them to correlated changes within itself. Hence, Plotkin casts the mechanisms of memory, learning, and reasoning as "knowledge gaining devices" which have arisen on the individual level as a result of selectional pressures.

By the same argument, cultural knowledge allows the organism to transcend the limits set by its personal experience. Access to a host culture (Plotkin, 1994, p.225) enables its members to come up with:

> ... behavioural adaptations to complex changing environments even more rapidly and effectively than intelligence acting in the lone individual. ... (It is) another form of Darwinian machine and hence another means of gaining knowledge of the world based on evolutionary processes ... In this case, the complete system of human knowledge would be a three level control hierarchy, each level operating on evolutionary principles ... and each sensitive to ever more fleeting short term stabilities.

The gist of the evolutionary epistemological position, therefore, is that the secondary and tertiary processes of individual and cultural learning—which allow for a more precise, fine-tuning of the organism to a changing world—are nested under and guided by the operations of primary, genetically specified adaptations. Accordingly, we will review some of the evidence taken to support this innate chain of control both as it is manifested on the individual and the collective level.

Innate human capacities for reasoning about physical events

Through study of the visual preferences of young infants it is possible to gain some insight into how they partition their visual world into discrete objects and how they use this information to draw inferences about the properties of their physical world. On the basis of a series of such studies, Spelke (e.g. 1991) has concluded that infants are born with certain domain-specific principles that serve to structure their interactions with physical objects. By applying these principles the infant comes to register a variety of object properties, such as "boundedness", "cohesion", and "rigidity" and is thus equipped with the means for predicting how these same objects are likely to interact with their containing environment.

The basic experimental procedure has involved habituating infants to a display in which an object is first revealed in one position prior to it moving out of sight behind a screen. The screen is then lifted and the same object is shown in a new position. Once the infant has habituated to a particular display, it is tested under new conditions which may or may not be consistent with natural laws. Habituation will have reduced the infant's interest in the original display but, if the infant has registered a physical constraint violation, it should show renewed interest in the critical test display.

Spelke (1991) used this habituation technique with 4-month and 6-month old infants by presenting a falling ball which came to rest in different positions. The infants were first habituated to the ball coming to rest on a surface and then viewed new demonstrations which either displayed a new (feasible) resting position or one that was not physically possible. In the first case, although the ball came to rest on a different surface location from the habituation phase, the movement was physically feasible. In the second case, the ball appeared to pass through a solid surface before coming to rest in the original location (see Fig. 14.1). If infants who had previously habituated to the display suddenly show a reawakening of interest this could be because the new display conflicts with what they have come to expect based on their original analysis of the scene.

Figure 14.1A illustrates the case where the ball falls behind a screen and, when the screen is lifted, it is shown to have come to rest on the floor of the apparatus. This constitutes the familiarisation phase of the experiment. Subsequently, a barrier is introduced above the floor and the infant is either shown the ball at rest on top of the barrier (a novel resting position compared with the first phase) or it is shown on the floor of the apparatus as before. Whereas the former arrangement is consistent with the principle of continuity, the latter arrangement violates both the constraints of continuity and solidity. It was found that even at 4 months the infants in the inconsistent condition looked longer at the display than those in the control condition, implying that they grasped something of the significance of continuity and solidity constraints for object movement. Equivalent results were reported when further experiments tested the same principles using different displays and younger age groups (2½–3 months).

In contrast, when 4-month-old infants were shown the ball remaining in mid-air, as in Fig. 14.1B, this arrangement had little effect on their response to the display. Knowledge of inertia, it seems, emerges more gradually than knowledge of continuity so that even around 10 months, displays that violated the former constraint were not "strong" enough to capture the infant's full attention. All of which suggests that in coming

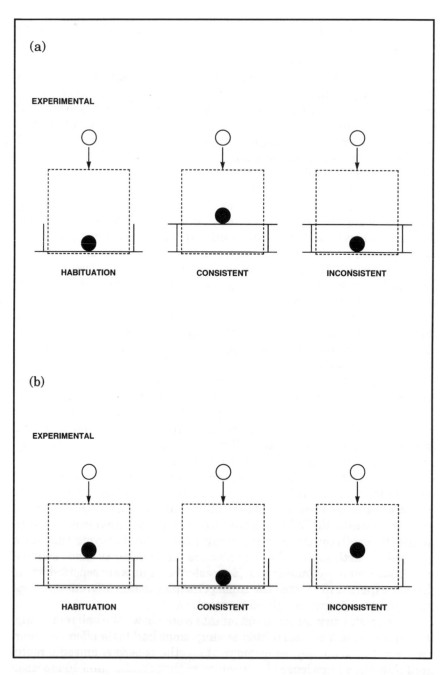

FIG. 14.1. Displays testing infants' knowledge of (a) continuity and (b) inertia. (From Spelke, 1991.)

to understand the physical world the child's attention is drawn at the outset to particular aspects of a visual scene which then constrain what is learned from the experience.

If infants have a relatively detailed knowledge of certain object-related properties, what form of knowledge is it? Spelke, Katz, Purcell, Ehrlich, and Breinlinger (1994) refer to infants having a "core knowledge" about physical objects which is retained at later stages of development, albeit enriched in various ways. This information is stored in a procedurally embedded format and this would seem to implicate I-level representations as posited by Karmiloff-Smith's (1992) knowledge redescription model. Spelke's investigations with infant subjects, therefore, point to the presence of innate, domain-specific principles bearing on the properties of the physical environment.

A rather different line of investigation, this time employing adult subjects, has postulated an innate cognitive mechanism bearing on the properties of the social environment. Its function is to facilitate how we comprehend the intricacies underlying social contracts.

Darwinian algorithms

According to Cosmides (1989) an innate and specialised learning mechanism has evolved as part of the architecture of the modern mind whose prime purpose is to oversee the course taken by a social exchange. A social exchange occurs when two (or more) people agree on a balance of costs and benefits. We may offer someone money in exchange for food or we may promise to work on their behalf in order to qualify for a reward. If all goes well, both participants should realise a net benefit; the payer receives food and the payee receives money. All will not go well if this credit balance is upset and we should seek to avoid transactions where the cost of participating is likely to exceed any attainable benefit. Calculating the potential costs and benefits of an exchange will be an important prerequisite to agreeing to its terms but it also calls for some rather complex computations to be made. Darwinian algorithms are said to have evolved as a response to these social pressures. Whenever two people enter into a social contract, the algorithm is likely to be activated, and it then it serves to direct their attention towards the costs and benefits that are likely to be involved. In particular, it alerts the participants to any cheating that might take place.

Expressed in more formal terms, detecting cheating means assessing whether the conditional rule ("If you take the benefit then you pay the cost") has been observed. In other words, it can be interpreted as a variant of the Wason selection task as discussed in Chapter 10. And, if what Cosmides has to say is correct, we should find that people are especially effective in testing whether a rule has been observed when it presents in the form of a social contract. Hence, an empirical test of these claims could proceed by monitoring the levels of success on the Wason task when subjects are led to believe that the conditional rule refers to a social contract rather than serving as a simple description.

Social contract theory predicts that people will fare significantly better when selecting the critical instances (P and Not Q) when the rule comes in the form of a social contract (even though this may be more unfamilar to them) than when the rule functions merely as a description. For example, subjects should find it easier to respond to the unfamiliar contractual rule "If a man eats cassava root then he must have a tattoo on his face", than to the rule "If a person goes into Boston then he takes a subway". In the former case, provided it is clear that cassava is a rationed benefit that needs to be earned, subjects will be alerted to possible cheating and thus transcend the usual difficulties associated with making the appropriate selections. In the latter case, the algorithm will not be triggered and subjects should show the typical error pattern.

The logically correct selection in the Wason task consists of the combination of the P and Not Q cards. Only these selections can falsify the conditional rule although, as has now been well documented, when the rule is given without contextual support, most subjects choose P alone or P and Q. Suppose, however, the rule is interpreted as a social contract. The subject should be alerted to its cost–benefit structure and should go on to adopt a "look for cheaters" approach. These are the cases where (1) a benefit has been accepted, and (2) a cost has not been paid. Only these cases involve potential cheating. Instances where the cost has been paid or the benefit has not been accepted carry no threat for the other participants. Hence, social contract theory claims to explain the contextual vagaries associated with the Wason task more efficiently than alternative theories such as content-free rules or pragmatic schemas. (Incidentally, by the same argument the other cases are not as irrelevant as is being proposed. If detecting cheaters is important for avoiding personal loss, detecting "suckers" would seem equally advantageous for personal gain.)

Cosmides designed her experimental programme so as to compare her predictions against those generated by two alternative theories; (1) where quality of performance is predicated on familiarity with the content of the rule, and (2) where the quality of reasoning derives from the use of pragmatic schemas. Her experimental procedure employed both a standard contractual version of the conditional rule and a switched version which, while logically equivalent, significantly altered the terms of the contract. The standard contract takes the form "If you take the benefit then you pay the cost" which entails, as possible outcomes: benefit accepted (P); benefit not accepted (Not P); cost paid (Q); and cost not paid (Not Q).

The switched contract takes the form "If you pay the cost then you take the benefit" where the possible outcomes are now: benefit accepted (Q); benefit not accepted (Not Q); cost paid (P); and cost not paid (Not P). In each case the correct logical response is to choose P and Not Q regardless of the expressed form (standard or switched). However, as the definition of cheating varies for each version, social contract theory predicts that responses should differ for the standard and switched forms. Thus, whereas social contract theory and a theory based on logical rules both predict the choices P and Not Q for the standard contract, they differ in their predictions for the switched version. In this case, the logical choices remain unchanged at P and Not Q, while cheating will be associated with Not P (cost not paid) and Q (benefit accepted).

Social contract theory also predicts that this response pattern of looking for cheaters will apply regardless of whether the content of the rule is familiar to the experimental subject or not. If the problem is taken as being an example of a social exchange this is all that is necessary to bring the algorithm into play. Hence, the independent variables in the experimental programme, consisted of, (1) standard and switched versions of the rule, (2) unfamiliar and familiar social contracts, and (for comparison), (3) familiar and unfamiliar descriptions.

Cosmides' initial experiments were aimed at testing whether perceiving the rule as a social contract, as opposed to a description, would elicit the choice of P and Not Q, even when the setting was unfamiliar. In fact, her results indicated that familiarity was not a relevant factor determining subject choice whereas perceiving the rule as a social contract did influence their responses. More subjects chose P and Not Q for an unfamiliar social contract version than did so when the rule took the form of a familiar description. All of which is consistent with the operation of a look for cheaters algorithm.

The next set of experiments then introduced the switched version of the rule. Once again it was found that the subjects' responses followed the social contract predictions; more subjects were drawn into selecting [Not P] and [Q] for the switched condition when the presentation led them to interpret the rule as a social contract. Subsequent experiments then tested standard social contract rules against permission rules using both familiar and unfamiliar settings. Here too, the social contract algorithm predicted the fluctuations in subjects' choices more effectively than a rival account based on permission schemas.

Taking stock, these experiments demonstrated that the conditions under which subjects achieve high solution rates on the Wason task are essentially those in which a specific algorithm for detecting cheating can be applied. Logical rules failed to cope with "switched contracts" because the subjects' responses shifted to the (non-logical) selections consistent with the detection of cheating. Availability explanations failed to the extent that contracts could still be evaluated in the presence of unfamiliar content. Permission or obligation rules, while handling some facilitation conditions, ran into trouble when the rule functioned as a permission but not as a social contract. With these rivals falling at different fences, this appeared to leave social contract theory ahead of the field as the only theory capable of handling all of the conditions where contextual facilitation in the Wason task had been found.

Evolution and social contract theory

If we now turn to the issue of the origins of the cognitive algorithm in question it may, as claimed, have evolved for the purpose of detecting cheating but it could also be accounted for via induction from our experiences with social transactions. However, Cosmides rejects an account based on induction from experience on the grounds that the nature of the algorithm is too specific. Why, she asks, should some domain-general, inductive process simply stop at the cost–benefit level of abstraction rather than continuing up to create the more abstract "action–precondition" representations postulated by pragmatic reasoning theory? As social contracts form a subset of the class of all permission rules, people must have had more experience in relating actions to preconditions than they have had in relating costs to benefits. Consequently, if induction were the source of the schemas used to detect violations of social contracts then the same process should have led to yet more abstract schemas capable of detecting the other types of violation commonly encountered with social events. As this was not the case, the possibility that a specialised algorithm has evolved for the express purpose of handling the costs and benefits of social exchanges invites serious consideration. We find such computations both easy and natural to carry out because, like seeing or hearing, we have recourse to Darwinian algorithms that have been specially selected to match up to the requirements of the task.

If Wason's original task led to a extended research programme in which no card was left unturned, Cosmides' variant has prompted yet another round with no exchanges barred. Although she provides an ingenious defence of her theory, this has not prevented her underlying reasoning from being severely challenged. Criticisms of her conclusions have focused on four main points; (1) the precise definitions of "cost" and "benefit" (Cheng & Holyoak, 1989), (2) possible changes in meaning brought about by the "switched rule" version (Pollard, 1990), (3) the supposedly automatic nature of looking for "cheating" (Politzer & Nguyen-Xuan, 1992), and (4) the effect of different varieties of cheating on subjects' choices, (Gigerenzer & Hug, 1992). None of these studies provides unequivocal support for Cosmides' arguments nor for her rejection of pragmatic reasoning schemas. The verdict, it seems, is that the claims for Darwinian algorithms are not as compelling as Cosmides makes out. However, her decision to focus theoretical attention on the evolutionary significance of detecting cases of cheating and deception does remain compelling. Not least because it carries interesting parallels with other, independent work currently underway in comparative and developmental psychology.

Comparative studies of Machiavellianism

Acts of deception call for an agent capable of entertaining thoughts about thoughts, as when we reason about the belief states present in minds other than our own. At minimum, an act of pretence seems to require agents capable of distinguishing between how their actions appear to them and how they will be interpreted by others. The evolutionary basis of such metacognitive skills may be unclear but these same skills can be seen to play a critical role as we come to understand other minds and their potential mental states. Furthermore, it is possible that humans are not the only species capable of employing these metacognitive skills.

Behaviour apparently involving the use of pretence has been reported in the repertoire of certain primates, implying that they can exhibit some understanding of the internal mental states of their conspecifics (Whiten & Byrne, 1988). Although much of the evidence is anecdotal, Whiten and Byrne have compiled a corpus of behavioural observations that do seem to point to tactical deception at work. Two examples, and their accompanying interpretations will suffice to illustrate what they have in mind (see Table 14.1).

Each of these episodes seems to involve a form of pretence behaviour where the tactical deception is aimed at misleading others to the agent's advantage. Thus, the behaviour described by Fossey is interpreted as the tactical use of "Inhibition of Attending". Its use seems to presuppose a mental representation being entertained by the deceiving *agent* of potential *targets* who are capable of using the *agent's* attention as a guide for their own attention. The *agent* seems to appreciate that the *target* can attend where she is looking and takes steps to circumvent it.

In the second vignette, the tactic has been classified as "Creating an Image", and underlying this deliberate tactic is an even more complex mental representation than before. Now the *agent* goes beyond registering what the *targets* can attend to by inferring the content of

TABLE 14.1
Examples of tactical deception

1: INHIBITION OF ATTENDING
"S's group travelling slowly between feeding sites in a relatively straight line along a narrow trail. Four other animals behind S in a line. S looks up into Hypericum tree and spies a nearly obscured clump of Loranthus vine. Without looking at those behind her, she sits down by the side of the trail and begins to self-groom intently until the others have passed her and all are out of sight some 15 feet ahead. Only then did S stop "self-grooming" to rapidly climb into the tree, break off the vine clump and descend with it to the trail to hastily feed on it before running to catch up with the group". (Number 2, Fossey, Gorillas)

2: CREATING AN IMAGE
"Yeroen hurts his hand during a fight with Nikki ... Yeroen walks past the sitting Nikki from a point in front of him to a point behind him and the whole time Yeroen is in Nikki's field of vision he hobbles pitifully but once he has passed Nikki his behaviour changes and he walks normally again". (Number 65, De Waal, chimpanzees)

From Whiten and Byrne, 1988.

what they are then likely to come to believe. At minimum this seems to entail the *agent* having a representation of the *target's* interpretation of the *agent's* behaviour.

Whiten and Byrne go on to press for similar modes of meta-analysis in a variety of other cases but the layers of recursion soon outstrip the evidence to hand and, despite the plausibility of their examples of primates acting as natural psychologists, the representational issues remain tantalisingly opaque. We simply cannot be certain whether chimps and apes develop some insight into the mental states of their companions. In principle, neither can we be certain that human children go down this route but adopting this shift in orientation does increase confidence that we are looking in the right place.

CHILDREN'S THEORY OF MIND

The ability to understand the actions of others and to predict their likely behaviour is a prime essential for any form of social life. Failure to arrive at an understanding of what people are thinking and feeling would make social interaction impossibly chaotic. Given that children will eventually show signs of making these types of inference it is important to understand what skills are entailed and how they become established.

Traditionally, (e.g. Piaget 1929), it had been held that the theory of mind is late developing and that children under 7 years of age cannot distinguish clearly between the properties of mental and physical acts. More recent studies disagree with this timetable. Wellman (1990) sets the point at which children start to adopt a theory of mind and to engage in belief/desire reasoning at 3 years although there are notable limitations on what can be represented. Three-year-olds may be able to distinguish between real and imagined entities but they do not seem to understand the significance of false beliefs (Wellman & Estes, 1986). In fact, how the child handles false belief has come to be seen as the critical test for assigning psychological insight into the mental states of others.

False beliefs

To justify mind-reading in humans (or other animals), it is not enough just to show that the actor can represent the other's belief, as an actor may simply attribute his or her own belief state indiscriminately to others (Premack & Woodruff, 1978). Rather, we need to go further by demonstrating that the actor can handle false beliefs appropriately—I may know that the box is empty but I also know that you believe it to be full. In this case, actors must be capable of setting their own beliefs about the true state of the world to one side in order to represent the false belief of the other—and, having done that, go on to use the false and not the true belief when predicting the other's behaviour. Consequently, we can place the child in these circumstances, and then ask for a prediction of how another (uninformed) child is likely to behave. If the prediction is based, not on what the child knows to be the case, but on the other's false belief, then we have grounds for the child attributing beliefs to other minds.

Although 3-year-olds do not handle this kind of task with much success, a significant advance comes at around 4 years when the child starts to make attributions based on false beliefs, and by 5 years of age the skill is well established. To understand the nature of this advance, we need to digress in order to draw a distinction between reasoning about propositional attitudes and reasoning about propositional contents. Making this distinction will allow us to understand more clearly the nature of the metacognitive operations contributing to the child's burgeoning theory of mind.

Propositional attitudes

Coming to understand statements containing the different propositional attitudes towards propositional contents (believing that, desiring that etc.) is not the same as coming to understand statements of propositional contents on their own. Whereas a statement about the world can be assessed as true or false (either the state is as described or it is not) assessing an attitude of belief towards that propositional content is not so straightforward. Something may be false but I may sincerely believe that it is true. Drawing a distinction between these two types of mental representation is essential for any theory of mind and the first manifestation of the distinction has been traced to the early use of pretence activity in infancy.

Leslie (1987) refers to an apparently paradoxical situation that can be detected in the behaviour of children of around 18 months to 2 years of age. At this stage, children are learning the extensional meanings of words but, at much the same time, they also start to indulge in pretend play. This coincidence seems perverse, as children who are just beginning to learn which animals are called "sheep" are doing themselves no favours if during pretend play they also treat something else as a "sheep". Pretence strikes out in quite the wrong direction to the primary representation and, if harmful interference is to be avoided, somehow the child must keep these two modes of representation apart.

The significant feature of primary representation is its "referential transparency", i.e. the way in which it refers directly to objects in the external world. Using primary representations it is possible to describe external objects in propositional terms and to use logically equivalent propositions as substitutes for each other. For example, the propositions "This is the author of the paper entitled Pretence and Representation" and "This is Alan M. Leslie" refer to the same person. What is true of the one is true of the other. Matters change, however, when instead of reasoning from "asserting that P", we reason from "believing that P". My "believing that this is the author ..." no longer allows for the direct substitution of "Alan M. Leslie". Somehow, the presence of the mental state term (believing) has operated to suspend the primary reference relationship. Similarly, "pretending that this is P" also suspends normal reference relations. In fact, pretence works against the sobriety of primary representation not only by introducing referential opacity, as discussed earlier, but also by attributing deviant properties to objects and, indeed, by creating imaginary objects. When the child invents imaginary objects, the entailment of existence has been suspended. And the same licence applies to mental state terms. "Believing that P" does not entail the existence of whatever is contained in the embedded proposition.

It is as though there are two kinds of mental representation. One kind consists of primary representations which directly represent states of the world. The other kind consists of pretence representations which are not representations of the world so much as "representations of representations". Having drawn this distinction, Leslie then argues that it can be used to explain how pretend play is quarantined from the primary representations underlying normal vocabulary growth.

Leslie (1987, p.417) proposes that during pretence, a primary expression is "elevated" into a new metarepresentational context:

This second-order context gives a report or quotation of the first-order expression. In doing this, it renders opaque the expression that was previously transparent. Its reference, truth and existence relations are suspended while it appears in this context ... the metarepresentational context decouples the primary expression from its normal input–output relations. Meanwhile the original primary representation, a copy of which was raised to a second order, continues with its definite and literal reference, truth and existence relations.

Thus, for Leslie, pretence marks the child's entrée into the mysteries of human intentionality by drawing upon a reflexive capacity that serves to represent cognition to itself. When decoupling the primary function of an object (say, treating a stick as an animal) the child is creating the same kind of metarepresentation as will eventually be needed to represent the mental state of another person. That such metarepresentation should be possible as early as 18 months is taken as evidence in favour of a distinct cognitive module innately dedicated to this task. (A more sceptical treatment of these claims can be found in Lillard, 1993 and Karmiloff-Smith, 1992.) It is through the workings of this module that we embark on constructing the folk psychology that enables each of us to deal with the mental states of others. Furthermore, it can be argued that the emergence of mind-reading skills in the course of evolution set in place the foundations for the construction of cultural knowledge.

Mind-reading and cultural learning

As we become skilled at reading the minds of others we become better equipped to learn from other people. This inter-relationship has prompted Tomasello, Kruger, and Ratner (1993) to conclude that it was the emergence of mind-reading skills during evolution that acted as the vital precursor for the more formal modes of learning associated with the transmission of cultural knowledge. They propose that primate cognition initially evolved in response to the competitive pressures arising from the conduct of social interaction. Then, as mind-reading skills were added to the organism's repertoire of cognitive functions, they were recruited to support new modes of cultural learning such as formal instruction and collaborative problem solving. This evolutionary progression has culminated in the current situation where children can be expected to benefit from increasingly complex modes of cultural learning in step with refinements in their own mind-reading skills. The more the child understands about the instructor's intentions, the more he or she can derive from the content of the instruction.

For example, *Imitative learning* typically occurs around 12 months and it requires no specialised mind-reading ability other than distinguishing between intentional agents and inanimate objects. In contrast, *instructed learning* requires the learner to entertain a modicum of insight into the mental state of the teacher if communication is to be sustained. The stage at which such learning becomes possible is located around 4 years of age, i.e. the point in development where the child can be expected to deploy the metacognitive skills necessary for interpreting the content of other minds. Further developments in social cognition are called for, however, if the child is to benefit from *collaborative learning*. In this case, the transmission of knowledge depends less on what is handed down "from on high" than on peers working together to construct something new for all concerned (see Chapter 12). For children to engage successfully in collaborative learning, quite subtle skills in mind-reading seem to be essential. Not only must the participants be capable of reflecting on their own mental states and not only must they be capable of registering different mental states in others, they must also be capable of taking the further step of reconciling these alternative states. Tomasello et al., somewhat tentatively, locate the stage at which collaborative learning becomes possible at around 6–7 years. They also note that it is around this time that the child shows evidence of understanding others as reflective agents; a level of skill that calls for the processing of second-order mental states—as when representations such as "You think that I think that P" are being entertained.

Tomasello et al. propose that this interdependence between individual mind-reading skills and the different modes of socially facilitated learning they support, when writ large, has led to the emergence of significant developments on the collective level. In effect, it has set in place a cultural "ratchet mechanism" whereby information could now be passed from one generation to the next without significant loss of content. Without such a mechanism, novel modifications in behaviour, instead of accumulating across generations, could easily be lost in the course of transmission. As it is, according to Tomasello et al. (1993, p.495):

> ... human beings transmit ontogenetically acquired behavior and information both within and across generations, with a much higher degree of fidelity than other animal species. The learning processes that ensure this fidelity serve to prevent information loss (the ratchet) and thus in combination with individual and collaborative inventiveness, form the basis for cultural evolution. Human

beings are able to learn from one another in this way because they have very powerful, perhaps uniquely powerful, forms of social cognition.

It has to be acknowledged that such arguments take us into extremely speculative territory where we can only surmise about the stages in the evolutionary sequence that have led up to the present day. And if this is true for specific components of the cognitive architecture and specific aspects of cultural change, it is especially so when it comes to describing the human story itself—the progressive stages in representational capacity that link the modern mind to its primate ancestors. Nonetheless, we embarked on this excursion into evolutionary epistemology with the aim of searching for a deeper understanding of the interplay that exists between the individual and the collective aspects of cognition. Consequently, rather than backing off in alarm at the audacity of the tale that is being spun, we will see just how much further the synthesis can be taken within the confines of the available data.

STAGES IN THE EVOLUTION OF
THE MODERN MIND

A singularly ambitious attempt at recounting the human story has orginated from Donald (1991). In fact, his account is so far-reaching that it is impossible to do justice here to the range of information he draws upon. Fossil evidence, tool making, cave paintings, memory organisation, and brain localisation are just some of the hares that he sets running. Nonetheless, we will accompany him for part of the chase because what he has to say bears closely upon a number of the themes that have cropped up earlier.

Donald proposes that the contemporary human mind has evolved from the primate mind via three transitional stages where, at each transition, new representational systems have emerged as supplements to earlier forms. The first transition was from an *episodic* mode of representation to a *mimetic* mode; the second transition introduced a *narrative* representational mode; and the third transition added *theoretic* representation to the armoury of representational forms. Whereas the first two transitions resulted in new features being added to the biological memory, the third transition breached the limits set by the biological memory as cognitive operations began to take on a socially distributed form. Donald locates the first major transition some two million years ago when the culture of *Homo erectus* came into being. The second transition is located around 200,000 years ago with the emergence of *Homo sapiens*. In contrast, the third transition is much more recent and is linked to the artificial symbol systems (such as writing and number) that function as external devices for representing and storing information. Each transition has led to major gains in voluntary access to stored information which, in turn, have allowed qualitatively new ways for accumulating and integrating information to emerge.

Episodic culture

Donald launches his account by observing that different cultures are typically classified according to their social organisation or tool use. Unfortunately, these descriptive criteria are not very helpful if the aim is to search for continuities in cognitive processing between humans and the rest of the animal kingdom and a classification of cultures in terms of their representational strategies would seem to offer a much more effective means for bridging this gap. Adopting this criterion, Donald proceeds to assign the behavioural repertoire of apes to a cognitive culture that is "episodic" in nature and reliant on a representational system specially adapted for sustaining a network of social relationships. On this interpretation (Donald, 1991, p.149), the lives of apes:

> ... are lived entirely in the present, as a series of concrete episodes and the highest element in their system of representation seems to be at the level of event representation. Where humans have abstract symbolic memory representations, apes are bound to the concrete situation or episode; their social behaviour reflects this situational limitation. Their culture might be therefore classified as an episodic culture.

Clearly, in mounting this argument, Donald does not accept the examples of primate deception cited earlier as evidence for attributing a theory of mind to apes. Rather, he attributes the emergence of the ability to reflect upon internal representations to a quite different cultural system—one that could make extensive use of mimetic activity for the purposes of communication.

Mimetic culture

The culture of *Homo erectus* is seen as constituting an intermediate stage that links the episodic mind to the modern mind and its symbolic representational systems. The bridge was put in place once intentional but non-linguistic representations came into existence. Such representations are to be found in the use of mime where the agent's body is used as a representational device. A social community capable of employing mimetic skills would have made a significant step towards the mutual sharing of knowledge about events. At this point, its members would be able to initiate a "self-triggered" rehearsal loop and thus gain voluntary access to information stored in memory. They would also have moved towards controlling the circumstances under which this same information could be shared with others within the community.

The further transition from a mimetic culture to a "mythic culture" is critically linked with the emergence of language. As linguistic skills came to be developed within the community, this meant that specific episodic experiences could be rehearsed and combined in the form of storylines that could be narrated to a wider audience. Once these narrative accounts became standardised in their retelling, the whole community would then have gained access to collective representations (myths) which dealt with issues of central importance for the lives of its members. It also meant that the properties of narrative structures could begin to be exploited as a new tool in the service of integrative thought.

Whereas the creation of myths marked the most striking achievement of pre-literate societies, a further advance was made once literacy skills appeared along with the external representations employed for reading and writing. At this point, extant knowledge could not only be readily accessed and communicated to others, it could also be readily interrogated on many different levels. Ultimately, it was the exercise of these metareflective operations that led to the belief systems that inform scientific activity and programmes of formal instruction, i.e. the central themes of the two previous chapters.

External symbolic storage (ESS)

In the modern world, external symbolic storage (ESS) can take many forms ranging from the pictures, books, and numerical tables typically available to previous generations, to the photographs, films, and electronic storage systems that have been developed in the present century. In each and every case, the presence of these devices has had the effect of lifting part of the burden of storing information from the individual mind and displacing it outwards onto physical structures in the external world. Although the "engram" (as an entry in biological memory) and the "exogram" (as an entry in external memory), share features in common, they also differ on certain critical points, as listed in Table 14.2. It is these differences that are said to have played a crucial role in setting in place the computational functions attributed to the modern mind.

TABLE 14.2
Some properties of engrams and exograms

Engrams	Exograms
Internal memory record	External memory record
Fixed physical medium	Virtually unlimited media
Constrained format	Unconstrained and reformattable
Impermanent	May be permanent
Large but limited capacity	Virtually unlimited
Limited size of single entries	Virtually unlimited
Not easily refined	Unlimited iterative refinement
Retrieval paths constrained	Retrieval paths unconstrained
Limited perceptual access in audition, virtually none in vision	Unlimited perceptual access especially in vision, spatial structure useful as an organisational device

From Donald, 1991

Whereas previously in the evolutionary record, qualitatively new modes of cognition had arisen as greater processing demands were placed upon different areas of the cortex, the appearance of exograms on the scene brought about a re-ordering of these pressures. For example, following the invention of graphic representations, a shift in the relative importance of auditory and visual representations in the cognitive economy could be expected to come into effect. Additionally, once a culture had access to a store of exograms, the boundary between internal and external modes of information processing had been breached. Now, by virtue of being inducted into this larger representational network, individuals came to inherit a new type of cognitive system whose capabilities were *jointly* determined by the individual's biological memory and by the properties of the external network.

The effect of redistributing the mental load of cognitive operations in this way was to usher in new techniques for editing and reformatting information whose powers far surpassed those of earlier versions. Editing and updating tasks that would have soon exhausted the individual's biological capacities were no longer quite so daunting once external records were to hand. For example, an oral listing of a communities' assets would lend itself to a distinctly limited set of manipulations due to the constraints on biological working memory. When converted into a visual list, however, such constraints were removed. In list form, it was possible for individual entries to be rearranged in different ways—allowing for similarities to be detected with listings compiled in other domains. Lists could also be preserved long after the original compilers had left the scene—allowing for the detection of similarities with listings compiled before and since. And lists could easily be revised—allowing for new information to be added and for older information to be reassessed. Thus, once graphic representations became available, extant knowledge could engage with a variety of new and powerful metarepresentational techniques which enabled the products of earlier cognitive operations to be interrogated in new contexts of interpretation. This dialectical exercise has culminated in the systems of analytic thought that have supplemented (or supplanted) the storylines derived from the application of narrative modes of representation. Individuals most likely to fare best under these circumstances will be those most capable of exploiting the computational properties of the distributed system—provided they have been taught the necessary skills.

Evidently, Donald has pieced together an intriguing version of the human enterprise which happens to tie together a number of subthemes that have surfaced elsewhere in the present account. Nonetheless, it has to be recognised that it is but one of the many storylines that could be imposed on the evolutionary record where the scope for disagreement over detail remains intolerably high. There are other versions of the evolutionary story that would arrange the pieces differently. Even so, certain themes are likely to remain in place.

Donald's emphasis on the functional significance of external symbol systems is entirely congruent with the arguments of Rumelhart, Smolensky, McClelland, and Hinton (1986) as outlined in Chapter 5. There it was argued that complex tasks can be made computationally more tractable provided the solver can bring external representations into play. An arithmetical calculation that calls for many subcomputations can be done the hard way (in the head of the solver) or the easy way (where the solver has recourse to pen and paper). In expanding on the nature of this distinction, Donald's arguments combine with those of the connectionists in raising serious questions concerning the psychological validity of the classical computational models described in Section 1. By ignoring the situated nature of cognition, classicists have been forced to tilt the balance of explanation in the wrong direction. Where exograms could have shouldered some of the computational load, classical theorists have chosen instead to postulate extended sequences of internal symbol manipulation as the means of plugging the gap.

Conjoining internal and external representations

This same point has been underlined by Zhang and Norman (1994, p.88). They refer to the failure of cognitive scientists to partition cognitive tasks into their internal and external components as the prime reason why they have been led to:

... postulate complex internal representations to account for the complexity of behavior, much of which, however, is merely a reflection of the complexity of the environment ...

To illustrate their case, Zhang and Norman refer to the various ways in which the external and internal representations of a given task can interact to create a problem space that then determines its perceived difficulty. For example, different versions of the Tower of Hanoi problem (where rings of different sizes have to be stacked in a set sequence) can be made easier by the simple device of mapping the content of the rules governing legitimate moves onto the structure of the physical apparatus itself. If an illegitimate move is made physically impossible to execute, the demands on the mental resources of the solver have been effectively reduced and they can then be directed to other ends (see also the discussion of Sweller's work on schematisation during problem solving in Chapter 12).

In general, wherever the external component of a problem configuration is minimal, it will call for a great deal of information to be computed internally. The mental load on the solver will be high and the route to a solution will be that much harder. Wherever the same task has been redesigned to displace some of the relevant information onto structures in the external environment, this will lead to a reduction in the solver's mental load and we can expect a commensurate reduction in the perceived difficulty of the task. Equally, we should expect to find equivalent trade-offs at work when we consider the systems of exograms that have evolved within particular cultures.

In Chapter 1, it was noted how numeral systems have evolved that make different demands on their users when they are put to use in arithmetical computations. In the light of the preceding discussion these demands can now be seen as dependent on the ways in which each numeral system partitions its representational functions between the mind of the user and the physical tokens being employed (Zhang & Norman, 1993). In the tally system it is left to the user to project the properties of base and power onto the physical tokens (as when distinguishing "2" from "3" or "20" from "30") as only the single dimension of quantity is externally represented. However, within the Arabic system we find two external devices being deployed to register the base and the power dimension. The base dimension is determined by the shapes of the digits (0, 1, etc.) and the power dimension is represented through the spatial position of the digits. Hence, as Zhang and Norman describe (1993, pp.1–2) the middle digit (4) in the number 447:

... has a value 4 on the base dimension and position 1 (counting from the rightmost digit, starting from zero) on the power dimension. The actual value it represents is 40 (the product of its values on the base and power dimensions, 4×10^1).

To the extent that different numeral systems vary in their explicit representation of base and power information they will also vary in the extent to which their users have to compute this information internally. The more this information is made available directly to perception, the fewer the internal demands made on the user, and hence the more efficient the system is likely to be. Of course, the affordances of different numeration systems depend on considerable amounts of prior learning—we will not see base and power information in Arabic numerals unaided. But the point remains that we can perform many cognitive tasks, not just in our heads, but via conjunctions of internalised and explicit representations and how this is managed makes a significant contribution to their intrinsic difficulty.

ECOLOGICAL THEORIES OF COGNITION

The preceding arguments fit rather awkwardly within the classical view of cognition which holds that the perceptual systems inform our understanding of the world only to the extent that their outputs engage with the mechanisms of central cognition. Within ACT* and SOAR, perceptual inputs exert an influence on thinking when and only when they trigger the conditions of production rules. From this perspective, the corrective movements of the steering wheel that a driver has to make to keep the car on the road, although they depend on perceptual inputs relating to the nature of the road ahead, require the intervention of a further processing stage before they can be executed. Only once this stage has been completed and the appropriate productions have been triggered is the driver in the position to turn the wheel as required.

In contrast, ecological theorists (e.g. Gibson, 1979) would put quite a different gloss on the driver's behaviour. Now, the steering adjustments are seen to arise as the driver attends to "invariants" in the external environment which afford information directly about what to do next. On this argument, there is simply no need for a further round of internal processing intervening between the perceptual input and the motor response. Affordance resides in the perceptual analysis of the situation and this analysis may be sufficient to give individuals direct access to information on how to respond. Such direct cognition arises wherever selectional pressures have worked to tune the organism's sensory systems to information that can be picked up from the properties of the external environment. The need for indirect cognition arises wherever cultural processes have reworked tacit knowledge into an explicit (symbolic) form that can be shared with others within the culture.

Reactions to ecological arguments of this kind have, in the main, been pretty dismissive. Thus, Vera and Simon (1993) have retorted that, although the pick-up of information from the environment may seem direct and effortless to the agent involved, this is only because the skill has been well practised and the relevant decision cycles can run their course free of impasses. Nonetheless, the work cited earlier suggests that this insistence on the primacy of individual, central cognition is too rigid. There are many everyday tasks whose performance defy explanation at this level alone. A convincing, if specialised, illustration is provided by Hutchins (1995) who demonstrates that the modern navigational techniques found at sea can *only* be understood through an analysis of the external physical and social scaffolding that serves to hold the computational details in place. The computations that keep a modern ship on course arise out of a complex distribution of responsibilities where individual problem solving both relies upon the extensive use of technical artefacts and on back-up from other people in the navigational team. And there are many other cases where similar distributional patterns have evolved within the host culture—not least, the practices of normal science as discussed in the previous chapter.

POSTSCRIPT

The aim of this chapter has been to try to inject a greater degree of coherence into our explanations of knowledge in mind by locating cognitive phenomena within an evolutionary setting. Hopefully, enough has been said by now to justify this diversion into evolutionary epistemology while at the same time conveying how difficult it can be to steer a course away from a series of "just-so" stories towards other versions that are scientifically acceptable. In this respect we are not helped by our human propensity for preferring "plot" over proof although, as noted earlier and elsewhere, combining individual and collective modes of knowing can go a long way towards detecting and refining ill-formed beliefs about the world. But we should not be too complacent about where all this can lead. Resort to collective reasoning, and to scientific method in particular, may have done much to redress imperfections in what we come to believe but there are fashions in social beliefs that sometimes override our individual common sense.

In the nineteenth century, Mackay (c.1860) produced an entertaining compendium in which he described numerous instances where people "go mad in herds [but] they only recover their senses slowly and one by one" (*Memoirs of extraordinary popular delusions and the madness of crowds*). There is no reason to suppose that such propensities were left behind at the turn of the last century or that they will be jettisoned at the turn of this millenium. Even science as a collective mode of belief fixation has been quite capable of generating its own intellectual pathologies. Pseudosciences, such as phrenology and astrology, have thrived, at least for a while, because their proponents sought and found cases that supported their claims while neglecting to search with equal zeal for cases that disproved their hypothesis (Young, 1970). These are clear and worrying cases where the confirmation bias has survived the transition to the collective level. Of course, such case histories can be dismissed precisely because they are pseudosciences, but the distinction is not always so sharply etched at the time. A more instructive example can be found in what happened to the biological sciences in the Soviet Union just after the Second World War.

In August 1948, the Lenin Academy of Agricultural Sciences called a meeting to discuss "The Situation in Biological Science" at that time (Proceedings, 1949). In fact, this meeting of some 700 or so participants had been deliberately stacked against the few geneticists in their midst who subscribed to Mendelian genetics. Arraigned against this small group was a much greater number of Academicians who held strongly to the neo-Lamarckian views of their President, Trofim D. Lysenko. That the minority view was also the received view in Western capitalist science obviously did not help.

The key victims in this debate had not been told of the meeting but this did not prevent their absence from being criticised. When they did attend to further their own defence, they were then placed under enormous group pressures to change their views. Not, it must be said, on the basis of the scientific evidence but by a much more straightforward process of collective bullying. Over the course of the week's proceedings the collective pressures on the minority view were deliberately stoked up and they were to have catastrophic consequences.

On the eighth day of sitting, Academician P.M. Zhukovsky addressed the meeting stating (Proceedings, 1949, p.456):

As regards the chromosome theory of heredity. It would be deplorable if the entire group of geneticists that has been labelled Mendelists-Morganists were, from this rostrum, to renounce the chromosome theory of heredity. I do not intend to do that.

By the tenth day of sitting, Zhukovsky returned to the rostrum to state (ibid. p.618):

There are moments in a man's life, especially in our historic days, which are to him of profound and crucial moral and political significance. This is what I experienced yesterday and today. The speech I made the day before yesterday was an unhappy one; ... it was my last speech from an incorrect biological and ideological standpoint [applause].

At its conclusion, the meeting passed a resolution that praised the majority view for its "great and fruitful work [in] exposing and shattering the theoretical positions of Mendelism-Morganism" (p.630).

The net consequences that followed from this resolution were that Soviet agriculture went on to experience severe setbacks as the promised benefits failed to materialise, and the whole of Soviet biological science was cast into disarray as Mendel's ideas were systematically purged from the teaching syllabuses in colleges and universities.

Once again, we may compartmentalise what has happened here by pointing to the necessity for keeping politics out of science. However, a little reflection indicates that scientific standards cannot be divorced from political values quite that easily. Kohn (1986, pp.72–73) having discussed this case under the heading Lysenko—Science and Politics, concluded, apparently without noting the irony, that:

When Khrushchev was deposed in 1964, Lysenko was deprived of his post as the director of the Institute of Genetics, and the Institute was dissolved. ... The fall of Khrushchev and of Lysenko led in 1965 to the reorganization of teaching in biology by culling Lysenkoist pseudoscience from it. It was another year before biology taught in Russian schools became similar to that prevalent in the West. [Italics added.]

The point behind this example is not that such culling has turned out be unjustified but rather to underline an obvious if uncomfortable observation—the knowledge we profess at any one time (including scientific knowledge) cannot be treated as infallible. Furthermore, recourse to a collective level of decision making provides no necessary escape from this tension between acceptance and doubt. It can make things worse as well as better and our present levels of understanding offer no guarantee that we are always wise enough to tell the direction in which we are heading.

In a different context, Sternberg (1990, p.3) has sagely remarked that "To understand wisdom fully and correctly probably requires more wisdom than any of us has". Exactly so, but it would be remiss to bring this account of knowledge in mind to its conclusion without passing some comment on the distinction in question. For Meacham (1990, p.181), it is a distinction that hinges upon the balance to be struck between the extent to which we trust in what we know and the extent to which it is open to questioning:

> ... the essence of wisdom is to hold the attitude that knowledge is fallible and to strive for a balance between knowing and doubting.

No doubt wisdom has other essences too, but individuals who fail through a lack of reflexivity to doubt the limits of their own knowledge—who act as though they alone are in possession of received truth—are acting unwisely by doubting too little. Equally, those individuals who, by virtue of doubting too much, devalue their beliefs indiscriminately, are also acting unwisely. There needs to be a creative tension between affirming and doubting if we are to use our acquired knowledge with discernment. It has not helped in achieving this accommodation that, as individuals, we find it easier to believe than to doubt and, as members of larger groups, we may find this bias to be amplified as well as attentuated.

Yet, somehow, in the course of the evolution of the modern mind there has been progress towards the intellectual state of detachment that attends getting this balance, if not right, then at least under control. The outputs of the perceptual systems continue to provide information about the environment that is accepted and unquestioned at one operational level while, on other operational levels—individually and collectively defined—this same information can be unaccepted and questioned.

Evolutionary accounts of cognition have repeatedly drawn attention to the way in which basic modes of cognition, originally selected for the registration of external events, have been recruited to form new cognitive regimes that treat their own products as grist for further processing. To take another example, Gilbert (1991) specifically attributes the affirmation bias in human reasoning to the manner in which the operations of perceptual system have come to be recruited into the processes of central cognition. In the course of perception we come to believe in what we see without feeling the need to question further. In central cognition we initially accept as true that which we have understood (see Chapter 10). According to Gilbert (1991 p.116), that the two systems should match in this respect is because:

... one (namely, the propositional system of representation that underlies cognition) is an evolutionary outgrowth of the other (namely, the imaginal system of representation that underlies perception)

When we have a clearer understanding of how this transition from "seeing" to "knowing" occurred during the course of biological evolution we will be in a stronger position to understand why and how similar processes have been set in train on other descriptive levels. We may then aspire to an account of human cognition that houses knowledge in mind without radically compromising its living requirements.

References

Abbot, V., & Black, J.B. (1986). Goal related inferences in comprehension. In J.A. Galambos, R.P. Abelson, & J.B. Black (Eds.), *Knowledge structures* (pp.123–142). Hillsdale, NJ: Lawrence Erlbaum Associates Inc.

Alba, J.W., & Hasher, L. (1983). Is memory schematic? *Psychological Bulletin, 93*, 203–231.

Alba, J.W., Alexander, S.J., Hasher, L., & Caniglia, K. (1981). The role of context in the encoding of information. *Journal of Experimental Psychology, Human Learning and Memory, 7*, 283–292.

Anderson, J. R. (1974). Retrieval of propositional information from long-term memory. *Cognitive Psychology, 6*, 451–474.

Anderson, J.R. (1978). Arguments concerning representations for mental imagery. *Psychological Review, 85*, 249–277.

Anderson, J.R. (1983). *The architecture of cognition*. Cambridge, MA: Harvard University Press.

Anderson, J.R. (1990). *The adaptive character of thought*. Hillsdale, NJ: Lawrence Erlbaum Associates Inc.

Anderson, J.R. (1993). *Rules of the mind*. Hillsdale, NJ: Lawrence Erlbaum Associates Inc.

Anderson, J.R., & Bower, G.H. (1973). *Human associative memory*. Washington: Winston & Sons.

Anderson, R.C., & Biddle, W.B. (1975). On asking people questions about what they are reading. In G.H. Bower (Ed.), *Psychology of learning and motivation, Vol. 9* (pp.89–132). New York: Academic Press.

Anderson, R.C., & Pichert, J.W. (1978). Recall of previously unrecallable information following a shift in perspective. *Journal of Verbal Learning and Verbal Behavior, 17*, 1–12.

Anderson, T.H. (1980). Study strategies and adjunct aids. In R.J. Spiro, B.C. Bruce, & W.F. Brewer (Eds.), *Theoretical issues in reading comprehension* (pp. 483–501). Hillsdale, NJ: Lawrence Erlbaum Associates Inc.

Annis, L.F. (1983). The processes and effects of peer tutoring. *Human Learning, 2,* 39–47.

Apter, M.J. (1982). *The experience of motivation: The theory of psychological reversals.* San Diego: Academic Press.

Asimov, S. (1993). More on Asimov's learning curve. *Psychological Science, 4,* 214.

Atkinson, R.C., & Shiffrin, R.M. (1968). Human memory: A proposed system and its control processes. In K.W. Spence (Ed.), *The psychology of learning and motivation: Advances in research and theory, Vol. 2* (pp. 89–195). New York: Academic Press.

Baddeley, A. (1990). *Human memory. Theory and practice.* Hove, UK: Lawrence Erlbaum Associates Ltd.

Baddeley, A. (1992). Is working memory working? The fifteenth Bartlett lecture. *Quarterly Journal of Experimental Psychology, 44A,* 1–31.

Bain, A. (1873). *Mind and body. The theories of their relation.* London: Henry King.

Bain, A. (1904). *Autobiography.* London: Longmans, Green.

Baker, L., & Wagner, J.L. (1987). Evaluating information for truthfulness; The effects of logical subordination. *Memory and Cognition, 15,* 247–255.

Baldwin, J. (1915). *Genetic theory of reality.* New York: Putnam.

Barsalou, L.W. (1985). Ideals, central tendency and frequency of instantiation as determinants of graded structure in categories. *Journal of Experimental Psychology: Learning, Memory and Cognition, 11,* 629–654.

Barsalou, L.W. (1992). *Cognitive psychology. An overview for cognitive scientists.* Hillsdale, NJ: Lawrence Erlbaum Associates Inc.

Barsalou, L.W. (1993). Flexibility, structure and linguistic vagary in concepts: Manifestations of a computational system of perceptual symbols. In A.F. Collins, S.E. Gathercole, M.A. Conway, & P.E. Morris (Eds.), *Theories of memory,* (pp. 28–98). Hillsdale, NJ: Lawrence Erlbaum Associates Inc.

Bartlett, F.C. (1932). *Remembering: A study in experimental and social psychology.* Cambridge: Cambridge University Press.

Bartlett, F.C (1958). *Thinking. An experimental and social study.* London: George Allen & Unwin Ltd.

Bates, E.A., & Elman, J.L. (1992). *Connectionism and the study of change.* CRL Technical Report 9202. Center for Research in Language, San Diego.

Bauer, P.J., & Mandler, J.M. (1989). One thing follows another: Effects of temporal structure on 1- to 2- year olds' recall of events. *Developmental Psychology, 25,* 197–206.

Bekerian, D.A., & Bowers, J.M. (1983). Eye witness testimony: Were we misled? *Journal of Experimental Psychology: Learning, Memory and Cognition, 9,* 139–145.

Billig, M. (1987). *Arguing and thinking. A rhetorical approach to social psychology.* Cambridge: Cambridge University Press.

Bjork, R.A. (1978). The updating of human memory. In G.H. Bower (Ed.), *The psychology of learning and motivation, vol. 12.* New York: Academic Press.

Blaney, P.H. (1986). Affect and memory: A review. *Psychological Bulletin, 99,* 229–246.

Boden, M.A. (1982). Is equilibration important? A view from artificial intelligence. *British Journal of Psychology, 73*, 165–173.

Boden, M. (1988). *Computer models of the mind. Computational approaches in theoretical psychology.* Cambridge: Cambridge University Press.

Boden, M.A. (1994). Précis of the creative mind: Myths and mechanisms. *Behavioral and Brain Sciences, 17*, 519–570.

Bookman, L.A., & Alterman, R. (1991). Schema recognition for text understanding: An analog semantic feature approach. In J.A. Barnden (Ed.), *Advances in connectionist and neural computation theory, Volume 1* (pp. 87–122). Norwood, NJ: Ablex Publishing Corporation.

Bornens, M-T. (1990). Problems brought about by "reading" a sequence of pictures. *Journal of Experimental Child Psychology, 49*, 189–226.

Bower, G.H. (1974). Selective facilitation and interference in the retention of prose. *Journal of Educational Psychology, 66*, 1–8.

Bower, G.H. (1981). Mood and memory. *American Psychologist, 36*, 129–148.

Bower, G.H. (1992). How might emotions affect learning? In S-A. Christianson (Ed.), *The handbook of emotion and memory: Research and theory.* Hillsdale, NJ: Lawrence Erlbaum Associates Inc.

Bower, G.H. (1994). Some relations between emotions and memory. In P. Ekman & R.J. Davidson (Eds.), *The nature of emotions* (pp. 303–305). Oxford: Oxford University Press.

Bower, G.H., Black, J.B., & Turner, T.J. (1979). Scripts in memory for text. *Cognitive Psychology, 11*, 177–220.

Bower, G.H., & Cohen, P.R. (1982). Emotional influences in memory and thinking. In M.S. Clark & S.T. Fiske (Eds.), *Affect and cognition* (pp. 291–331). Hillsdale, NJ: Lawrence Erlbaum Associates Inc.

Bower, G.H., & Mayer, J.D. (1985). Failure to replicate mood-dependent retrieval. *Bulletin of the Psychonomic Society, 23*, 39–42.

Bower, G.H., Thompson-Schill, S., & Tulving, E. (1994). Reducing retro-active interference: An interference analysis. *Journal of Experimental Psychology: Learning, Memory and Cognition, 20*, 31–66.

Bower, G.H., & Winzenz, D. (1969). Group structure, coding and memory for digit series. *Journal of Experimental Psychology, 80*(2, Part 2), 1–17.

Braine, M.D.S., & O'Brien, D.P. (1991). A theory of If: A lexical entry reasoning program and pragmatic principles. *Psychological Review, 98*, 182–203.

Bransford, J.D., Barclay, J.R., & Franks, J.J. (1972). Sentence memory: A constructive versus interpretive approach. *Cognitive Psychology, 3*, 193–209.

Bransford, J.D., & McCarrell, N.S. (1974). A sketch of a cognitive approach to comprehension: Some thoughts about understanding what it means to comprehend. In W. Weimer & D. Palermo (Eds.), *Cognition and the symbolic processes* (pp.189–229). Hillsdale, NJ: Lawrence Erlbaum Associates Inc.

Brewer, W.F. (1980). Literary theory, rhetoric and stylistics: Implications for psychology. In R.J. Spiro, B.C. Bruce, & W.F. Brewer (Eds.), *Theoretical issues in reading comprehension* (pp.221–239). Hillsdale, NJ: Lawrence Erlbaum Associates Inc.

Brewer, W.F., & Nakamura, G.V. (1983). The nature and functions of schemas. In R.S. Wyer & T.S. Krull (Eds.), *Handbook of social cognition.* Hillsdale, NJ: Lawrence Erlbaum Associates Inc.

Brewer, W.F., & Treyens, J.C. (1981). Role of schemata in memory for places. *Cognitive Psychology, 13*, 207–230.

Broadbent, D.E. (1975). The magic number seven after fifteen years. In A. Kennedy & A. Wilkes (Eds.), *Studies in long term memory* (pp. 3–18). London: John Wiley & Sons.

Brooks, L.R. (1967). The suppression of visualization by reading. *Quarterly Journal of Experimental Psychology, 19,* 289–299.

Brown, D. (1953). Stimulus similarity and the anchoring of subjective scales. *American Journal of Psychology, 66,* 199–214.

Brown, R. (1986). *Social psychology.* Second Edition. New York: The Free Press.

Brown, R., & Kulik, J. (1977). Flashbulb memories. *Cognition, 5,* 73–99.

Bruner, J. (1959). Inhelder and Piaget's *The growth of logical thinking.* A psychologist's viewpoint. *British Journal of Psychology, 50,* 363–370.

Bruner, J. (1990). *Acts of meaning.* Cambridge, MA: Harvard University Press.

Bryant, P.E. (1982). The role of conflict and agreement between intellectual strategies in children's ideas about measurement. *British Journal of Psychology, 73,* 242–251.

Bryant, P.E. (1986). Theories about the causes of cognitive development. In P. Van Geert (Ed.), *Theory building in developmental psychology* (pp.167–187). North Holland: Elsevier.

Bryant, P.E., & Kopytynska, H. (1976). Spontaneous measurement by young children. *Nature, 260,* 773.

Burke, A., Heuer, F., & Reisberg, D. (1992). Remembering emotional events. *Memory and Cognition, 20,* 277–290.

Butler, K. (1991). Towards a connectionist architecture. *Mind and Language, 6,* 252–272.

Carey, S. (1988). Reorganisation of knowledge in the course of acquisition. In S. Strauss (Ed.), *Ontogeny, phylogeny and historical development* (pp. 1–27). Norwood, NJ: Ablex Publishing Co.

Carrasco, M., & Ridout, J.B. (1993). Olfactory perception and olfactory imagery: A multidimensional analysis. *Journal of Experimental Psychology, Human Perception and Performance, 19,* 287–301.

Chambers, D., & Reisberg, D. (1985). Can mental images be ambiguous? *Journal of Experimental Psychology: Human Perception and Performance, 11,* 317–328.

Chambers, D., & Reisberg, D. (1992). What an image depicts depends on what an image means. *Cognitive Psychology, 24,* 145–174.

Chase, W.G., & Ericsson, K.A. (1981). Skilled memory. In J.R. Anderson (Ed.), *Cognitive skills and their acquisition* (pp. 141–189). Hillsdale, NJ: Lawrence Erlbaum Associates Inc.

Chase, W.G., & Simon, H.A. (1973). Perception in chess, *Cognitive Psychology, 4,* 55–81.

Cheng, P.W., & Holyoak, K.J. (1985). Pragmatic reasoning schemas. *Cognitive Psychology, 17,* 391–416.

Cheng, P.W., & Holyoak, K.J. (1989). On the natural selection of reasoning theories. *Cognition, 33,* 285–313.

Chi, M.T.H., Bassok, M., Lewis, M., Reimann, P., & Glaser, R. (1989). Self-explanations: How students study and use examples in learning to solve problems. *Cognitive Science, 13,* 145–182.

Chi, M.T.H., De Leeuw, N., Chiu, M.H., & LaVancher, C. (1994). Eliciting self-explanations improves understanding. *Cognitive Science, 18,* 439–477.

Chi, M.T.H., Feltovich, P.J., & Glaser, R. (1981). Categorisation and representation of physics problems by experts and novices. *Cognitive Science*, 5, 121–152.

Chiesi, H.L., Spilich, G.J., & Voss, J.F. (1979). Acquisition of domain related information in relation to high and low domain knowledge. *Journal of Verbal Learning and Verbal Behavior*, 18, 257–273.

Christianson, S-A. (1989). Flashbulb memories: Special but not so special. *Memory and Cognition*, 17, 435–443.

Christianson, S-A., & Loftus, E.F. (1990). Some characteristics of people's traumatic memories. *Bulletin of the Psychonomic Society*, 28, 195–198.

Christianson, S-A., & Loftus, E. (1991). Remembering emotional events. *Cognition and Emotion*, 5, 81–108.

Churchland, P. (1981). Eliminative materialism and the propositional attitudes. *Journal of Philosophy*, 78, 67–90.

Cialdini, R., Vincent, J., Lewis, S., Catalan, J., Wheeler, D., & Darby, B. (1975). Reciprocal concessions procedure for inducing compliance: The-door-in-the-face technique. *Journal of Personality and Social Psychology*, 31, 206–215.

Clark, A. (1987). From folk psychology to naive psychology. *Cognitive Science*, 11, 139–154.

Cleeremans, A. (1993). *Mechanisms of implicit learning. Connectionist models of sequence processing*. Cambridge, MA: MIT Press.

Clement, J. (1988). Observed methods for generating analogies in scientific problem solving. *Cognitive Science*, 12, 563–586.

Collins, A.M., & Loftus, E.F. (1975). A spreading-activation theory of semantic processing. *Psychological Review*, 82, 407–428.

Collins, A.M., & Quillian, M.R. (1969). Retrieval time from semantic memory. *Journal of Verbal Learning and Verbal Behavior*, 8, 240–247.

Cooper, L.A., & Shepard, R.N. (1973). Chronometric studies of the rotation of mental images. In W.G. Chase (Ed.), *Visual information processing* (pp.75–176). New York: Academic Press.

Cooper, R., & Shallice, T. (1995). SOAR and the case for unified theories of cognition. *Cognition*, 55, 115–149.

Cosmides, L. (1989). The logic of social exchange: Has natural selection shaped how humans reason? Studies with the Wason selection task. *Cognition*, 31, 187–276.

Craik, K. (1943). *The nature of explanation*. Cambridge: Cambridge University Press.

Crossman, E.R.F.W. (1959). A theory of the acquisition of speed-skill. *Ergonomics*, 2, 153–166.

Cummins, R. (1989). *Meaning and mental representation*. Cambridge, MA: MIT Press.

Cunningham, J.G., & Weaver, S.L. (1989). Young children's knowledge of their memory span: Effects of task and experience. *Journal of Experimental Child Psychology*, 48, 32–44.

Dampier-Whetham, W.C.D. (1929). *A history of science and its relations with philosophy and religion*. Cambridge: Cambridge University Press.

Daneman, M., & Carpenter, P.A. (1980). Individual differences in working memory and reading. *Journal of Verbal Learning and Verbal Behavior*, 19, 450–466.

Dawes, E.A. (1979). *The great illusionists*. NJ: Chartwell Books Inc.

Debus, A.G. (1977). *The chemical philosophy. Paracelsian science and medicine in the sixteenth and seventeenth centuries, Vol 2*. New York: Science History Publications.

DeCasper, A.J., & Fifer, W.P. (1980). Of human bonding: Newborns prefer their mothers' voices. *Science, 208*, 1174–1176.

Dee-Lucas, D., & Larkin, J.H. (1990). Organization and comprehensibility in scientific proofs. *Journal of Educational Psychology, 82*, 701–714.

De Groot, A.D. (1965). *Thought and choice in chess*. The Hague: Mouton.

De Groot, A.D. (1966). Perception and memory versus thought: Some old ideas and recent findings. In B. Kleinmuntz (Ed.), *Problem solving; Research, method and theory* (pp.19–50). New York: John Wiley & Sons.

De Kleer, J., & Brown, J.S. (1981). Mental models of physical mechanisms and their acquisition. In J.R. Anderson (Ed.), *Cognitive skills and their acquisition* (pp. 285–309). Hillsdale, NJ: Lawrence Erlbaum Associates Inc.

Dell, G.S., McKoon, G., & Ratcliff, R. (1983). The activation of antecedent information during the processing of anaphoric reference in reading. *Journal of Verbal Learning and Verbal Behavior, 22*, 121–131.

Denis, M., & Carfantan, M. (1985). People's knowledge about images. *Cognition, 20*, 49–60.

Dennett, D.C. (1983). Artificial intelligence and the strategies of psychological investigation. In J. Miller (Ed.), *States of mind. Conversations with psychological investigators* (pp. 66–81). London: British Broadcasting Corporation.

Dennett, D.C. (1987). Cognitive wheels. The frame problem of AI. In Z.W. Pylyshyn (Ed.), *The robot's dilemma. The frame problem in artificial intelligence* (pp. 41–64). Norwood, NJ: Ablex Publishing Corp.

Dodson, C., & Reisberg, D. (1991). Indirect testing of eyewitness memory: The (non)effect of misinformation. *Bulletin of the Psychonomic Society, 29*, 333–336.

Doise, W., & Mugny, G. (1984). *The social development of the intellect*. Oxford: Pergamon Press.

Donald, M. (1991). *Origins of the modern mind. Three stages in the evolution of culture and cognition*. Cambridge, MA: Harvard University Press.

Donaldson, M. (1978). *Children's minds*. London: Fontana.

Dreyfus, H.L., & Dreyfus, S.E. (1988). Making a mind versus modelling the brain: Artificial intelligence back at a branchpoint. In S.R. Graubard (Ed.), *The artificial intelligence debate. False starts, real foundations*. Cambridge, MA: MIT Press.

Dulaney, D.E., Carlson, R.A., & Dewey, G.I. (1985). On consciousness in syntactical learning and judgement. A reply to Reber, Allen and Regan. *Journal of Experimental Psychology: General, 114*, 25–32.

Dunbar, K. (1996). How scientists really reason: Scientific reasoning in real-world laboratories. In R.J. Sternberg & J. Davidson (Eds.), *The nature of insight*. Cambridge, MA: MIT Press.

Duncker, K. (1945). On problem solving. *Psychological Monographs, 58*, (Whole Number 270).

Durso, F.T., & Shore, W.J. (1991). Partial knowledge of word meaning. *Journal of Experimental Psychology: General, 20*, 190–202.

Ebbinghaus, H. (1885). *Uber das Gedachtnis*. Leipzig: Duncker. [Translated H. Ruyer & C.E. Bussenius (1913). *Memory*. New York: Teacher's College Press.]

Edelman, G. (1992). *Bright air, brilliant fire. On the matter of mind*. Allen Lane: The Penguin Press.

Eiser, J.R., & Stroebe, W. (1972). *Categorisation and social judgement*. London: Academic Press.

Ekman, P. (1994). Strong evidence for universals in facial expressions: A reply to Russell's mistaken critique. *Psychological Bulletin, 115*, 268–287.

Emler, N., & Valiant, G. (1982). Social interaction and cognitive conflict in the development of spatial co-ordination skills. *British Journal of Psychology, 73*, 295–303.

Ericsson, K.A., & Polson, P.G. (1988). An experimental analysis of the mechanisms of a memory skill. *Journal of Experimental Psychology: Learning, Memory and Cognition, 14*, 305–316.

Erikson, T.D., & Mattson, M.E. (1981). From words to meaning: A semantic illusion. *Journal of Verbal Learning and Verbal Behavior, 20*, 540–551.

Estes, W.K. (1988). Toward a framework for combining connectionist and symbol-processing models. *Journal of Memory and Language, 27*, 196–212.

Farr, R.M., & Moscovici, S. (1984). *Social representations*. Cambridge: Cambridge University Press.

Ferguson-Hessler, M.G.M., & de Jong, T. (1990). Studying physics texts: Differences in study processes between good and poor performers. *Cognition and Instruction, 7*, 41–54.

Fillmore, C.J. (1968). The case for case. In E. Bach & R.T. Harms (Eds.), *Universals of linguistic theory* (pp. 1–90). New York: Holt, Rhinehart & Winston.

Finke, R.A. (1989). *Principles of mental imagery*. Cambridge, MA: MIT Press.

Finke, R.A., Johnson, M.K., & Shyi, G.C-W. (1988). Memory confusions for real and imagined completions of symmetrical visual patterns. *Memory and Cognition, 16*, 133–137.

Finke, R.A., Pinker, S., & Farah, M. (1989). Reinterpreting visual patterns in mental imagery. *Cognitive Science, 13*, 51–78.

Flanagan, O.J. (1984). *The science of mind*. Cambridge, MA: MIT Press. [2nd. Edition; 1991.]

Flavell, J.H., Beach, D.R., & Chinsky, J.M. (1966). Spontaneous verbal rehearsal in a memory task as a function of age. *Child Development, 37*, 283–299.

Flavell, J.H., Friedrichs, A.G., & Hoyt, J.D. (1970). Developmental changes in memorization processes. *Cognitive Psychology, 1*, 324–340.

Flesch, R. (1948). A new readability yardstick. *Journal of Applied Psychology, 32*, 221–233.

Fletcher, C.R., & Bloom, C.P. (1988). Causal reasoning in the comprehension of simple narrative tasks. *Journal of Memory and Language, 27*, 235–244.

Fodor, J.A. (1983). *The modularity of mind*. Cambridge, MA: MIT Press.

Fodor, J.A., & Pylyshyn, Z.W. (1988). Connectionism and cognitive architecture: A critical analysis. *Cognition, 28*, 3–71.

Foley, M.A., Johnson, M.K., & Raye, C.L. (1983). Age-related changes in confusion between memories for thoughts and memories for speech. *Child Development, 54*, 51–60.

Foley, M.A., Santini, C., & Sopasakis, M. (1989). Discriminating between memories: Evidence for children's spontaneous elaborations. *Journal of Experimental Child Psychology, 46*, 146–169.

Franklin, N., & Tversky, B. (1990). Searching imagined environments. *Journal of Experimental Psychology: General, 119*, 63–76.

Freedman, J., & Fraser, S. (1966). Compliance without pressure: The foot-in-the-door technique. *Journal of Personality and Social Psychology, 4,* 195–202.

Freud, S. (1905). *Jokes and their relation to the unconscious* [Translated by J.Strachey, 1957.] Standard Edition, vol. 8. London: Hogarth Press.

Galotti, K.M. (1989). Approaches to studying formal and everyday reasoning. *Pychological Bulletin, 105,* 331–351.

Galton, F. (1880). Statistics of mental imagery. *Mind, 5,* 301–318.

Galton, F. (1908). *Memories of my life.* London: Methuen.

Garnham, A., & Oakhill, J. (1992). Discourse processing and text representation from a "mental models" perspective. *Language and Cognitive Processes, 7,* 193–204.

Garrod, S.C., & Sanford, A.J. (1977). Interpreting anaphoric relations: The integration of semantic information while reading. *Journal of Verbal Learning and Verbal Behavior, 16,* 77–90.

Gauld, A., & Stephenson, G.M. (1967). Some experiments relating to Bartlett's theory of remembering. *British Journal of Psychology, 58,* 39–49.

Gehring, R.E., & Toglia, M.P. (1988). Relative retention of verbal and audio-visual information in a national training programme. *Applied Cognitive Psychology, 2,* 213–221.

Gelman, S.A. (1989). Children's use of categories to guide biological inferences. *Human Development, 32,* 65–71.

Gelman, S.A., & Markman, E.M. (1986). Categories and induction in young children. *Cognition, 23,* 183–209.

Gelman, S.A., & O'Reilly, A.W. (1988). Children's inductive inferences within superordinate categories: The role of language and category structure. *Child Development, 59,* 876–887.

Gentner, D., & Toupin, C. (1986). Systematicity and surface similarity in the development of analogy. *Cognitive Science, 10,* 277–300.

Gergen, K.J., & Gergen, M.J. (1991). Toward reflex methodologies. In F. Steier (Ed.), *Research and reflexivity* (pp. 76–95). London: Sage Publications.

Gernsbacher, M.A. (1994). *Handbook of psycholinguistics.* San Diego: Academic Press.

Gibson, J.J. (1979). *The ecological approach to visual perception.* Boston: Houghton Mifflin.

Gick, M.L., & Holyoak, K.J. (1980). Analogical problem solving. *Cognitive Psychology, 12,* 306–355.

Gick, M.L., & Holyoak, K.J. (1983). Schema induction and analogical transfer. *Cognitive Psychology, 15,* 1–38.

Gigerenzer, G. (1993). The bounded rationality of probabilistic mental models. In D.E. Over & K.L. Manktelow (Eds.), *Rationality. psychological and philosophical perspectives* (pp. 284–313). London: Routledge.

Gigerenzer, G., & Hug, K. (1992). Domain-specific reasoning: Social contracts, cheating and perspective change. *Cognition, 43,* 127–171.

Gilbert, D.T. (1991). How mental systems believe. *American Psychologist, 46,* 107–119.

Gilbert, D.T., Krull, D.S., & Malone, P.S. (1990). Unbelieving the unbelievable: Some problems in the rejection of false information. *Journal of Personality and Social Psychology, 59,* 601–613.

Gilbert, D.T., Taforodi, R.W., & Malone, P.S. (1993). You can't not believe everything you read. *Journal of Personality and Social Psychology, 65,* 221–233.

Gilbert, G.M. (1951). Stereotype persistence and change among college students. *Journal of Abnormal and Social Psychology, 46*, 245–254.

Girotto, V., Light, P., & Colbourn, C. (1988). Pragmatic schemas and conditional reasoning in children. *Quarterly Journal of Psychology, 40*, 469–482.

Glenberg, A.M., & Epstein, W. (1985). Calibration of comprehension. *Journal of Experimental Psychology: Learning, Memory and Cognition, 11*, 702–718.

Glenberg, A.M., & Epstein, W. (1987). Inexpert calibration of comprehension. *Memory and Cognition, 15*, 84–93.

Glenberg, A.M., & Langston, W.E. (1992). Comprehension of illustrated text: Pictures help to build mental models. *Journal of Memory and Language, 31*, 129–151.

Glover, J.A., & Krug, D. (1988). Detecting false statements in text: The role of outlines and inserted headings. *British Journal of Educational Psychology, 58*, 310–306.

Gluck, M.A., & Bower, G.H. (1988). Evaluating an adaptive network model of human learning. *Journal of Memory and Language, 27*, 166–195.

Glynn, S.M., & Di Vesta, F.J. (1977). Outline and hierarchical organisation as aids for study and retrieval. *Journal of Educational Psychology, 69*, 89–95.

Goldman, A. (1986). *Epistemology and cognition*. Cambridge, MA: Harvard University Press.

Goldstone, R.L. (1994). The role of similarity in categorization: Providing a groundwork. *Cognition, 52*, 125–157.

Gomulicki, B.R. (1956). Recall as an abstractive process. *Acta Psychologica, 12*, 77–94.

Graesser, A.C., & Goodman, S.M. (1985). Implicit knowledge, question answering and the representation of expository text. In B.K. Britton & J.B. Black (Eds.), *Understanding expository text. A theoretical and practical handbook for analyzing explanatory text* (pp.109–171). Hillsdale, NJ: Lawrence Erlbaum Associates Inc.

Graesser, A.C., Singer, M., & Trabasso, T. (1994). Constructing inferences during narrative text comprehension. *Psychological Review, 101*, 371–395.

Graesser, A.C., Woll, S.B., Kowalski, D.J., & Smith, D.A. (1980). Memory for typical and atypical actions in scripted activities. *Journal of Experimental Psychology, Human Learning and Memory, 6*, 503–515.

Green, R.E.A., & Shanks, D.R. (1993). On the existence of independent explicit and implicit learning systems.: An examination of some evidence. *Memory and Cognition, 21*, 304–317.

Groner, R., Groner, M., & Bischoff, W.F. (1983). *Methods of heuristics*. Hillsdale, NJ: Lawrence Erlbaum Associates Inc.

Haberlandt, K. (1980). Story grammar and reading time of story constituents. *Poetics, 9*, 99–116.

Haberlandt, K., Berian, C., & Sandson, J. (1980). The episode schema in story processing. *Journal of Verbal Learning and Verbal Behavior, 19*, 635–650.

Halpern, A.R. (1992). Musical aspects of auditory imagery. In D. Reisberg (Ed.), *Auditory imagery* (pp.1–28). Hillsdale, NJ: Lawrence Erlbaum Associates Inc.

Hamilton, D.L., Sherman, S.J., & Ruvolo, C.M. (1990). Stereotype-based expectancies: Effects on information processing and social behavior. *Journal of Social Issues, 46*, 35–60.

Harley, T.A. (1995). *The psychology of language. From data to theory*. Hove, UK: Psychology Press.

Harris, R.J., & Monaco, G.E. (1978). Psychology of pragmatic implications: Information processing between the lines. *Journal of Experimental Psychology: General, 107*, 1–22.

Hartley, D. (1791). *Observations on man. His frame, his duty, his expectations* (2nd Edition). London: J. Johnson.

Hasher, L., & Griffin, M. (1978). Reconstructive and reproductive processes in memory. *Journal of Experimental Psychology, Human Learning and Memory, 4*, 318–330.

Haviland, S.E., & Clark, H.H. (1974). What's new? Acquiring new information as a process of comprehension. *Journal of Verbal Learning and Verbal Behavior, 13*, 515–521.

Hayes, N.A., & Broadbent, D.E. (1988). Two modes of learning for interactive tasks. *Cognition, 28*, 249–276.

Hayes, P.J. (1987). What the frame problem is and isn't. In Z.W. Pylyshyn (Ed.), *The robot's dilemma: The frame problem in artificial intelligence* (pp. 123–138). Norwood, NJ: Ablex Publishing Corp.

Head, H. (1920). *Studies in neurology, Vols 1 & 2*, London: Frowde.

Hebb, D.O. (1949). *The organisation of behavior*. New York: John Wiley & Sons.

Heuer, F., & Reisberg, D. (1990). Vivid memories of emotional events: The accuracy of remembered minutiae. *Memory and Cognition, 18*, 496–506.

Hilton, D.J., & Slugoski, B.R. (1986). Knowledge-based causal attribution: The abnormal conditions focus model. *Psychological Review, 93*, 75–88.

Hinton, G.E. (1991). *Connectionist symbol processing*. Cambridge, MA: MIT Press.

Hobhouse, L.T. (1901). *Mind in evolution*. New York: Macmillan.

Hodges, A. (1983). *Alan Turing. The enigma of intelligence*. London: Unwin Paperbacks.

Hofstadter, D. (1988). Common sense and conceptual halos. *Behavioral and Brain Sciences, 11*, 35–37.

Holyoak, K.J. (1990). Problem solving. In D.N. Osherson & E.E. Smith (Eds.), *An invitation to cognitive science. Vol. 3, Thinking* (pp. 117–146). Cambridge, MA: MIT Press.

Holyoak, K.J. (1991). Symbolic connectionism: Toward third generation theories of expertise. In K.A. Ericsson & J. Smith (Eds.), *Toward a general theory of expertise. Prospects and limits* (pp.301–335). Cambridge: Cambridge University Press.

Holyoak, K.J., & Koh, K. (1987). Surface and structural similarity in analogical transfer. *Memory and Cognition, 15*, 332–340.

Holyoak, K.J., & Thagard, P. (1989). Analogical mapping by constraint satisfaction. *Cognitive Science, 13*, 295–355.

Hubbard, T.L., & Stoeckig, K. (1992). The representation of pitch in musical images. In D.Reisberg (Ed.), *Auditory imagery* (pp. 199–235). Hillsdale, NJ: Lawrence Erlbaum Associates Inc.

Humphrey, G. (1951). *Thinking: An introduction to its experimental psychology*. London: Methuen.

Hutchins, E. (1991). The social organisation of distributed cognition. In L.B. Resnick, J.M. Levine, & S.D. Teasley (Eds.), *Perspectives on socially shared cognition* (pp. 283–307). Washington: American Psychological Association.

Hutchins, E. (1995). *Cognition in the wild*. Cambridge, MA: MIT Press.

Inhelder, B., & Piaget, J. (1958). *The growth of logical thinking from childhood to adolescence*. New York: Basic Books.

Inhelder, B., & Piaget, J. (1964). *The early growth of logic in the child*. London: Routledge & Kegan Paul.

Intons-Peterson, M.J. (1992). Components of auditory imagery. In D. Reisberg (Ed.), *Auditory imagery* (pp. 45–72). Hillsdale; NJ: Lawrence Erlbaum Associates Inc.

Intons-Peterson, M.J., & Fournier, J.A. (1986). External and internal memory aids: When and how often do we use them. *Journal of Experimental Psychology: General, 115*, 267–280.

Intons-Peterson, M.J., & Roskos-Ewaldson, B.B. (1989). Sensory-perceptual qualities of images. *Journal of Experimental Psychology: Learning, Memory and Cognition, 15*, 188–199.

Izard, C.E. (1994). Innate and universal facial expressions: Evidence from developmental and cross-cultural research. *Psychological Bulletin, 115*, 288–299.

Janoff-Bulman, R. (1992). *Shattered assumptions: Towards a new psychology of trauma*. New York: The Free Press.

Jaspers, J.M.F., Hewstone, M.R.C., & Fincham, F.D. (1983). Attribution theory and research: The state of the art. In J.M.F. Jaspars, F.D. Fincham, & M.R.C. Hewstone (Eds.), *Attribution theory: Essays and experiments* (pp. 3–36). London: Academic Press.

Johnson, H.M., & Seifert, C.M. (1994). Sources of the continued influence effect: When misinformation in memory affects later inferences. *Journal of Experimental Psychology: Learning, Memory and Cognition, 20*, 1420–1436.

Johnson, M.K., Foley, M.A., & Leach, K. (1988). The consequences for memory of imagining in another's voice. *Memory and Cognition, 16*, 337–342.

Johnson, M.K., Foley, M.A., Suengas, A.G., & Raye, C.L. (1988). Phenomenal characteristics of memories for perceived and imagined autobiographical events. *Journal of Experimental Psychology: General, 117*, 371–376.

Johnson, M.K., & Raye, C.L. (1981). Reality monitoring. *Psychological Review, 88*, 67–85.

Johnson, M.K., & Suengas, A.G. (1989). Reality monitoring judgements of other people's memories. *Bulletin of the Psychonomic Society, 27*, 107–110.

Johnson, R.E. (1970). Recall of prose as a function of the structural importance of the linguistic units. *Journal of Verbal Learning and Verbal Behavior, 9*, 12–20.

Johnson-Laird, P.N. (1983). *Mental models: Towards a cognitive science of language, inference and consciousness*. Cambridge: Cambridge University Press.

Johnson-Laird, P.N. (1988). *The computer and the mind. An introduction to cognitive science*. London: Fontana Press.

Johnson-Laird, P.N. (1993). *Human and machine thinking*. Hillsdale, NJ: Lawrence Erlbaum Associates Inc.

Johnson-Laird, P.N., & Byrne, R.M.J. (1991). *Deduction*. Hove, UK: Lawrence Erlbaum Associates Ltd.

Johnson-Laird, P.N., Byrne, R.M.J., & Schaeken, W. (1992). Propositional reasoning by model. *Psychological Review, 99*, 418–439.

Johnson-Laird, P.N., Legrenzi, P., & Legrenzi, M.S. (1972). Reasoning and a sense of reality. *British Journal of Psychology, 63*, 395–400.

Johnson-Laird, P.N., & Oatley, K. (1989). The language of emotions. *Cognition and Emotion, 3*, 81–123.

Jones, E.E., & Nisbett, R.E. (1971). The actor and the observer: Divergent perceptions of the causes of behavior. In E.E. Jones, D.E. Kanouse, H.H. Kelley, R.E. Nisbett, S. Valins, & B. Weiner (Eds.), *Attribution: Perceiving the causes of behavior* (pp. 79–94). Morristown, NJ: General Learning Press.

Just, M.A., & Carpenter, P. A. (1987). *The psychology of reading and language comprehension*. Boston: Allyn & Bacon.

Karmiloff-Smith, A. (1979). Micro- and macrodevelopmental changes in language acquisition and other representational systems. *Cognitive Science, 3*, 91–118.

Karmiloff-Smith, A. (1986). From meta-processes to conscious access: Evidence from children's metalinguistic and repair data. *Cognition, 23*, 95–147.

Karmiloff-Smith, A. (1992). *Beyond modularity. A developmental perspective on cognitive science*. Cambridge, MA: MIT Press.

Katz, D., & Braly, K.W. (1933). Racial prejudice and racial stereotypes. *Journal of Abnormal and Social Psychology, 30*, 175–193.

Keller, H. (1908). *The world I live in*. New York: The Century Co.

Kintsch, W. (1974). *The representation of meaning in memory*. Hillsdale, NJ: Lawrence Erlbaum Associates Inc.

Kintsch, W. (1988). The role of knowledge in discourse comprehension: A construction–integration model. *Psychological Review, 95*, 163–182.

Kintsch, W., Welsch, D., Schmalhofer, F., & Zimny, S. (1990). Sentence memory: A theoretical analysis. *Journal of Memory and Language, 29*, 133–159.

Kirsner, K., & Speelman, C. (1993). Is lexical processing just an "ACT"? In A.F. Collins, S.E. Gathercole, M.A. Conway, & P.E. Morris (Eds.), *Theories of memory* (pp. 303–326). Hove, UK: Lawrence Erlbaum Associates Ltd.

Kitcher, P. (1993). *The advancement of science. Science without legend, objectivity without illusions*. Oxford: Oxford University Press.

Klatzky, R.L., & Lederman, S. (1988). The representation of objects in memory: Contrasting perspectives from vision and touch. In M.M. Gruneberg, P.E. Morris, & R.N. Sykes (Eds.), *Practical aspects of memory: Current research and issues* Vol 2, (pp. 426–433). Chichester, UK: John Wiley & Sons.

Klatzky, R.L., Lederman, S., & Reed, C. (1987). There's more to touch than meets the eye: The salience of object attributes for haptics with and without vision. *Journal of Experimental Psychology, General, 116*, 356–369.

Kohn, A. (1986). *False prophets. Fraud and error in science and medicine*. Oxford: Basil Blackwell.

Kolodner, J.L. (1983). Maintaining organization in a dynamic long-term memory. *Cognitive Science, 7*, 243–280.

Kosslyn, S.M. (1980). *Image and mind*. Cambridge, MA: Harvard University Press.

Kosslyn, S.M., Ball, T.M., & Reiser, B.J. (1978). Visual images preserve metric spatial information: Evidence from studies of image scanning. *Journal of Experimental Psychology: Human Perception and Performance, 4*, 47–60.

Kozminsky, E. (1977). Altering comprehension: The effect of biasing titles on text comprehension. *Memory and Cognition, 5*, 482–490.

Kreutzer, M.A., Leonard, C., & Flavell, J.H. (1975). An interview study of children's knowledge about memory. *Monographs of the Society for Research in Child Development, 40* (No. 159), 1–58.

Kroll, N.E., Ogawa, K.H., & Nieters, J.E. (1988). Eye witness memory and the importance of sequential information. *Bulletin of the Psychonomic Society*, *26*, 395–398.

Kuhn, D. (1991). *The skills of argument*. Cambridge: Cambridge University Press.

Kuhn, T.S. (1962). *The structure of scientific revolutions*. Chicago: University of Chicago Press. [2nd Edition, 1970; University of Chicago Press.]

Kulkarni, D., & Simon, H.A. (1988). The process of scientific discovery: The strategy of experimentation. *Cognitive Science*, *12*, 139–175.

Kunda, Z., Miller, D.T., & Claire, T. (1990). Combining social concepts: The role of causal reasoning. *Cognitive Science*, *14*, 551–577.

Lakoff, G. (1987). *Women, fire and dangerous things*. Chicago: University of Chicago Press.

Landauer, T.K. (1986). How much do people remember? Some estimates of the quantity of learned information in long-term memory. *Cognitive Science*, *10*, 477–493.

Langer, J. (1988). A note on the comparative psychology of mental development. In S. Strauss (Ed.), *Ontogeny, phylogeny and historical development. Human development, Vol. 2* (pp. 68–85). Norwood, NJ: Ablex Publishing Corp.

Langley, P., Simon, H.A., Bradshaw, G.L., & Zytkow, J.M. (1987). *Scientific discovery. Computational explorations of the creative processes*. Cambridge, MA: MIT Press.

Lardner, D. (1835). Babbage's calculating machine. *Arcana of Science and Art* (p.79). London: John Limbird.

Lawler, R.W. (1981). The progressive construction of mind. *Cognitive Science*, *5*, 1–47.

Lefcourt, H.M., & Martin, R.A. (1986). *Humor and life stress. Antidote to adversity*. New York: Springer-Verlag.

Legrenzi, P., Girotto, V., & Johnson-Laird, P.N. (1993). Focusing in reasoning and decision making. *Cognition*, *49*, 37–66.

Lehman, D.R., Lempert, R.O., & Nisbett, R.E. (1988). The effects of graduate training on reasoning. *American Psychologist*, *43*, 431–442.

Lehman, D.R., & Nisbett, R.E. (1990). A longitudinal study of the effects of undergraduate training on reasoning. *Developmental Psychology*, *26*, 952–960.

Lehnert, W.G. (1981). Plot units and narrative summarization. *Cognitive Science*, *4*, 293–331.

Lehnert, W.G. (1984). Paradigmatic issues in cognitive science. In W. Kintsch, J.R. Miller, & P.G. Polson (Eds.), *Methods and tactics in cognitive science*. Hillsdale, NJ: Lawrence Erlbaum Associates Inc.

Lehnert, W.G, Robertson, S.P., & Black, J.B. (1984). Memory interactions during question answering. In H. Mandl, N.L. Stein, & T. Trabasso (Eds.), *Learning and comprehension of text* (pp. 355–377). Hillsdale, NJ: Lawrence Erlbaum Associates Inc.

Leslie, A.M. (1987). Pretense and representation: The origins of "Theory of Mind". *Psychological Review*, *94*, 412–426.

Levy, J. (1988, 11 August). Computers that learn to forget. *New Scientist*, 36–39.

Lewis, C.H., & Anderson, J.R (1976). Interference with real world knowledge. *Cognitive Psychology*, *8*, 311–335.

Ley, P. (1977). Psychological studies of doctor-patient communication. In S. Rachman (Ed.), *Contributions to medical psychology* (pp. 9–42). Oxford: Pergamon Press.

Lifton, R.J. (1961). *Thought reform and the psychology of totalism. A study of "brain-washing" in China.* London: Gollancz.

Lillard, A.S. (1993). Pretend playskills and the child's theory of mind. *Child Development, 64,* 348–371.

Lindsay, D.S., & Johnson, M.K. (1989). The reversed eye witness suggestibility effect. *Bulletin of the Psychonomic Society, 26,* 395–398.

Linton, M. (1975). Memory for real world events. In D.A. Norman & D.E. Rumelhart (Eds.), *Explorations in cognition* (pp. 376–404). San Francisco: Freeman.

Lloyd, D. (1988). *Simple minds.* Cambridge, MA: MIT Press.

Loftus, E.F., & Burns, T. (1982). Mental shock can produce retrograde amnesia. *Memory and Cognition, 10,* 318–323.

Loftus, E.F., & Loftus, G.R. (1980). On the permanence of stored information in the human brain. *American Psychologist, 35,* 409–420.

Loftus, E.F., Miller, D.G., & Burns, H.J. (1978). Semantic integration of verbal information into a visual memory. *Journal of Experimental Psychology: Human Learning and Memory, 4,* 19–31.

Loftus, E.F., Schooler, J.W., & Wagenaar, W.A. (1985). The fate of memory: Comment on McCloskey and Zaragoza. *Journal of Experimental Psychology: General, 114,* 375–380.

Lyman, B.J., & McDaniel, M.A. (1986). Effects of encoding strategy on long-term memory for odours. *Quarterly Journal of Experimental Psychology, 38A,* 753–765.

Mackay, C. (ca 1860). *Memoirs of extraordinary popular delusions and the madness of crowds.* London: George Routledge & Sons.

Maki, R.H., Foley, J.M., Kajer, W.K., Thompson, R.C., & Willert, M.G. (1990). Increased processing enhances calibration of comprehension. *Journal of Experimental Psychology: Learning, Memory and Cognition, 16,* 609–616.

Mandler, J.M., & Goodman, M.S. (1982). On the psychological validity of story structures. *Journal of Verbal Learning and Verbal Behavior, 21,* 507–523.

Markman, E.M., & Wachtel, G.F. (1988). Children's use of mutual exclusivity to constrain the meanings of words. *Cognitive Psychology, 20,* 121–157.

Martin, R.M. (1975). Effects of familiar and complex stimuli on infant attention. *Developmental Psychology, 11,* 178–185.

Masur, E.F., McIntyre, C.W., & Flavell, J.H. (1973). Developmental changes in apportionment of study time among items in a multitrial free recall task. *Journal of Experimental Child Psychology, 15,* 237–246.

Mayer, R.E. (1985). Structural analysis of science prose: Can we increase problem solving performance? In B.K. Britton & J.B. Black (Eds.), *Understanding expository text: A theoretical and practical handbook for analysing explanatory text* (pp. 65–87). Hillsdale, NJ: Lawrence Erlbaum Associates Inc.

Mayer, R.E., & Gallini, J.K. (1990). When is an illustration worth 10,000 words? *Journal of Educational Psychology, 82,* 715–726.

McCarthy, J., & Hayes, P.J. (1969). Some philosophical problems from the standpoint of artificial intelligence. In B. Meltzer & D. Michie (Eds.), *Machine intelligence 4.* Edinburgh: Edinburgh University Press.

McClelland, J.L., & Elman, J.L. (1986). The TRACE model of speech perception. *Cognitive Psychology, 18*, 1–86.

McClelland, J.L., & Jenkins, E. (1991). Nature, nurture and connections: Implications of connectionist models for cognitive development. In K. VanLehn (Ed.), *Architectures for intelligence. The twenty-second Carnegie Mellon symposium on cognition* (pp. 41–73). Hillsdale, NJ: Lawrence Erlabum Associates Inc.

McClelland, J.L., & Rumelhart, D.E. (1985). Distributed memory and the representation of general and specific information. *Journal of Experimental Psychology: General, 114*, 159–188.

McClelland, J.L., Rumelhart, D.E., & Hinton, G.E. (1986). The appeal of parallel distributed processing. In D.E. Rumelhart, J. L. McClelland & the PDP Research Group. *Parallel distributed processing. Vol. 1* (pp. 3–44). Cambridge, MA: MIT Press.

McClelland, J.L., Rumelhart, D.E., & the PDP Research Group. (1986). *Parallel distributed processing: Explorations in the microstructure of cognition. Vol. 2: Psychological and biological models.* Cambridge, MA: MIT Press.

McCloskey, M., & Kargon, R. (1988). The meaning and use of historical models in the study of intuitive physics. In S. Strauss (Ed.), *Ontogeny, phylogeny and historical development* Vol. 2 (pp.49–67). Norwood, NJ: Ablex Publishing Corp.

McCloskey, M., Wible, C.G., & Cohen, N.J. (1988). Is there a special flash-bulb memory mechanism? *Journal of Experimental Psychology: General, 117*, 171–181.

McCloskey, M., & Zaragoza, M. (1985). Misleading postevent information and memory for events: Arguments and evidence against memory impairment hypotheses. *Journal of Experimental Psychology: General, 114*, 1–16.

McCulloch, W.S., & Pitts, W.H. (1943). A logical calculus of the ideas immanent in nervous activity. *Bulletin of Mathematical Biophysics, 5*, 115–133.

McKoon, G., & Ratcliff, R. (1992). Inference during reading. *Psychological Review, 99*, 440–466.

McKoon, G., Ratcliff, R., & Seifert, C. (1989). Making the connection: Generalised knowledge structures in story understanding. *Journal of Memory and Language, 28*, 711–734.

Meacham, J.A. (1990). The loss of wisdom. In R.J. Sternberg (Ed.), *Wisdom: Its nature, origins and development* (pp. 181–211). Cambridge: Cambridge University Press.

Medicus, G. (1992). The inapplicability of the biogenetic rule to behavioral development. *Human Development, 35*, 1–8.

Medin, D.L., & Shoben, E.J. (1988). Context and structure in conceptual combination. *Cognitive Psychology, 20*, 158–190.

Mehler, J., & Dupoux, E. (1994). *What infants know. The new cognitive science of early development.* Cambridge, MA: Blackwell.

Meringoff, L.K. (1980). Influence of the medium in children's story apprehension. *Journal of Educational Psychology, 72*, 240–249.

Metcalfe, J. (1990). Composite holographic associative recall model (CHARM). and blended memories in eye witness testimony. *Journal of Experimental Psychology: General, 119*, 145–160.

Meudell, P.R., Hitch, G.J., & Kirby, P. (1992). Are two heads better than one? Experimental investigation of the social facilitation of memory. *Applied Cognitive Psychology, 6*, 525–543.

Meyer, D., & Schvaneveldt, R. (1971). Facilitation in recognising pairs of words: Evidence of a dependence between retrieval operations. *Journal of Experimental Psychology*, *90*, 227–234.

Miall, D.S. (1989). Beyond the schema given: Affective comprehension of literary narratives. *Cognition and Emotion*, *3*, 55–78.

Middleton, D., & Edwards, D. (1990). *Collective remembering*. London: Sage Publications.

Miller, G.A. (1956). The magical number seven, plus or minus two: Some limits on our capacity for processing information. *Psychological Review*, *63*, 81–97.

Miller, G.A. (1983). The background to modern psychology. In J. Miller (Ed.), *States of mind. Conversations with psychological investigators* (pp.12–28). London: British Broadcasting Corporation.

Miller, G.A., Galanter, E., & Pribram, K.H. (1960). *Plans and the structure of behavior*. New York: Holt, Rinehart & Winston.

Miller, J.R., & Kintsch, W. (1980). Readability and recall of short prose passages: A theoretical analysis. *Journal of Experimental Psychology: Human Learning and Memory*, *6*, 335–353.

Minsky, M. (1975). A framework for representing knowledge. In P.H. Winston (Ed.), *The psychology of computer vision* (pp. 211–277). New York: McGraw-Hill.

Minsky, M. (1984). Jokes and the logic of the cognitive unconscious. In L.Vaina & J. Hintikka (Eds.) *Cognitive constraints on communication* (pp. 175–200). Dordrecht: D.Reidel Publishing Co.

Minsky, M., & Papert, S. (1969). *Perceptrons*. Cambridge, MA: MIT Press.

Moely, B.E., Olson, F.A., Halwes, T.G., & Flavell, J.H. (1969). Production deficiency in young children's clustered recall. *Developmental Psychology*, *1*, 26–34.

Morrow, D.G., Bower, G.H., & Greenspan, S.L. (1989). Updating situation models during narrative comprehension. *Journal of Memory and Language*, *28*, 292–312.

Morrow, D.G., Greenspan, S.L., & Bower, G.H. (1987). Accessibility and situation models in narrative comprehension. *Journal of Memory and Language*, *26*, 165–187.

Morton, J., Hammersley, R.H., & Bekerian, D.A. (1985). Headed records: A model for memory and its failures. *Cognition*, *20*, 1–23.

Moscovici, S. (1961). *La psychanalyse, son image et son public*. Paris: Presses Universitaires de France.

Moscovici, S. (1988). Notes towards a description of social representations. *European Journal of Social Psychology*, *18*, 211–250.

Murray, F.B. (1987). Necessity: The developmental component in school mathematics. In L.S. Liben (Ed.), *Development and learning: Conflict or congruence?* (pp.51–69). Hillsdale, NJ: Lawrence Erlbaum Associates Inc.

Murray, H.G. (1985). Classroom teaching behaviors related to college teaching effectiveness. In J.G. Donald & A.M. Sullivan (Eds.), *Using research to improve teaching* (pp.21–34). San Francisco: Jossey Bass.

Myers, J.L., O'Brien, E.J., Albrecht, J.E., & Mason, R.A. (1994). Maintaining global coherence during reading. *Journal of Experimental Psychology: Learning, Memory and Cognition*, *20*, 876–888.

Neisser, U. (1967). *Cognitive psychology*. New York: Appleton-Century-Crofts.

Neisser, U. (1982). John Dean's memory: A case study. In U. Neisser (Ed.), *Memory observed. Remembering in natural contexts* (pp. 139–159). San Francisco: W.H. Freeman & Company.

Nelson. K. (1988). Where do taxonomic categories come from? *Human Development, 31,* 3–10.

Nelson, T.D., & Dunlosky, J. (1991). When people's judgments of learning (JOLs) are extremely accurate at predicting subsequent recall: The "delayed-JOL effect". *Psychological Science, 2,* 267–270.

Neves, D.M., & Anderson, J.R. (1981). Mechanisms for the automatization of cognitive skills. In J.R. Anderson (Ed.), *Cognitive skills and their acquisition* (pp. 57–84). Hillsdale, NJ: Lawrence Erlbaum Associates Inc.

Newell. A. (1980). Physical symbol systems. *Cognitive Science, 4,* 135–183.

Newell, A. (1990). *Unified theories of cognition.* Cambridge, MA: Harvard University Press.

Newell, A., Rosenbloom, P.S., & Laird, J.E. (1990). Symbolic architectures for cognition. In M.E. Posner (Ed.), *Foundations of cognitive science* (pp. 93–131). Cambridge, MA: MIT Press.

Newell, A., & Simon, H.A. (1972). *Human problem solving.* Englewood Cliffs, NJ: Prentice Hall.

Nezu, A.M., Nezu, C.M., & Blissett, S.E. (1988). Sense of humor as a moderator of the relation between stressful events and psychological stress. A prospective analysis. *Journal of Personality and Social Psychology, 54,* 520–525.

Nickerson, R.S. (1988). Counting, computing and the representation of numbers. *Human Factors, 30,* 181–189.

Norman, D.A. (1980). Twelve issues for cognitive science. *Cognitive Science, 4,* 1–32.

Novick, L.R., & Holyoak, K.J. (1991). Mathematical problem solving by analogy. *Journal of Experimental Psychology: Learning, Memory and Cognition, 17,* 398–415.

Oaksford, M., & Chater, N. (1993). Reasoning theories and bounded rationality. In K.I. Manktelow & D.E. Over (Eds.), *Rationality. Psychological and philosophical perspectives* (pp. 31–60). London: Routledge.

Ohlsson, S. (1992). The learning curve for writing books: Evidence from Professor Asimov. *Psychological Science, 3,* 380–382.

Ornstein, P.A., Naus, M.J., & Liberty, C. (1975). Rehearsal and organizational processes in children's memory. *Child Development, 46,* 818–830.

Ortony, A., & Clore, G.L. (1989). Emotions, moods and conscious awareness. *Cognition and Emotion, 3,* 125–137.

Ostrom, T. (1989). Three catechisms for social memory. In P. Solomon, G.Goethals, C. Kelley, & B. Stephens. (Eds.), *Memory: Interdisciplinary approaches* (pp.201–220). New York: Springer Verlag.

Over, D.E., & Manktelow, K.L. (1993). Rationality, utility and deontic reasoning. In K.L. Manktelow & D.E. Over (Eds.), *Rationality. Psychological and philosophical perspectives* (pp. 231–259). London: Routledge.

Paivio, A. (1971). *Imagery and verbal processes.* New York: Holt, Rhinehart & Winston.

Paivio, A. (1986). *Mental representations: A dual coding approach.* Oxford: Oxford University Press.

Palmer, S., & Rock, I. (1994). Rethinking perceptual organisation: The role of uniform connectedness. *Psychonomic Bulletin and Review, 1,* 29–55.

Papert, S. (1988). One AI or many? In S.R. Graubard (Ed.), *The artificial intelligence debate: False starts, real foundations.* Cambridge, MA: MIT Press.

Paris, S.G., & Lindauer, B.K. (1976). The role of inference in children's comprehension and memory for sentences. *Cognitive Psychology, 8*, 217–227.

Pennebaker, J.W., & O'Heeron, R.C. (1984). Confiding in others and illness rate among spouses of suicide and accidental death victims. *Journal of Abnormal Psychology, 93*, 473–476.

Pennington, N., & Hastie, R. (1986). Evidence evaluation in complex decision making. *Journal of Personality and Social Psychology, 51*, 242–258.

Pennington, N., & Hastie, R. (1988). Explanation-based decision making: Effects of memory structure on judgment. *Journal of Experimental Psychology: Learning, Memory and Cognition, 14*, 521–533.

Pennington, N., & Hastie, R. (1992). Explaining the evidence: Tests of the story model for juror decision making. *Journal of Personality and Social Psychology, 62*, 189–206.

Pennington, N., & Hastie, R. (1993). Reasoning in explanation-based decision making. *Cognition, 49*, 123–163.

Penrose, R. (1989). *The emperor's new mind. Concerning computers, mind and the laws of physics.* Oxford: Oxford University Press.

Penrose, R. (1990). Précis of the emperor's new mind: Concerning computers, minds and the laws of physics. *Behavioral and Brain Sciences, 16*, 643–705.

Penrose, R. (1994). *Shadows of the mind. A search for the missing science of consciousness.* Oxford: Oxford University Press.

Perkins, D.N. (1986). *Knowledge as design.* Hillsdale, NJ: Lawrence Erlbaum Associates Inc.

Perret-Clermont, A-N., Perret, J-J., & Bell, N. (1991). The social construction of meaning and cognitive activity in elementary school children. In L.B. Resnick, J.M. Levine, & S.D. Teasley (Eds.), *Perspectives on socially shared cognition* (pp. 41–62). Washington: American Psychological Association.

Perrig, W.J., & Perrig, P. (1988). Mood and memory: Mood congruity effects in the absence of mood. *Memory and Cognition, 16*, 102–109.

Pettigrew, T.F., & Meertens, R.W. (1995). Subtle and blatant prejudice in Western Europe. *European Journal of Social Psychology, 25*, 57–75.

Piaget, J. (1926). *The language and thought of the child.* London: Routledge & Kegan Paul.

Piaget, J. (1929). *The child's conception of the world.* London: Routledge & Kegan Paul.

Piaget, J. (1980). *Experiments in contradiction.* Chicago: University of Chicago Press.

Piaget, J., & Garcia, R. (1989). *Psychogenesis and the history of science.* New York: Columbia University Press.

Piaget, J., & Inhelder, B. (1969). *The psychology of the child.* London: Routledge & Kegan Paul.

Piaget, J., & Inhelder, B. (1973). *Memory and intelligence.* New York: Basic Books.

Pichert, J.W., & Anderson, R.C. (1977). Taking different perspectives on a story. *Journal of Educational Psychology, 69*, 309–315.

Plotkin, H. (1994). *The nature of knowledge. Concerning adaptations, instinct and the evolution of intelligence.* London: The Penguin Press.

Politzer, G., & Nguyen-Xuan, A. (1992). Reasoning about conditional premises and warnings: Darwinian algorithms, mental models, relevance judgements or pragmatic schemas? *Quarterly Journal of Experimental Psychology, 44A*, 401–421.

Pollard, P. (1990). Natural selection for the selection task: Limits to social exchange theory. *Cognition, 36*, 195–204.

Post, E.L. (1943). Formal reductions of the general combinatorial decision problem. *American Journal of Mathematics, 65*, 197–268.

Postman, L. (1975). Verbal learning and memory. *Annual Review of Psychology, 26*, 291–335.

Potts, G.R., St John, M., & Kirson, D. (1989). Incorporating new information into existing world knowledge. *Cognitive Psychology, 21*, 303–333.

Pratkanis, A.R., & Aronson, E. (1991). *Age of propaganda. The everyday use and abuse of persuasion.* New York: W.H. Freeman & Co.

Premack, D., & Woodruff, G. (1978). Does the chimpanzee have a theory of mind? *Behavioral and Brain Sciences, 1*, 516–526.

Proceedings of the Lenin Academy of Agricultural Sciences of the USSR. (1949). *The situation in biological science.* Moscow: Foreign Languages Publishing House.

Pylyshyn, Z.W. (1973). What the mind's eye tells the mind's brain. *Psychological Bulletin, 80*, 1–24.

Pylyshyn, Z.W. (1984). *Computation and cognition. Toward a foundation for cognitive science.* Cambridge, MA: MIT Press.

Qin, Y., & Simon, H.A. (1990). Laboratory replication of scientific discovery processes. *Cognitive Science, 14*, 281–312.

Ratcliff, R., & McKoon, G. (1978). Priming in item recognition: Evidence for the propositional structure of sentences. *Journal of Verbal Learning and Verbal Behavior, 17*, 403–417.

Read, S.J., & Cesa, I.L. (1991). This reminds me of the time when … Expectation failures in reminding and explanation. *Journal of Experimental Social Psychology, 27*, 1–25.

Reber, A.S. (1989). Implicit learning and tacit knowledge. *Journal of Experimental Psychology: General, 118*, 219–235.

Reder, L.M. (1982). Plausibility judgments versus fact retrieval: Alternative strategies for sentence verification. *Psychological Review, 89*, 250–280.

Reder, L.M. (1987). Strategy selection in question answering. *Cognitive Psychology, 19*, 90–138.

Reder, L.M., & Anderson, J.R. (1980). A partial resolution of the paradox of interference: The role of integrating knowledge. *Cognitive Psychology, 12*, 447–472.

Reed, S.K., & Johnsen, J.A. (1975). Detection of parts in patterns and images. *Memory and Cognition, 3*, 569–575.

Resnick, L.B., Levine, J.M., & Teasley, S.D. (1991). *Perspectives on socially shared cognition.* Washington: American Psychological Association.

Rinck, M., Glowalla, U., & Schneider, K. (1992). Mood congruent and mood incongruent learning. *Memory and Cognition, 20*, 29–39.

Rips, L.J., & Collins, A. (1993). Categories and resemblance. *Journal of Experimental Psychology, General, 122*, 468–486.

Robinson, L.B., & Hastie, R. (1985). Revision of beliefs when a hypothesis is eliminated from consideration. *Journal of Experimental Psychology: Human Perception and Performance, 11*, 443–456.

Rojhan, K., & Pettigrew, T.F. (1992). Memory for schema-relevant information: A meta analytic resolution. *British Journal of Social Psychology, 31*, 81–109.

Rorty, R. (1980). *Philosophy and the mirror of nature.* Oxford: Basil Blackwell.

Rosch, E. (1973). On the internal structure of perceptual and semantic categories. In T.E. Moore (Ed.), *Cognitive development and the acquisition of language* (pp. 111–144). New York: Academic Press.

Rosch, E., & Mervis, C.B. (1975). Family resemblances: Studies in the internal structure of categories. *Cognitive Psychology, 7*, 573–603.

Rosch, E., Mervis, C.B., Gray, W., Johnson, D., & Boyes-Braem, P. (1976). Basic objects in natural categories. *Cognitive Psychology, 8*, 382–439.

Rosenblatt, F. (1962). *The principles of neurodynamics.* New York: Spartan.

Ross, B.H. (1987). This is like that: The use of earlier problems and the separation of similarity effects. *Journal of Experimental Psychology: Learning, Memory and Cognition, 13*, 629–639.

Ross, L., Amabile, T., & Steinmetz, J. (1977). Social roles, social control and biases in the social perception process. *Journal of Personality and Social Psychology, 37*, 485–494.

Ross, S., & DiVesta, F. (1976). Oral summary as a review strategy for enhancing the recall of textual material. *Journal of Educational Psychology, 68*, 689–695.

Roth, E.M., & Shoben, E.J. (1983). The effect of context on the structure of categories. *Cognitive Psychology, 15*, 346–378.

Rouse, J. (1990). The narrative reconstruction of science. *Inquiry, 33*, 179–196.

Royer, P. (1977). Effects of specificity and position of written instructional objectives on learning from lectures. *Journal of Educational Psychology, 69*, 40–45.

Rumelhart, D.E. (1975). Notes on a schema for stories. In D.G. Bobrow & A.M. Collins (Eds.), *Representation and understanding: Studies in cognitive science* (pp. 211–236). New York: Academic Press.

Rumelhart, D.E. (1980). Schemata: The building blocks of cognition. In R.J. Spiro, B.C. Bruce, & W.F. Brewer (Eds.), *Theoretical issues in reading comprehension* (pp. 33–57). Hillsdale, NJ: Lawrence Erlbaum Associates Inc.

Rumelhart, D.E., Hinton, G.E., & Williams, R.J. (1986). Learning internal representations by error propagation. In D.E. Rumelhart, J.L. McClelland & the PDP Research Group. *Parallel distributed processing*, Vol. 1, (pp. 318–362). Cambridge, MA: MIT Press.

Rumelhart, D.E., & McClelland, J.L. (1986). PDP models and general issues in cognitive science. In D.E. Rumelhart, J.L. McClelland & the PDP Research Group. *Parallel distributed processing, Vol. 1*, (pp. 110–146). Cambridge, MA: MIT Press.

Rumelhart, D.E., McClelland, J.L., & the PDP Research Group. (1986). *Parallel distributed processing. Explorations in the microstructure of cognition. Vol. 1: Foundations.* Cambridge: MA: MIT Press.

Rumelhart, D.E., Smolensky, P., McClelland, J.L., & Hinton, G.E. (1986). Schemata and sequential thought processes. In J.L. McClelland, D.E. Rumelhart & the PDP Research Group. *Parallel distributed processing*, Vol. 2, (pp. 7–57). Cambridge, MA: MIT Press.

Russell, J.A. (1994). Is there universal recognition of emotion from facial expressions? A review of the cross cultural studies. *Psychological Bulletin, 115*, 102–141.

Ryan, J. (1969). Grouping and short-term memory: Different means and patterns of grouping. *Quarterly Journal of Experimental Psychology, 21*, 137–147.

Sachs, J.S. (1967). Recognition memory for syntactic and semantic aspects of connected discourse. *Perception and Psychophysics, 2,* 437–442.

Salomon, G. (1993). *Distributed cognitions. Psychological and educational considerations.* Cambridge: Cambridge University Press.

Sanford, A.J., & Garrod, S.C. (1981). *Understanding written language.* Chichester, UK: John Wiley & Sons.

Schab, F.R. (1991). Odor memory: Taking stock. *Psychological Bulletin, 109,* 242–251.

Schank, R.C. (1982). *Dynamic memory. A theory of reminding and learning in computers and people.* Cambridge: Cambridge University Press.

Schank, R.C. (1987). Question and thought. In P. Morris (Ed.), *Modelling cognition* (pp. 21–56). Chichester, UK: John Wiley & Sons.

Schank, R. C., & Abelson, R.P. (1977). *Scripts, plans, goals and understanding.* Hillsdale, NJ: Lawrence Erlbaum Associates Inc.

Schawenflugel, P.J., & Shoben, E.J. (1983). Differential context effects in the comprehension of abstract and concrete verbal materials. *Journal of Experimental Psychology, Learning, Memory and Cognition, 9,* 82–102.

Schooler, J.W., & Tanaka, J.W. (1991). Composites, compromises and CHARM: What is the evidence for blend memory representations? *Journal of Experimental Psychology: General, 120,* 96–100.

Schustack, M.W., & Anderson, J.R. (1979). Effects of analogy to prior knowledge on memory for new information. *Journal of Verbal Learning and Verbal Behavior, 18,* 565–583.

Schyns, P.G. (1991). A modular neural network model of concept acquisition. *Cognitive Science, 15,* 461–508.

Searle, J.R. (1980). Minds, brains and programs. *Behavioral and Brain Sciences, 3,* 417–457.

Searleman, A., & Carter, H. (1988). The effectiveness of different types of pragmatic implications found in commercials to mislead subjects. *Applied Cognitive Psychology, 2,* 265–272.

Segal, S.J., & Fusella, V. (1970). Influence of imaged pictures and sounds on detection of visual and auditory signals. *Journal of Experimental Psychology, 83,* 458–464.

Seibert, P.S., & Ellis, H.C. (1991). Irrelevant thoughts, emotional mood states and cognitive task performance. *Memory and Cognition, 19,* 507–513.

Seifert, C.M., & Black, J.B. (1983). Thematic connections between episodes. *Proceedings of the fifth annual conference of the Cognitive Science Society.* New York: Rochester.

Seifert, C.M., McKoon, G., Abelson, R.P., & Ratcliff, R. (1986). Memory connections between thematically similar episodes. *Journal of Experimental Psychology: Learning, Memory and Cognition, 12,* 220–231.

Shafir, E., Simonson, I., & Tversky, A. (1993). Reason-based choice. *Cognition, 49,* 11–36.

Shaver, P., Schwartz, J., Kirson, D., & O'Connor, C. (1987). Emotion knowledge: Further exploration of a prototype approach. *Journal of Personality and Social Psychology, 52,* 1061–1086.

Siegler, R.S. (1981). Developmental sequences within and between concepts. *Monographs of the Society for Research on Child Development, 46,* Number 189, 1–74.

Singer, M., Graesser, A.C., & Trabasso, T. (1994). Minimal or global inferencing during reading. *Journal of Memory and Language, 33,* 421–441.

Skinner, B.F. (1985). Cognitive science and behaviorism. *British Journal of Psychology*, 76, 291–301.

Skinner, B.F. (1989). The origins of cognitive thought. *American Psychologist*, 44, 13–18.

Smith, E.E., Adams, N., & Schorr, D. (1978). Fact retrieval and the paradox of interference. *Cognitive Psychology*, 10, 438–464.

Spelke, E.S. (1991). Physical knowledge in infancy: Reflections on Piaget's theory. In S. Carey & R. Gelman (Eds.), *The epigenesis of mind: Essays on biology and cognition* (pp. 133–169). Hillsdale, NJ: Lawrence Erlbaum Associates Inc.

Spelke, E.S., Katz, G., Purcell, S.E., Ehrlich, S.M., & Breinlinger, K. (1994). Early knowledge of object motion: Continuity and inertia. *Cognition*, 51, 131–176.

Spiro, R.J. (1980). Constructive processes in prose comprehension and recall. In R.J. Spiro, B.C. Bruce, & W.F. Brewer (Eds.), *Theoretical issues in reading comprehension* (pp. 245–278). Hillsdale, NJ: Lawrence Erlbaum Associates Inc.

Sternberg, R.J. (1990). *Wisdom:. Its nature, origins and development.* Cambridge: Cambridge University Press.

Stich, S. (1983). *From folk psychology to cognitive science: The case against belief.* Cambridge, MA: MIT Press.

Stich, S. (1992). What is a theory of mental representation? *Mind*, 101, 243–267.

Stillings, N.A., Feinstein, M.H., Garfield, J.L., Rissland, E.L., Rosenbaum, D.A., Weisler, S.E., & Baker-Ward, L. (1987). *Cognitive science. An introduction.* Cambridge, MA: MIT Press.

Strauss, S. (1987). Educational–developmental psychology and school learning. In L.S. Liben (Ed.), *Development and learning: Conflict or congruence?* (pp.133–157). Hillsdale, NJ: Lawrence Erlbaum Associates Inc.

Sweller, J. (1988). Cognitive load during problem solving: Effects on learning. *Cognitive Science*, 12, 257–285.

Sweller, J., Chandler, P., Tierney, P., & Cooper, M. (1990). Cognitive load as a factor in the structuring of technical material. *Journal of Experimental Psychology: General*, 119, 176–192.

Sweller, J., Mawer, R.F., & Ward, M.R. (1983). Development of expertise in mathematical problem solving. *Journal of Experimental Psychology: General*, 112, 639–661.

Tajfel, H. (1957). Value and the perceptual judgment of magnitude. *Psychological Review*, 64, 192–204.

Tajfel, H. (1981). *Human groups and social categories.* Cambridge: Cambridge University Press.

Tajfel, H., & Wilkes, A.L. (1963). Classification and quantitative judgement. *British Journal of Psychology*, 54, 101–114.

Taylor, W.L. (1953). Cloze procedure: A new tool for measuring readability. *Journalism Quarterly*, 30, 415–433.

Thagard, P. (1989). Explanatory coherence. *Behavioral and Brain Sciences*, 12, 435–467.

Thagard, P. (1992). *Conceptual revolutions.* Princeton, NJ: Princeton University Press.

Thorndyke, P.W. (1977). Cognitive structures in comprehension and memory of narrative discourse. *Cognitive Psychology*, 9, 77–110.

Tomasello, R., Kruger, A.C., & Ratner, H.H. (1993). Cultural learning. *Behavioral and Brain Sciences, 16,* 495–582.

Trabasso, T., & Sperry, L.L. (1985). Causal relatedness and importance of story events. *Journal of Memory and language, 24,* 595–611.

Trabasso, T., & Suh, S. (1993). Understanding text: Achieving explanatory coherence through on-line inferences and mental operations in working memory. *Discourse Processes, 16,* 3–34.

Tulving, E. (1983). *Elements of episodic memory.* New York: Oxford University Press.

Tulving, E. (1985). How many memory systems are there? *American Psychologist, 40,* 385–398.

Turing, A.M. (1936). On computable numbers, with an application to the Entscheidungsproblem. *Proceedings of the London Mathematical Society,* Series 2, *42,* 230–265.

Tversky, A., & Kahneman, D. (1974). Judgement under uncertainty: Heuristics and biases. *Science, 185,* 1124–1131.

Tye, M. (1991). *The imagery debate.* Cambridge, MA: MIT Press.

Ucros, C.G. (1989). Mood state dependent memory: A meta analysis. *Cognition and Emotion, 3,* 139–167.

Valentine, E.R. (1989). Neural nets: From Hartley and Hebb to Hinton. *Journal of Mathematical Psychology, 33,* 348–357.

van den Broek, P. (1994). Comprehension and memory of narrative texts. In M.A. Gernsbacher (Ed.), *Handbook of psycholinguistics* (pp. 539–588). San Diego: Academic Press.

van der Meij, H. (1990). Question asking: To know that you do not know is not enough. *Journal of Educational Psychology, 82,* 505–512.

van Dijk, T.A., & Kintsch, W. (1983). *Strategies of discourse comprehension.* New York: Academic Press.

Vera, A.H., & Simon, H.A. (1993). Situated action: A symbolic interpretation. *Cognitive Science, 17,* 7–48.

Vicente, K.J., & Brewer, W.F. (1993). Reconstructive remembering of the scientific literature. *Cognition, 46,* 101–128.

Vipond, D. (1980). Micro- and macroprocesses in text comprehension. *Journal of Verbal Learning and Verbal Behavior, 19,* 276–296.

von Neumann, J., & Morgenstern, O. (1947). *Theory of games and economic behavior.* Princeton, NJ: Princeton University Press.

Vygotsky, L.S. (1962). *Thought and language.* New York: MIT Press and J. Wiley & Sons Inc.

Wagenaar, W.A. (1986). My memory: A study of autobiographical memory over six years. *Cognitive Psychology, 18,* 225–252.

Wagenaar, W.A., & Groeneweg, J. (1990). The memory of concentration camp survivors. *Applied Cognitive Psychology, 4,* 77–87.

Wade, N. (1990). *Visual allusions. Pictures of perception.* Hove, UK: Lawrence Erlbaum Associates Ltd.

Walker, S.F. (1990). A brief history of connectionism and its psychological implications. *AI and Society, 4,* 17–38.

Warren, H.C. (1921). *History of the association psychology.* London: Constable & Co. Ltd.

Wason, P.C. (1966). Reasoning. In B.M. Foss (Ed.), *New horizons in psychology.* Harmondsworth, UK: Penguin.

Weaver, C.A. (1990). Constraining factors in calibration of comprehension. *Journal of Experimental Psychology: Learning, Memory and Cognition, 16,* 214–222.

Weaver, C.A. (1993). Do you need a "flash" to form a flashbulb memory? *Journal of Experimental Psychology: General, 122,* 39–46.

Webber, B.L. (1980). Syntax beyond the sentence: Anaphora. In R.J. Spiro, B.C. Bruce & W.F. Brewer (Eds.), *Theoretical issues in reading comprehension* (pp. 141–164). Hillsdale, NJ: Lawrence Erlbaum Associates Inc.

Wegner, D.M. (1988). Stress and mental control. In S. Fisher & J. Reason (Eds.), *Handbook of life stress, cognition and health* (pp. 683–697). Chichester, UK: John Wiley & Sons.

Wegner, D.M. (1994). Ironic processes of mental control. *Psychological Review, 101,* 34–52.

Wegner, D.M., Erber, R., & Raymond, P. (1991). Transactive memory in close relationships. *Journal of Personality and Social Psychology, 61,* 923–928.

Wegner, D.M., Schneider, D.J., Carter, S., & White, T. (1987). Paradoxical effects of thought suppression. *Journal of Personality and Social Psychology, 53,* 1–9.

Weinberg, H.I., Wadsworth, J., & Baron, R.S. (1983). Demand and the impact of leading questions on eyewitness testimony. *Memory and Cognition, 11,* 101–104.

Weisberg, R.W. (1969). Sentence processing assessed through intra-sentence word associations. *Journal of Experimental Psychology, 82,* 332–338.

Weisberg, R.W. (1992). *Creativity. Beyond the myth of genius.* New York: W.H. Freeman & Co.

Wellman, H.M. (1990). *The child's theory of mind.* Cambridge, MA: MIT Press.

Wellman, H.M., & Estes, D. (1986). Early understanding of mental entities. A re-examination of childhood realism. *Child Development, 57,* 910–923.

Wenzlaff, R.M., Wegner, D.M., & Klein, S.B. (1991). The role of thought suppression in the bonding of thought and mind. *Journal of Personality and Social Psychology, 60,* 500–508.

Wertsch, J.V. (1985). *Vygotsky and the social formation of the mind.* Cambridge, MA: Harvard University Press.

Whiten, A., & Byrne, R.W. (1988). Tactical deception in primates. *Behavioral and Brain Sciences, 11,* 233–273.

Wilkes, A.L. (1972). Reading pauses during serial list learning with fixed or randomly changing groups. *Journal of Experimental Psychology, 94,* 206–209.

Wilkes, A.L., & Alred, G. (1978). Prose and prejudice: Some effects of priming context on the immediate recall of information. *British Journal of Psychology, 69,* 123–133.

Wilkes, A.L., & Leatherbarrow, M. (1988). Editing episodic memory following the identification of error. *Quarterly Journal of Experimental Psychology, 40A,* 361–387.

Wilkes, A.L., Lloyd, P., & Simpson, I. (1972). Spontaneous pausing strategies during serial list learning. *Quarterly Journal of Experimental Psychology, 24,* 48–54.

Wilkes, A.L., & Wade, N.J. (in press). Bain on neural networks. *Brain and Cognition.*

Wilson, S.G., Rinck, M., McNamara, T.P., Bower, G.H., & Morrow, D.G. (1993). Mental models and narrative comprehension: Some qualifications. *Journal of Memory and Language, 32,* 141–154.

Wineberg, S.S. (1991). Historical problem solving: A study of the cognitive processes used in the evaluation of documentary and pictorial evidence. *Journal of Educational Psychology, 83*, 73–87.

Wiser, M. (1988). The differentiation of heat and temperature: History of science and novice-expert shift. In S.Strauss (Ed.), *Ontogeny, phylogeny and historical development*, Vol. 2, (pp. 28–48). Norwood, NJ: Ablex Publishing Corp.

Wyer, R.S., & Collins, J.E. (1992). A theory of humor elicitation. *Psychological Review, 99*, 663–688.

Yates, F.A. (1966). *The art of memory*. London: Routledge & Kegan Paul.

Young, R.M. (1970). *Mind, brain and adaptation in the nineteenth century*. Oxford: Clarendon Press.

Zangwill, O.L. (1972). Remembering revisited. *Quarterly Journal of Experimental Psychology, 24*, 123–138.

Zhang, J., & Norman, D.A. (1993). A cognitive taxonomy of numeration systems. *Proceedings of the Fifteenth Annual Conference of the Cognitive Science Society*. Hillsdale, NJ: Lawrence Erlbaum Associates Inc.

Zhang, J., & Norman, D.A. (1994). Representations in distributive cognitive tasks. *Cognitive Science, 18*, 87–122.

Author index

Subject index

ACME, 273-274
ACT*, 6, 79, 88-95, 106, 209, 387, 407
  as general purpose architecture, 79, 94-95
  knowledge compilation in, 91-94
  power law of learning, 93-94
  procedural memory, 87, 88-94
  rule matching, 90-91
ACT-R, 94-95, 387
  and identifiability problem, 94
Affect, 212
  and attentional focusing, 210, 222-224
  and cognition, 211-233
  see also Mood states, Emotion
Alchemists, 377
Algorithms, 15-19, 25-26
  see also Heuristics
Ambiguous figures, 64-66
Amodal codes, 6, 53, 75-77
Analogical problem solving, 159-160, 250, 268-274

and categorisation, 76-77
  and group problem solving, 382-383
  transparency and systematicity, 269-274
  as constraint satisfaction, 271-274
  see also Problem solving
Anaphoric reference, 40-41, 240-242, 258
Architecture of cognition, 5-6, 21, 56, 77
  and connectionism, 109-139
  and symbol processing, 87-108
Argumentation, 313-322
  simulation studies, 319-322
  styles of, 316-318
Associationism, 27, 110-114
Associative networks, 60-61, 84-86, 89-90, 146-149, 260, 271
  and emotion nodes, 216-217

Assumptive schemas, 230-232
Autoassociator, 118-120
Autobiographical memory, 82-84

Babbage's analytical and difference engine, 16
Backward error propagation, 125-126, 133-135
BACON, 370-373, 378-379
  and discovery of scientific laws, 371-373
Beam balance task, 101-105, 133-135, 206
Behaviourism, 12-13, 27
Beliefs, 8-11, 20, 23-24
  establishing true and false beliefs, 292-294, 326, 411-412
  justification of, 313-318 see also Scientific beliefs

Categories, 29-38
  internal structure of, 34, 76-77